Performance in Contemporary Art

Performance in Contemporary Art

Catherine Wood

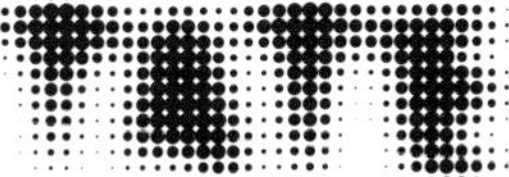

First published 2018 by order of the Tate Trustees
by Tate Publishing, a division of Tate Enterprises Ltd,
Millbank, London SW1P 4RG
www.tate.org.uk/publishing

Paperback edition first published 2022

Reprinted 2024

A catalogue record for this book is available from
the British Library
ISBN 978 1 84976 823 8

Distributed in the United States and Canada
by ABRAMS, New York

Library of Congress Control Number applied for

Project Editor: Nicola Bion
Production: Juliette Dupire
Picture Researcher: Deborah Metherell
Designed by Sarah Boris
Colour reproduction by Alta Image, London
Printed in Wales by Cambrian Printers

Front cover: Anne Imhof, *Aqua Leo, 1st of at least two* from *Parade*, Portikus, Frankfurt am Main, 2013
Back cover: Francis Alÿs, *When Faith Moves Mountains* 2002 (see p.145)
p.6: Sylvia Palacios Whitman, *Green Hands* 1977
pp.30–1: Xavier Le Roy, *Self Unfinished* 1998 (detail, see p.83)
pp.112–3:Tania Bruguera, *Tatlin's Whisper #5* 2008 (detail, see p.164)
pp.174–5: Senga Nengudi, R.S.V.P. sculptures 1977 (detail, see p.185)

Measurements are given in centimetres, height before width and depth

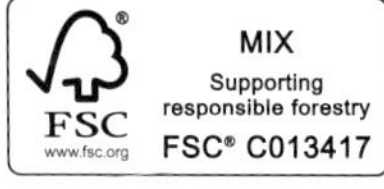

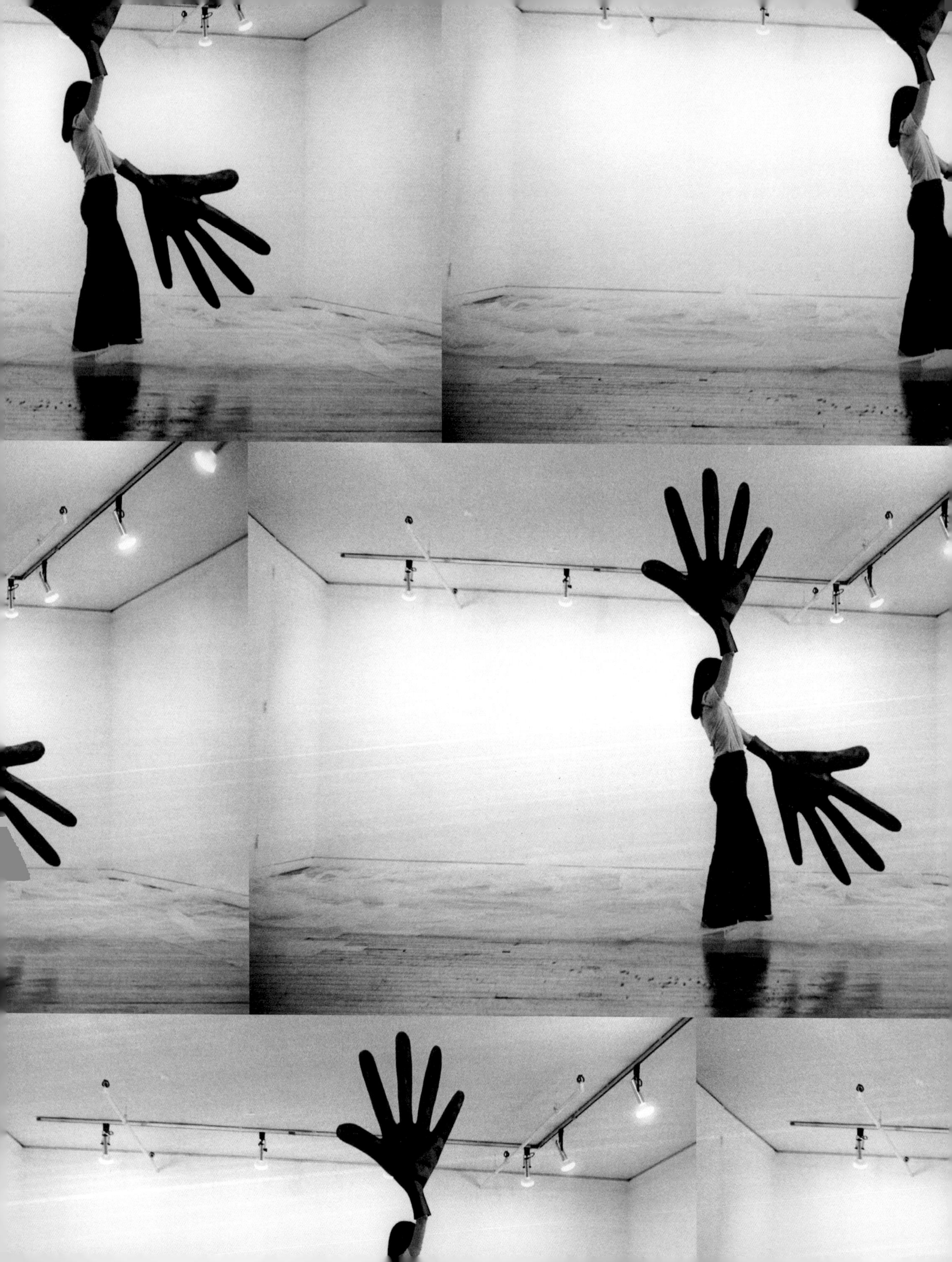

Introduction

Art that moves

Performance has become a highly visible feature of contemporary art. Since the early 2000s, visual artists have increasingly turned to live action or situations, movement and participation. In parallel, both artists and art audiences have become newly fascinated by the history of performance. This book looks at what we mean by performance in the context of contemporary art, and considers how current practices are rooted in approaches to art that emerged in the first half of the twentieth century, and which developed significantly, internationally, after the 1950s. Charting the evolution of performance since the 1950s, it asks how this art form has come to play a key role in shaping our very understanding of what art is today.

What we call 'performance' might, from a certain perspective, be understood as a way of enlarging the frame around what was previously considered to be the work of art, as a material object, to include also the active presence of its maker and viewers. This book is split into three sections which aim to provide a lens for looking at the component parts of the performance situation, as it has been staged within art. Each section looks at performance through the point of view of one of three actors: *I*, *We* and *It*, which stand for the self, the collective and the material object respectively, or, as these are expressed in the art encounter: the artist, the audience and the artwork. Typically, most works that involve performance make visible the relationship between these three elements, the balance of which can also shift. Works are discussed in each of these sections, then, not because they are exclusively appropriate to that aspect, but as a way of considering which of these perspectives has a degree of prominence in the work.

An example of an artist working now in this vein helps to begin addressing these questions: New York-based, Japanese artist Ei Arakawa. Arakawa has made work that resembles a club night, an opera or a parade. His practice combines performance, participation, art historical research and activism, woven through the lens of autobiography. Frequently collaborative, Arakawa's events tend to look like live experiments, in which relations between the artist, artwork and viewer are deliberately unstable. Staging himself as part of the work, Arakawa plays host to, or compères, ready-made formats for live action, within which he creates images of community, and often uses artworks by other artists as props and prompts within these scenes.

In 2012, as part of the programme 'Art in Action' in the Tanks at Tate Modern, for example, Arakawa invited two Japanese art historians – Harumi Nishizawa and Miwako Tezuka – to participate in a performance. Their research into postwar Japanese art, including the historical photographs of avant-garde performance that they unearthed, was used by the artist as a score for a group event combining live re-enactments and a public discussion about performance. Arakawa stood onstage with Nishizawa and Tezuka, and arranged around them a hastily corralled group of friends and colleagues. Everyone had been given fringed black wigs and white brocade shirts to wear, resembling Russian peasant costumes, inspired by the radical 1920s Japanese art group Mavo. We (because I was also included) assembled and remained present onstage as a chorus for the lectures and discussions that took place. Now and then, we were invited to participate in re-enacting some of the photographs of historical Japanese works; sometimes we asked questions, and got into discursive asides, serving as an impromptu

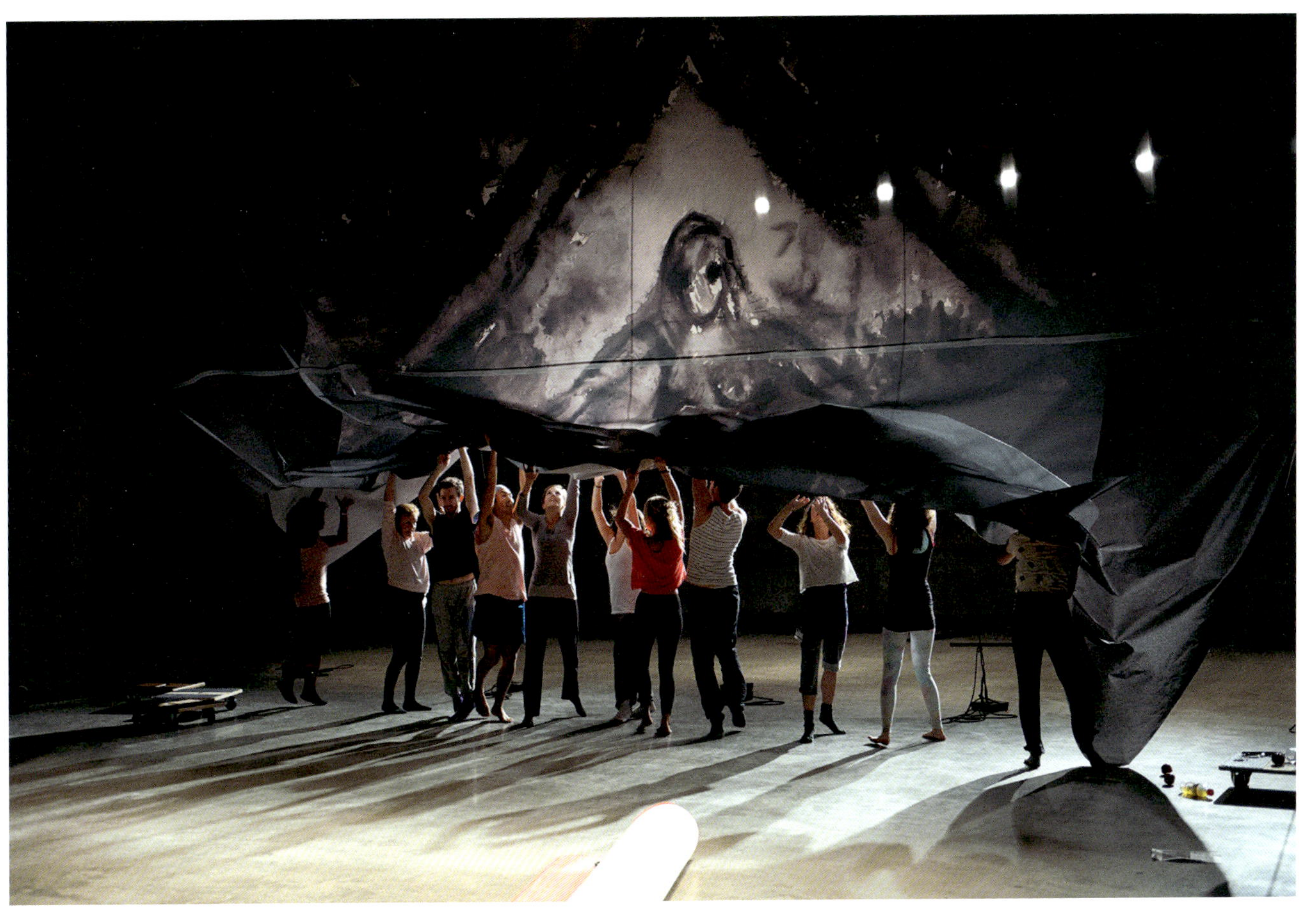

Ei Arakawa, *Singles Night*, with paintings by Jutta Koether and music by Sergei Tcherepnin, as part of Art in Action, The Tanks, Tate Modern, 2012

community of interest around the material under discussion. But given the fancy dress, it was also a bit like performing as a cheering campaign for the esoteric research area being explored onstage. And it was a party of sorts, too – one that included the gathered audience, because Arakawa's commentary and finely judged sense of playfulness appealed to everyone directly. The event became an extraordinary and vivid reflection on performance's live presence and its history. Arakawa's role as an artist was less a point of focus than the entire situation that he manipulated into being.

Performance history is, for Arakawa, a set of templates and patterns that can be used actively to share a story about art that helps to make sense of the present. It is also an alternative way for a temporary community to come together. His work suggests a way to summon a new version of the past, which points towards possible new futures. Alongside this seminar, Arakawa presented one of his own performances, a *Single's Night*, in which audience members were invited to improvise dances using painted panels by the artist Jutta Koether as props, to themed soundtracks composed by artist Stefan Tcherepnin. Embarrassed at first, visitors soon found partners and made up dances with abandon. And for a project for Frieze Art Fair in 2014, Arakawa created a deliberately ambiguous situation in which he gave away free soup, made by his mother using ingredients from her home town, Fukushima: the site of a recent, high-profile nuclear explosion.

Those who opted for soup made from UK ingredients instead had to pay £3.50. Information about the potential effects of radiation on Japanese food production clipped from newspapers and researched online was pasted on the booth wall.

I begin with Arakawa, and the complex ecology of his art practice, because in its breadth it encompasses so much of what performance might mean within visual art today. With an attitude of camp playfulness, he questions whether the live presence of the artist is, or needs to be, authentic, and even what authenticity is in the media-savvy twenty-first century. His work demonstrates the activity of witnessing to be as important as performing, by foregrounding the roles of participants and interlocutors. And he stages the art object – often signified by painting in his work – as something that gains meaning through the collective rituals that surround it, rather than simply on its own terms.

Through this brief description of Arakawa's approach to performance, we immediately see its shifting shapes: it might be a form of participatory exchange, or stylised movement presented onstage; pop entertainment, or political activism. Much as Arakawa's work includes dancing, the artist also casts paintings – whether by Koether, Silke Otto-Knapp or the historic Gutai group – as standards paraded in processions, or pushed about on wheels, and frames the audience's own decision-making capacities as part of the work. Significantly, for Arakawa 'liveness' is not just an attribute of the human actors involved but a state of *potentiality* embodied in how all the elements of his work might move and change.

As performance has become increasingly prevalent in the field of contemporary art, this renewal of interest has put a spotlight, also, on its backstories. In their desire to invent forms of live art, artists have sought to summon its relatively invisible histories. There is new attention to both the living practitioners who pioneered performance art in the 1970s, such as Joan Jonas, VALIE EXPORT or Sanja Iveković, and its historical roots in, say, Bauhaus and Constructivist theatre of the 1920s and 30s, or the actions by the Gutai group and the Nouveaux Réalistes in the 1950s. But a 'secret history' has also emerged, one embedded in the object histories of expanded sculpture, action painting and immersive installation in the second half of the twentieth century. Performance in contemporary art, then, might essentially be said to connote a space not just for performed action, but *a space of active relations*: *a space in which things happen*. Performance is a mode of working that draws attention to, and initiates transgressions of, art's defining frame. As London-based artist Cally Spooner (see p.229) has described it, performance for her generation is about a kind of art that 'refuses to settle'.[1] It represents a crucible of aesthetic relations between people and things that persists in a speculative state. Through this unsettling attitude of taking the whole situation of the art encounter apart and re-making it, we could say that performance is not only related to revelation of process, but it exaggerates or extends the propositional state of art: the 'is-it-art?' or rather 'this is art'[2] that Marcel Duchamp initiated with the probative placing of a shop-bought urinal or bottle rack in a gallery, his famous 'readymade'. Recognising that it was the declarative action that made this gesture into art, rather than the object itself, we see that questions of agency, intention and reception are essential to our understanding of what contemporary art is today. And these are the questions that are often dramatised in performance situations.

Yoko Ono performing *Cut Piece* 1964, Sogetsu Art Centre, Tokyo, 1964

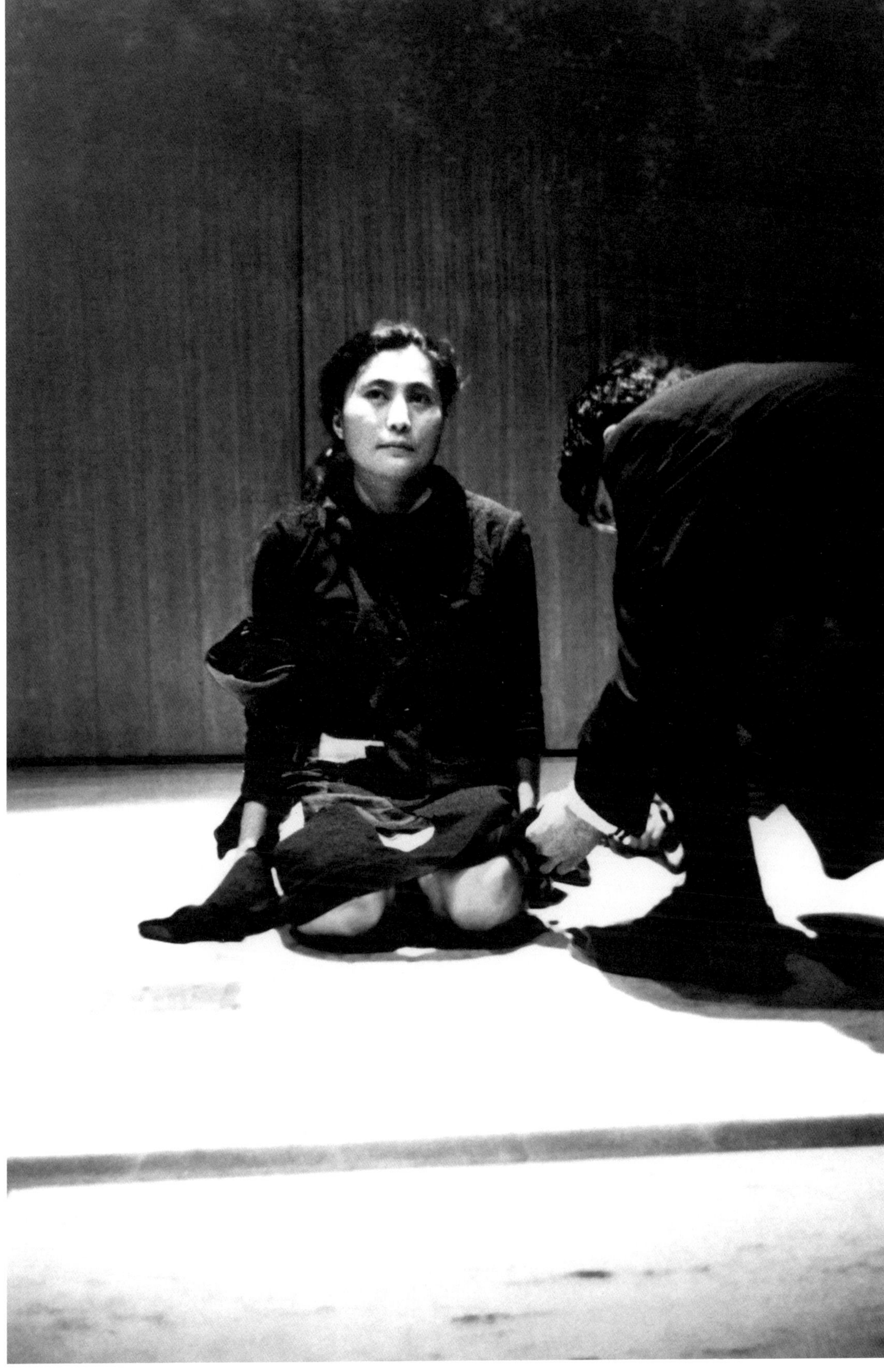

Performance art

Why is this kind of work being made, more and more often, now? The landscape of contemporary art is increasingly rich with works that, because they are about action and the body, or are simply live events, might be loosely termed as performance. But the term is broad, and the nature of the performance aspect within these works is widely varied almost to the point of dispersion. It is a term that younger artists often reject as a specialised area of activity. Aversion to this label rests largely upon its strong associations with a notion of historical 'performance art' centred on the body in the 1960s and 1970s. But, nevertheless, it is essential to acknowledge that such historical experiments opened up possibilities, or created new templates for art-making, that are highly relevant to the way many artists are working now.

What we know as performance art in a historical sense can be said to originate with a key period of experimental art made in multiple locations internationally between the 1950s and the late 1970s. Discourses and practices of performance art also emerge in other periods, movements and ways. For example, in China and Indonesia discourses and practices of contemporary art rise, including an emergence of performance actions, during the 1980s and 1990s. Likewise in Singapore during the 1990s, linked to important discussions on bodies and spaces for the presentation of performance art.[3] The 1950s to 1970s high period might be loosely identified as the foundation of performance art as a genre or movement, during a time when artists explicitly identified themselves as 'performance artists', a label which few younger artists in a Western context use today. Although the term 'performance' (or its equivalent in translation) was not, of course, used by artists in all the geographical regions in which live actions, events, body art or communal happenings were taking place, it was quite common by the late 1970s in a Western European and American context, as is evidenced in the title of several publications and events of the period.[4] It is therefore useful as a label for the general nature of what was happening, and how much of it was framed, at this time.

From the 1950s, a fresh wave of expressly live or event-based actions were seen in the work of the Gutai artists in Japan; the experimental *Theater Pieces* of John Cage, Merce Cunningham and Robert Rauschenberg, begun at Black Mountain College in North Carolina; or the early satirical actions of Yves Klein and Piero Manzoni in Paris and Milan respectively. These early examples opened up the space of what emerged in the later 1960s and 1970s as 'performance' or 'performance art' proper across the globe: work by artists as varied as Joseph Beuys, Marina Abramović, Milan Knížák, Chris Burden, the Vienna Actionists, Lygia Pape, Yoko Ono and Hi-Red Center, all of whom experimented with live, body-centred practices as a counterpart to, or in confrontation with, the market and traditional media of sculpture and painting. A second kind of performance-based work arguably emerged from the late 1970s to 1980s: loosely speaking, a more media-literate form of self-presentation made possible by innovations in video technology, which can be seen as a precursor for the seamless inhabitation of the image in the work of many artists working today. Key protagonists in this second wave (which was, in fact, entangled with the first) are Joan Jonas, Luigi Ontani, Cosey Fanni Tutti, Michel Journiac, General Idea, Michael Smith, IRWIN, Lorraine O'Grady, Cindy Sherman and Yasumasa Morimura.

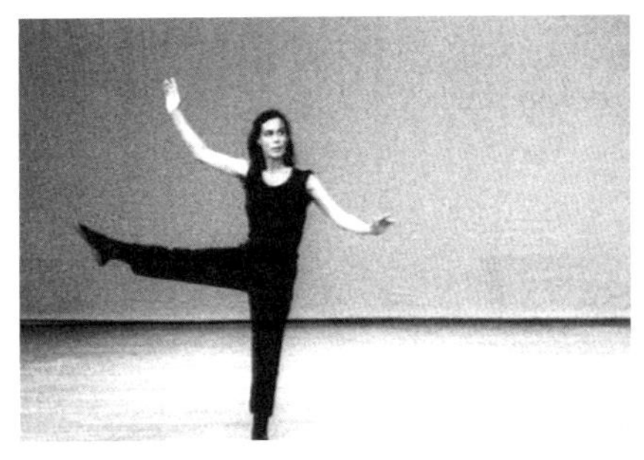
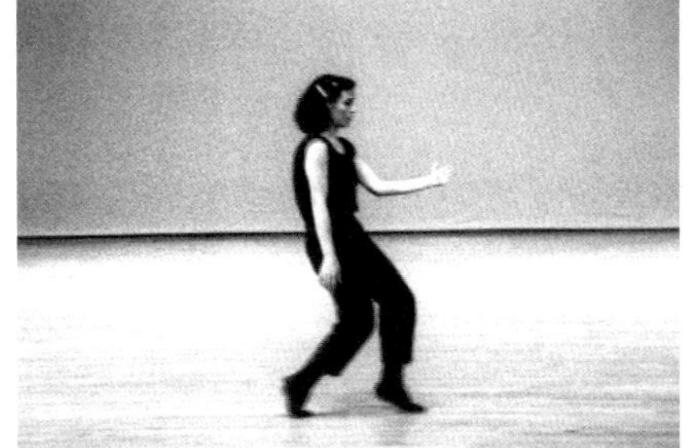
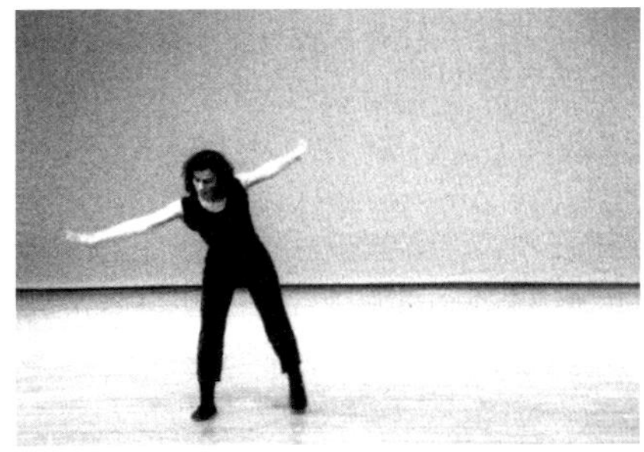
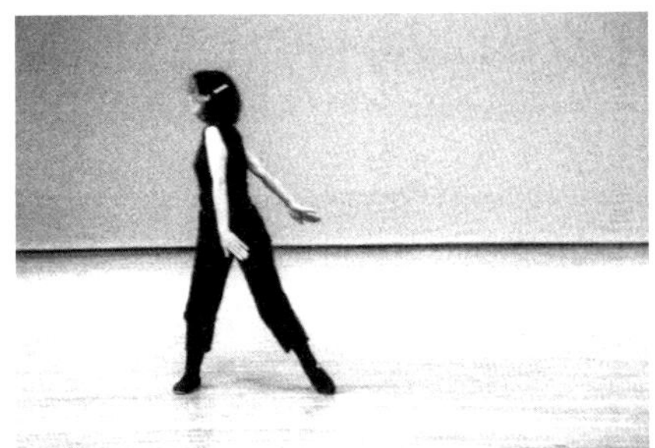
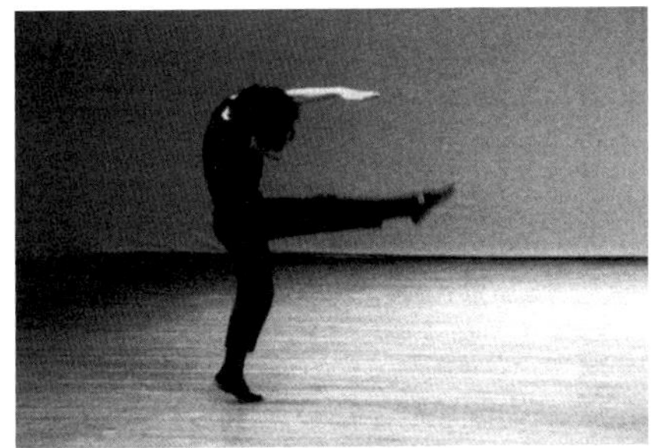

Yvonne Rainer, *Trio A*
1966, video (black and white, sound), 10:21 min., recorded 1978

In this book, I will refer to this high period of performance art and happenings as an important but somewhat narrow reference point for contemporary practice. From today's perspective, the notion of performance art can be understood as a genre of sorts, albeit an extraordinarily and – by its own definition – necessarily permissive, open-ended one. What is especially new and valuable in the work developed during the 1960s and 1970s, and into the 1980s, is the introduction of a set of templates activating relations between the artist, viewer and artwork: a redistribution of the relations making up this triad, which had already been implicitly initiated with Duchamp, and which arguably connects with pre-modern and non-Western ideas about the role of art in a social context. These radical reconfigurations of primary relations offer a complex starting point from which I wish to build a more expansive understanding of the reach of performance and the more virulently dispersed notion of the performative today.

The irruption of 'performance art' is habitually described in terms of rupture: a radical break with traditional forms of art-making that stripped art of many of its accumulated habits and political associations. Yet, when the initial acts that I shall describe as 'proto-performance' emerged in the late 1940s and 1950s, themselves building upon attitudes initiated by the Dadaists, Futurists and Surrealists, society was already undergoing radical changes across the world. Early twentieth-century totalitarian regimes were being taken apart and, in parallel, various grassroots left-wing movements were assembling – numerous African independence movements, the American Civil Rights movement and second-wave feminism – which would gather pace in the 1960s. Artist Graciela Carnevale observed, from her point of view in Rosario, Argentina, at this time, 'The concept of revolution was very present in 1968: the Cuban revolution, the life of Che Guevara, the Vietnam War, all these very important events were affecting us.'[5] The spirit of May 1968 protests in Paris was inherently entwined with a theatrical attitude towards demonstrating in public spaces. In tandem, the so-called 'global village' was being

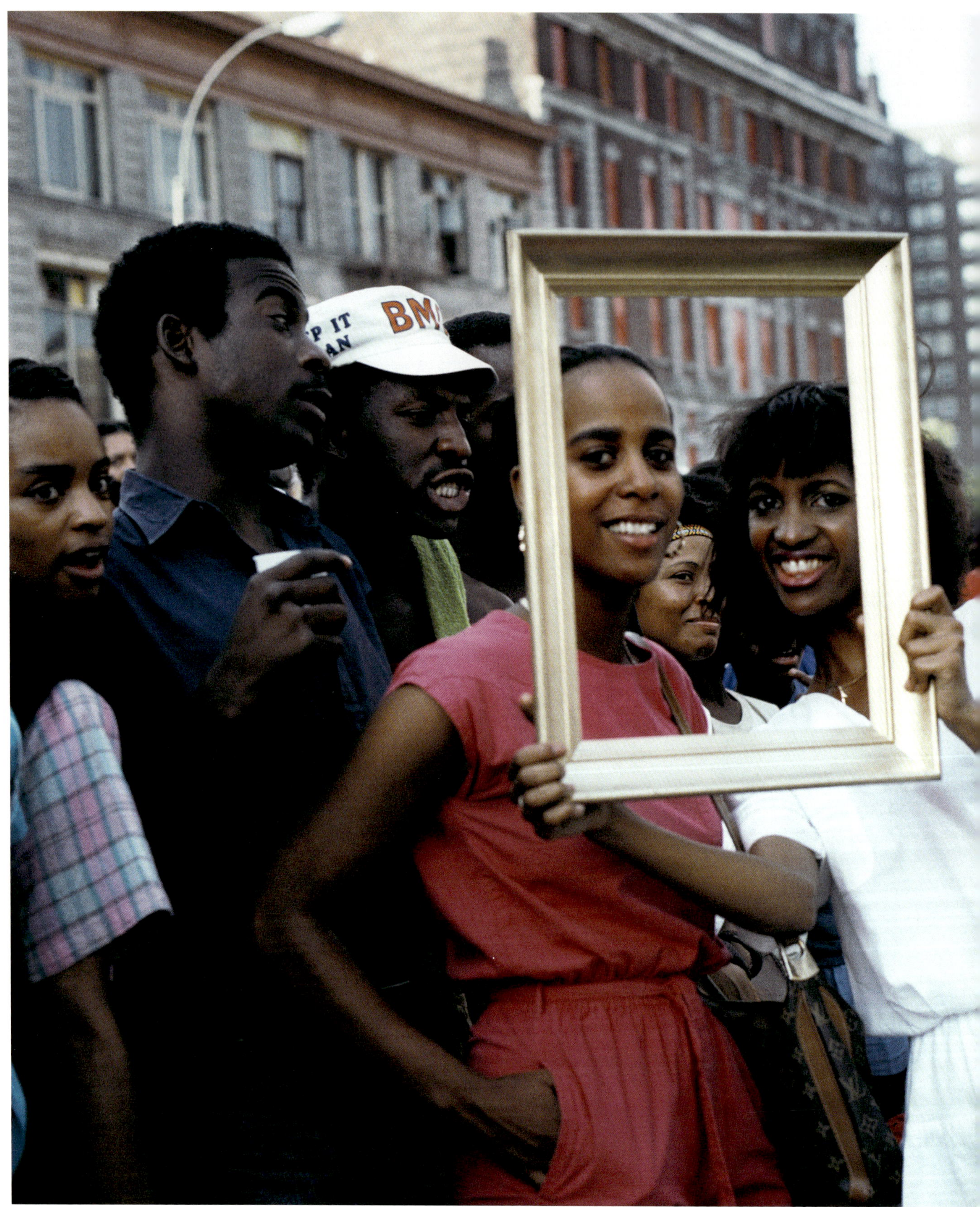

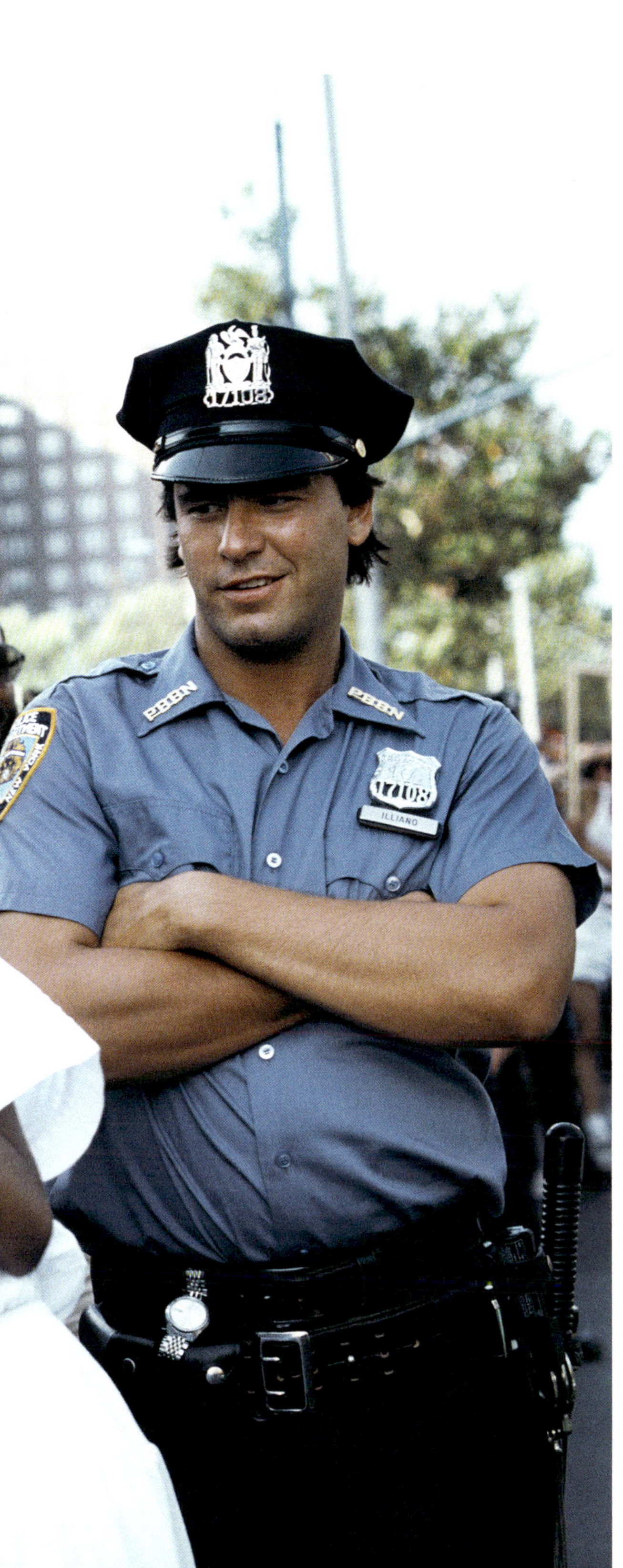

Lorraine O'Grady, *Art Is ... (Woman with Man and Cop Watching)* 1983/2009

born: the introduction of live television newscasts gave a more immediate view into people's lives in different countries and cultures, lending a different level of self-awareness. New relativistic and critical views on the institutions of authority thus emerged, both governmental and familial. This came hand in hand with a new sense of fracture between the immediacy of one's own life and the consumption of mediated reality.

French theorist Guy Debord wrote, in *The Society of the Spectacle* (1967), that the spectacle had become the mediator of all social relations, making authenticity impossible: 'all that was once lived directly has become mere representation'.[6] From such a perspective, performance appeared, at this moment, as an arena for a new, apparently unmediated culture in the present tense. American postmodern choreographer Yvonne Rainer's programme notes for her evening-length dance concert *The Mind Is a Muscle* 1968 declare her body to be 'the enduring reality' in opposition to her experience of global politics via television. Rainer protests that she can see a Vietnamese person shot dead during a war report, but can switch it off 'as though after a bad Western'.[7] In an age of increasing reliance on technology for industry and communication, a return to the body as a primary actor manifesting agency made some sense.

These socio-political factors, and the overriding traumas of the Second World War in large parts of the world, as well as the early stages of the Cold War, can be seen to have had a bearing on the thinking of artists, but they should not be substituted too literally for the nuances of the art historical context. The live performances that were created in these decades were not only a rejection of the institutions of art, as is habitually assumed: the museum and either market- or state-sanctioned conventions, depending on the context, that many artists were reacting against. The reinstatement of the figure within the frame of art, through performance, also posed a driving question about art's capacity to tell stories, and its ritual basis. This reappearance of the figure was, in certain ways, an alternative and fresh *continuation* of what art had been up until then. In a context of increasingly dominant abstraction in painting and sculpture, performance proposed new forms of figuration via narrative and picture-making, and also potential for explicit political content, which high modernism had absented. Instead of just being a radical alternative to gallery art, performance in the 1950s was a way of making a place for art among people: creating a scene in which the art object had meaning, or a vision of artistic activity that located art within life once again.

On the one hand, then, performance arguably supplemented the blank formalism of modernist abstraction with a reinstatement of the figure. Through the 1940s and 1950s, that shadow side of abstraction – of human agency – had been more or less repressed within a dominant Western narrative of modernism, in favour of the aesthetic objects displayed in the white cube. But as contemporary artists such as Paulina Ołowska, Daria Martin, Mai-Thu Perret and Shahryar Nashat have reminded us in their recent, performative re-imaginings of Bauhaus and Constructivist visions, geometric abstraction in sculpture and painting with its attendant aspirations towards utopian architectural and interior design arguably opened up a space of imaginative possibility: a space where the figure could emerge differently, performing against a new ground.

On the other hand, however, by making live images, the body-art kind of performance could be seen to extend early twentieth-century concerns with expressionist figuration towards a literal, and often extreme, picture of raw

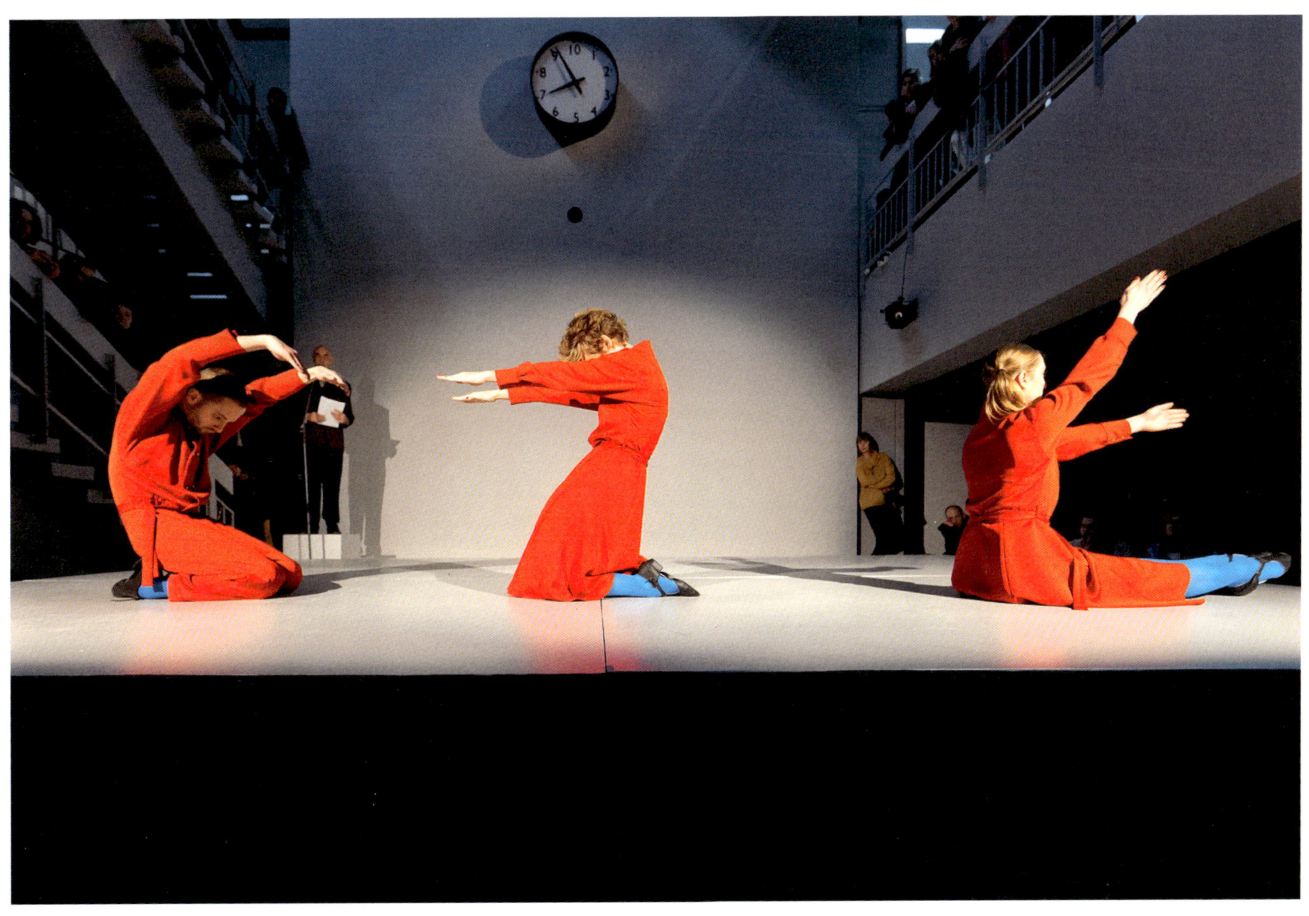

Paulina Olowska, *Alphabet* 2005, Museum of Modern Art, Warsaw, 6 January 2014

authenticity. The expressive staging of the body in Vienna Actionism and after – the transgression, scarification, decoration of the body's skin – might be traced back not only to Antonin Artaud's passionate and convulsive 'theatre of cruelty' of the 1920s and 30s but also to naïve ideas of 'primitivism' born of fantasies of non-Western artefacts and cultures. The work of Paul Gauguin, Pablo Picasso and others in the early twentieth century problematically lumped together notions from Balinese or African art with the unselfconsciousness of art by children. This body art is also connected with the Freudian expressionism of Gustav Klimt, Egon Schiele and Oskar Kokoschka in turn-of-the-century Vienna and the non-academic art forms, or 'art brut', that inspired Jean Dubuffet during the postwar period. If those artists sought, in different ways, to express interiority by identifying with the so-called other – the outsider, the exotic subject, the child – they also sought to access a seemingly authentic mode of expression, borrowed from these 'found' practices, to counter the cultured stylisation of academic European sculpture and painting. The staging of the naked, raw physicality of the subject, often in situations of extreme endurance, in the performance art of the Vienna Actionists can be seen as a literalised extension of this desire. In the 1970s, artists such as Gina Pane, Stuart Brisley, Marina Abramović and Petr Štembera took these ideas to their limit, to create powerful images of alternatively fragile and abject bodies that push interiority to the surface.

Artists working in different contexts in this period demonstrated a desire to strike out against accepted forms and start from scratch. These artists were often working on their own bodies as a signifier of a mode of primary existence, imagining the body as a territory and a material that could be claimed and presented on its own terms. This focus on the body offered, in turn, potential for rethinking the culture of art-making. Performance art was often about being an amateur, experimenting, rather than a skilled performer, in order that apparently authentic exposure of the self, or exchange with others, might occur. Working with notions of intimacy, reciprocity, community and communality, and challenging the boundaries of the artwork as a fixed material object, artists began, rather, to show its significance within a visible conversation between people: to show its base in social relations. The relative statuses of the *I* (the artist as maker and subject), *We* (the viewers or participants in the work) and *It* (the art object as an externalisation of the artist's subjectivity) were being newly staged and reimagined.

These questions and tendencies are evident in the practices that emerged in this period in different parts of the world, which were connected in a limited fashion via artists' networks such as mail art and touring festivals and exhibitions. For example, according to historian William Marotti, in the Japanese Anti-Art movements of the 1960s 'all artistic conventions and practices, from object to performance, were subject to scrutiny, experiment, and revisions in the service of a critical investigation of daily life'.[8] Artists began to create direct action on the streets, as is the case of the events orchestrated by the group Hi-Red Center (Jiro Takamatsu, Genpei Akasegawa and Natsuyuki Nakanishi) in public spaces around Tokyo, which were intended to cause agitation. These included performing with sculptural objects while riding on the train and staging a cleaning event prior to the 1964 Tokyo Olympics that parodied the government's desire to show the city off to a new global audience. In parallel, in the 1960s in Europe, the Vienna Actionists sought to re-awaken the senses in the stultifying context of denial that prevailed in bourgeois postwar Austria by creating – in their studios – live tableaux including blood and naked flesh in combination with the raw pigments, and the traditional materials and support, of painting. In the same period, artists Allan Kaprow in the US, Jean-Jacques Lebel in Paris, and Marta Minujín in both Paris and Buenos Aires staged large-scale, game-like participatory events called 'happenings' that blurred the boundaries between artist, artwork and spectators, and segued into daily life, while in Korea individual artists such as Kim Ku-lim and Lee Kang-So performed eccentric or intimate gestures, often in public spaces, to propose micro-alternatives to state-led mass conformity.

It is useful, initially, to draw our frame of study closely around this burst of body-centred performance action, this moment that destabilised clear divisions between spectator and artist-actor, which built momentum in the late 1950s. We might propose it as a kind of 'degree zero' for a thread that reaches backwards to early twentieth-century experiments, and forwards to what performance in art means today. Performance, in the mid-twentieth century, proposed a way of re-connecting art and life. It conjured alternatives to the dominant ideologies under which art and life operated, demonstrating art's role within a specific context, and a community of shared interest, and yet challenging prevalent political or institutional agendas. Its directness could offer a new kind of sincerity, confound expectations with an emphasis on risk, and foreground the fundamental relations between making, showing and witnessing that constitute the art experience. At a time of incipient globalism, such shifts were part of a wider,

Minoru Hirata, *Hi Red Center's Dropping Event, Ikenobo Hall, Tokyo, 10 October 1964*

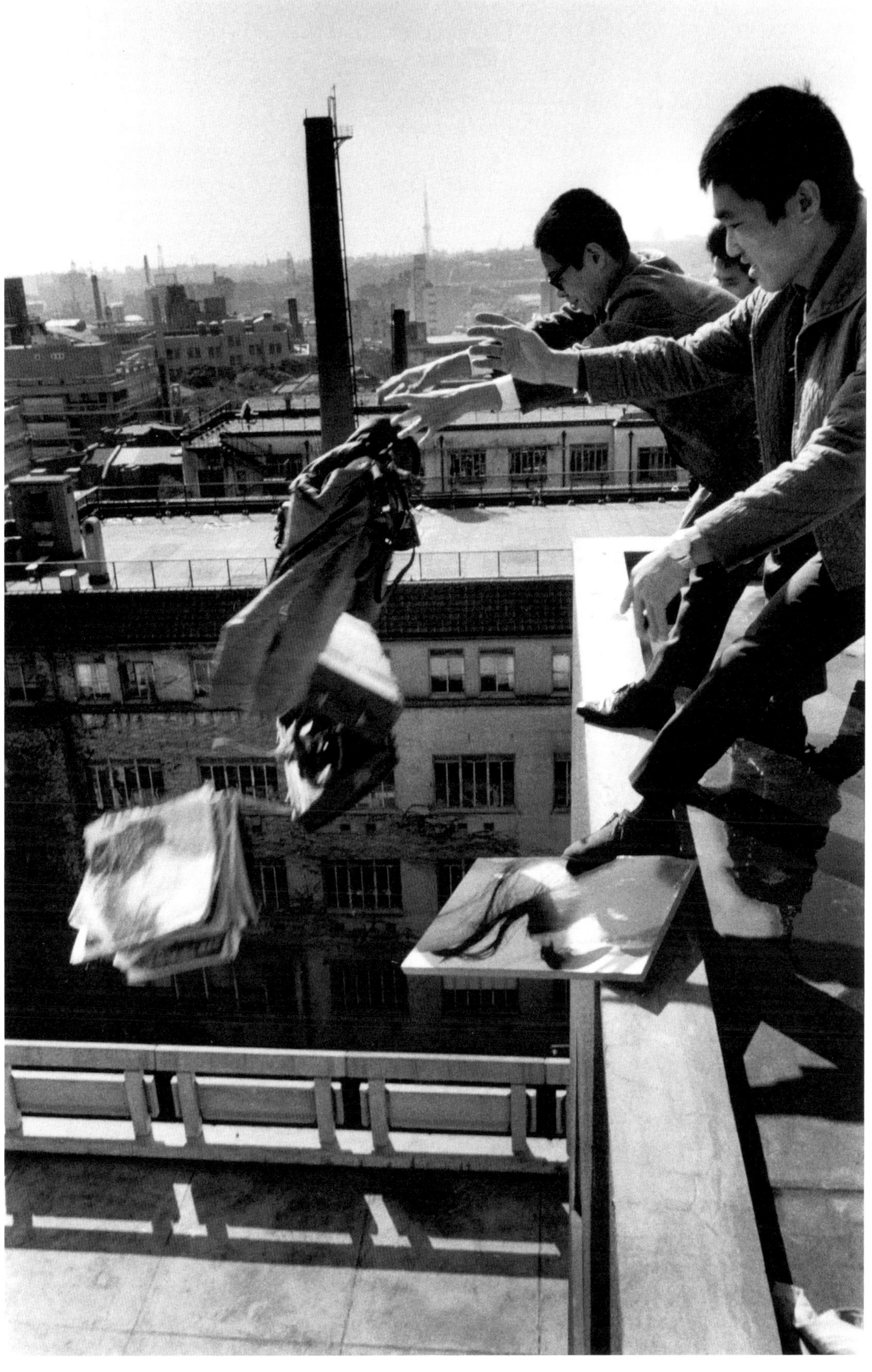

emergent post-colonial challenge to an idea of who the 'we' of the audience might be, too. This was not to be taken for granted. If 'what is art?' was in question for Duchamp in the early twentieth century, after the upheavals of two world wars, it was overwritten by the bigger contextual question: 'what is society?'

Performance and performativity

Before we begin to deal with what performance means, and has meant, in an art context over the past fifty years, it is worth considering the ways in which the word itself is fundamentally, and productively, slippery. Several terms have been used for this kind of art: 'live art', 'action', 'happening', 'event' and 'situation', in English alone. But 'performance' is the English term that has most currency internationally at present: it is routinely used by artists, writers and curators to describe work with a live dimension in the contexts of conversation, critical writing, marketing materials and programming.[9] As a result, it has become ever more potent and pervasive. It functions, as writer Bert O. States has observed, as 'one of those terms that Raymond Williams calls "keywords"': words 'whose meanings are "inextricably bound up with the problems [they are] being used to discuss"'.[10] That is, words that in themselves create the conceptual space that enables the existence of what they describe.

The etymology of the term is instructive in a study of performance within art, especially because it helps us to understand its entanglement with the language-basis of conceptualism. 'To perform' at one time meant simply 'to do'. Later, around the seventeenth century, its meaning shifted towards completing a task or behaviour for an audience, 'to enact doing'. In contemporary business terminology, 'to perform' is 'to succeed', hence the notion of assessment through 'key performance indicators'. Today, 'performance' and its related theoretical term 'the performative' connote something more reflexive, like the (artificial) constitution of reality by 'enacting-as-doing' and 'doing-as-enacting'. Within art, the term 'performative' is commonly, and a little confusingly, used both as an adjective, intended to mean 'performance-like', or 'involving live performance', and in its theoretical sense, after the linguistic theory of J.L. Austin. Austin coined the term in the 1950s to refer to the citation (or performed repetition) of socially instituted scripts via utterances such as oaths or declarations, which form the foundation of a shared agreement about reality, such as a law, or institutional rules and codes.[11] In a slightly messy overlap of these dual uses of the term, 'performative' has come to suggest a state of self-awareness that is fundamentally woven into the undertaking of practical action: a capacity for iteration as opposed to passive description. In her important book *Gender Trouble* (1990), philosopher Judith Butler borrowed this linguistic concept to consider the 'acts' that constitute normative patterns of behaviour in society: the way in which a person's individual subjectivity is produced through the unwitting repetition of acts learned at school, in the family and through the media – one's social performance – and is thus potentially open to change.[12] Performativity as a concept is concerned, then, with the mutual influences between how we imagine the *I*, *We* and *It*, and how language is part of this game.

Questions around performance within visual art can be partially, but not substantially, articulated in relation to the academic discipline of performance studies, whose territory expands well beyond that of visual art towards a broader anthropological study of rites and cultural enactment as they intersect with theatre. Richard Schechner, one of the founders of this discipline, has described performance in a general sense as 'twice-behaved behaviour'.[13] Marvin Carlson, author of *Performance: A Critical Introduction* (1996), points to the difficulty of judging where performing might begin and end, stating, 'the recognition that our lives are structured according to repeated and socially sanctioned modes of behaviour' suggests that 'all human activity could potentially be considered as "performance" … or at least all activity carried out with a consciousness of itself'.[14] But in art terms, performance is treated not so much as an anthropological condition of our social state of being (although this might be implicit in certain works) but, in the first instance, as a medium: a way of working with a live situation. In a more developed sense, performance conveys a certain attitude: a degree of self-consciousness about art as live activity, which might also be carried through to our understanding of all other forms of art-making, even those in purportedly traditional media.

The mapping of this territory within the field of visual art has been given more and more attention in recent decades. RoseLee Goldberg, author of the essential first survey of performance art, *Performance: Live Art, 1909 to the Present* (1979), has stated that, as a baseline, performance art is 'live art by artists', elaborating that it is 'a medium that insists on actual presence, on the experience of "being there"'.[15] Birgit Pelzer, also writing in the 1970s, defined performance as 'an activity that declares itself as an activity'.[16] British artist Bruce McLean, a sculptor who made important live work that muddled disciplinary boundaries, such as *Pose Work for Plinths* 1971, in which he himself appears as the figure on the plinth, has humorously described it as 'a word that was invented by the Arts Council to categorise "difficult" work'.[17] Equivalent translations of 'performance' were used in many contexts. For example, Diana Taylor notes that in Latin America, 'where the term finds no satisfactory equivalent in either Spanish or Portuguese, "performance" has commonly referred to performance art'.[18] But other terms also emerged in that context to identify specific practices. Harper Montgomery remarks that the term 'arte no-objetual' (non-object-based art), coined by Peruvian art historian Juan Acha in the 1970s, aimed to account for 'experimental practices that incorporated performance, media art, and other ephemeral and interventionist tactics'.[19] Or, discussing the history of performance in Korea, for example, Joan Kee has said: 'The social import of performance art in Korea is vividly manifested by the Korean terms used to refer to such works. *P'ŏp'omŏnsŭ*, the romanised term for performance, was not widely used until the 1980s. Instead the earliest performances, which took place in the late 1960s, were often called "happenings", a term likely borrowed from Allan Kaprow.'[20]

In a contemporary context, theorist Bojana Kunst describes performance as 'an antagonistic knot … a conglomerate of contradictory forces (human, non-human, spatial, natural, etc.) that constitute the moment of the present, and the invention of its political potential'.[21] In common art-world parlance, 'performance' in art often means something much simpler: more or less, a work of art that is staged as a live event, or has live presence. Even if the term is inadequate, it can work as a basic medium description alongside other basic categories of painting, sculpture, video, and so on. And yet the term's purchase within the field of contemporary art has evolved in ways that are, as Kunst notes, to do with its revelation of art's socio-political base, and how it might be applied to technology and objects too. Performance and performativity represent attitudes or perspectives as much as media in current practice.

Daniel Buren, *Photo-Souvenir: Affichage sauvage, travail in situ*, Paris, May 1969 (detail)

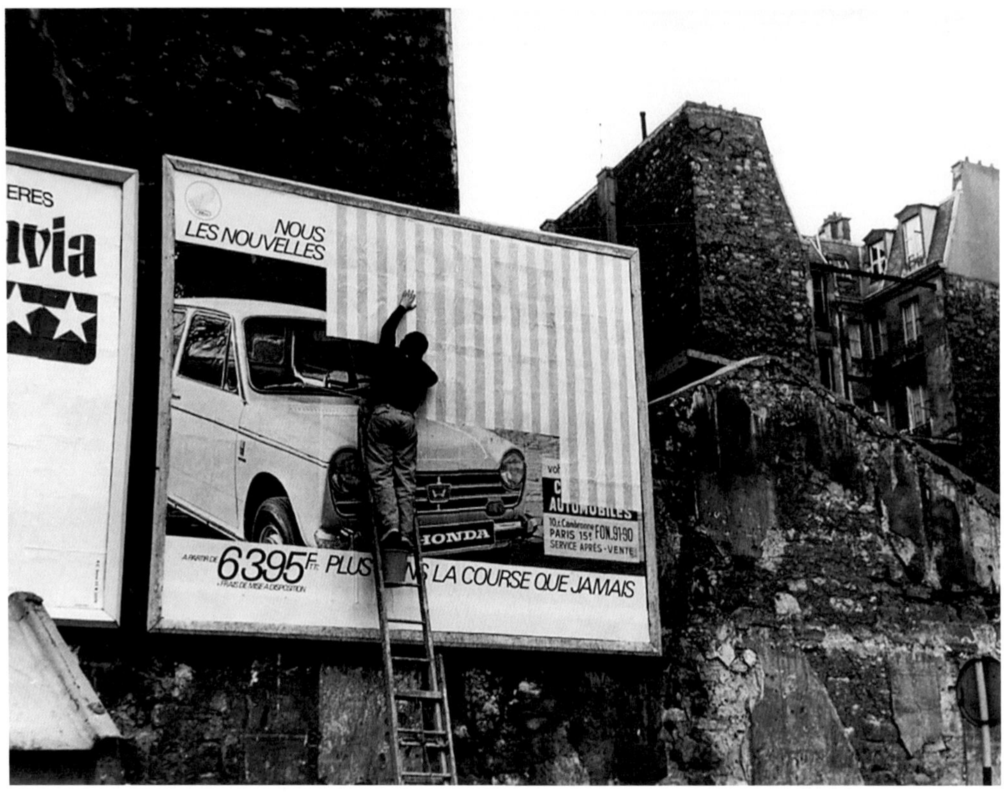

In her important book *How to Do Things with Art* (2010), art historian Dorothea von Hantelmann shows how both objects and installations, as well as actors, can perform within an art context.[22] Her approach to performativity in contemporary art deliberately opens this idea up to consider how paintings by Daniel Buren or the video installations of James Coleman might be citational. In drawing our attention to the theatrical nature of the gallery's white walls, or the ritual of viewing a video – which either iterate or deviate from pre-existing social and institutional scripts – von Hantelmann makes the essential point that structures and objects perform actively as much as people do. But von Hantelmann's separation of this iterative quality of art from the literal theatre of historical performance art seems too neat, especially as regards its development in the 1960s, 1970s and 1980s. Literal acts of performance art, as events, haunt performativity as its metaphorical ancestors.

In the last fifty years, the action-basis of performance has drawn attention to the instability of the repeated rituals of so many aspects of art-making and presentation. Actual performances occurring within the field of art have, arguably, prompted us to see the whole field differently. Just as conceptual art began as a discrete perspective on practice, foregrounding concept and language, but has come to underwrite our understanding of contemporary art practice ubiquitously, so the performance perspective on visual art production – what we have learned to see as its made-ness, its transactional character, its impermanence, and its reliance upon repeated conventions of display – comes to inflect our understanding of what art is and means in the broadest sense.

The kinds of performance art that emerged in the 1960s instigated a dissolution of traditional disciplinary boundaries. The attitude of Cage, Cunningham and Rauschenberg towards indeterminacy and improvisation across their respective disciplines of music, dance, and painting and sculpture has been a strong influence on our understanding of this area of practice, and its legacy dominates Western art history. But for artists in the twenty-first century, performance is not the free or undefinable space of cross-disciplinarity that some mythology around the work suggests. It is, often, a way of testing art's own frame and its protocols as regards audience-artist-artwork relations. Performance can be about singular acts or events created for an audience, but it can also be about drawing our attention to the active relations between people and things in more subtle ways that are not clearly bracketed in time. Performance is now defined by a double-layered understanding: as both the making of live events for a temporary community and the more pervasive conceptual attitude of performativity, which marks an openness to the possibility that things might act, and that social and institutional scripts might be acting through us.

Understanding what performance in art today means is less about fetishising liveness as defined by the presence of the living body, as much writing on performance has done, and more about considering a broader state of *changeability* or instability that is live: to consider how subject and object positions might be destabilised, and how subjectivity and society might be reciprocally shaped. Such a state is what makes performance thrilling, but it also makes it difficult to define its limits. Without the clear material boundaries of a painting or a sculpture, where does a work of performance begin and end? How does the zone of possibility that performance initiates intersect with other disciplines?

Performance has emerged afresh as a vital area of exploration for artists in the past decade, perhaps because of its potential to be direct, expressive, political and unstable, as well as seductive, experiential and visually compelling. Performance seems to offer a space where the acts of making and showing, the process of exhibiting, are heeded; a space where a temporary reality might be produced and inhabited, shared by a community who gather to focus their attention for a period of time. Performance heightens our perception of art's components: they are making, we are watching, this is the work of art. It creates an expanded zone of contemplation that gives attention to art's foundation in deliberate acts and decisions, value systems and beliefs. And in a twenty-first-century context, where the optical field is dominated by seductive images on screens, this kind of work puts an emphasis, instead, on the conventional frame of art – the gallery – as not just a viewing space, but a public space in which to gather.

I – We – It

If performance is elusive in its definitions, it is equally slippery as an object of study. Much has been made in art historical and theoretical writing of performance's ephemerality, its status as material fragments or remains. There are different ways in which I have accessed the works discussed in this book: much of the contemporary work has been experienced through direct encounters with it, or even working with the artists to produce it, yet most historical work has been viewed through documentation. What remains of past events is a mixed bag: photographs, sketches, video, scores, stage sets, reviews, costumes, props, rumours, witness memories. Though these fragments offer only glimpses of the original work, they build nevertheless to form an imperfectly partial but powerfully intoxicating foundation myth for our understanding of performance art. These pictures and accounts are, first, forms and formats in themselves,[23] but I am taking permission to treat them, also, as prompts to the imagination, which can give us forceful, primary images of artistic activity.

In the past fifty years, a new lexicon of art-making has emerged that re-casts the roles conventionally ascribed to the participants in the art encounter: the individual subject (*I*), the audience or community (*We*) and the artwork (*It*). Performance has given us an arena in which to look, explicitly, at the testing of dynamic positions between artist, audience or artwork; positions that proffer concrete new patterns for presenting, paying attention to, and participating in art. From these templates, performance has emerged bolder, more theoretical and nuanced. Ideas coming out of the raw, early period of performance art are now woven into the fabric of much more wide-ranging art practices in ways that are highly fragmented and dispersed. Arguably, the very logic of performance as an event-based art form contained a drive towards the further disintegration of its own boundaries: a radical flexibility that is about much more than the electric charge of immediate liveness.

I was drawn to the area of performance within art because it was in motion, and because it is an experience of art in which one can never be sure where it is going or what is next, which offers a tantalising sense of infinite possibility. And as a student of a more conventional art history in the early 1990s, I had always wanted to widen the frame around the work of art to see how its aesthetic form was not only informed by, but also merged with, its social, and thus political, base. Performance incorporates live actions, but it also feels closer to lived life in its refusal to stay in one place, its persistence in transgression. Thrillingly, the rules never quite fit. In this sense, it is an area of practice that disrupts prevailing definitions of authorship and ownership; even the fact that performances are now bought and sold is an experiment with the rules of the market. That is not to say that it is a free-for-all area without conventions. Conventions, drawn from its evolution through the history of art, and through dialogue with its neighbouring disciplines, exist, but are visibly open to contestation, or to being replayed and reimagined.

More familiar forms of art can, of course, also be all these things, but under the banner of performance we experience them, arguably, more directly, and often as a two-way conversation, or a situation that we are implicated in. At the same time, since Gerhard Richter, Sigmar Polke and others playfully planted a group of paintings in the front garden outside the Wupperthal villa of their soon-to-be dealer, Rudolf Jahrling, in 1964, performance actions can also be used as a means of gaining exposure in late capitalism. Performance, then, is a notion that can speak eloquently about the anxious position of being alive, and the need to be paid, in the twenty-first century: having to negotiate new online pressure for hyper-visibility in work and leisure.

The history of performance that has been written so far has attempted to situate performance as a medium that equates with other art historical mediums: painting, sculpture, installation and so on. Goldberg has, appositely, proposed that the roots of performance art can be identified in the experiments of the avant-gardes of the early twentieth century. Her book has been incredibly important in setting out such a history, from a Western perspective, and in attempting to make sense of the work that Goldberg was experiencing in New York and London at the time of her writing it. But one of the potential limits of this kind of method, based on classical art history, is that despite its championing of the quality of liveness, such a mode of tracking the evolution of a language through time, appropriate to painting or sculpture, is applied to what is, by and large, a fundamentally different medium and attitude. Performance, and the attendant difficulty in retrieving it, rests upon a succession of disappearing acts that operate in a different cyclical kind of progression of iteration and repetition and, in this sense, it has to be thought about differently.

Chronology that was designed for stories of object-based media makes less sense for ephemeral and time-based formats, with their own cycles of appearance and disappearance. Moreover, there is an emphasis in Goldberg on liveness's service to the object, which remains as the prized evidence. 'When the members of such groups [Futurists, Constructivists, Dadaists, Surrealists] were still in their twenties or early thirties,' she observes, 'it was in performance that they tested their ideas, only later expressing them in objects.'[24] The extraordinarily rich and important exhibition *Out of Actions: Between Performance and the Object 1949–79* similarly focused on 'the paintings, sculptures, installations, objects and documentation that form the residue, the work of art, that resulted from [the] performance work' of artists and collectives such as Gutai, Yves Klein, Mike Kelley and others.[25] And yet, what we actually see in the work of an artist like Rauschenberg is a continuous movement back and forth between work made for the gallery and work made for the stage, a desire to 'keep painting alive', and a productive influence both ways.

From a museological point of view, the retrieval of this performance history, and the preservation of performance work, is a current concern for many institutions (alongside Tate, museums including the Museum of Modern Art in New York, the Stedelijk Museum in Amsterdam, the Van Abbemuseum in Eindhoven and the Serralves Museum in Porto are actively engaged in this process). It is worth noting that this movement, across art institutions, might be set within the context of a broader, emerging interest in live traditions internationally; UNESCO have begun to preserve 'intangible cultural heritage' alongside monuments and artefacts, for example. In the museum, we must infer the liveness of historical work that appears as documentation: its summoning of attention to the unique quality that performance necessarily embodies, that of being in the 'present tense'.[26] But what is available to represent that history is usually only secondary material: those paintings, sculptures, installations and photographs – and one might add scores and instruction pieces that come with contracts. In this way, it is important that the above institutions are not only collecting but also programming live work.

In 2018, at a time when artists of the current generation are working on ways of scoring, or otherwise devising strategies through which live work can be exhibited and collected in its primary form, we might begin by trying to think about what seems essential to our understanding of that high period between the 1950s and 1970s from a contemporary perspective. The museological problem of how this period of performance work can be collected and displayed is fundamentally related to the question of how this work is embedded in art historical narratives as much as in the space and time in which we encounter it today. In the first instance, it might be necessary to get a little lost in the fiction suggested by the fragments, to allow ourselves to imagine the live impact of seeing arrows shot

Atsuko Tanaka wearing her Electric Dress suspended from the ceiling at the 2nd Gutai Art Exhibition, Tokyo, 1956

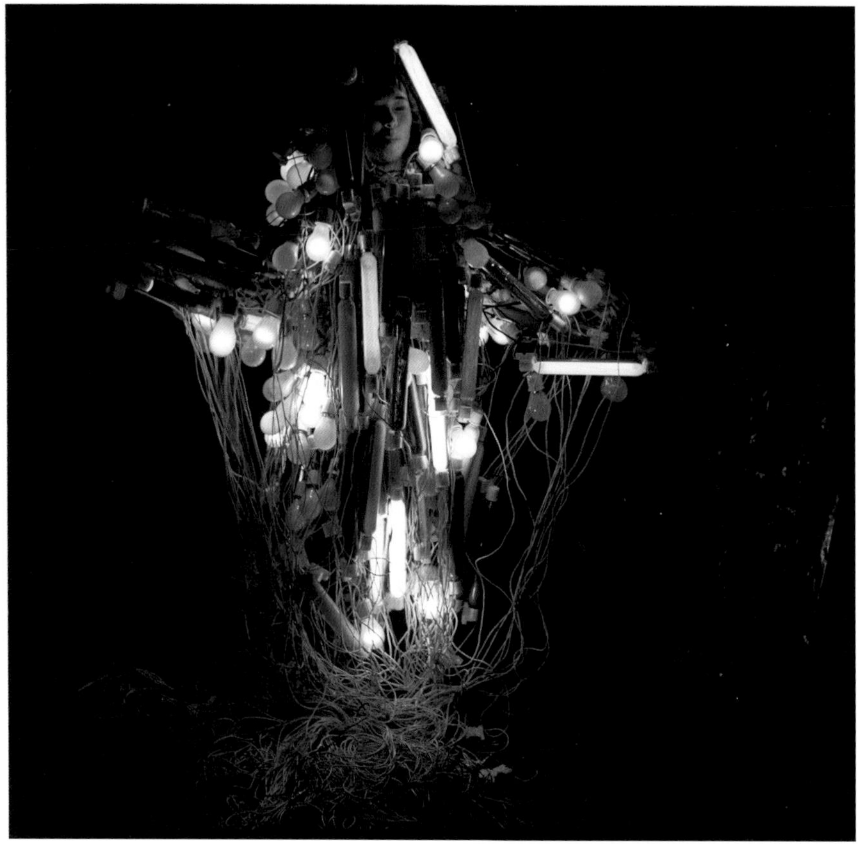

through canvases and smoke ring sculptures in *Gutai Art on the Stage* 1957–8, as though we can access it via the transparent information contained in documentation, which otherwise – considered as the remains of a historical event – returns us to the material present. Yet the texture of the remnants also opens up ways of looking at objects that come from a different, performative perspective. In his analysis for the research project 'Performance at Tate', Jonah Westerman observes that the two polar approaches to past performances that define the territory are those of Peggy Phelan and Philip Auslander: the former believing in the unique presence of the live event, that 'one had to be there', the latter arguing that only the event's mediation enables us to recognise it as a performance as such. Westerman suggests a third, 'inframedial' approach that has to do with the space between witness and document, a space where performance 'lies and lives'.[27]

If we are to understand what performance means for art now, attempting to trace the art historical evolution of a form or genre akin to painting or installation seems inadequate. To begin exploring this territory from a fresh perspective, we might observe that the current generation of artists working with performance manifest a flatter relationship with history than the teleological narrative that dominates art historical accounts. We are, arguably, in a post-modern, post-internet world in which all of history appears to be available simultaneously, or at least images thereof. Work of the current generation thus often stages an interplay between live acts, performed attitudes, vintage images and films, and networks of translation and connection: a territory in which historical change does not happen as a succession of formal questions being passed one to the next, but as a complex back-and-forth between past and present, and between multiple presents or multiple localities. In the past decade, many artists, including Tino Sehgal, Marina Abramović, Ei Arakawa, Keren Cytter, Tania Bruguera and Rabih Mroué, have made works that iterate potted histories of performance – both canonical surveys and individual re-enactments – as new works.[28] They are summoning passing history and making it palpable in the present. And so performance history does not behave around questions of authenticity, originality, reproducibility, stability and historical narrative in the way that more traditional art objects do, or can.

It is also important to note, in looking at the pivotal period of experimentation in the 1960s and 1970s, that 'performance art' as a term is heavily associated with work made in the US.[29] American work has also been the most extensively theorised and tracked art historically. As a result, the attitudes associated with this work – the conception of subjectivity, psychology, gender relations, and society – are inflected by an American worldview. While acknowledging the richness of these practices and the influence that this work has had internationally, it is essential to consider, in parallel, different ways of understanding the categories *I*, *We* and *It*, as they have been put forward by a wider global network of artists during this same period, with diverging understandings of the relation between individuality and collectivity, privacy and publicness.

Work that was made in Korea, Russia, the former Yugoslavia, Africa, Latin America and elsewhere is often clearly in dialogue with American and western European notions of performance art, and we know that images of actions, performances and events were circulating globally, via diplomatic networks and art magazines, as well as through unofficial channels such as mail art and Fluxus. It is also true that, often, similar gestures or actions were performed in different geographical contexts, taking on different inferences and creating a disjointed conversation of near doublings and *faux amis* across continents. But part of the richness of this territory, and the peculiar nature of this kind of work, is that such back-and-forth between live action, image, transmission and description was taking place actively, and that different conceptions of what performing meant – by whom and for whom – emerged in different places. David Joselit's distinction between a desire to track 'global' art history and the potentially more accurate perspective of the 'international', or transnational, is pertinent here,[30] as is Édouard Glissant's preference for the archipelago format of connected concrete localities in his concept of 'mondialité' over pan-globalism.[31]

This book is not a history of performance art as a genre, unto itself. Neither is it a comprehensive survey covering every form of performance in art since the 1950s. Rather, I have worked backwards from the present, trying to understand how we got here by looking at a necessarily limited selection of artists who are representative of historical imperatives in this area, and trying to relate them to the contemporary by setting them into a broader pattern. My perspective on the territory is inevitably skewed by geography, built from my own bias as a London-based curator at Tate Modern with a fundamentally Western perspective and sphere of experience, but my own work and research in a context of Tate's rich international research programmes have provided me with awareness of multiple international histories and the extraordinary chance to work with very many of the artists discussed here.

Borders

The map of this moving territory is difficult to chart. We might imagine a Venn diagram, in which contemporary art appears as a series of intersecting rings, which partly overlap with neighbouring disciplines – theatre, music, dance, as well as architecture, science, film and political activism. It is the movement of these 'other' disciplinary practices – as ready-made formats – into contemporary art's frame that makes for part of the performative attitude that is current.

Some of the practitioners in neighbouring fields find a place within the zone of contemporary art because their approach speaks to art's concerns. Mutual curiosity prompts such movements. And a number of such practitioners operate in both areas, moving in and out of the space of art: Lucy McKenzie (working with designer Beca Lipscombe) operates a commercial fashion and design company – Atelier E.B. – alongside and enmeshed with her painting-based art practice; Tarek Atoui works across the world of electro-acoustic music and the gallery or museum context; with his 'dancing museum', Boris Charmatz choreographs works for the stage of the contemporary dance theatre as well as for the public plaza or the gallery; and, indeed, Steve McQueen directs Hollywood movies and continues to show in museums with his video installations. The space of art readily ingests all manner of other forms, seeming to offer a temporary home that draws attention to disciplinary values and formats in a critical context. Art is also, apparently, hungry to learn from its neighbouring practices.

Artists have begun to invite the crafts of dancing, acting and performing into their practices on a continuum with approaches to materials more commonly associated with the visual arts, whether painting on canvas, collage or editing high-res video. They might work with dancers to make a living picture, or borrow an academic lecture format. Indeed, visual artists are importing whole ready-made conventions, the theatre piece being a prime example: Elmgreen & Dragset, Goshka Macuga, Paulina Ołowska and Keren Cytter have all appropriated theatre formats for art, finding new spaces and possibilities within them. Equally, since the late 1970s, the US artist Suzanne Lacy has instigated media activism campaigns while producing aesthetic representations of the work for gallery display. And so on.

At the same time, institutions have increasingly been inviting practitioners in other fields – choreographers, musicians, filmmakers – into the space of art. Why? The cross-disciplinary nature of earlier performance opened this door; it suggested that such a trespass might be possible and productive. And in a field where artists readily borrow from the disciplines in proximity, such displacements can stimulate attention to the nuances inherent in the different practices being gathered together. Even if an artist working with dancers and a choreographer proper might be coming from different places, their cohabitation forces comparison, it compels the acknowledgement of meeting points, or contrast. Since the early 2000s, the field of contemporary art has seen a period of expansion where such clashes and collaborations have been tested.

Inviting dance, music or film into the frame of art – literally into the gallery – can make us ask, 'is it art?', just as Duchamp's urinal did. But this movement is more important than its probative question. What that movement between disciplinary boundaries brings is a productive cross-contamination: the encounter with dance in the museum not only offers comparative freedom for the choreographer to experiment, it extends the possibilities for art; it adds expertise, nuance and depth to the ways in which the traditionally material-focused world of visual art understands the place of living bodies, of people performing and working together. How does the highly trained, practiced, disciplined and often communally produced dance-conception of the body impact and influence the representation and presence of the human figure as it is presented in a visual arts context? And, conversely, how does the specific approach of the musician both lend new approaches to co-operation, or improvisation, and also benefit from the space of the propositional art context, which might return an extended appreciation of its complex and practiced possibilities? In this book, these crossovers feature more significantly than the many artists who operate solely within those neighbouring disciplines, who have made work that is indirectly relevant to, and influential upon, an art context.

Despite a focus on familiar works from the Western canon that have been thus far acknowledged as the precursors and drivers of performance it is essential for future research to pay attention to unique practices, such as the Jikken Kōbō in 1950s Japan, or the Laboratoire Agit'Art in Senegal in the 1970s. These groups were not necessarily influential in the Western narrative of performance, because being either underground or outside of the major market centres they were not widely known, or photographed, or written about. Nevertheless, they are examples of approaches that provide new models of art that help us to understand contemporary practice, and to imagine new futures for it by offering backstories from which we can retrospectively project. Within our emergent understanding of the transnational, performance is one of the areas of art practice that makes global networks of exchange visible. In the long-distance conversations between practitioners in the past fifty years we can see mutual awareness and exchange; appropriation and adaptation of forms and styles, whose reach is only now beginning to be tracked.

This book's three sections ('I', 'We', 'It') are not intended to create exclusive boundaries between works. Rather, they are tools for considering the primary impact of different kinds of work, and how various artists emphasise the components of the art they make to different degrees. The high point of performance art radically changed the field of art, by attending to what had built it up to this point, and imagining how it could develop from there. But this perspective on performance poses questions, too. How does such active testing of art's boundaries and its modes of working with time threaten our understanding of contemporary art as an area of practice? And what is *not* performative within this perspective? Is there a space outside its reach? To understand contemporary art, an understanding of how it performs is necessary. This book offers a guide to the evolution of that story, both in the dynamics of the art encounter and as a conversation between artists, taking select examples from the past six decades and across continents.

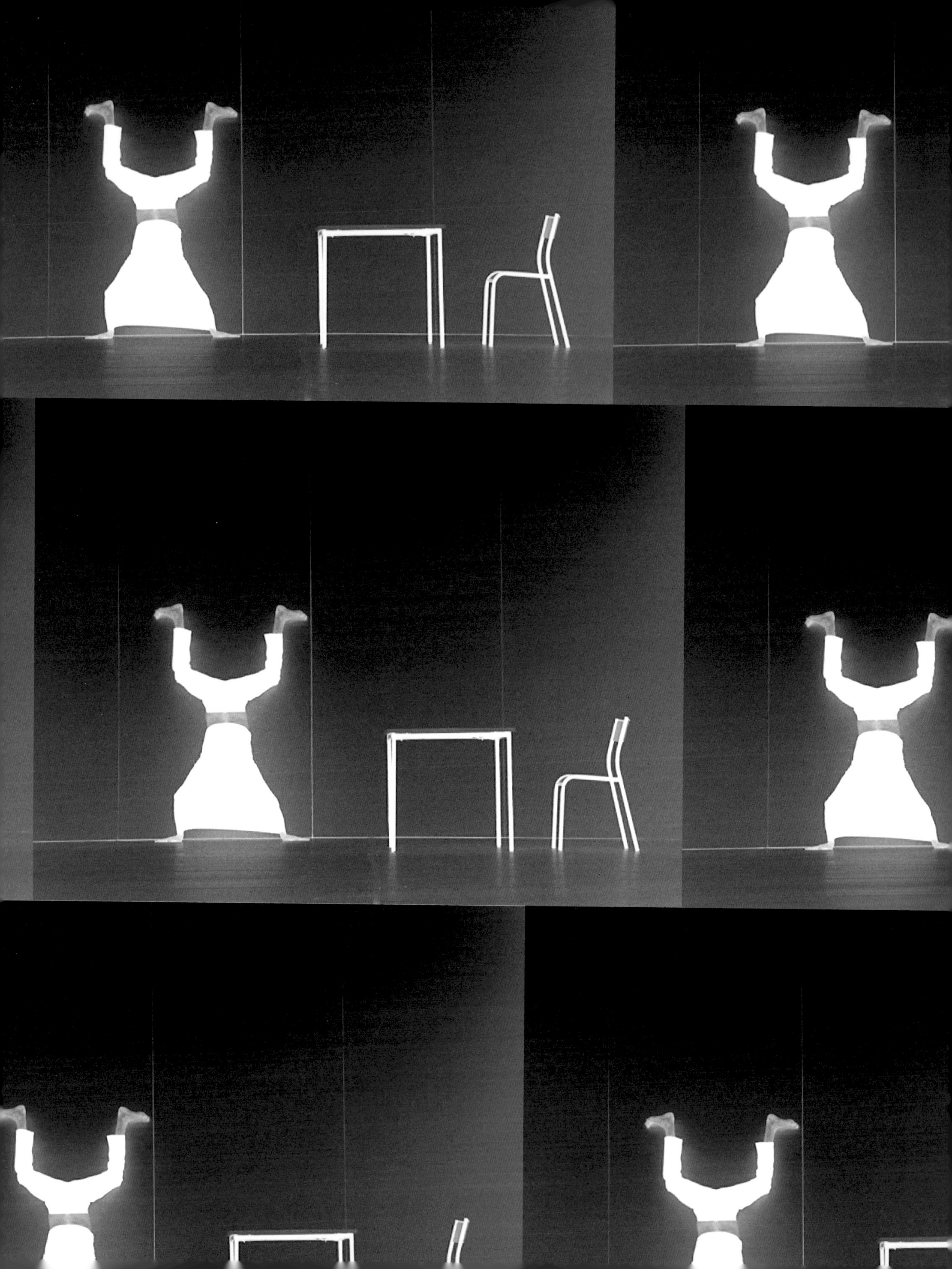

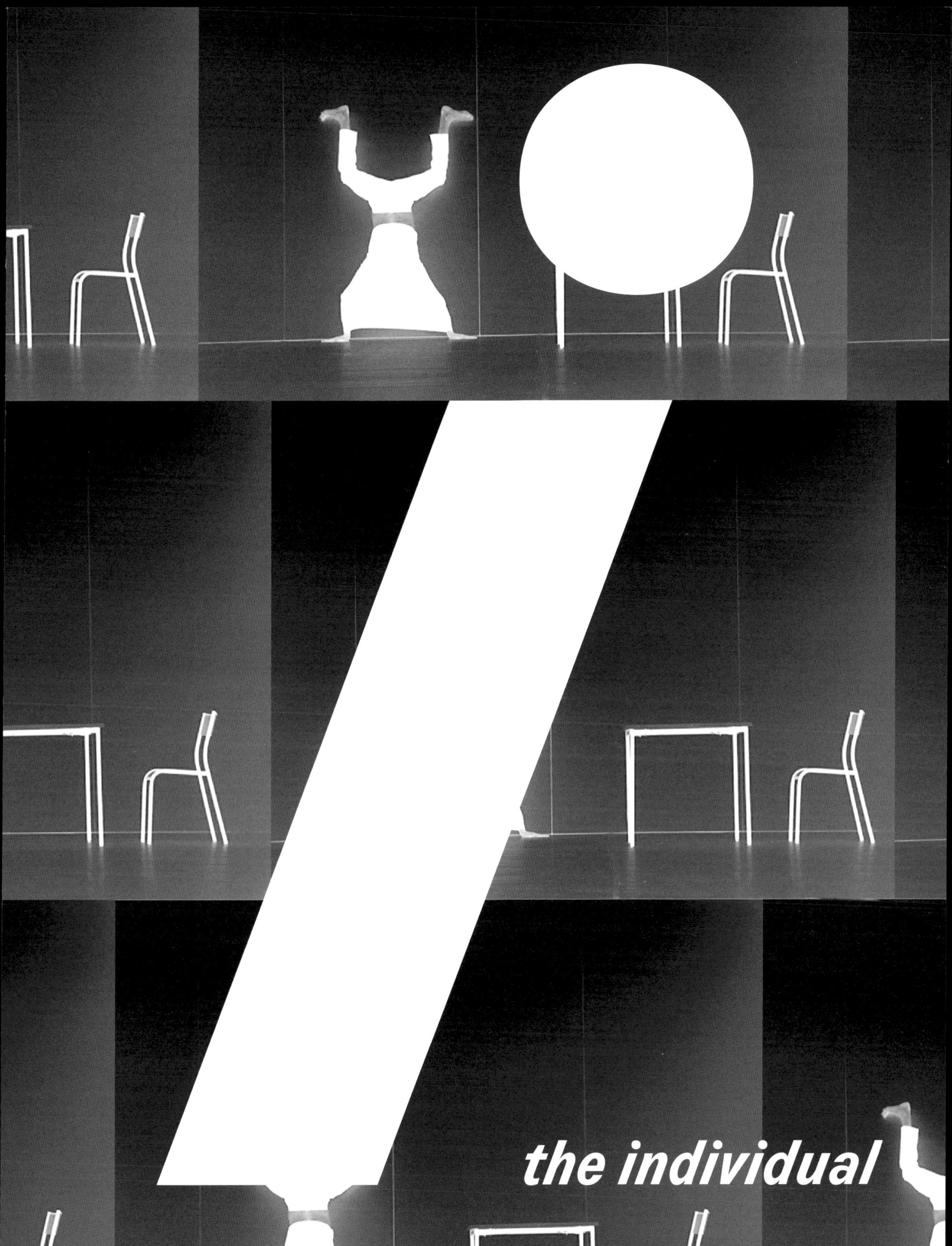
the individual

The artist's presence

Every day, for eight hours a day, over three months in the spring of 2010, the artist Marina Abramović sat silent and still in the atrium of the Museum of Modern Art, New York (MoMA). This feat of endurance was part of *The Artist Is Present*, a work in which Abramović herself was material and medium. A table and two chairs were set out in the middle of a square arena of sorts, lit by four bright lamps. Abramović, dressed in a specially designed dress of heavy cloth (alternating daily between red and white), sat on a chair, while the other was to be occupied by visitors. Anybody could join, one at a time, for as long as they wanted to sit with her. Some pushed this to extremes. Despite the event's popularity resulting in mass attendance, the atmosphere was meditative and serious, and visitors usually held the artist's eye contact. Abramović said that she wanted to be 'like a mountain', 'like a rock'. She claimed that because she did 'nothing', the performance 'became life itself'. The work contained 'no story, no objects, just pure presence', she said.[1]

The figure of the artist presented by Abramović in this work has come to stand for 'performance art' as it is popularly understood today. Against the backdrop of her retrospective unfolding upstairs in the museum – an exhibition that included the live re-enactment of many of her iconic earlier works from the 1970s and 1980s – the singularity of this piece resonated loudly with visitors, and created ripples of attention through New York's saturated media landscape, as well as internationally. Abramović, unmoving at the centre of all this, nevertheless moved those who encountered the piece. She became a kind of living saint or shaman, prompting tearful and ecstatic experiences in turn. People queued to experience this invitation to connect with her. But the impact of the artist's apparently pure presence in real time was also powerfully multiplied by her celebrity profile – she counts actor James Franco and pop star Lady Gaga among her fans – producing a new hybrid, populist version of the previously marginalised image of performance art.

Abramović was born in Belgrade in 1946. She began making performances in the late 1960s, alongside film and video works. Her early work placed an emphasis on endurance, risk and intimacy, using daily rituals such as eating and sleeping, and staging the body's vulnerability to pain. One of her most significant works is her *Rhythm* series 1973–74: a sequence of individual body-art performances exploring her research on 'the body when conscious and unconscious'.[2]
In *Rhythm 10* 1973, the first in the series, Abramović used a collection of twenty knives to repeatedly stab at a piece of paper between her fingers. Each time she cut herself, she changed knives, until she had used all the knives. The series also includes *Rhythm 5*, in which the artist lay on the floor, framed by a burning, five-point star formation (symbolic of Tito's Yugoslavia) made of wood shavings soaked in petrol. In *Rhythm 0* 1974, Abramović appeared seated next to a table, upon which were set seventy-two items suggesting either pain or pleasure, to be utilised at will by the audience on the artist. The action ended when audience members intervened after someone held a gun to her head. Between 1976 and 1988, she worked in collaboration with Frank Uwe Laysiepen (known as Ulay) on works such as *Imponderabilia* 1977, a piece in which viewers attempting to enter a gallery space had to squeeze between the naked bodies of the artists standing either side of the doorway, and *Rest Energy* 1980, a video in which the couple pull a loaded crossbow between them, aimed at Abramović. Their epic work made

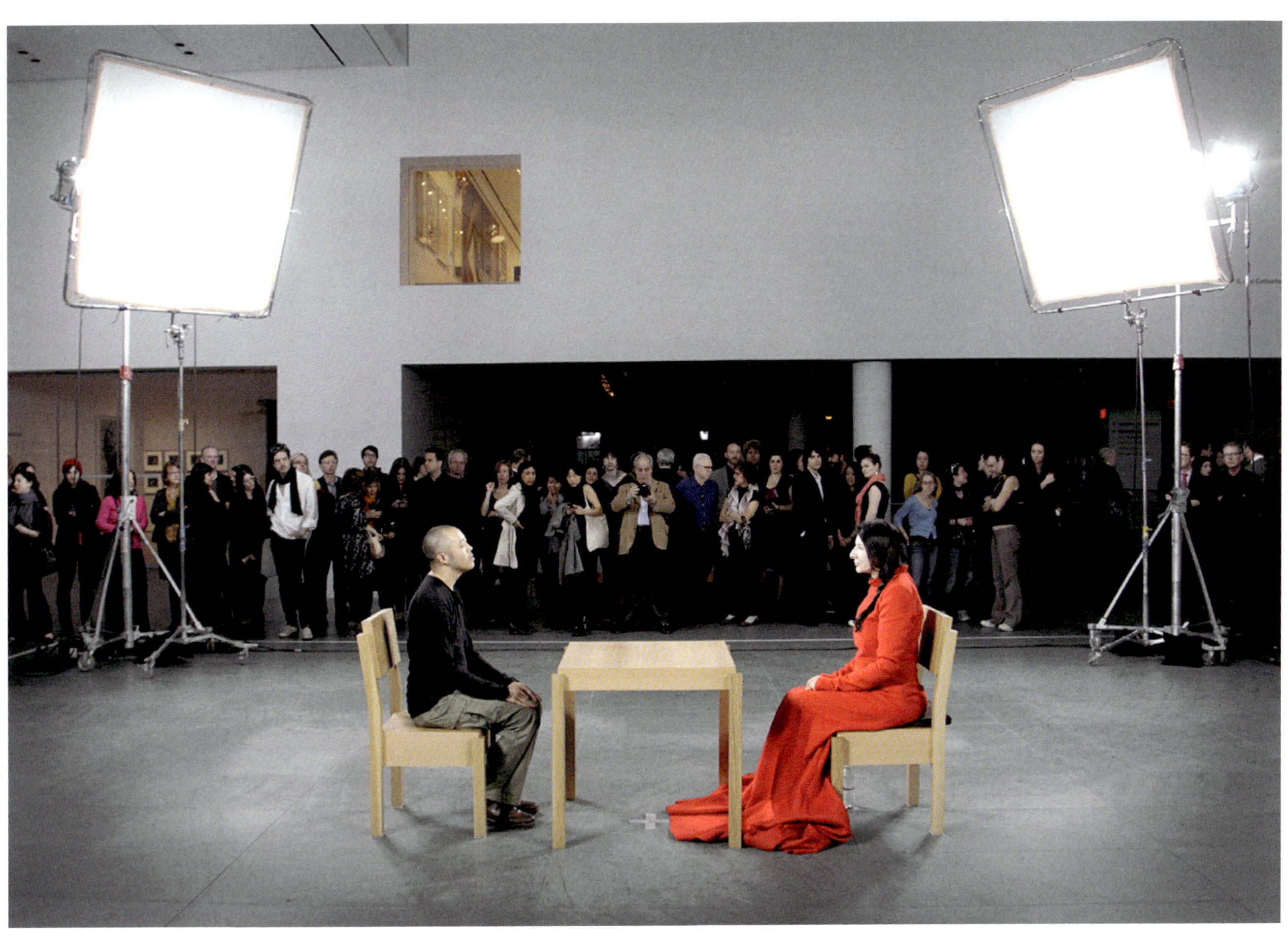

Marina Abramović, *The Artist is Present*, The Museum of Modern Art, New York, 14 March – 31 May 2010

in China, *The Lovers: The Great Wall Walk* 1988, ended both their romantic and artistic relationships in the same year. Abramović's staging of 'pure presence' at MoMA spoke of an idea of authenticity associated with that genre of performance art of the 1970s and, according to Ulay, drew influence from travels during which they lived temporarily among an Aboriginal community in Australia in the 1980s. It was then, Ulay explains, that they together devised the idea that being simply present might be enough to create a kind of perceptual energy that could be art, underwritten by a notion of the artist as a special conduit for a kind of heightened or rarefied perception.[3]

Abramović's performance at MoMA conflates the two major paradigms that define a Western idea of the artist's 'self-performance' in the postwar period: the presentation of the authentic self via the body as a real, vulnerable, physical and emotional presence, often involving ritual duration, on the one hand, and the idea of presenting oneself as a mediated image, on the other. This is not to say that Abramović's is the best work in performance made in this period. The work's own understanding of its authentic basis is questionable in relation to its theatricality. The artist's fast-track invitation to intimacy in such a high-profile setting might be seen as a form of kitsch. In fact, how can one be authentic when performing as a quasi-celebrity? Or is this the only way to present oneself realistically within a twenty-first-century landscape dominated by the image? Abramović arguably builds on the strategies that she developed in the radically different socio-political context of socialist Yugoslavia, and later with Ulay in the West, such as slowing time and creating an intimate rapport between artist and viewer, and spectacularises them to make images suitable for consumer-friendly, twenty-first-century America.

Marina Abramović with Ulay, *Rest Energy*, Dublin 1980, performance for video, 4 min.

But Abramović's performance undoubtedly touches upon something significant in its invitation to a kind of contact – within a form of quasi-mystical contemplation – rarely acknowledged in the contemporary museum. *The Artist Is Present* put forward an idea of being over doing, which seems thrillingly unproductive, perhaps. It appears strangely out of time in its transposition of ideas relevant to the 1970s into the networked, image-obsessed digital age. But the piece gives us a useful way in to chart the evolution of this kind of staging of the self: now, and then. The example of Abramović's work opens up a way to explore not only this transition from marginalised counterculture to the mainstream – a movement that is very familiar in the arena of, say, pop music – but a split view of what it means to present or perform the body: on the one hand, as a kind of raw material and, on the other hand, through constructing one's identity, finding ways to assimilate to the power of the image.

Performance art, as a genre, remains overridingly associated with a similar notion of authenticity to that posed by Abramović's real presence at MoMA. The powerful images that come to mind are of individual artists, surrounded by witnesses, engaged in expressive acts. Canonical images include Yoko Ono's serenely passive expression as her clothes are cut away from her body by an audience member in *Cut Piece* 1964, or Chris Burden's blanched look of shock as he holds his bleeding arm in the surviving photograph of *Shoot* 1971, just after he was shot at by a friend, the flesh of his upper arm penetrated by a real bullet that was fired from only a short distance away (p.36).

Typically, performance art is represented by a singular, experimental and anarchic act. It often involves nakedness, vulnerability and risk, invariably putting the artist-performer face-to-face with the audience. Setting itself up as a counterpoint to the crafted and rehearsed nature of theatre, performance in art was about the un-skilled performer who might reveal something about themselves, unmasked, as it were. The 'I' of the self, in this kind of work, is delineated by the physical boundaries of the artist's body, and the probing thereof is often a kind of literal demonstration of psychological implications: one's inside is shown on the skin. Abramović's *The Artist Is Present* drew heavily upon this history, and one might say that subtle, original aims at authenticity were prostituted in the service of its mass consumption in the museum. But looking back at the roots of performance, a relationship to publicity and press might be seen to play a fundamental role from the start, as inherently intertwined with existential questions regarding what it means to be human.

Live acts by artists proliferated from the early 1950s to the late 1970s in many locations internationally. Artists with diverse approaches to staging the body, and radically different understandings of the status of what *I* meant in this period, include Yves Klein, Niki de Saint Phalle, Shiraga Kazuo, Atsuko Tanaka, Günter Brus, Otto Muehl, Carolee Schneemann, Gina Pane, Petr Štembera, Ana Mendieta and Ion Grigorescu. These practices were variously inflected by existentialism,

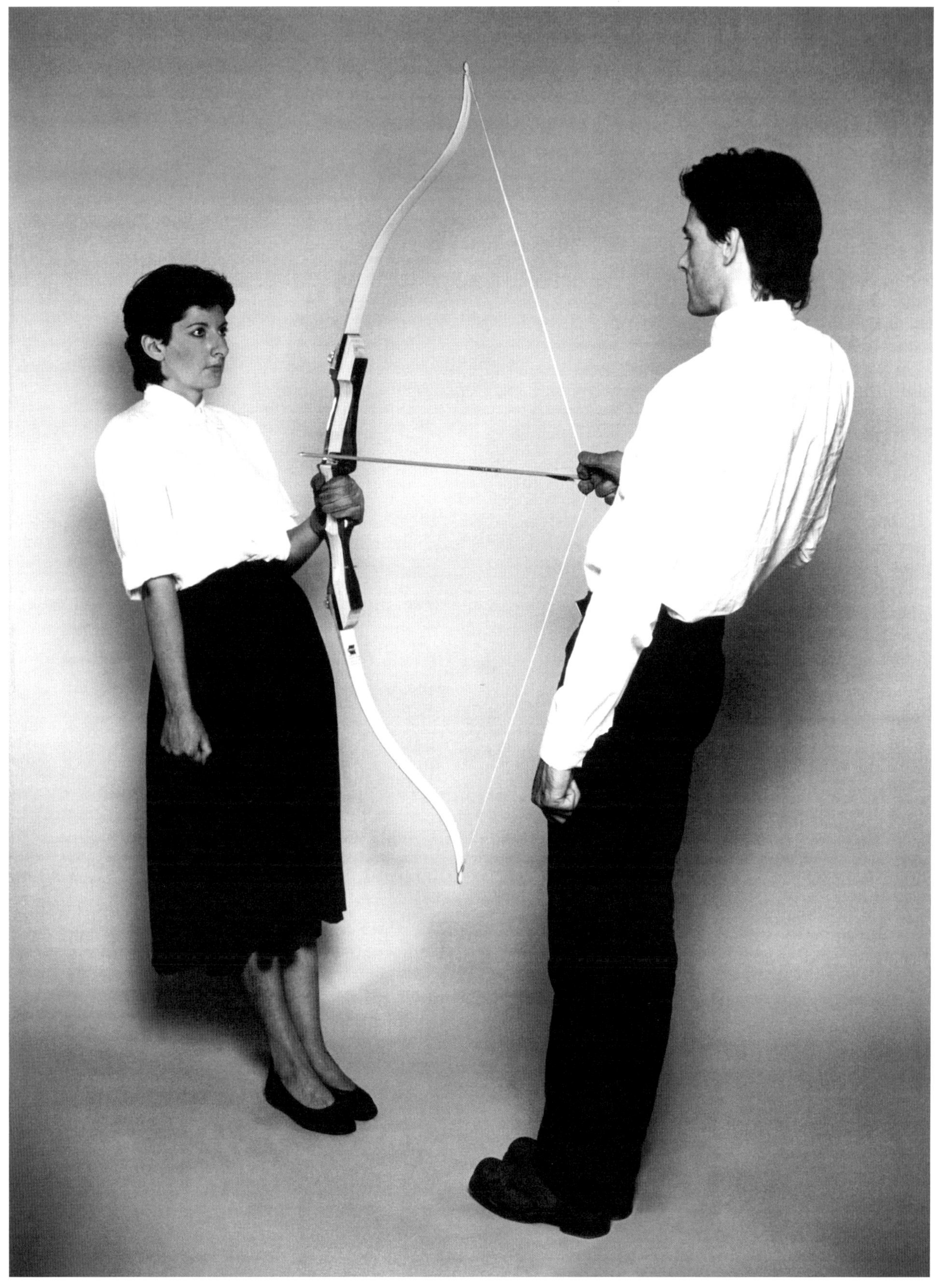

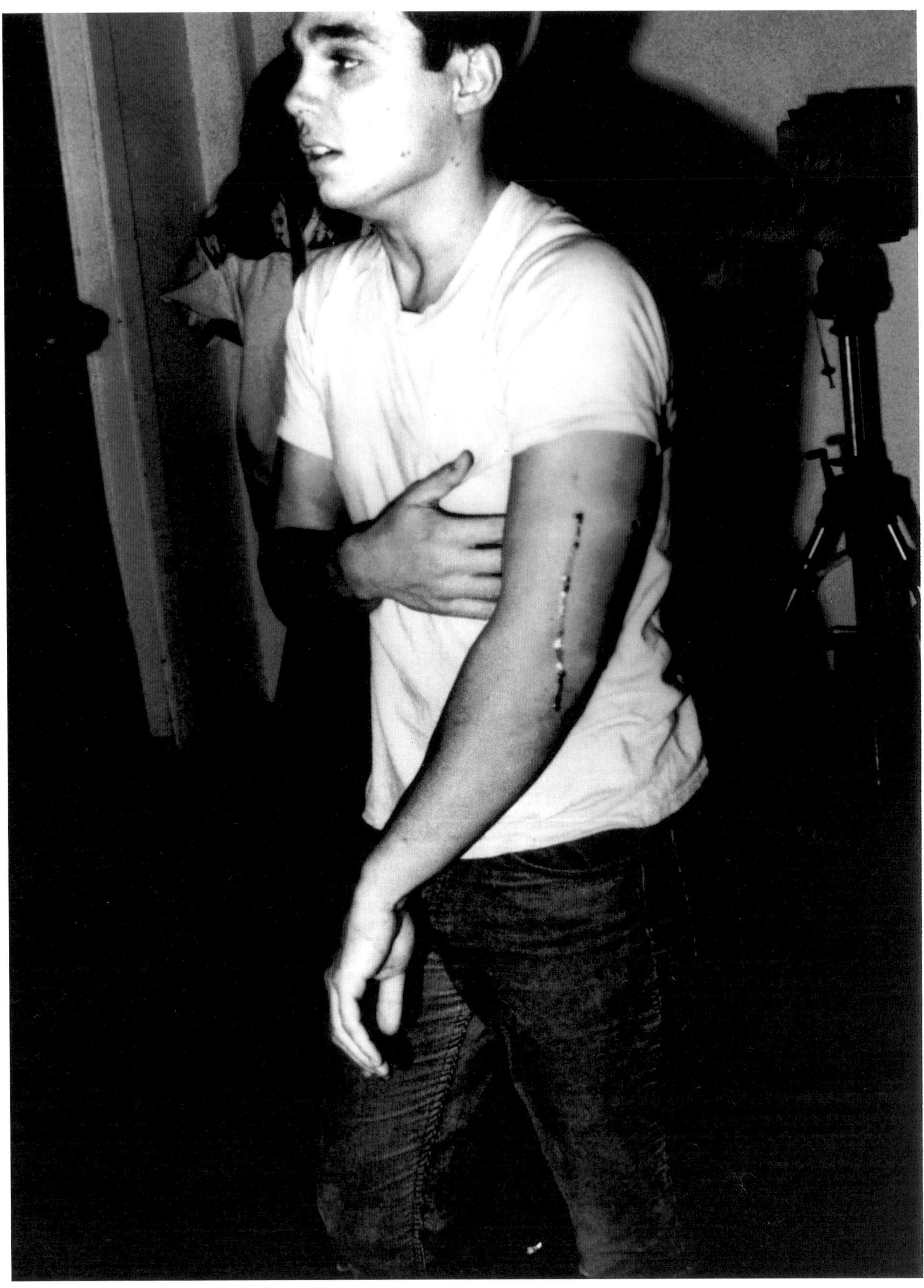

Chris Burden, *Shoot*. *F Space*, Santa Ana, CA, 19 November 1971. At 7:45 p.m. I was shot in the left arm by a friend. The bullet was a copper jacket .22 long rifle. My friend was standing about fifteen feet from me.

psychoanalysis, structuralism and post-structuralism, and the birth of second-wave feminism. All these ideas, in different ways, explored how our personalities and sense of being individual people are shaped, building upon the growing understanding that human subjects are both formed by external disciplinary structures and unique entities unto themselves, with their own consciousness, perspective and set of experiences. In the field of art, there were new explorations of subject-object relations, particularly of the relationship between artwork, maker and viewer: how a sense of self (*I*) is shaped by one's relation to others (*We*) and externalised as an art object (*It*).

In the three decades following the end of the Second World War, the staging of the body can be crudely divided into three major phases: firstly, what I call a proto-performance phase, in which the body appears as an active agent in revealing the *process* of making art, and then, secondly and thirdly, overlapping, two strands of body art, in which the body is either stripped bare (experimenting on the limits of the self), or appears in camouflage (transforming into an image, often as a form of drag).

In all of this work, the figure of the artist-performer appears as a singular and powerful presence, even in moments that expose failure or vulnerability. These kinds of actions moved from a revelation of process to propose, radically, that with barely any other materials, one could transform oneself into art. One powerful, punning template for understanding the role of the artist as medium was suggested by Bruce Nauman who often used his own body in his video work, and made a 1967 neon sign, which read: *The True Artist Helps the World by Revealing Mystic Truths*. We could say that performance art proper, then, began with the proposition of a self that one directs to aesthetic and political ends: the posing of an *I* as a new kind of art object. This simple idea was one of the most important building blocks set out by artists after the 1950s.

Post-1950 Proto-performance: the artist as agent, maker and producer

Before looking at artists' staging of the body as material, it is worth stepping back for a moment to consider a key transition in art history: from attention to the material object itself (the painting or sculpture) to the action or process of making it. Prior to defining a genre of bodily performance art per se, certain artists in the 1950s and early 1960s began to enact their roles as makers explicitly for the public, and frequently for the camera. We might see this move emerging from the cult of personality around key artists such as Pablo Picasso and Salvador Dalí in the interwar period, whose performances of their roles as artists became as visible and powerful as their own work. But by the time Yves Klein starts making work in the late 1940s, there is clearly an increasingly self-conscious move from a clear separation between artist and object towards artist-as-artwork.

In the immediate postwar period, the ways in which artists began to perform or were presented explicitly as makers took some important new directions. There were artists, like Jackson Pollock, Helen Frankenthaler and Karel Appel, whose appearances working on the canvas appeared somewhat heroic, demonstrating intense or grand physical gestures. At the same time, the trickster attitude of Klein and Piero Manzoni, after Duchamp, was playfully critical of such grandeur: they were already posing as artists whose notion of the self was heavily inflected by what we would now call branding and marketing. Yet the example of Gutai artists in Japan, such as Jirō Yoshihara, offered an emphasis on visible process that proposed a radically new sensitivity towards the formal relations between materials and actions within the frame of art. Theirs is one of the early approaches that feels highly relevant to contemporary practice. In Gutai, the artist was presented as an instigator of action, creating gestures in balance with materials, rather than wilfully mastering them.

Writing in the late 1950s, the artist Allan Kaprow – founder of 'happenings', which I shall discuss in the second chapter – famously understood Hans Namuth's photographs of Jackson Pollock at work in his studio as a tipping point in 'the blurring of life'.[4] Indeed, these pictures were circulated nationally and internationally in magazines such as *Life*, with significant impact. We might now read Pollock's 'dance' on the canvas as a proto-form of performance as we understand it today, although this was explicitly not the artist's original intention.

Yet this shift in the mythology around an artist at work was far from an isolated example. From the late 1950s onwards, after Pollock, many artists began to recognise that the circulation of images of their work, and indeed the activity of making it, was becoming as important as the work itself, creating a theatrical double frame that conflated real and representational space. Photography played a key role, both at the time and retrospectively. In the postwar period, a painting or sculpture might be encountered not just as a mechanical reproduction, as Walter Benjamin had observed in 1936, but via *images of its making*, or via images of its subsequent placement in different installation set-ups.[5] Not only the artist, but also the work became a performer in itself. American critic Leo Steinberg remarked that artists began, in this period, to want to get away from 'art' (with its connotations of 'artifice'), towards art as 'activism', thus choosing to make their artistic labour visible.[6]

In both live presentations and photographic and film documentation, artists disclosed the process of making as an extension of the imaginative space of the work. Beyond the depiction of Pollock, angst-ridden in his studio, or Helen Frankenthaler, photographed at work by Ernst Haas in the later 1960s, as individuals expressing their innermost impulses in their action paintings, Niki de Saint Phalle and Georges Mathieu fully embraced staging the working process, being documented for the press and even televised, in the case of Saint Phalle. The Dutch, CoBrA-associated painter Karel Appel collaborated with filmmaker Jan Vrijman to such an extent that he made a painting with a rectangular hole in it so that he could be filmed from the other side of the canvas in the intense moment of creating it. The resulting film, *The Reality of Karel Appel* (1962), stages the artist intently attacking and daubing his work as the 'barbarian painter', before sitting down and drinking a rather dainty cup of tea.

If this idea of exposing the private process of making to apparently reveal the artist's unconscious impulses staged one conception of the artist's subjectivity, in terms drawn from Jungian and Freudian psychoanalytic theory, other approaches to performing the act of making posed the artist very differently. From the 1950s, Klein produced events that enacted art-world conventions with

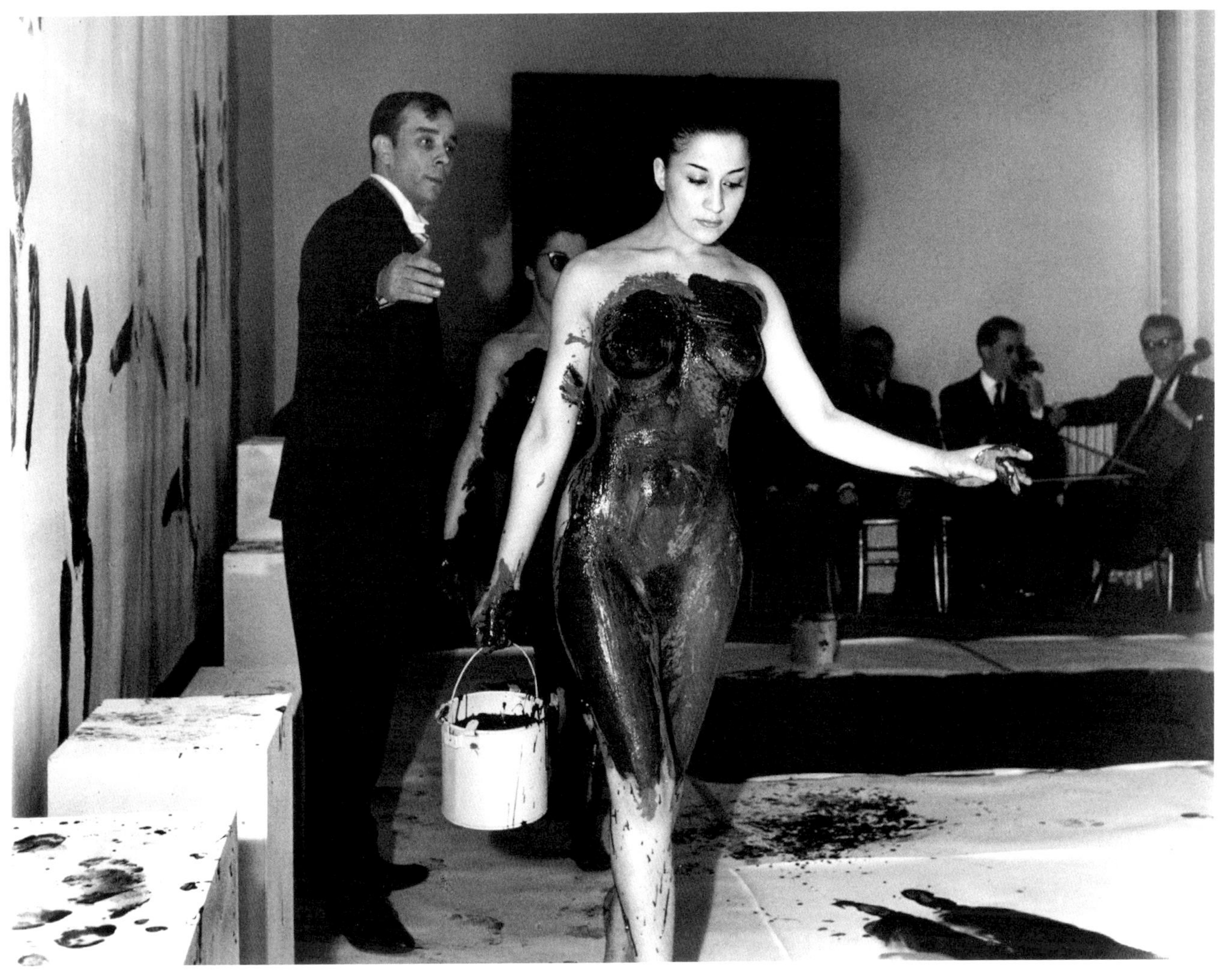

Yves Klein, *Anthropometries of the Blue Period*, Galerie Internationale d'art contemporain, Paris, 1960

a spirit of mischievous play, and cast himself as compère: an / that had little to do with interiority. For Klein, ahead of his time, and in the wake of Duchamp's readymade, making art was as much about the frame of presentation as it was about manipulating paint or clay. As an artist who did not want to get his hands dirty, as it were, his most famous works, the *Anthropometry* performances, were highly theatrical: in early iterations, naked female models, such as his artist friend Elena Palumbo, were covered in blue paint and directed by Klein, dressed in evening wear, to press their bodies onto large sheets of paper to create imprints, while a string quartet played his *Monotone Symphony* (1949) for the audience in formal dress, seated on gold chairs and sipping champagne, or International Klein Blue cocktails.

Criticised by Benjamin Buchloh, among others, as the 'artist par excellence of advanced capitalism',[7] Klein put forward a version of art-making not as authentic expression of his subjectivity but as premised upon delegation, an approach which is highly relevant to our understanding of contemporary art made within a late capitalist economy built upon outsourced labour. That is, neither his nor

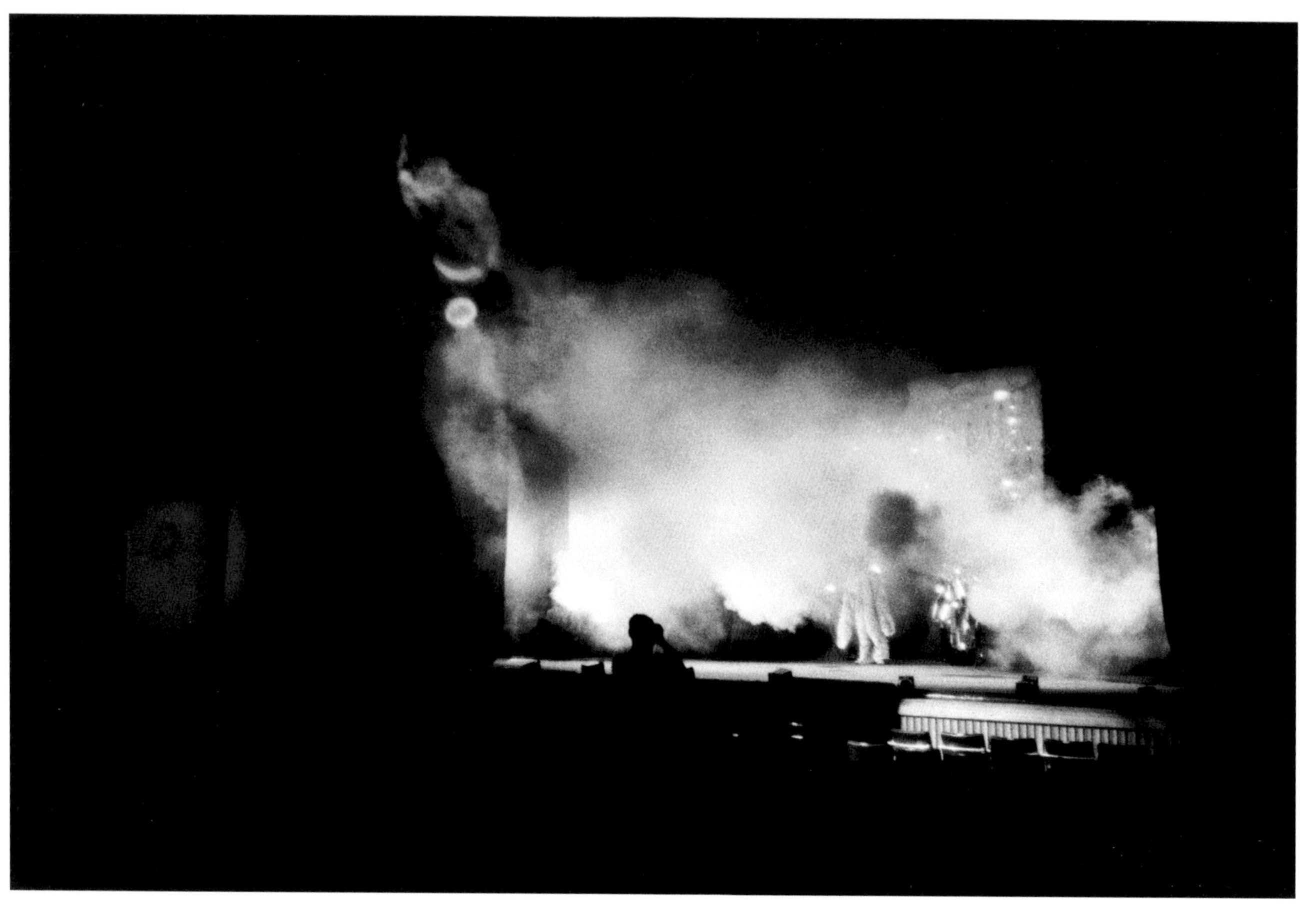

Gutai Exhibition on stage, 1957 Sadamasa Motonaga *Smoke*

his performers' actions were expressions of their inner worlds, and neither were they body art as such. Rather, Klein built on Picasso and Dalí's cults of the artist-persona. His complex actions from the late 1950s both dramatised the process of making art and posed a critique of its institutions, which framed the artist as a brand. Klein's interventions into the art world's habitual scripts and formats, both commercial and institutional, drew attention to their performative nature. He showed how it was not just art that was made; he revealed the whole situation around making, exhibiting and selling art as a kind of theatre, one in which both artist and audience willingly participate.

If Klein presented himself as a critical agent playing art's game, the artists of the Gutai group in Japan incorporated the agency of the artist into a different picture of making. In their extraordinary experimental exhibitions, *Gutai Art on the Stage*, presented in 1957 and 1958, artists appeared as quasi-magicians: drawing smoke rings in the air, dressed in costumes made of electrically powered light bulbs, and jumping through paper screens. The Gutai group created a new kind of active sculpture and painting via formal rituals that combined materials and gestures. Koichi Nakahashi threw dozens of paint-covered balls at a white canvas and Yasuo Sumi splashed buckets of paint at a vinyl scrim. In the same year, Kazuo Shiraga performed *Ultra Modern Sanbasō*, a dance in a 'No drama', which involved archers shooting a hundred arrows through a white cotton backcloth.[8] This kind of work staged choice materials and artists' actions in equilibrium. Gutai foregrounded the individual's capacity to act and make change, presenting the work of art as a live entity. The group's attitude was more philosophical than trickster-like, in the Klein sense. One of the best-known figures in the Gutai movement, Saburo Murakami, stated that 'the Gutai Group's urge for discovery demands the element of time as well as the element of space in order to give a full aesthetic impact'.[9]

The Gutai Art Association was founded by Jirō Yoshihara in Osaka, Japan, in 1954 with the aim of discovering an equivalence between the artist's presence or behaviour and that of the materials, a dynamically reciprocal relationship embodied in the group's title: Gu (meaning tool), tai (meaning body). Gutai was partly inspired by images of Pollock's action painting circulated in magazines, their work was founded upon a fundamentally different value system from abstract expressionism, where priority was given to the resulting, static material object.[10] As well as responding to American and European expressionist painting, Gutai was explicitly influenced by Japanese ideas of Zen Buddhism and Kendo martial arts: the artists embodied a desire to transcend subjectivity rather than to express it as such.[11] In this sense, it offers a model of the artist or self – of the *I* – that is more relevant to the current generation than the psychological interiority of abstract expressionism.

The staging of the artist and his or her body in relation to the artwork within Gutai was also less of an art-world publicity game than it had been for the Nouveaux Réalistes, and more to do with a desire to devise a reciprocal relationship between the material artwork and the energy of life. Formats for sharing work were imaginative. Kazuo Shiraga made his paintings in collaboration with his wife, Fujiko Shiraga, also a painter, who appears within the frame of documentation. Splodges of paint were placed on the canvas by her as he swung from a rope, smearing the canvas about with his feet. In an important early experiment with liveness and mediation, one of his earliest works, *Challenging Mud* 1955, was presented at the *1st Gutai Art Exhibition* and also broadcast live on the television news. 'Gutai does not alter matter. Gutai Art imparts life to matter!' Yoshihara claimed.[12] By presenting artwork not only in galleries but also on the stage, on television and in outdoor spaces such as parks, as early as the 1950s, the Gutai group were crucial drivers of our contemporary understanding of performance in art. They balanced the agency of the performing artist against the production of aesthetic objects, and set the individual within a clear context of collaboration with others, as well as initiating what today we would dub a 'multi-platform' approach to presentation. Looking for an understanding of the *I* that neatly matches Western artistic practice, here, is misleading. Instead, we may draw contemporary relevance from the Gutai group's attitudes towards the interrelated nature of movement between people and things on its own terms. As curator Midori Yoshimoto explains: 'The body was essential yet the body was not prioritised over the materials themselves. It was rather seen as collaborating with the material.'[13]

The notion of self at stake here is distinct: *I* appears as a more fundamentally relational concept than the Freudian. According to art historian Ming Tiampo, the Gutai group also developed a new kind of relationship between individuality and collectivity: a 'collective spirit of individuality'.[14] The group understood that building a community of interest was important to provide a space for individual creativity, but at the same time there was suspicion in 1950s post-occupation Japan about the development of ideological groups, or identifying under specific political banners. Gutai took on a horizontal system of community as opposed to a hierarchical one, believing individualism to be a potentially positive counterpoint to external pressures, such as the psychological forces of fascism and other forms of totalitarian group control.

The body talks: the emergence of 'performance art' in the 1960s and 1970s

The ways in which these artists staged the process of making are indicative of the dramatic changes taking place within the field of art during the mid-twentieth century. In the later 1960s and 1970s, a further shift began to occur: artists staged their own role not only as makers but, instead, merged the *I* of the artist-subject with the *It* of the object. The self became the material proper. This kind of art made with the body took two broad directions. I shall describe the first in terms of the 'body art' practitioners emerging in the late 1960s and 1970s, and into the 1980s, who began to stage themselves as so-called authentic subjects. The second was concerned with constructing the self as fantasised image, and will be discussed in the next section.

Body art was a form that imagined the possibility of presenting oneself as real and raw, as existing prior to cultural or social convention: subject rather than citizen. Self-inflicted pain, nudity and endurance became markers of a new level of expressive realism. Artists staged themselves in the equivalent role of an initiate in a rite of passage. Key artists in this regard are the Vienna Actionists, Carolee Schneemann, VALIE EXPORT, Chris Burden, Marina Abramović (with and without Ulay), Petr Štembera, Ion Grigorescu, Gina Pane, Stuart Brisley and Letícia Parente, to name but a few. This was work that was often founded upon exposure of the artist's own body to risk and violence, but it was usually also concerned with formal composition.

Nevertheless, this work has been theorised in terms that emphasise its realness and authenticity as qualities of value – qualities often posed as being deliberately at odds with the perceived value system of fine art. Performance theorist Peggy Phelan has asserted that such body-centred work revalues 'a belief in subjectivity and identity which is not … representable' within 'the ideology of the visible'[15] and that to 'be in the present tense [the quality which, for her, defines performance's essence] one has to be an amateur, not knowing what you're doing, with the capacity to fail'.[16] Writing in the 1970s, the critic Lea Vergine observed: 'Most of the time, the experiences we are dealing with are authentic, and they are consequently cruel and painful. Those who are in pain will tell you they have the right to be taken seriously.' According to Vergine, these artists sought to 'eliminate culture', or cultivated ways of living in order to express an authentic interiority.[17] However, in the examples that follow, questions about the possibility of such apparent authenticity emerge.

Schneemann was one of the first artists to link her painting practice with tough questions about her bodily experience, to make this equation between *I* (the self) and *It* (the art object) explicit as a set of viewing – or voyeuristic – positions,

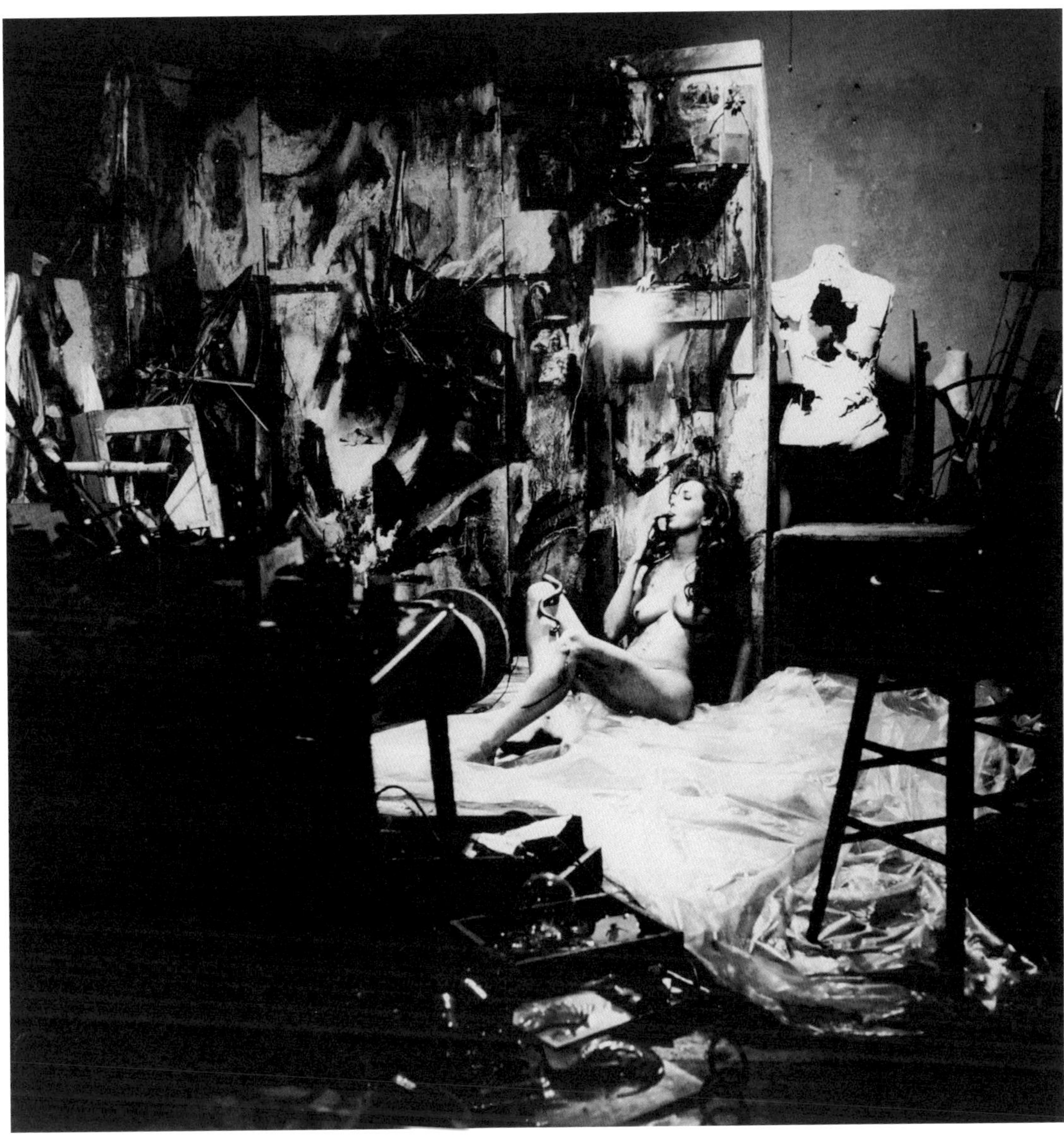

Carolee Schneemann, *Eye Body #2 from Eye Body: 36 Transformative Actions for the Camera* 1963

deliberately speaking from the position of an embodied woman. The pun of her title *Eye-Body: 36 Transformative Actions* 1963 is pertinent. In this series, Schneemann is photographed – by her friend, the painter Erró – within a painterly environment including broken mirrors, plastic sheeting, umbrellas and toy snakes. Her own naked body and face are painted and seem to be part of, or continuous with, the assemblage that makes up the work. Schneemann has said, 'I wanted my actual body to be one with the work, an integrated material … [to be] both image maker and image.'[18]

Although Schneemann began her career as an artist making abstract expressionist paintings, in the 1960s her work evolved into the performance-based environments and actions for which she is best known. Essential to Schneemann's transition from action painting to performance art was her explicit focus on female desire

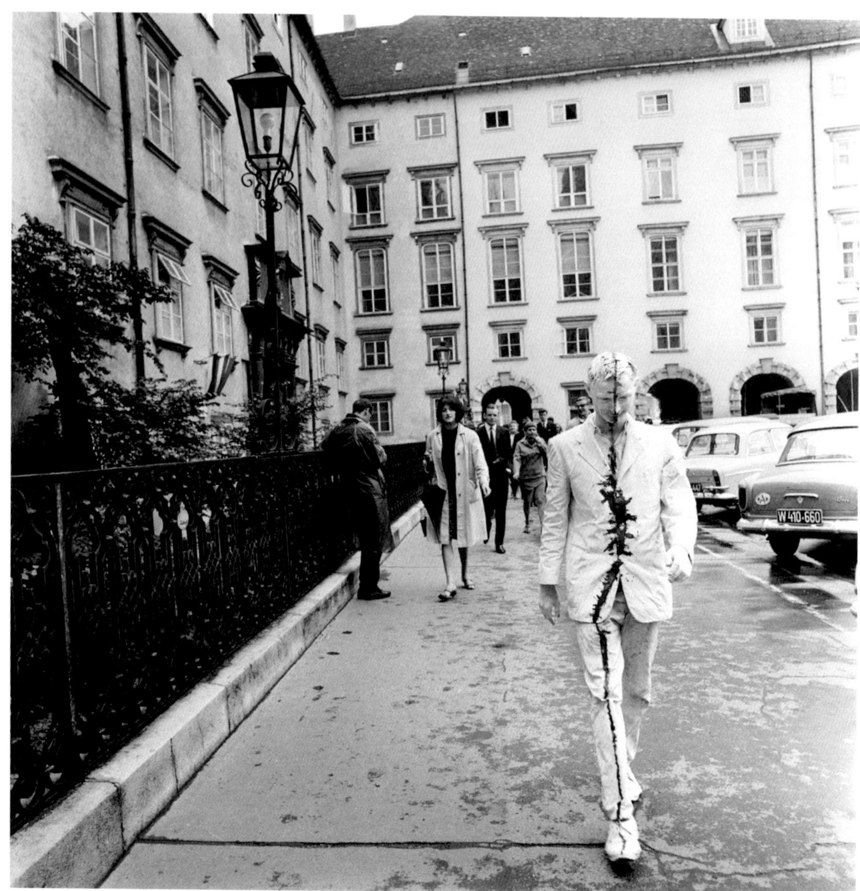

Günter Brus, *Vienna Walk*
1965

and her challenge to the status of the female body as image. *Eye-Body* was pioneering in its foregrounding of feminist questions about the relationship between production and representation. As art historian Kristine Stiles observes, these are 'the first visual images that constitute the lexicon of an explicitly feminist avant-garde vocabulary' – one that anticipates contemporary understandings of the relations between image and experience.[19] But against a backdrop of heroic modernist abstraction, the work was criticised at the time for being too autobiographical and narcissistic, reinforcing the stereotype that the female I is local, while the male equivalent is universally representative.

Schneemann's work of the 1960s and 1970s dramatised the idea of turning the interior to the exterior, but not in terms of psychological expressionism. Her work posed a continuity between vision and sex, surface and skin. In one of her best-known works, *Interior Scroll* 1975, she announced that she would perform a reading from her book *Cézanne, She Was a Great Painter* (1976), before pulling a scroll of text from her vagina and reading it out to the audience.[20] In staging such an intimate relationship with the idea of conceptual art via performance, Schneemann re-figured the image of the female nude in art. She posed as both author and subject, painter and painted: an approach to the construction of the self as both authentic and image-like that prefigures the charged ambivalence of Abramović's MoMA presentation.

The work of the Vienna Actionists in the 1960s – whose core members were Günter Brus, Hermann Nitsch, Otto Muehl and Rudolf Schwarzkogler – represents the emergence of a psychological, or psychoanalytical, idea of body art par excellence in Europe. Like Schneemann, whom their early work had an impact upon, they built their practice from painting, although it was not referred to as 'performance' per se, but as 'action'. This group of primarily male artists shared a focus on creating abject, painterly scenes rooted in physical presence, in violent transgression and on probing the boundaries delimiting the individual body, in relation to its environment as well as to others. Coming after the violence of the Second World War, in which their parents' generation had played a part, their work was avowedly an attempt to begin again, and to re-sensitise the arena of art as a space in which what it means to be human could be more honestly depicted and explored, via imagining a new and more real form of painting.

Actionism's limit is represented by Günter Brus's most extreme performance event, *Art and Revolution*, presented at the University of Vienna in 1968. During the piece, Brus urinated into a glass, defecated, then proceeded to cover his body in his own excrement, and ended the piece by drinking his own urine. He also sang the Austrian national anthem while masturbating, and subsequently vomited. The artist was arrested for making this work, as he had been earlier, in 1965, when performing his *Vienna Walk* – a piece in which he strolled around the city with his entire head and face painted in thick white oil paint, with a black line running down his body, as if he had been cut in half. Brus used this dramatic probing of the image, functions and limits of his own body as a means of representing his own fallible humanity: a naked and vulnerable subject, exposed to pain and degradation that was self-inflicted, or could be inflicted at will. His work represents an extreme point in staging the self in this way, bringing on a self-willed state of disintegration.

The gender politics of Vienna Actionism appear problematic today. Here, and especially in Muehl's orgiastic painting actions, such as *Material Action (Mama and Papa)* 1964, the body, as an active agent, is considered as almost universally male. As in the work of Klein and Manzoni, in Actionism female bodies serve primarily as props for the work of the male artists whose subjectivity is being expressed. It was as though the female nude had been transposed from iconographic motif to material support or surface to be painted on. In these works, it was most often the male artist whose body was actively doing or making; the female body remained passive. Schneemann's work, with its combination of action painting and expressions of female sexual desire, represented a deliberately feminist counterpoint to this attitude.

A key figure emerging from this context, but moving away from the notion of the apparently universal (male) subject towards an understanding of gender politics, is VALIE EXPORT. Born Waltraud Lehner, EXPORT changed her name in 1967, branding herself with an ambiguous, and androgynous, name, after the name of a popular brand of cigarettes. She was the only woman to be associated with Actionism, but was soon critical of its phallocentrism and its neutralising ideas of the body, given the distinctions between the ways in which women's and men's bodies were being staged in this work. EXPORT represents the crossover point between the apparently authentic, fallible body and the staging of a persona that is deliberately manipulated and performatively constructed – and, in this sense, fits also into a pop art landscape.

VALIE EXPORT, *TAP and TOUCH Cinema* 1968

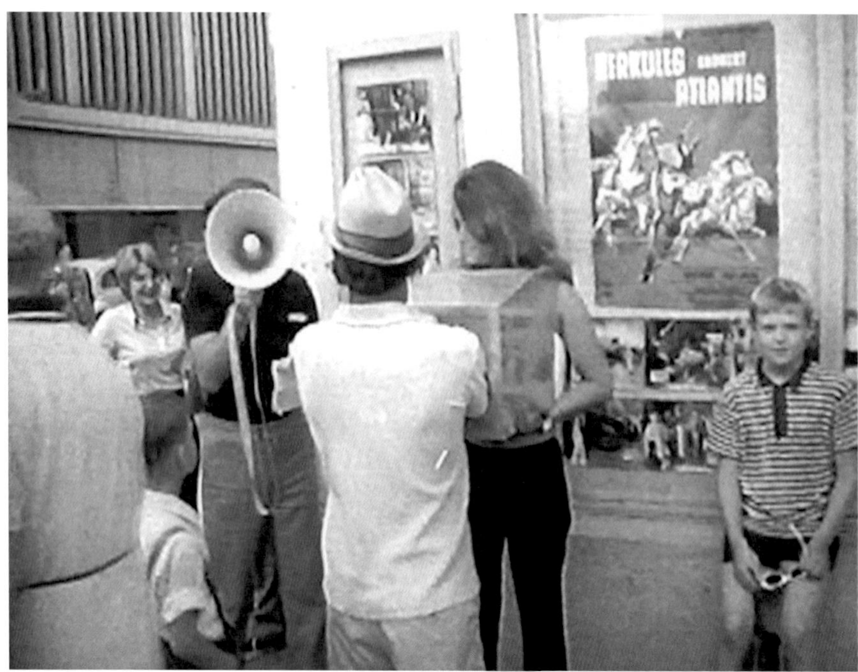

As a counterpoint to this male-dominated work, EXPORT began to make work dealing explicitly with the representation of the female body – her body – finding ways to transgress passive consumption of images of women. *Tap and Touch Cinema* 1968 was one of her first works: during an experimental film festival in Vienna, EXPORT walked around the city with a black box strapped to her naked torso. The front of the box was covered by a curtain, and she invited passers-by to put their hands inside it and grope her breasts. Her intention was to reverse the voyeuristic set-up of cinema, in which women's bodies often appear naked onscreen, for consumption by (implicitly male) viewers who remain unseen, in the dark. EXPORT presented her own real body as a startling interruption to this accepted norm of spectatorship.

Artists in the 1970s would take this idea of the self-as-canvas further. The figures involved in this work are too numerous to mention individually, and the territory is diverse to an extreme, but to give a sense of its range I will briefly describe a few key works which might be understood as emblematic, offering up a set of templates that these practices inscribed into the field of art at the turn of the 1960s to the 1970s. The early actions of Marina Abramović are significant in the history of this strain of Western body art, as is the work of Gina Pane, a French artist of Italian descent. Pane created works, surviving mostly as photographic documents, that present a painful and poetic vision of her body as a surface to be worked upon: composing with organic materials (flowers, food), combined with instruments of pain, through highly ritualised passages of action. Pane is best known for her work *The Conditioning* 1973, in which she lies on a metal bedframe placed over an arrangement of burning candles. Her self-inflicted suffering – which involved cutting and piercing her skin, ingesting food to the point

Gina Pane, *Azione Sentimentale* 1974

of nausea, and enduring pain from heat and sharp implements – was elevated through her aesthetic choices, which turned the masochistic experience into something sacrificial or saint-like, at the service of the making of art. Pane's work stages not only a sense of the externalisation of interior psychology, like the Actionists, but also a sense that the endurance of physical pain might effect some kind of transcendence, or the suggestion of a spirit at odds with the flesh. In this sense, Pane's practice has much in common with that of Cuban American artist Ana Mendieta, although Mendieta's work – emerging directly from a practice in painting – was primarily concerned with the creation of images that staged her hunger for primeval relations between the body and nature (p.48). Using earth, feathers, grass, cow's blood and paint in combination with her own naked body, Mendieta's sacrificial scenarios at times evoke pain and refer to violence against women explicitly, rather than documenting the artist's physical endurance thereof. But her extraordinary body of work moves on from post-Aktionist sensibility in the mid 1970s to invoke a vision of her 'earth body' dialogue with nature as a 'maternal source' as expressed by Ana Mendieta in her application for the Prix de Rome 1983. The performances were often enacted solely for the camera and the artist liked the sense of longing created by the mediation of film.

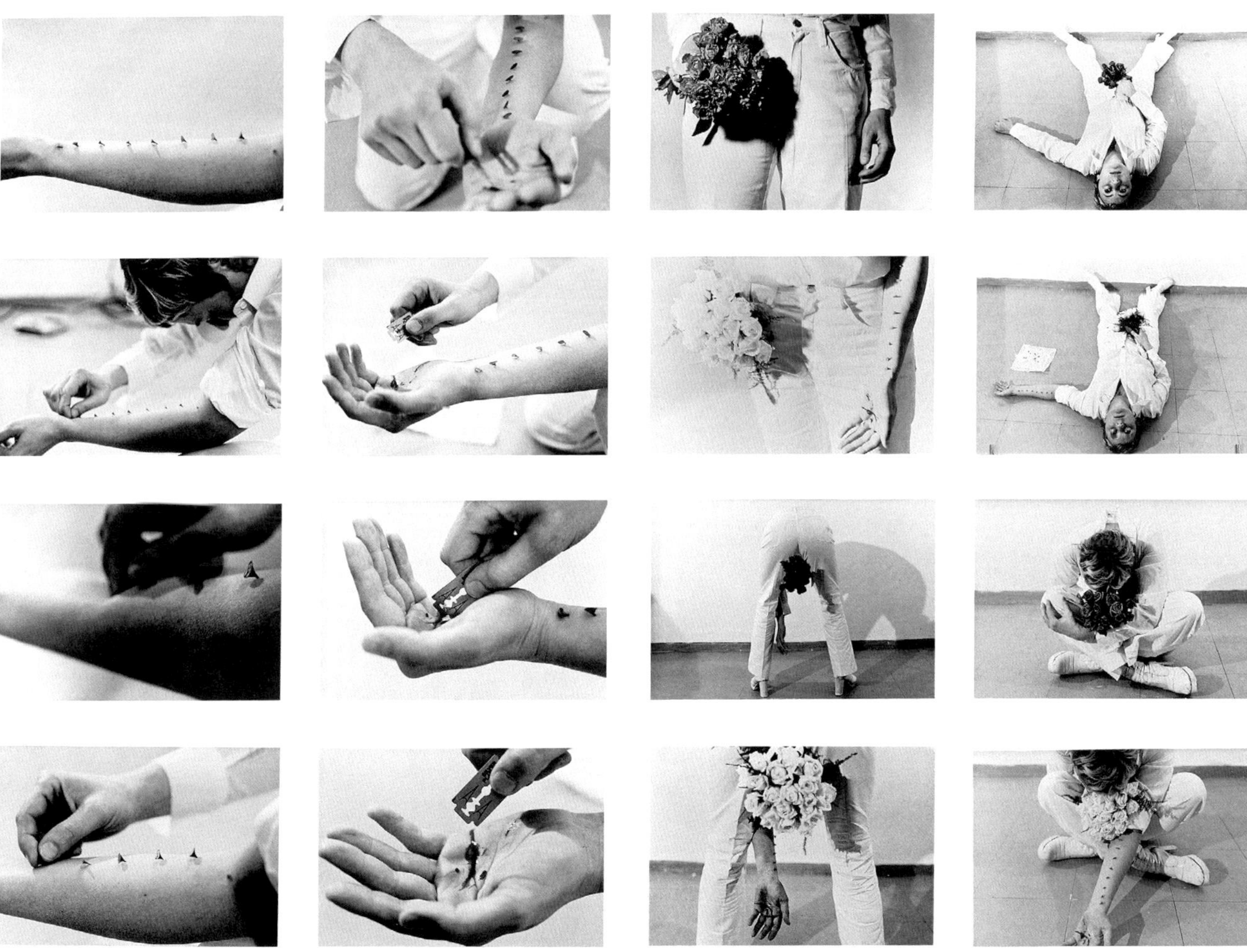

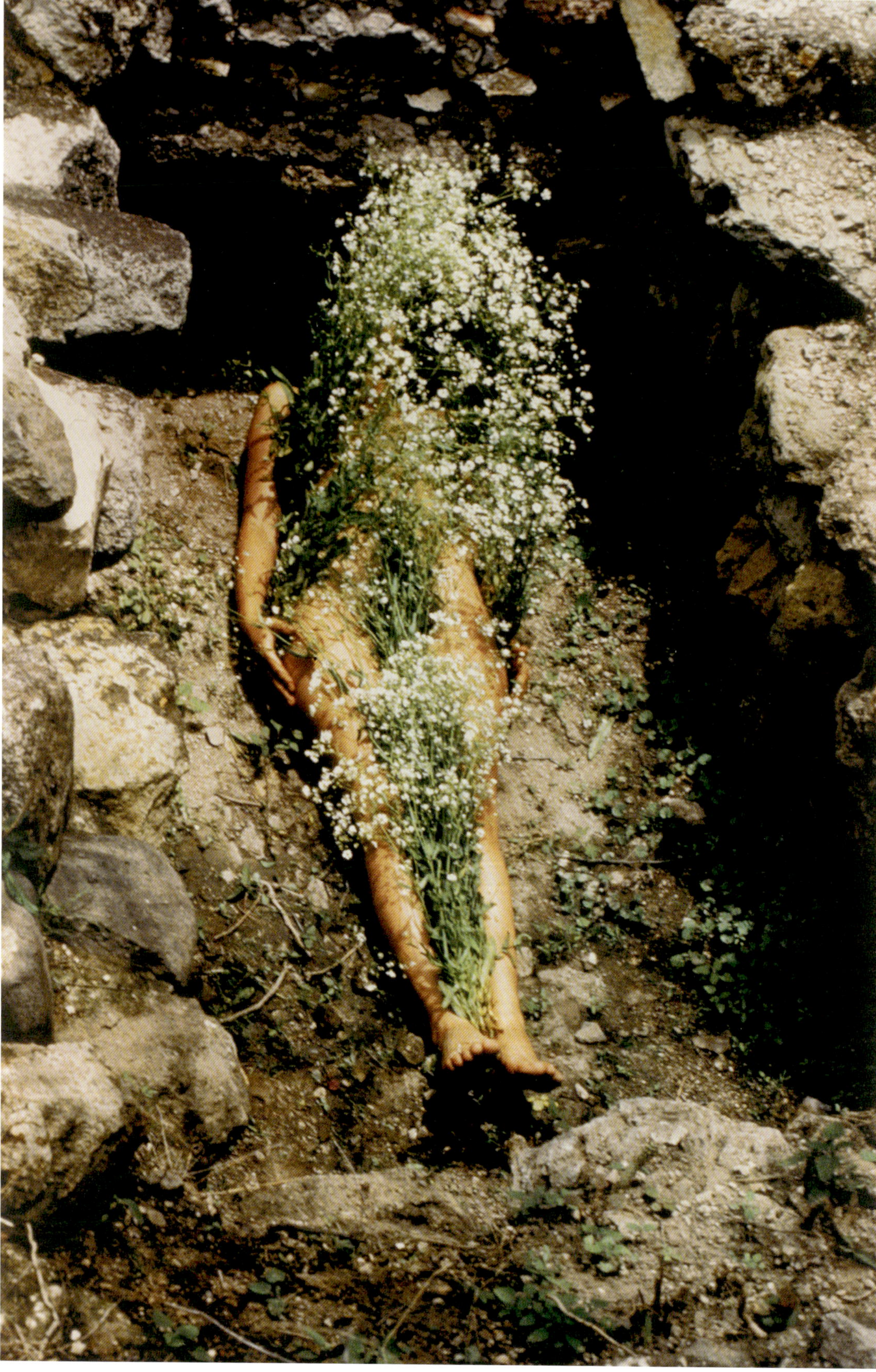

Ana Mendieta, *Untitled: Silueta Series*, Mexico, 1973

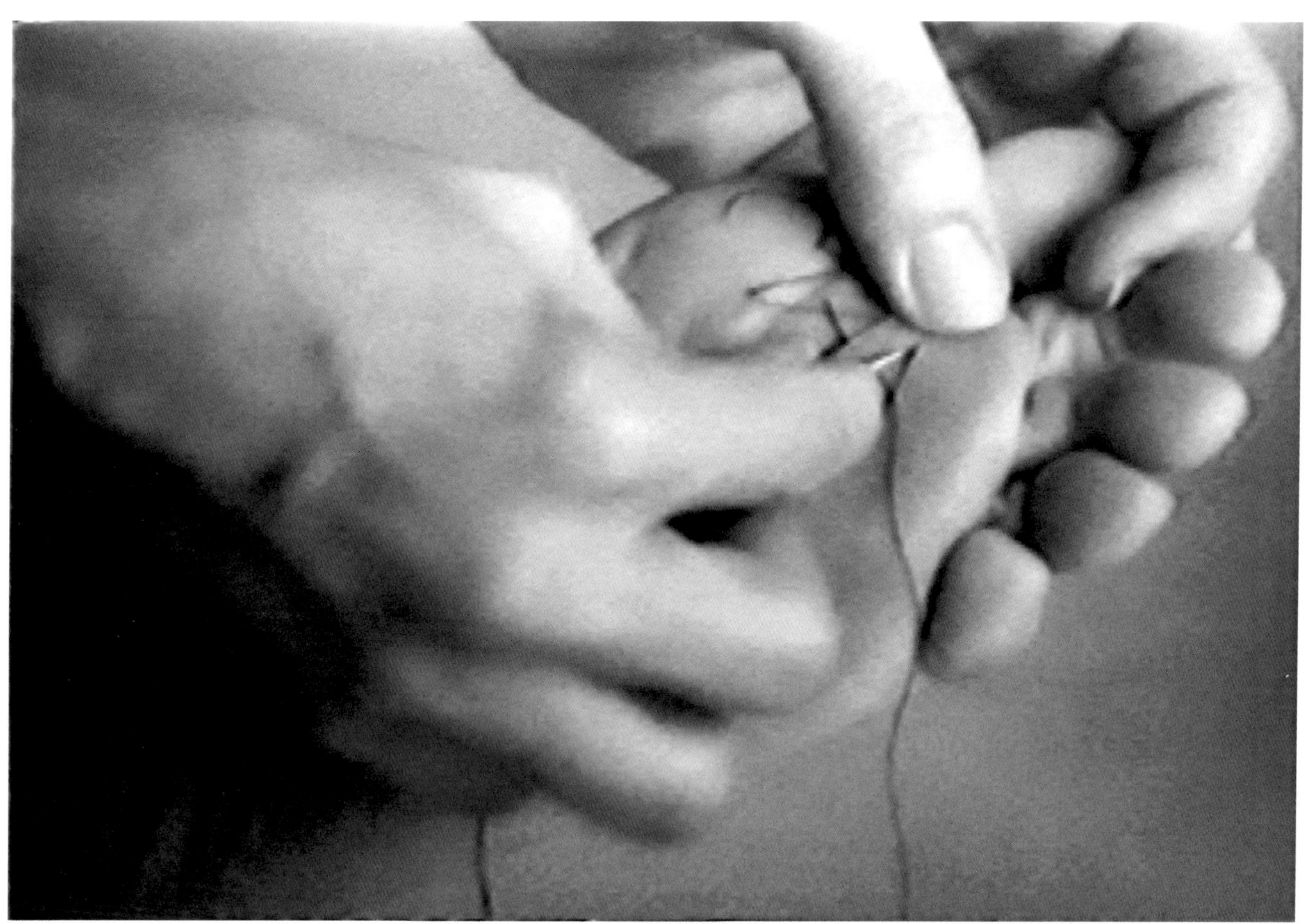

Leticia Parente, *Trademark* 1975, video still

In *Sentimental Action*, presented at Galleria Diagramma in Milan in 1973, Pane pressed the thorns of a rose into her arm, creating pricks of blood along it, and cut the palm of her hand with a razor blade, in order to make a drawing of a rose. These actions and installations often took place in private, and were shown via documentation. Like the comparable but distinct work of Brazilian pioneer of body art, Letícia Parente – such as the videos *Trademark* 1975, in which she sews the words 'Made in Brazil' onto the sole of her foot, referring to the Brazilian regime's use of electric shock torture to the soles of prisoners' feet, and *Preparation II* 1976, in which she gives herself four injections of vaccines labelled 'anti-cultural colonialism', 'anti-racism', 'anti-political mystification' and 'anti-art mythification' – Pane's performances use the artist's own body as a site for describing relations of power, pain and subjection. But whereas Pane's work operates at a poetic level, invoking religious sacrifice and the spiritual transcendence of soul over body, Parente's dramatisation of her own body's vulnerability to pain speaks specifically to the brutal military regime in Brazil and its use of torture. She tortures herself, mimicking the behaviour of state power, and yet stages her ownership of her own female body, simultaneously controlling its imprisonment by pain, and performing the possibility of resistance.

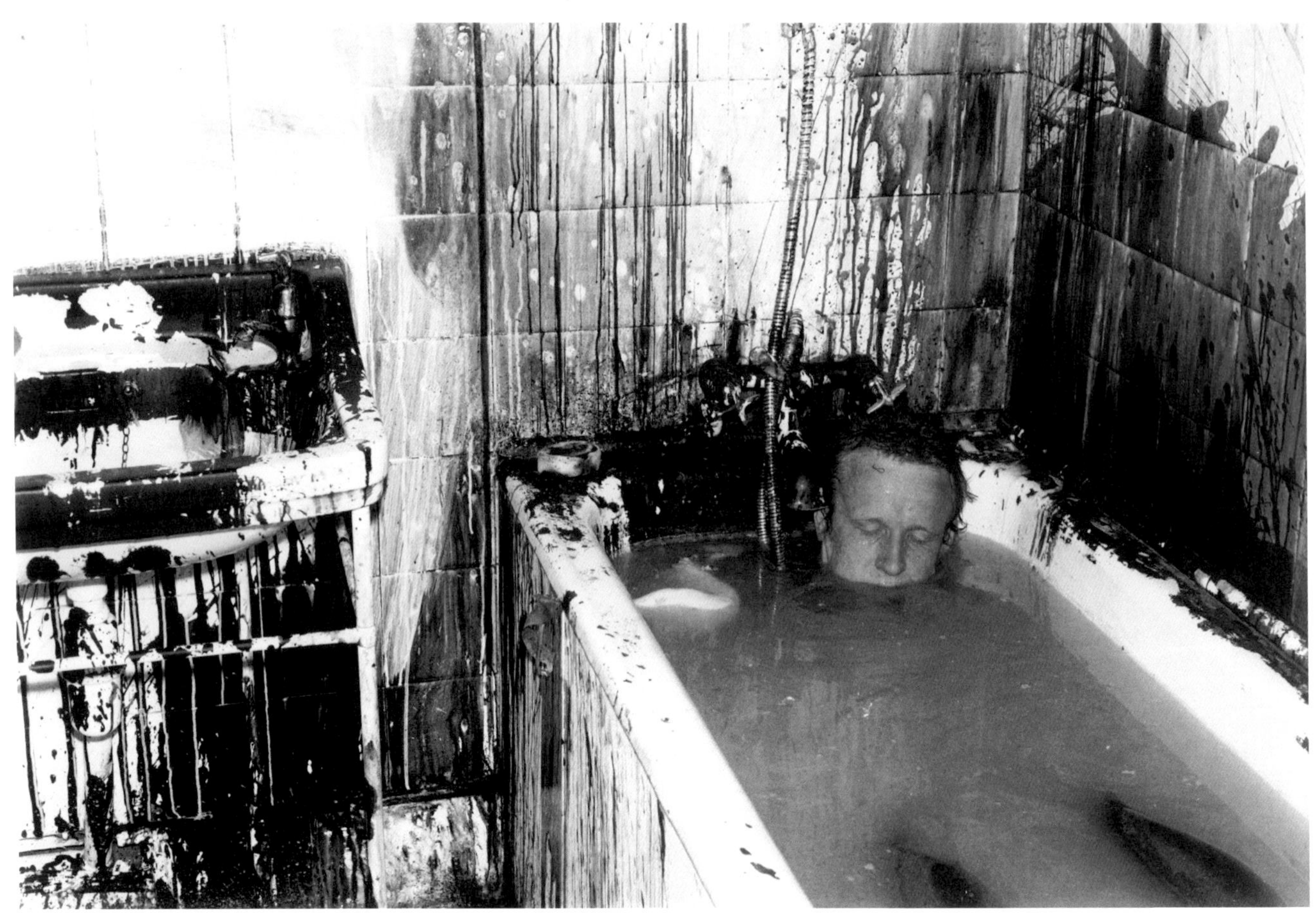

Stuart Brisley, *And for today ... nothing* 1972, Gallery House, Goethe Institute, London

Like Pane and Parente, the British artist Stuart Brisley also staged the testing of the limits of his body as a medium, with a greater degree of bluntness and sometimes brutality. Like Pane, Brisley drew upon aesthetic questions derived from his training in drawing and painting, qualities often manifest in his highly composed photographic documentation. But Brisley's body actions also connected with other facets of his practice that were directly political. Brisley's first event, *White Meal* 1968, involved the artist and another participant dressed in white, blindfolded and with their faces painted white, eating a three-course meal composed of white food. This early piece connected the workings of a living body (ingestion, digestion, excrement, waste) with the practice of painting – of smearing paint, suggesting it in Freudian terms as faecal matter – and with the institution of the dinner party as a form of social etiquette.

In one of his best-known works, *And for today ... nothing* 1972, Brisley lay in a bath filled with black water for two hours a day, during a period of two weeks. Adjacent, he laid out some offal that decayed through the course of the exhibition, with maggots and flies feeding on it. Viewers could just about see into the low-lit space through a door left ajar. The artist recalls: 'The only sign of movement was that of a body rising and falling in the water when breathing in and out. The stench of offal was overpowering.'[21] In this way, Brisley staged his body with a resemblance to the psychological expressionism of Actionism, but his approach to the entirety of the situation – the architectural set-up, the smell, the question of ordure or waste – went beyond the visual formalism of that work. Brisley took the representation of the body outside the frame of art and situated it in life's real systems. In this sense, his work is related to his driving involvement in socially committed organisations from the 1960s, such as the Artists' Union and the Artist Placement Group (an organisation that placed artists within industry or government departments in an attempt to respond to those contexts, and to initiate dialogue with workers). Brisley had also been a leading protagonist in the Hornsey College of Art sit-in of 1968, which called for a radical reconfiguration of social relations. His broader body of work manifests an important dual approach to aesthetic and political form: a relationship between symbolic and direct action, even if these activities were not necessarily occurring simultaneously within the same work. In this sense, Brisley's work stages the dependence of the exposed and vulnerable self upon the social body: alongside the subjection of the self, it introduces an activist impetus for the *We*.

Mona Hatoum is a Lebanese-born, UK-based artist of the subsequent generation to Brisley whose approach to the body furthered and made more explicit its situatedness in a political context, and within a practice largely focused on the making of sculpture. Hatoum first became known in the early 1980s for a series of performance and video pieces which used her own body as a site for exploring the fragility and strength of the human condition under duress. For the performance *Under Siege* 1982, she appeared naked, covered in mud and trapped inside a large transparent container. She repeatedly tried and failed to stand up inside the tank, its glass sides becoming increasingly smeared with body marks. Meanwhile, revolutionary songs in Arabic, French and English were played in the gallery, along with bits of news reporting from the Middle East. *Roadworks* 1985 was one of three street performances which Hatoum carried out in Brixton, London, for an exhibition of the same name, organised in 1985 by the Brixton Artists Collective. This time, the artist walked barefoot through the crowded streets of Brixton for nearly an hour, with Doc Marten boots, usually worn by both police and skinheads, attached to her ankles by their laces. Hatoum used apparently simple body actions invoking torture and endurance to bring political stories into art's frame, especially those related to the protracted conflicts in Palestine, where her parents were born, and Lebanon, where she grew up

In Los Angeles during the 1970s, Barbara T. Smith's work was typical of a new American feminist approach to the use of domestic ritual in intimate performance, and a counterpoint to the Actionists, Pane's masochism or the (albeit critical) machismo of work by male peers such as Vito Acconci and Chris Burden. The latter were engaged in quasi-scientific acts testing their physical and psychological limits. For *Trans-Fixed* 1974, Burden lay face up on the boot of a Volkswagen Beetle car parked in a garage in Venice, California, and had his hands nailed to the roof of the car, as if he were being crucified. The car was pushed out of the garage, and the engine revved for two minutes before being pushed back in. In *Seedbed* 1971, Acconci lay hidden underneath a gallery-wide ramp – a false floor that he had installed at the Sonnabend Gallery in New York – masturbating while describing out loud his fantasies about the visitors walking above him. Both of these artists drew upon stereotypes of masculinity, exaggerating and in different ways overidentifying with them as a critical strategy that disturbed social norms.

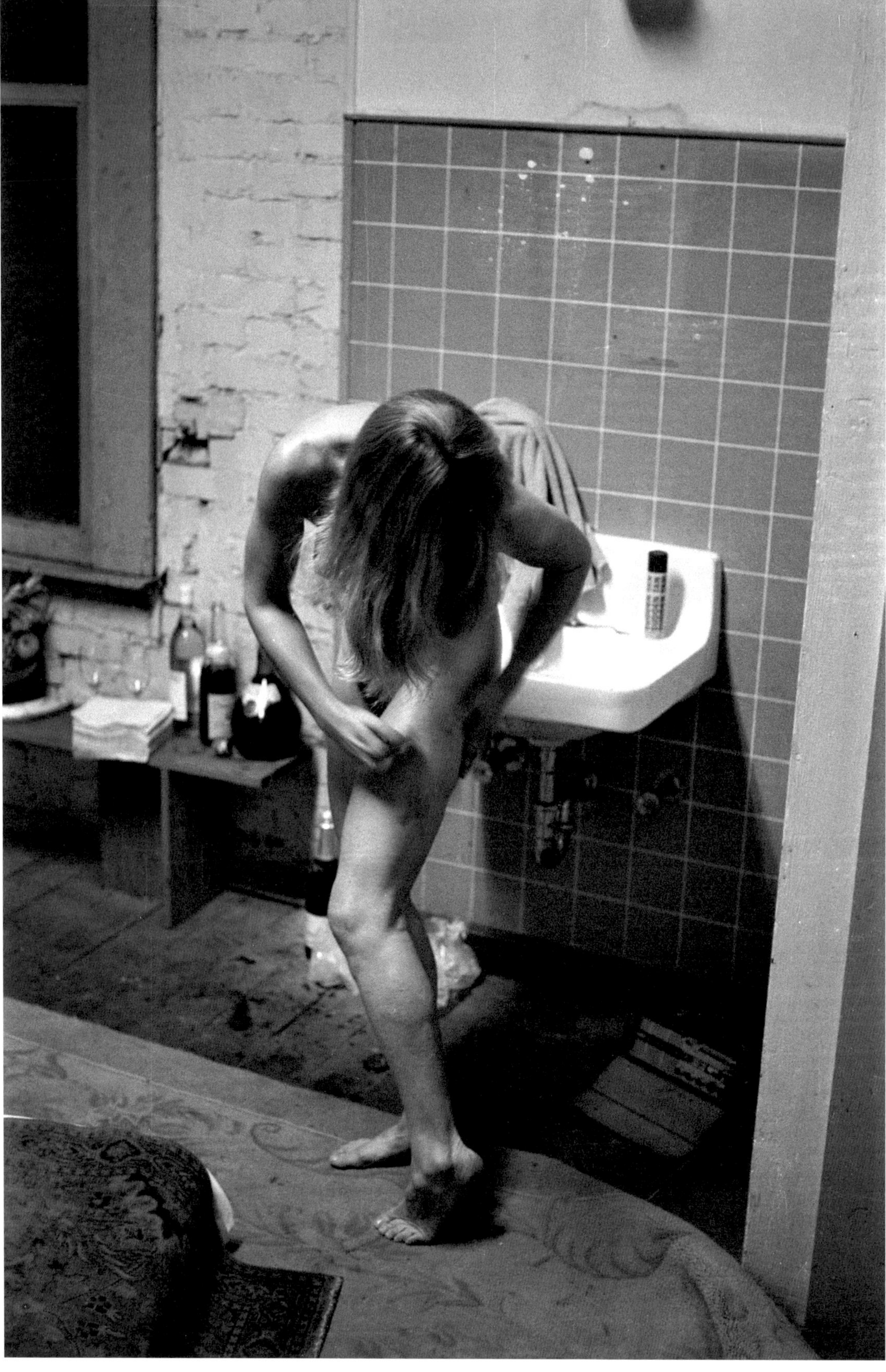

Barbara T. Smith,
Feed Me, Womanhouse,
Los Angeles, 1973

Smith's best-known work, *Feed Me* 1973 (p.52), took place between sunset and sunrise in the women's toilets at the Museum of Conceptual Art in San Francisco during an event called 'All Night Sculptures'. It involved the artist sitting naked, installed in the room and surrounded by items of food, pleasure and ornamentation. One person at a time was allowed to enter (sixteen men and three women came in). A tape loop in a corner played the artist's voice saying 'feed me' over and over again. Smith's intention was that people who entered the room would have to discover what she wanted, what would please or nurture her, by either asking or offering.[22] This was a significant early work dealing with intimacy and social interaction from a feminist perspective, in so far as it presented the artist as an ambiguous figure whose desires were not known. She appeared to be open to the offerings of visitors. The key transformation in the piece relied on the fact that the (generally) male visitor had to change his expectation of satisfying his lust to deducing a means of nurturance and offering it to Smith, thus switching the vulnerability of female subjectivity to an empowered position of accepting or rejecting his offering.

In parallel, in New York, the Taiwanese artist Tehching Hsieh began to make an extraordinary series of endurance performances dealing with the rituals of domestic life and the effort to survive as an immigrant in the city in the late 1970s and 1980s. His work tested his own physical limits to the extreme, exploring precariousness, marginality and struggle. 'Life is a life sentence. Life is passing time. Life is freethinking', Hsieh has said of the philosophy of his work.[23] Hsieh's *One Year Performances* began with his *Cage Piece* 1978–9, in which the artist locked himself inside a wooden cage with only basic washing and sleeping facilities, and no communications or entertainment, for the duration of a year, inviting people to view him at intervals. For *One Year Performance (Time Clock Piece)* 1980–81, Hsieh subjected himself to a rigorous hourly schedule: every hour, he would punch into a time-clock card, take a single photograph of himself and expose a single frame of a 16mm film. For this performance, Hsieh wore a uniform of sorts, and began the piece by shaving his head so that we see his hair grow through the documentation. For *One Year Performance (Outdoor Piece)* 1981–2, the artist lived outdoors in Manhattan with only a sleeping bag and basic clothing, sleeping rough and documenting his daily rituals – including eating, washing and defecating – in a map-diary, noting times and locations (p.54). Hsieh's extreme commitment to these durational performances marks a high point of performance art in this period. The pieces are well documented, but this was less about preserving the artwork and more to do with the artist's concern with legitimising and verifying his authentic execution of the proposed tasks. The meticulously gathered evidence betrays a quasi-legalistic anxiety about proving the seriousness of his position, despite his apparent espousal of marginal roles, that asserts his subject position despite this precarity.

Concentrating less on the visible exterior of the body, and more on its internal functions, the Colombian artist Sandra Llano-Mejia was innovative in considering her own subjectivity in bio-technological terms. She used computers and medical equipment to create forms of portraiture or self-portraits made from signals and data about her or others' physical condition. Her piece *In-pulso* (In-pulse) 1978, was the first video installation in Colombia, presented at the 4th Salón Atenas in Bogota (p.55). In this work, a participatory action, she and museum-goers recorded their heartbeats on an electrocardiogram: a procedure which involves having electrodes attached to the body, and the data they transmit recorded. The artist recalls how 'a doctor provided me with an electrocardiograph, which

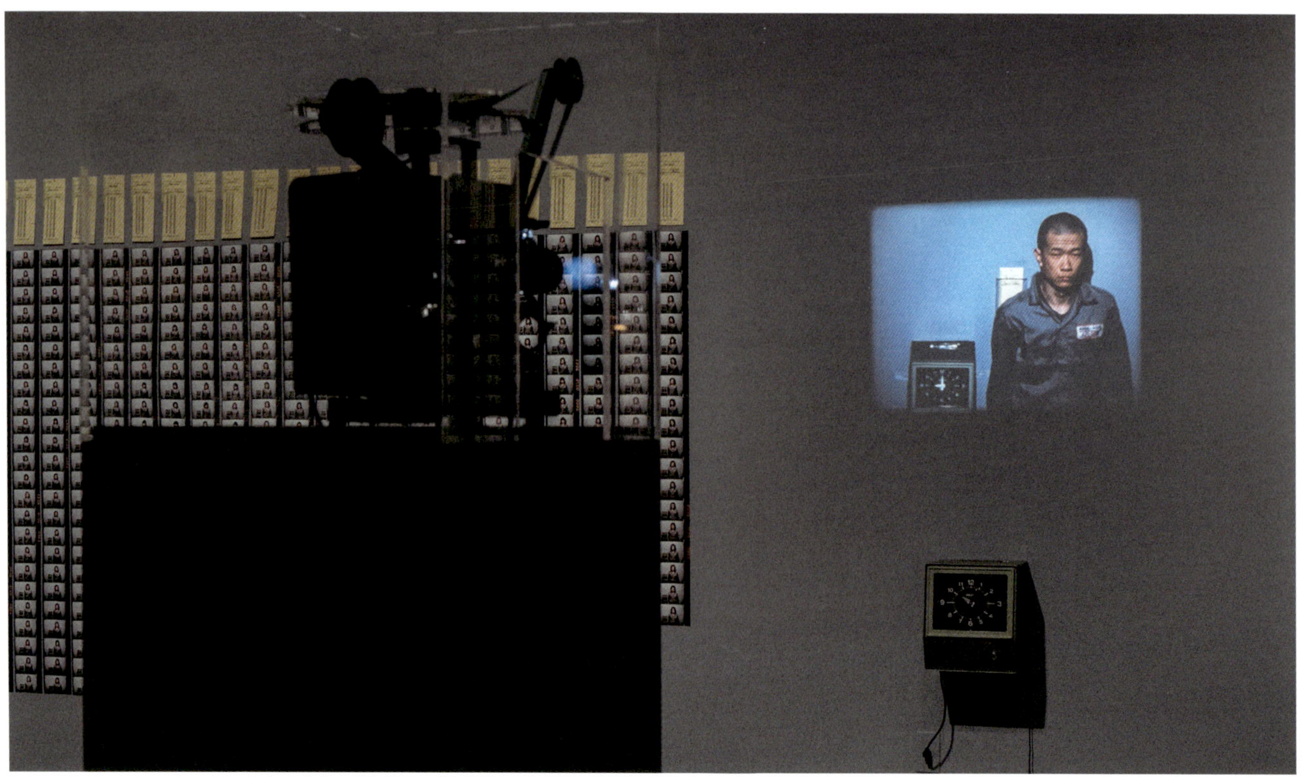

Tehching Hsieh, *One Year Performance* 1980–1, installation view, Tate Modern, 2017

I placed on a small table next to a chair adjacent to the wall where my work was. The idea was for viewers to take their emotions with them in the form of those cardiac images.'[24] In this work, and in others in which she used brain scans, Llano-Mejia used data patterns created by the signals that science and technology use to capture signs of life, whether one's own life or the lives of others. In displacing this medical data and imagery typically utilised for analytical purposes into the space of art, she created an alternative image of apparently truthful bodily, and emotional, presence: a form of a biometric portrait.[25]

As I have mentioned in the beginning of this chapter, Marina Abramović had emerged from a radically different context than twenty-first-century New York: she grew up in the former Yugoslavia and as a young artist she was in dialogue with artists elsewhere in Eastern Europe, where performance history has powerful roots. Key protagonists such as Ion Grigorescu (in Romania), Petr Štembera (in today's Czech Republic), Tibor Hajas (in Hungary), Natalia LL (in Poland) and Sanja Iveković (in today's Croatia) are a few of the artists who made influential performances during this period. The artists I have described thus far in Western Europe and America had been working in conditions of relative freedom and either developed communities or staged self-imposed limitations. It was, arguably, 'soft' psychological norms and attitudes that were being played against individual subjectivity. In *Body and the East* (1999), art historian and curator Zdenka Badovinac observes that in Eastern and Central Europe of this period, performance was a preferred medium because of direct oppression and censorship under communism: 'In the countries with the lowest level of personal

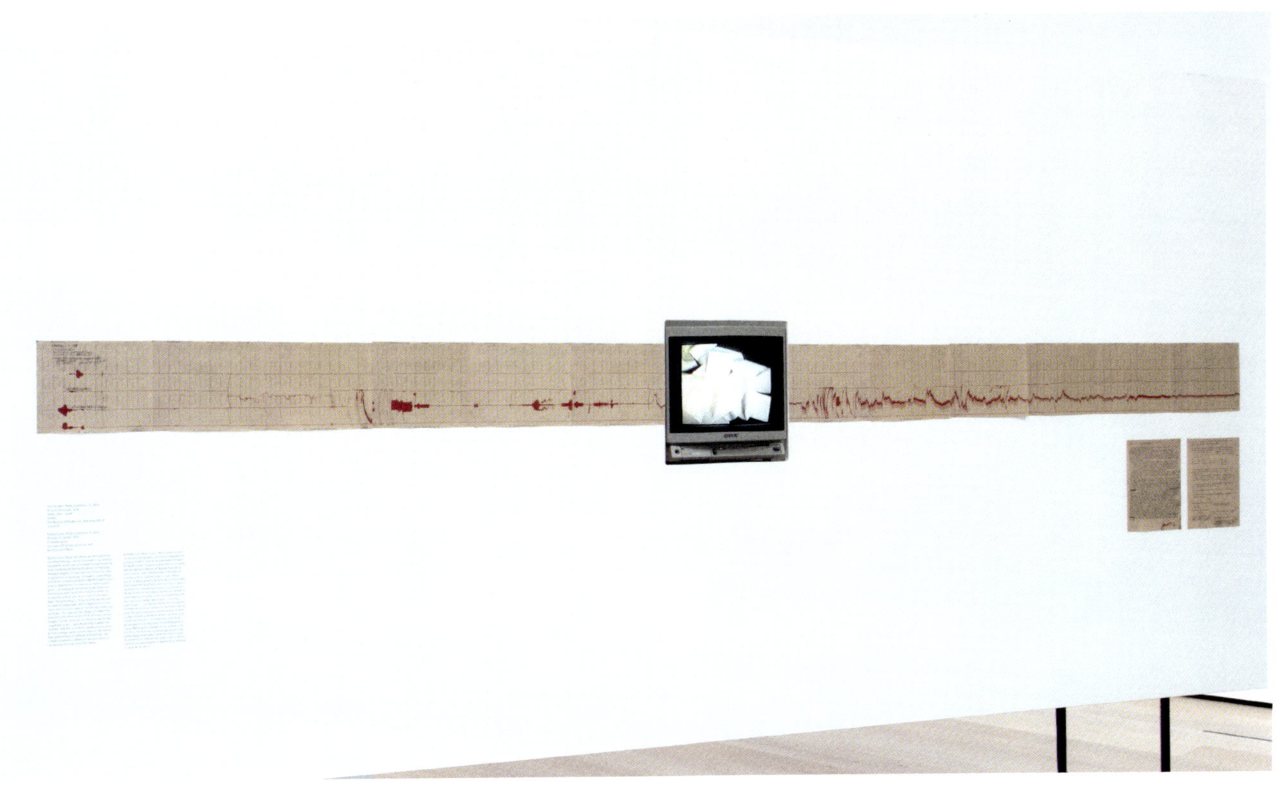

Sandra Llano Mejia, *In-pulso (In-pulse)* 1978. Installation view at *Radical Women: Latin American Art, 1960–1985*, Hammer Museum, Los Angeles, 15 September – 31 December 2017

freedom, special conditions emerged for carrying out performance practices.' Grigorescu, for example, staged his performance actions at home, only in front of a photographic or film camera, since 'this kind of activity was prohibited in public spaces'.[26] The film *Boxing* 1977, in which he appears naked, boxing his own shadow, suggests a psychological state of alienation, at the same time as it poses the artist as a force of violent energy. "Grigorescu, like his peers, grappled with living in a situation of 'absolute and unendurable coercion, constraint and surveillance which the artist turned back onto himself'.[27] Grigorescu did not have access to a public space that would allow him the freedom to appear as an artist performing actions in this way. He thus turned to the intimacy of solitary performances for the camera to create this space.

Štembera also made highly ritualistic actions that, in comparison with those of Abramović, had a more exaggeratedly symbolic-spiritual dimension. In *Narcissus No.1* 1974, he stood gazing at a portrait of himself placed on an improvised altar lit with candles. Fellow artist Jan Mlčoch drew blood from his vein with a hypodermic syringe and Štembera mixed the blood with his own urine, hair and nail clippings, and drank the mixture in front of his altar. Stiles observes that such an action recalls (or, I would suggest, invokes a fantasy of) 'shamanistic and voodoo practices for accumulating power, protecting against evil spirits and generally guarding the soul'. In the performance *Grafting* 1975 (p.57), Štembera attempted to graft a branch taken from a shrub to his arm, embedding it into his vein using gardening chemicals that were likely toxic, so as to 'make contact with a plant'.[28] The artist explained that 'the essence of these ideas was the discovery of one's own body, of physical experience and physical being in the world', adding that 'the actual form of [his] performances evolved under the direct influence of Western art'.[29] Štembera cites American artists Terry Fox, Tom Marioni and Chris Burden as influences, but decisively dissociates his aesthetic from the so-called old Europe of the Actionists. Štembera doesn't simply utilise his body as a material; by grafting a plant to his body he proposes an alternative ecosystem in which human and non-human might be symbiotically connected – a new order of adaptive organic life that disturbs the hierarchy of species, underwriting how we understand selfhood.

It is important to note that, even in this earlier period, artists communicated and shared work quite widely internationally: as documentation – through mail art, and in magazines as both photographs and written descriptions – and through participating in experimental film, music and performance festivals. Often this work was able to circulate more freely than traditional art objects could, even within oppressive regimes. In September 1975, for example, Los Angeles-based artist Tom Marioni travelled to Prague as part of the research for a special issue on Eastern European experimental art of the American *Vision Magazine*, and there he created an action titled *Joining*, together with Štembera. The idea of the action was to join the bodies of a Western and an Eastern artist into one, and was effected by creating two circles around themselves made of condensed milk and cocoa, and releasing hundreds of so-called hungry ants, who either ate the food or bit the artists.

In Korea, where communist society enforced a higher degree of conformity than in Eastern Europe, performance was an important facet of avant-garde art production, which was often related to forms of political activism, especially in the late 1960s and early 1970s. On 17 October 1968, artists Kuk-jin Kang, Kang-ja Jung and Ch'an-sŭng Chŏng were buried in soil, up to their necks, under the Second Bridge over the River Han, for a performance titled *Murder at the Han Riverside* – one of the first happenings to be staged in Korea. The audience and a reporter poured water over their heads, and they climbed out of the pit, wet. Over their wet bodies they wore vinyl covers, each written with words that translate as 'Culture Con-man (pseudo-artist)', 'Culture Dodger (idealist)', and so on.[30] They read these aloud, and then burned and buried them. The work has been described as 'an expression of their urge to burn the old monotonous culture system that gravitated around the corrupt National Art Exhibition, and to bring back respectability to Korean modern art'.[31]

According to art historian Joan Kee, in early 1970s Korea 'happenings' were popular as an 'exotic' foreign import.[32] Artists in Seoul learned about American performance via the magazines available at US Information Centres and via news of Korean-born Nam June Paik's success abroad: his collaboration with Charlotte Moorman and especially her appearance onstage naked were widely reported in the mainstream press. But performance was important in Korea as an alternative to the dominance of painting, drawing and sculpture taught via official channels, too, and must be understood against a context of mass conformity comprising mandatory exercises, for pupils as well as for workers, and the policing of one's appearance (men's haircuts, women's skirt lengths, etc.). Artists were interested in creating images of disobedience that countered the strict regulation of daily life and allowed for individuality to emerge. They performed deliberately idiosyncratic actions, often informally in public spaces, to develop an alternative form of / against a presumptive *We* imposed from above. In Lee Kun-yong's performance

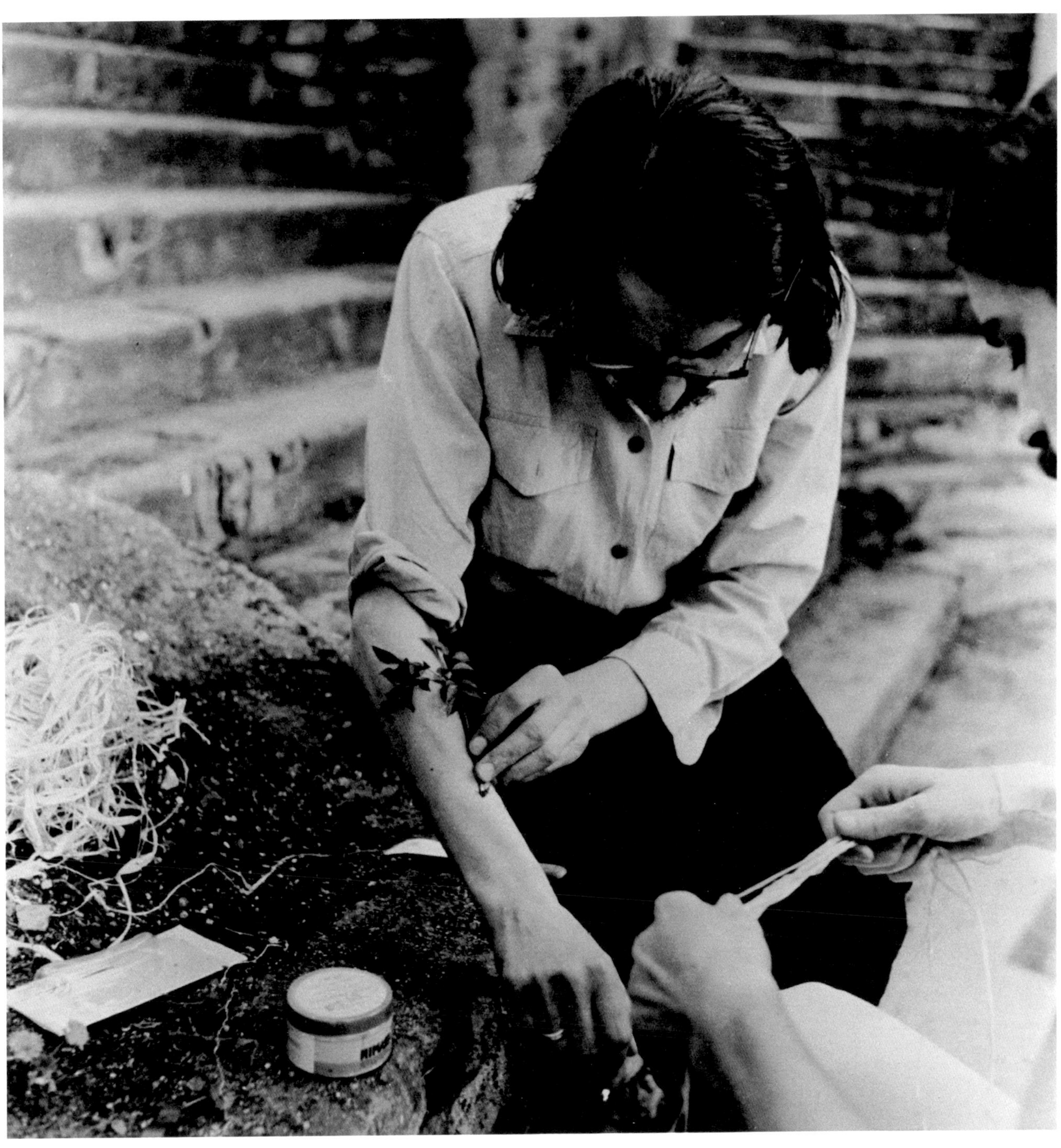

Petr Štembera, *Grafting*,
Prague, April 1975

Eating Hardtack 1975, for example, the artist struggled to perform the apparently simple action of eating this dry snack food while one arm was bandaged with a splint.[33] Such repetition of simple ordinary acts out of context represented a metaphorical form of resistance.

In *Painting (Event-77-2)* 1977, Lee Kang-So, who went on to make more explicitly theatrical assemblage paintings on canvas in the 1980s, painted directly onto his body and exhibited the photographic documentation of the action in series, beside a painted cloth that lay crumpled on the floor, like a shed skin. This work was ambiguous in staging the artist's body and simultaneously creating a camouflage situation, where the self was obliterated by the medium. In 1973, Lee also organised an early participatory performance whereby he set up a drinking bar in the Myongdong Gallery in Seoul. But getting people to participate (to alter their habitual gallery behaviour by drinking wine) was difficult because of the implied breach of social etiquette. He had to put up a sign saying 'please drink the wine', which he then felt defeated the purpose, and was disappointed by the work's failure. Even so, performance works did draw crowds, and, as Joan Kee notes, 'attracting … a high number of attendees could itself be seen as a distinctly subversive act in light of state restrictions on any form of collective gathering'.[34] Ku-lim Kim's body painting performances involved applying decorative paintings onto women's bodies, creating, like his later land art actions, living artworks that would eventually vanish, leaving no trace behind. Kim was a member of the Korean avant-garde Fourth Group, whose goal was to destroy existing conventions of art and construct afresh.

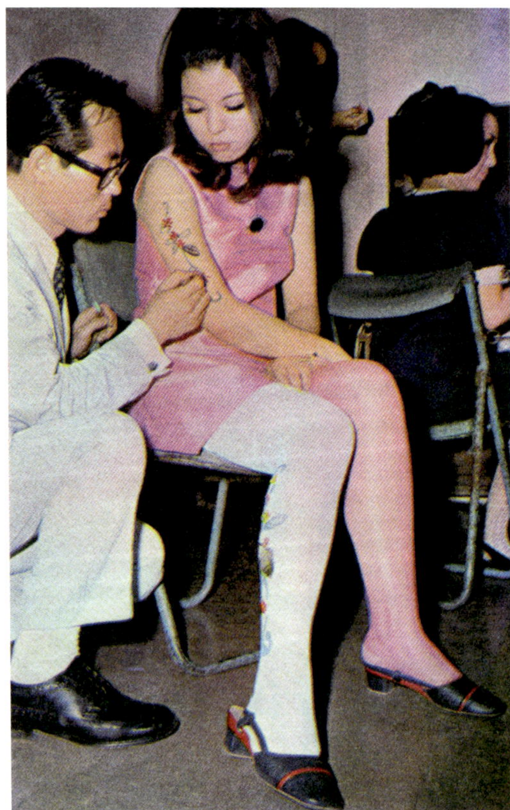

Ku-lim Kim, *Body Painting Performance* Documentation of performance 1969

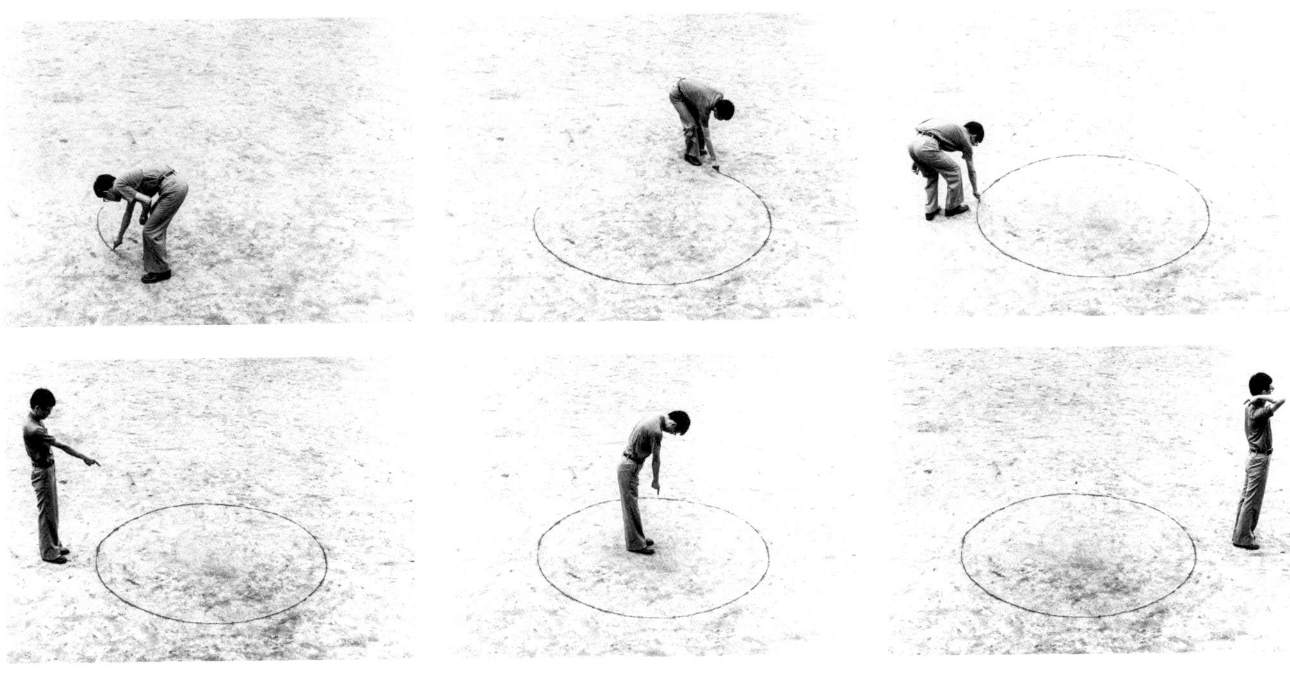

Lee Kun-yong, *Logic of Place* 1975

In China, from the late 1970s to the 1980s, following the end of the Cultural Revolution in 1976, a general shift towards body art occurred, too, but a little later than in Japan and the West, and in a situation of relative isolation from international networks. Initially, distinct from body art practice by individuals, Chinese performance emerged from experimentation with group actions and collective work with a political agenda.[35] The earliest Fluxus-style experiments with performance began to emerge around 1979 when Kwok Mang Ho (also known as Frog King) visited from Hong Kong – a more open context that offered greater opportunity for exchange internationally – and staged a series of land art-like events titled *Plastic Bag Happenings in China*. Important collectives such as the Stars group and Xiamen Dada began to make actions around this time. First, in September 1979, the Stars group conceived of a way to connect art more directly with the public by displaying a group of artworks without permission, attached to railings adjoining the China Art Gallery in Beijing, where the Fifth National Art Exhibition was taking place. They were forced to remove the works, and subsequently organised a large protest march. As a result, they were given permission to exhibit their art in the China Art Gallery in 1980 – an event that was attended by more than eighty thousand people. The Xiamen Dada followed on from this outdoor action by exhibiting and then burning a group of paintings in *Burning Event* 1986.

In a sense, distinct from the Korean context, these groups' endeavours replicated the dominant pattern of official culture under communism, in so far as they focused on group action, rather than the individual, yet they attempted to break given norms and conventions of communality with their actions, and to find new, unofficial ways of connecting art with the public. Things began to change as greater scope for international information exchanges opened up. Artist Huang Yong Ping describes it thus: 'At the end of the 1970s, policies changed and bookstores re-opened, offering an increasing number of translations of Western

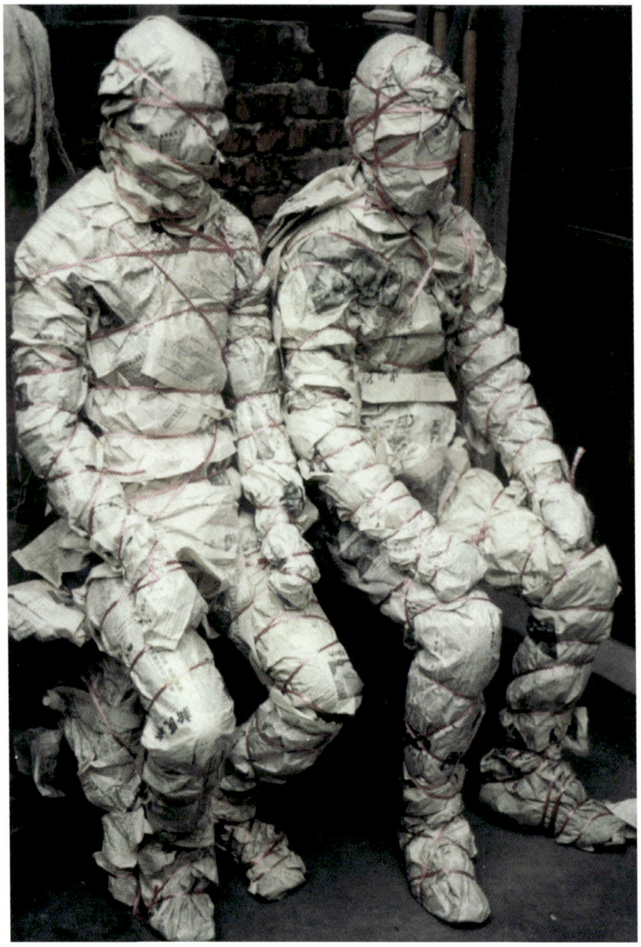

Zhang Peili and Geng Jianyi, *Wrapping Up – King and Queen*, Beijing, November 1986

texts, as well as some traditional Chinese texts. This period has been called "Reading Fever". […] I would say there were three solid legs (a trinity) of thought I felt an affinity to at the time: Wittgenstein, Duchamp and Zen Buddhism.'[36] Attention to the individual body in isolation – to a notion of the '*I*' that could be distinguished from such variations on the '*We*' – came subsequently when ideas of individual expression began to circulate. Concepts from psychoanalysis and expressionism in art were beginning to be encountered in China in the early 1980s. In February 1981, the Chinese art journal *Meishu* published an article about the concept of self-expression and existentialism in relation to Jean-Paul Sartre, for example. It is also significant that an exhibition titled *250 Years of French Painting* was held in the autumn of 1982 at China Art Gallery. The artist Song Dong has said that this 'exhibition presented for the first time an opportunity to see human figures painted with expression and engaged in movement and action'.[37]

Chinese artists in this early period had not been concerned with personal expression in the same way as Western artists immersed in psychoanalytic theory, nor was their conception of the body premised upon a Western mind/body dualism. Instead, in Chinese culture the body is a process and an embodied exchange between physical body and spirit (*shenti*), bringing our corporeal existence into contact with the entire universe. In his book *Performance Art in China*, Thomas Berghuis observes that the Chinese conception of the 'lived body' – body/life or body/substance – connects and equalises the notions of *I/We/It*.[38] Berghuis makes the important observation that, distinct from Western ideas of existentialism, psychoanalysis or phenomenology, in the Chinese intellectual context of this period 'the internal function of the body and its external behaviour in society are dependent upon each other, as can be seen, for example, in the Taoist notion that the internal system of the body represents a landscape'.[39] This is a philosophy that is highly relevant to contemporary artists' fascination with bodily practice as a counterpoint to language-driven conceptualism.

It was not until 1985 that Wang Qiang staged what Berghuis says 'can be considered one of the first private performance works' in China: 'he posed as a living statue, wearing a suit and covered entirely in paint and plaster, with his head wrapped in a white cloth'.[40] One year before, in 1984, Wang Peng had staged a performance 'action' work (*xingdong yishu*), titled *84 Performance*, for which he covered his body in Chinese ink and made imprints on sheets of *xuan* paper. Subsequently, the artists Zhang Peili and Geng Jianyi staged *Wrapping Up – King and Queen* 1986 in a private setting in Luoyang, wrapping their bodies, very tightly, in newspaper and rope. Zhang and Geng's work represented a new, expressive kind of self-suffocation with psychoanalytic connotations, rather than seeking to make 'an impact on the overall conditions of society'.[41] Artist Ma Liuming, who staged solo performances and participated in the performance titled *Suicide Project* by Wei Guanqing in 1988, involving wrapping of the body, states how he became influenced by the 'wrapping' installations of French artist duo Christo and Jeanne-Claude, whose work he encountered through documentation.[42] This was before a significant revival of body art by Ma Liuming, Zhang Huan, Zhu Ming – artists of the Beijing East Village – and others in the 1990s that could be compared in spirit to Vienna Actionism, often taking extreme and challenging forms, and producing work involving the naked body that posed the artist more clearly as an expressive agent shaping his or her own sense of self, rather than as a manipulator of materials.

Inhabiting the image

The body art practices discussed in the previous section emerged, broadly speaking, from the exploration of existential questions. But artists during this period also considered the place of the physical body in the natural ecosystem, and its potentially spiritual dimensions. Overall these works stage the possibility of a kind of transparency of the body: a continuity between inner and outer self, encapsulated in the idea that one's physical expression – one's skin, naked body, tolerance of pain – could serve as an index of interiority, or could point to this as a fantasy, sometimes critically. But a parallel strand of work on the body developed explicitly, despite having traceable roots in earlier periods, through the 1970s and into the 1980s. Within the emergent context of postmodernism, performances by artists such as Sanja Iveković, Luigi Ontani or Cindy Sherman suggested that the gendered self was not biologically innate or authentic, but was something that could be created through the enactment of fantasy or desire. One of the primary ways in which postmodernism deconstructed the fantasy of apparently authentic existence was via forms of 'passing' or 'drag', an approach that has been elaborated further and more fluidly still by the subsequent generation.

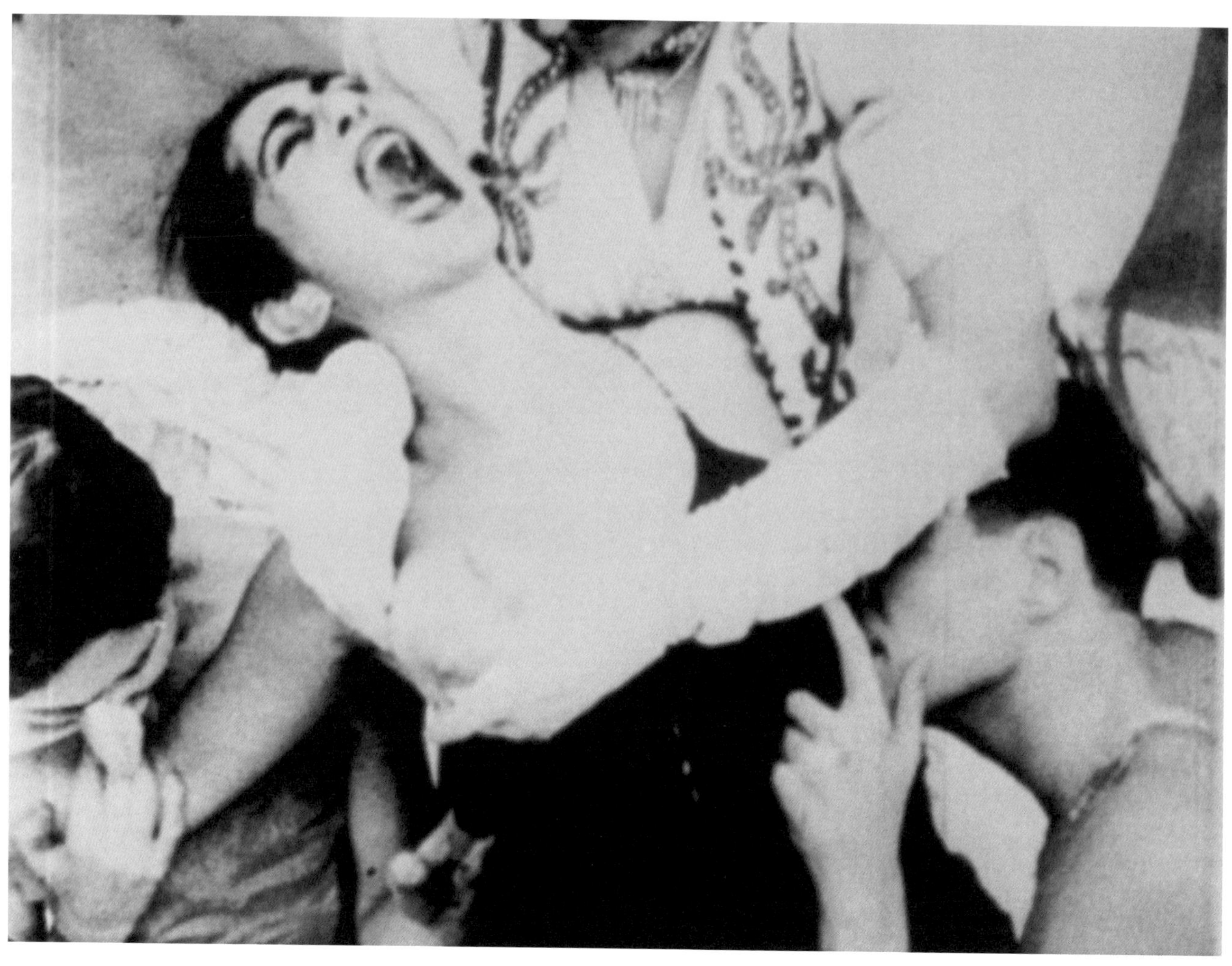

Jack Smith, *Flaming Creatures* (film still), 1962–3

The presumptive opposition of body art and image is crude, however, and key figures such as American experimental filmmaker Jack Smith productively muddle it. The greasepaint-caked faces and figures set within Smith's downtown New York apartment might be seen as one of the first instances of a form of drag performance camouflaging itself within a kind of 'total painting' situation, which also dealt with the body as abject matter. In his short story 'The Memoirs of Maria Montez' (1963–4), itself also a form of narrative drag, appropriating popular style, Smith describes the B-movie star who inspired much of his work in painterly terms that resonate with the space he was living in and his provisionally constructed stage sets: 'Maria Montez was propped up beside the pool which reflected her ravishing beauty. A chunk fell off her face, showing the grey under her rouge.'[43] Smith's vividly material description of the construction of identity and glamour relates directly to the paint-pasted faces of the characters appearing in his photographs and home-made films from the early 1960s, such as *Flaming Creatures* 1963 and *Normal Love* 1963, as well as the set itself: his ramshackle apartment, decorated with exotic elements of Eastern architecture and painted scenes presenting, in his mind, an alternative to the pristine 'eggshell walls of MoMA'.[44]

Through the 1970s, we see a shift from the early, queer self-transformations of Smith and his (proto-Warholian) co-stars, with their painterly low-fi glamour, and his influence on artists including Joan Jonas, who attended his performances, towards the concerns of those artists such as Sherman and Ontani, who were ever more engaged within an accelerating media culture of lens-derived images. In this period, artists responded to the proliferation of television, magazines and the increased availability of hand-held image-capture technologies like video (notably, the Super-8 or Portapak camera), shifting the early focus on forms of masquerade (masks or camouflage) towards an entangled relationship with photographic images and their surface. Inhabiting the image was becoming, from the 1970s towards the 1980s, not a possibility but an apparent necessity. The question of how one appeared, as much as what one depicted, came to be a foundation for art practice in the decades building up to our highly performative attention economy in the early twenty-first century. Andy Warhol was an artist

Luigi Ontani, *San Sebastiano Indiano* 1976, photograph hand-painted by the artist

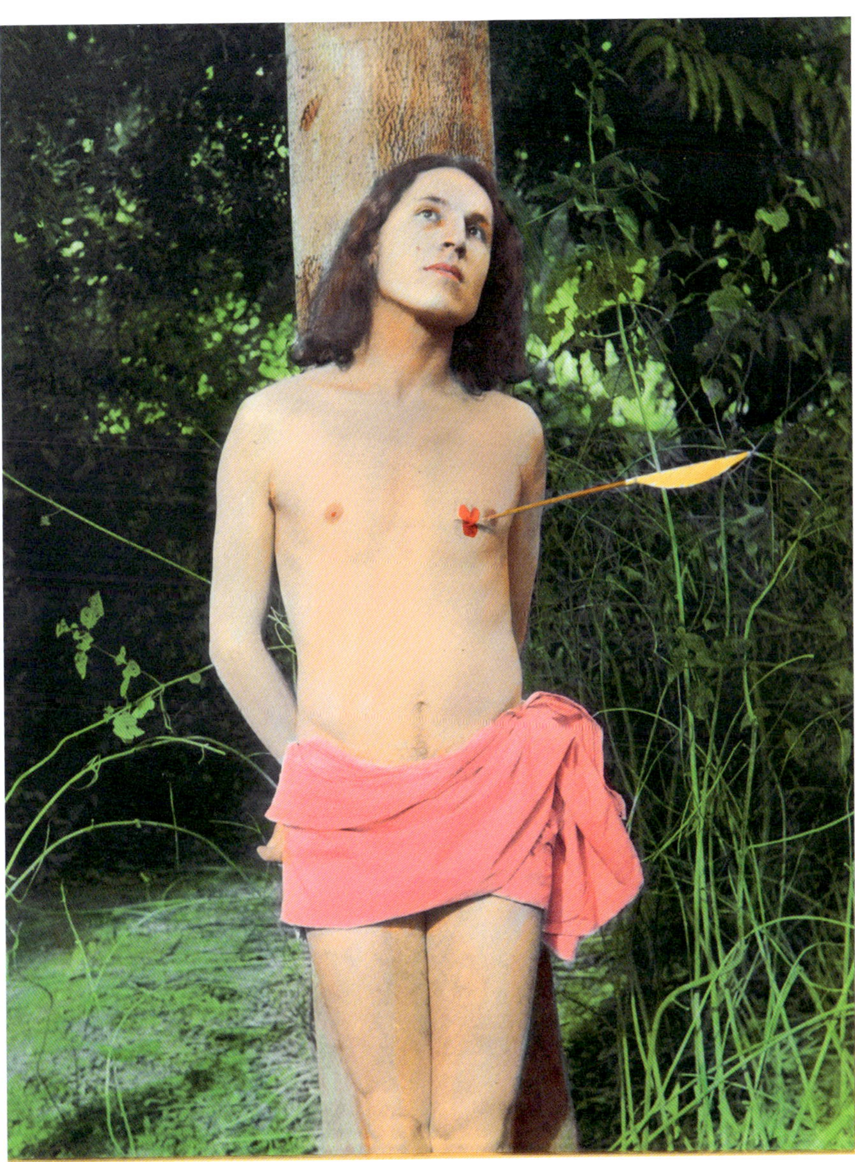

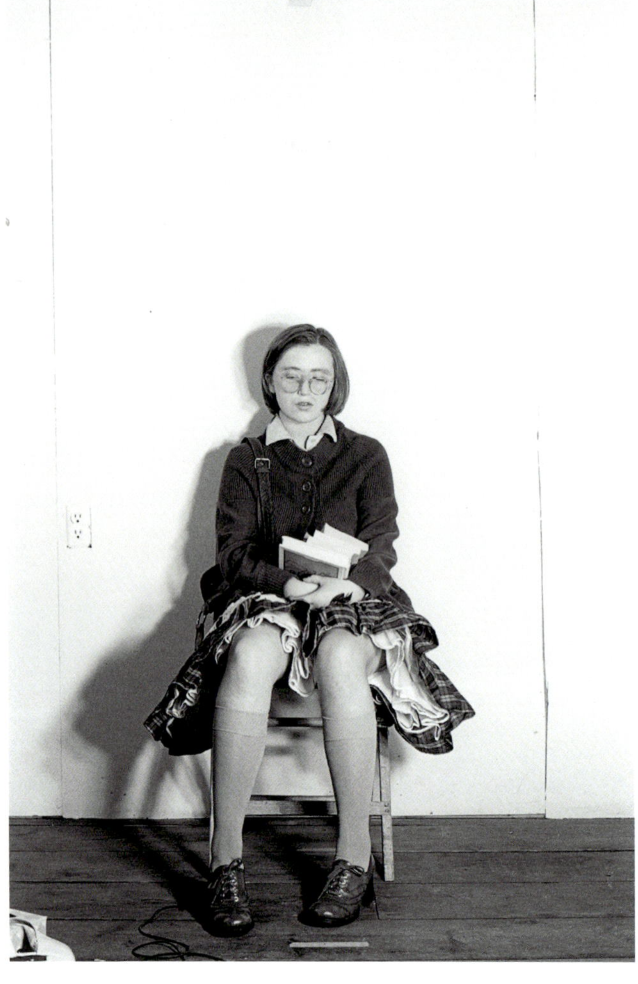

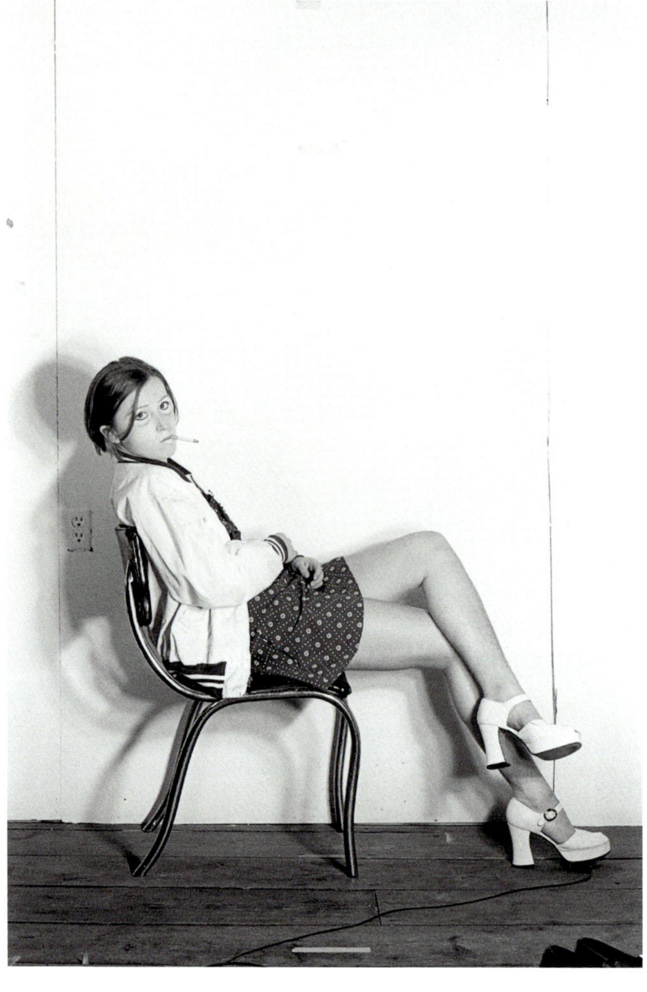

Cindy Sherman, *Untitled*,
from the series *Bus Riders*
1976–2000

Sanja Ivekovic, *Make-Up – Make-Down*, video still, 1978

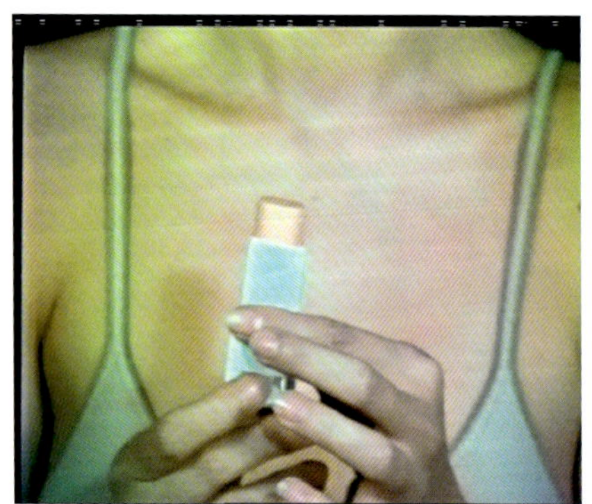

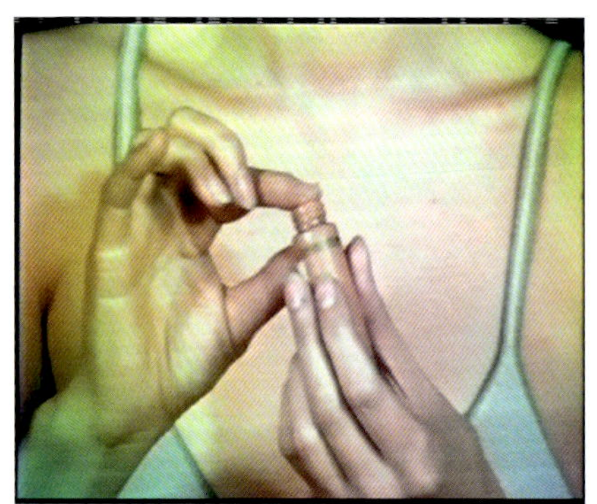

who anticipated this state of affairs, from early in the 1960s, through his cultivation of a deadpan camp persona in a blond shock wig, his castings of an entourage of 'superstars' in his films, and his embrace of with celebrity glamour in his paintings, all set within the theatre of his Factory and relishing 'documentation' by the paparazzi.

Two important exhibitions staged key questions about drag and identity-play during this period, presenting early conceptualisations of how a picture might represent a performance: *Transformer: Aspects of Travesty* (1974), curated by Jean-Christophe Ammann at Kunstmuseum Lucerne, and *Pictures* (1977), curated by Douglas Crimp at Artists Space in New York.[45] These shows investigated how image-making for artists had become entangled with the circulation of media images, which insistently reiterated ideals of beauty and gender norms, and how artists might appropriate or even colonise advertising imagery. This move was part of a wider shift in pop culture, encapsulated by the multiple personae inhabited by David Bowie in his transition from rock and roll to glam rock. Bowie had stunned critics by abandoning his superstar creation Ziggy Stardust at the height of his fame, in 1973, and re-inventing himself from there. The star summed up something of this shape-shifting attitude, saying of his own strategy, 'I felt more like an actor on stage than a rock 'n' roll star. I was not *in* rock and roll, I was using it.'[46]

Work by women artists of the period, such as Eleanor Antin, Sanja Iveković, Lorraine O'Grady, Joan Jonas, Cindy Sherman and Adrian Piper marked a series of important transitions, from the Actionists' use of the female body as a signifier of beauty towards the reclamation and transformation of the female body by the artist herself. These artists bluntly rejected stereotypical notions of femininity, both via parody and by asserting the possibilities of new identities. In the video *Representational Painting* 1971, Antin appears applying make-up in front of the camera, as though it were paint. Likewise, in *Make-Up – Make-Down* 1978, Iveković films her torso while she handles lipstick, face powder and mascara in a fetishistic manner that suggests the ritual of making oneself up as a seductive process in itself, commenting critically on the construction of identity and femininity as it is peddled in women's magazines. In *Double Life* 1975–6, the artist sourced snapshots from her own life and juxtaposed them with glossy advertisements for perfume or underwear to create a series of poignant and parodic diptychs that register the gap between reality and idealisation. By contrast, Jonas drew upon woman's status as image to play out fiction more explicitly. In 1972, after a trip to Japan where she was influenced both by new video-camera technology and Noh and Kabuki theatre, she invented an alter ego called Organic Honey, what Jonas has described as a masked 'erotic seductress', who wore a doll-like mask, a headdress and different costumes, representing a mechanised ideal female figure.[47] In the performance *Organic Honey's Visual Telepathy* 1972, Jonas was filmed and the image relayed on video, effecting an onstage split between live and mediated reality, which doubled the existing split between her own real presence and her masquerading character image. Jonas's live work marked a significant step away from body art towards a postmodern staging of presence entangled with image technology.

Cindy Sherman, an important artist featured in Crimp's *Pictures* article of 1979, also turned to make-up and costume to create a cast of characters from her own face and body. Where the artist herself was – her *I* – is hard to locate. Her work offers the self as a series of deferrals, in line with Simone de

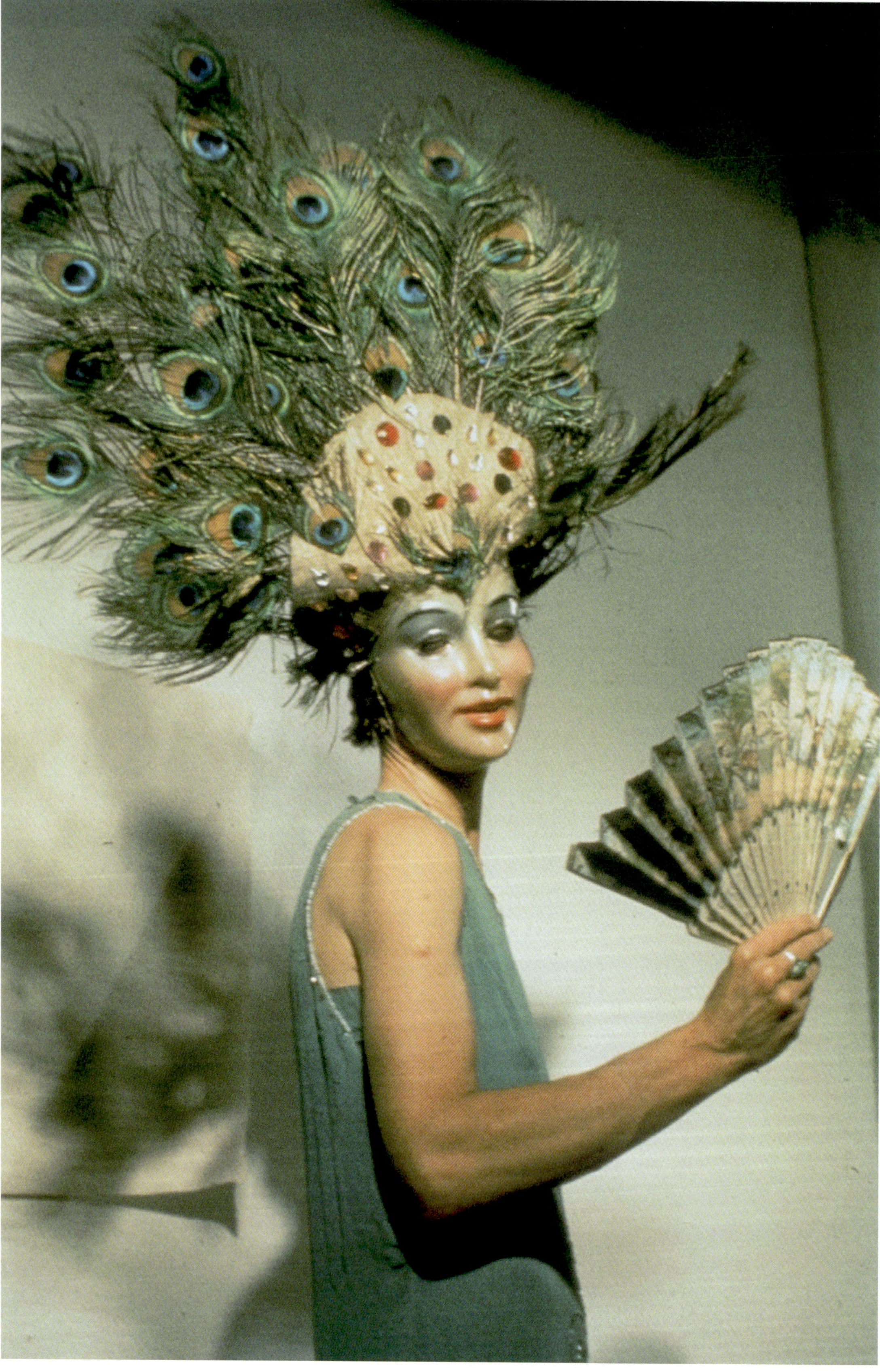

Joan Jonas, *Organic Honey's Visual Telepathy* 1972

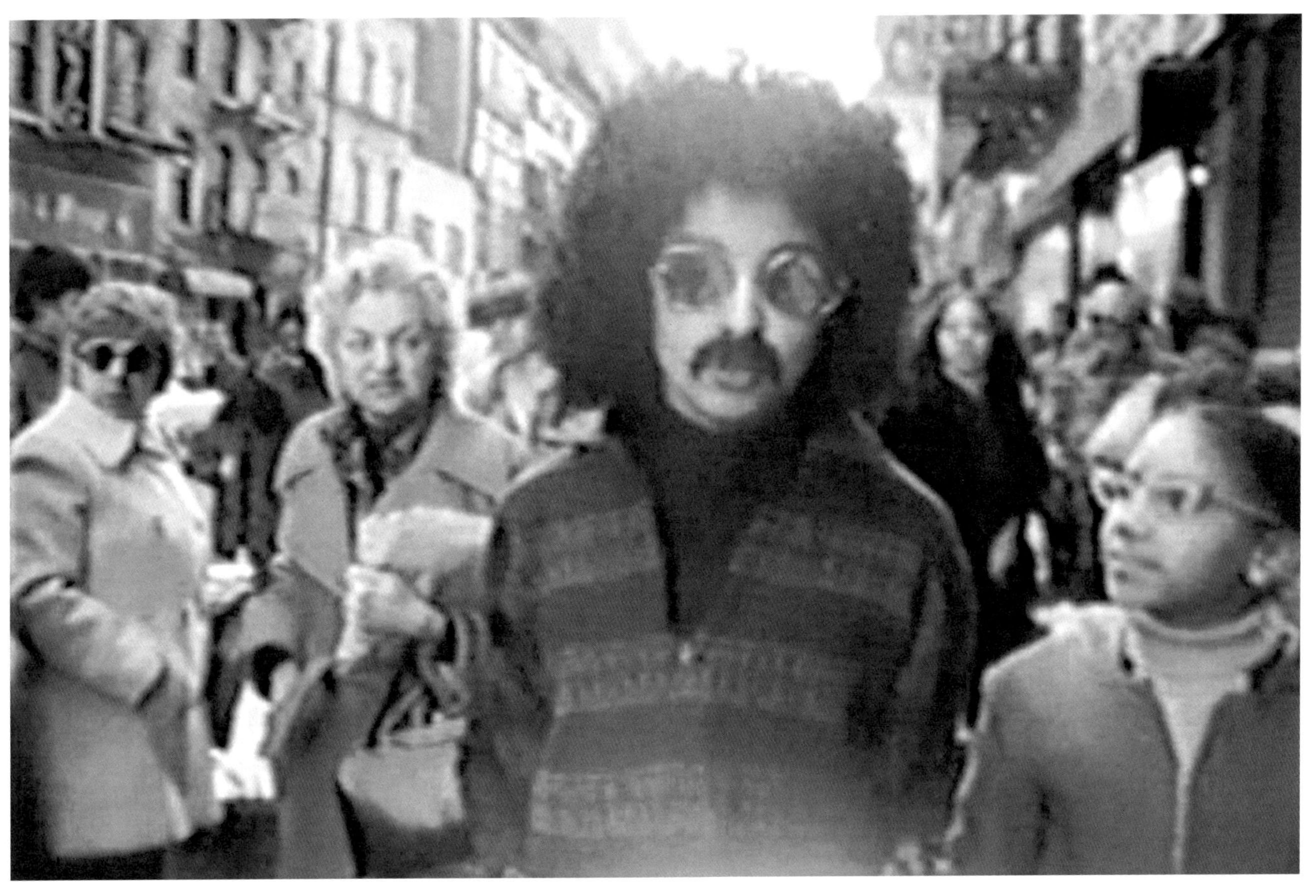

Adrian Piper, *The Mythic Being* 1973, video, 8 min; excerpted segment from the film *Other Than Art's Sake* by the artist Peter Kennedy (detail: video still at 00:06:02)

Beauvoir's assertion that one is not born but becomes a woman – or becomes many women, in Sherman's case.[48] Her personae – whether in her *Untitled Film Stills* from the late 1970s, her parodies of fashion photographs of the 1980s, or the history portraits and clowns from the 1990s – range from feminine ideals to exaggerated archetypes, and shift between naturalism, abstracted grotesquerie and glamour. Swiss artist Urs Lüthi and Italian artist Luigi Ontani – both key artists in the *Transformer* exhibition – similarly made live performance and photography to create experimental forms of drag, posing queer constructions of identity in ambiguously gendered terms. Ontani, for example, identifies himself with the authority of art history by inserting his image into the frame of old master paintings, whether as Saint Sebastian or Leda and the Swan, after Titian or Michelangelo.

The work of these artists is emblematic of emergent articulations of both feminist and queer politics in this period, a deconstructive and critical approach to received gender norms and ideas of 'straightness' which have subsequently been theorised by writers including Eve Kosofsky Sedgwick and Judith Butler. The implications of this notion of / move on from existentialism in a significant way. Here the self is not to be discovered, or probed at by going deep into one's psyche, but is constructed and projected towards the world, shaped in relation to social norms and expectations, whether with or against. This new performative attitude represents a fundamental shift not only in the psychology of the artist, but also in the relationship between artist and artwork. It opens up the possibility of a new continuum between the self and the surface of the work, where the apparently superficial might be more truthful than what lies beneath. 'If you want to know about me, look at the surface of my pictures', Warhol famously said.

During this period, artists investigated ideas of self not only in relation to gender norms, and social constructions of beauty, but also in terms of race and class. In the 1970s, the American artist Adrian Piper began a series of performance interventions in public space titled *Catalysis*. The work included painting her clothes with wet white paint, stuffing a huge white towel into her mouth or covering herself in a mixture of vinegar, eggs, milk and cod liver oil before travelling on the New York subway and elsewhere in the street. The *Catalysis* performances were intended to perform social disruption: her actions represented 'catalysts' that challenged social norms in terms of etiquette, dress codes and the normative boundary between what is considered to be appropriate behaviour for public or private spheres, or between sanity and insanity.

From 1972, Piper created an alter ego in which she 'dressed in drag as a young, black male' whom she titled the 'Mythic Being', for a series of performances begun in 1973 and continuing until 1975.[49] Her costume comprised an afro wig, moustache and sunglasses, with a t-shirt and jeans, and the artist adopted forms of behaviour that were apparently 'masculine', with an aggressive edge, conjuring up the figure of a lower-class black male; a figure she knew many white people perceived as an especially dangerous threat. As the character, Piper says that she 'crashed various contexts in New York cultural life [...] I went to the movies [...] I crashed art world openings [...] I went to the Opera; I did all the sorts of things I normally did except with this masculine guise.'[50] Piper's 'Mythic Being' first appeared in a series of seventeen photo-advertisements in *The Village Voice*. Photographed as the 'Being' at home, Piper pasted thought bubbles containing words from her own diaries onto her portrait images. The the status of her photographs as 'documentation' of her actions was provocatively undercut by the addition of these autobiographical journal entries. The combination of public revelation and private contemplation was an exorcism of sorts, the artist has explained. 'The experience of the Mythic Being thus becomes part of the public history and is no longer a part of my own.'[51]

In the 1980s, the American artist Lorraine O'Grady created the character Mlle Bourgeoise Noire – a critical answer to Antin's 1970s 'first black ballerina' character, in the performance of Eleanora Antinova. Mlle Bourgeoise Noire was a beauty queen persona appearing at art openings in a ballgown made of 180 pairs of white gloves. She moved around, when she appeared at openings, continuously hitting herself with a white cat-o'-nine-tails, while shouting out poems protesting against the racially segregated art world of that time. O'Grady's work in photography, performance and film has, since then, dealt with the subjects of diaspora, hybridity and black female subjectivity, often using her own position to bring into visibility wider social issues. In *Art Is …* 1983, O'Grady created her own float for the annual African American Day Parade in Harlem. With fifteen collaborators dressed in white, O'Grady's float paraded down the main boulevard, displaying an enormous, ornate, gilded frame, reminiscent of the frames used for old master paintings (pp.14–15). The words 'Art Is …' were emblazoned across the bottom of the float. At various points along the route, O'Grady and her collaborators jumped off the float and held up the empty picture frames, inviting people to pose in them. Parade onlookers and Harlem residents

Yasumasa Morimura,
M's self-portrait No.56/B (or 'as Marilyn Monroe')
1996

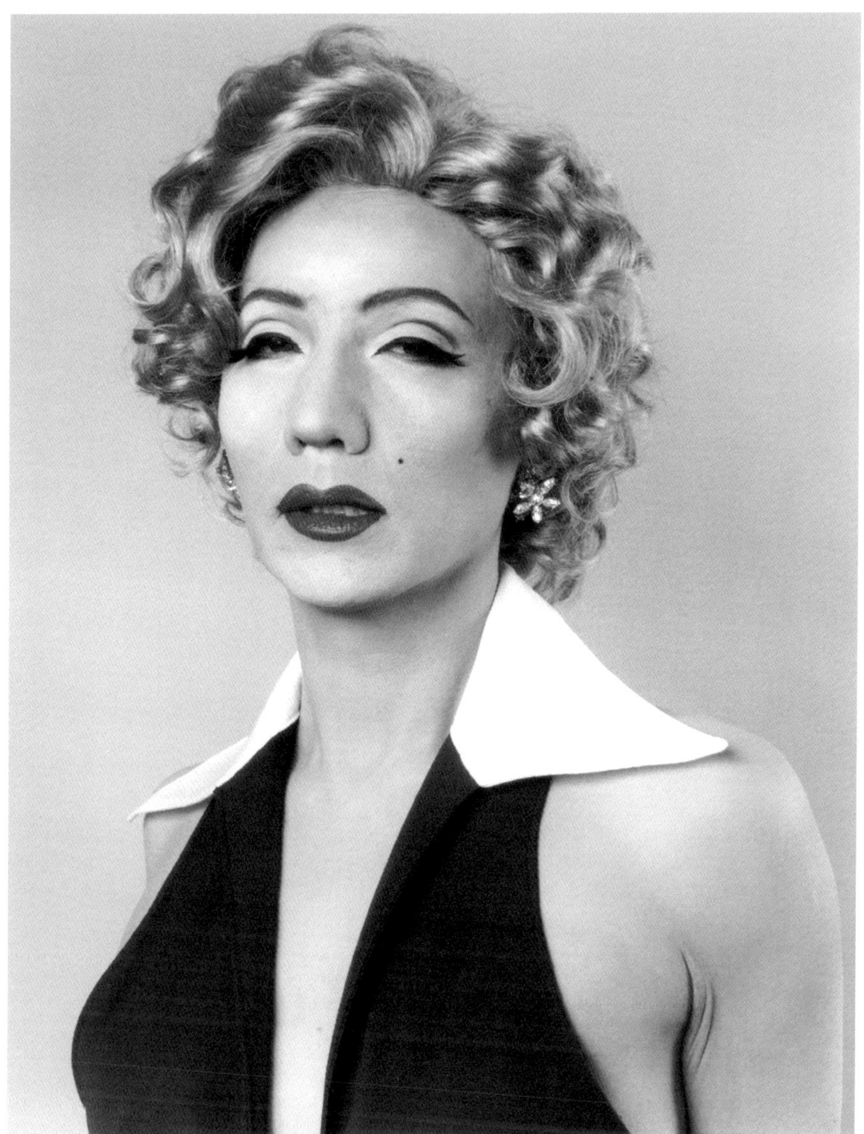

turned into the subject of her live portraits, inviting a collective switching of subject position from audience (*We*) to subject (*I*), through the frame of the artwork (*It*). This work offers a perfect example of how art can direct attention towards life by offering a frame or lens through which to look anew, and a switching of hierarchy between so-called 'high culture' and vernacular community art.

O'Grady's *Miscegenated Family Album* 1994 is a series of paired photographs that grew out of the 1980 performance *Nefertiti/Devonia Evangeline*. This piece examined the troubled relationship between the artist and her late sister, Devonia Evangeline, via the juxtaposition of images of the Ancient Egyptian queen Nefertiti and her sister Mutnedjmet. O'Grady was fascinated by the physical and biographical resemblances between Nefertiti and her own sister.

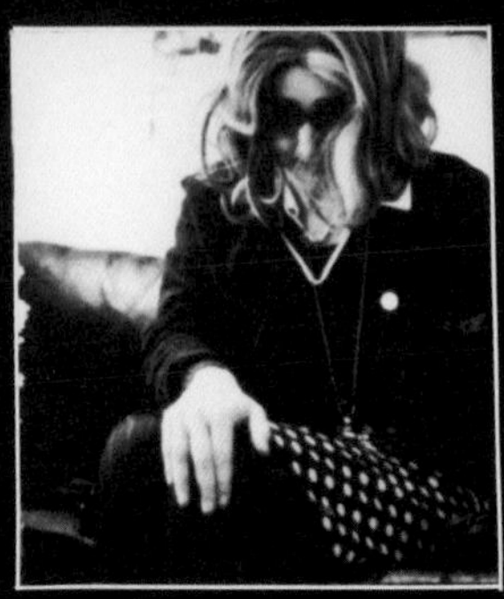

"Americans show greater differences gesturally"

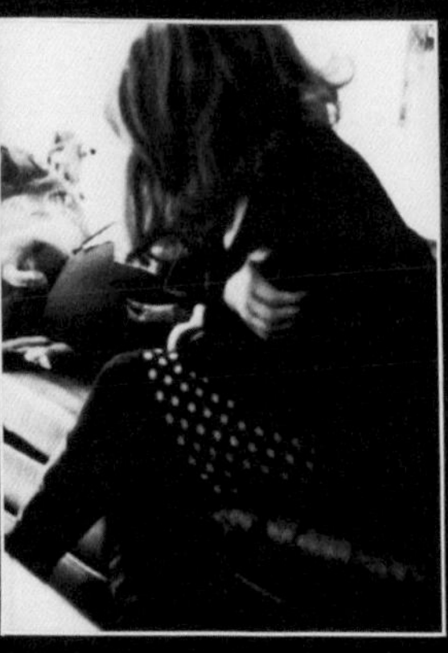

"Do crossed arms mean that 'I am frustrated?"

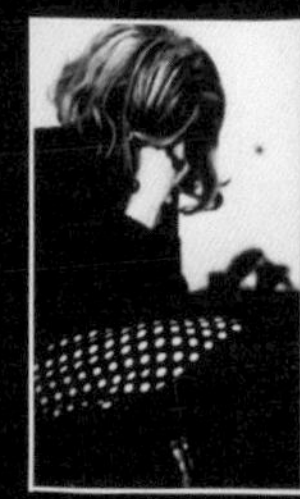

"A hand to the face may serve as a barrier"

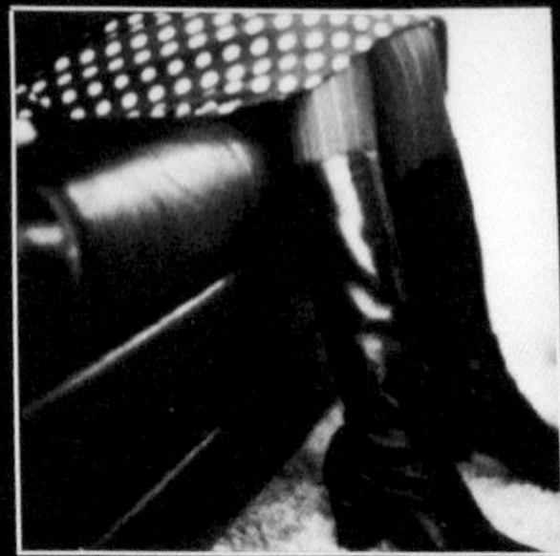

"Crossed legs point to each other. "

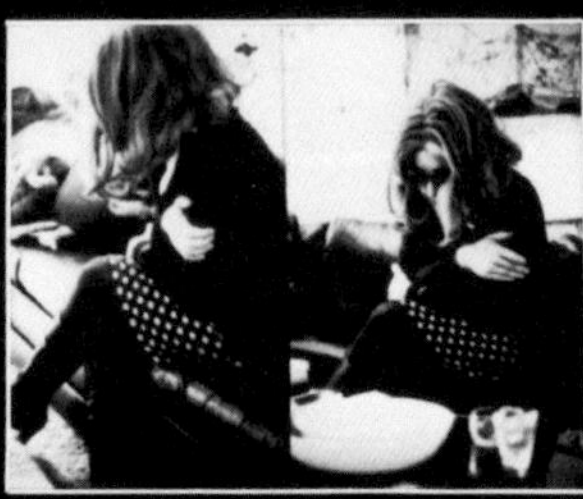

"Crossed arms do the same thing"

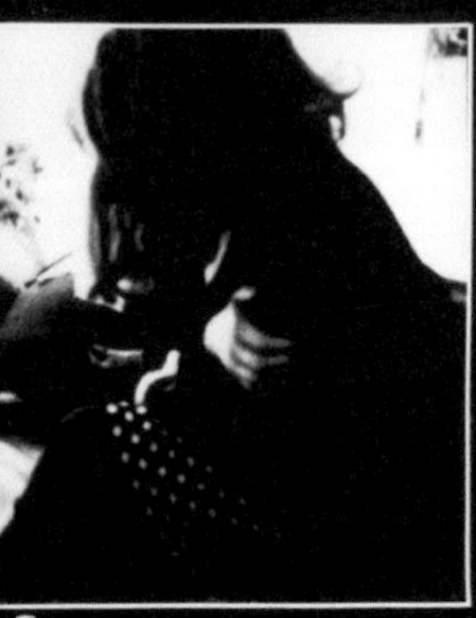

"Crossing arms defines posture"

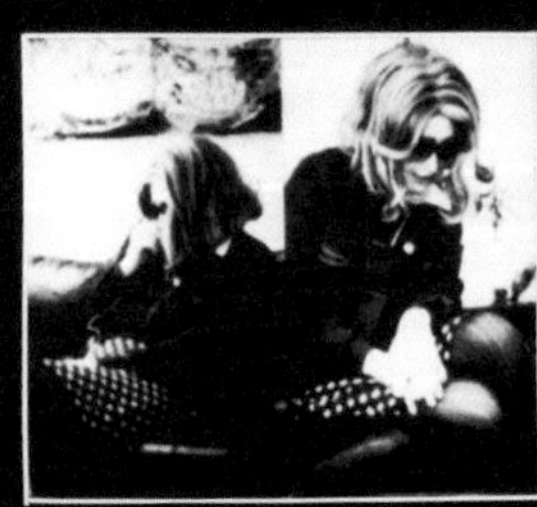

"Does she try to avert attention avoiding your eyes?"

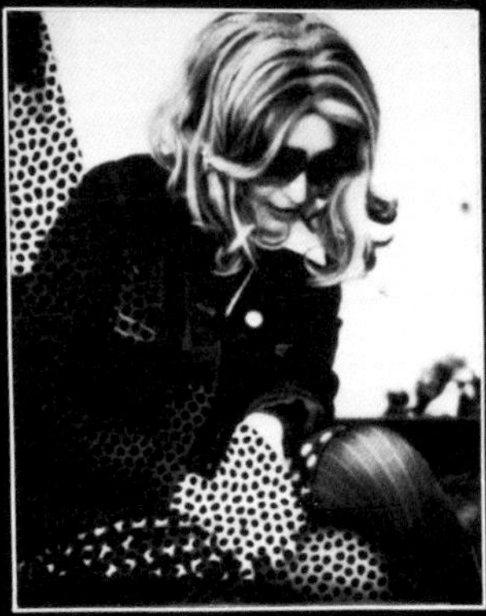

"Is she sitting stiffly and not relaxed?"

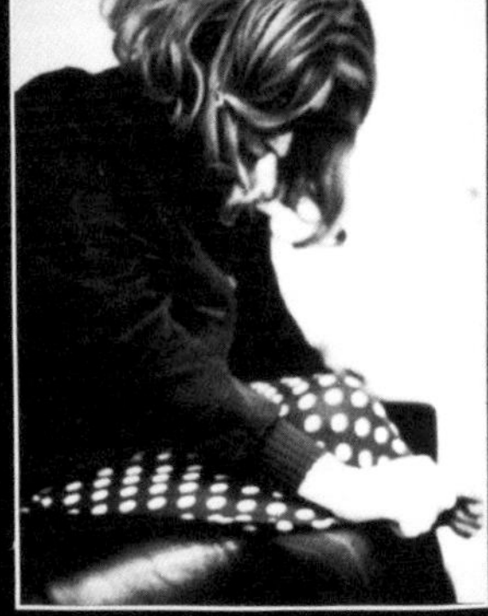

"Covering legs reveals frigidity, fear of sex."

ROBERTA'S BODY LANGUAGE CHART

(photographed during a psychiatric session)

January 24, 1978

Lynn Hershman, *Roberta's Body Language Chart* 1978

Though the artist's subject matter is deeply personal, she used images that were familiar within a shared understanding of history to address issues of class, racism, ethnography and African American art, approximating her own intimate experience to visual archetypes in the public imagination.

Japanese artist Yasumasa Morimura is, relatedly, known for his photographic remakes of iconic images from art history and pop culture, in which he himself plays the role of famous subjects (p.69). The work is a form of appropriation of mainstream culture, via assimilation. The artist often disregards the original gender or race of the subjects represented, inhabiting their images nevertheless through make-up and costume. In his *Art History* photographs, begun in the early 1990s, he painstakingly re-stages well-known paintings by the likes of Rembrandt, Goya and Frida Kahlo. In the *Actress* series, from 1998, he assumes the persona of Hollywood luminaries such as Marilyn Monroe and Elizabeth Taylor, and in his series *Requiem*, from 2007, he recreates iconic photographs relating to political and cultural life, from Adolf Hitler to Albert Einstein and Chairman Mao. Morimura's fascination with the self-portrait, celebrity, gay and transgender life, art history and popular culture align him closely with the work of Andy Warhol, to whom he pays homage, as well as Cindy Sherman's practice. His desiring insertion of himself into these pictures also comments upon the way in which Western culture has been absorbed and appropriated in his home context of Japan, flagrantly staging a kind of submissive complicity to which he appears personally subject.

American artist Lynn Hershman Leeson's project *Roberta* 1973–8 extended the artist's experiments with the construction of an ur-feminine character that she originally built from a composite of magazine images – blonde, made-up, in feminine clothing – into everyday life. For the best part of a decade, Hershman Leeson lived in the fracture between her apparently real self and her persona, Roberta Breitmore. She recorded her encounters in photographs (taken by a private detective she had commissioned) and in her own diary writings. Hershman Leeson's live portrait as a female stereotype proposed a complex performance of a normative ideal embedded in her real-life situations, thus theatricalising not only her own everyday activities and encounters, but also the wider social context in which Roberta appeared. It is hard to say where this performance begins and ends: what is clear is that the artist's commitment to her performance was extreme, especially given that she was caring for her daughter while managing this dual identity.

Instead of borrowing stereotyped images of femininity from magazine images and replaying them, or exposing their artifice, British artist Cosey Fanni Tutti – who also performed with Genesis P-Orridge in COUM Transmissions in the 1970s and was a founding member of the band Throbbing Gristle in 1976 – took a paid job as a model in porn magazines (p.72). In this way, she put her own image as model into circulation, as well as working as a stripper in the Raymond Revuebar in Soho, London. Her attitude was highly controversial at the time, both in the mainstream press and within feminist networks. Cosey Fanni Tutti, whose name was taken from the Mozart opera *Così fan tutte* ('they [women] all do the same'), pushed the idea of overidentifying with the image of femininity or female sexuality to an extreme – desiring to become, and literally becoming, that image herself by appearing as the object of desire. But as an artist from a low-income, working-class background, estranged from her family, Cosey Fanni Tutti also engaged with the politics of wage labour, as both a real necessity and a way to create a representation that was embedded in real industry. She did not announce herself

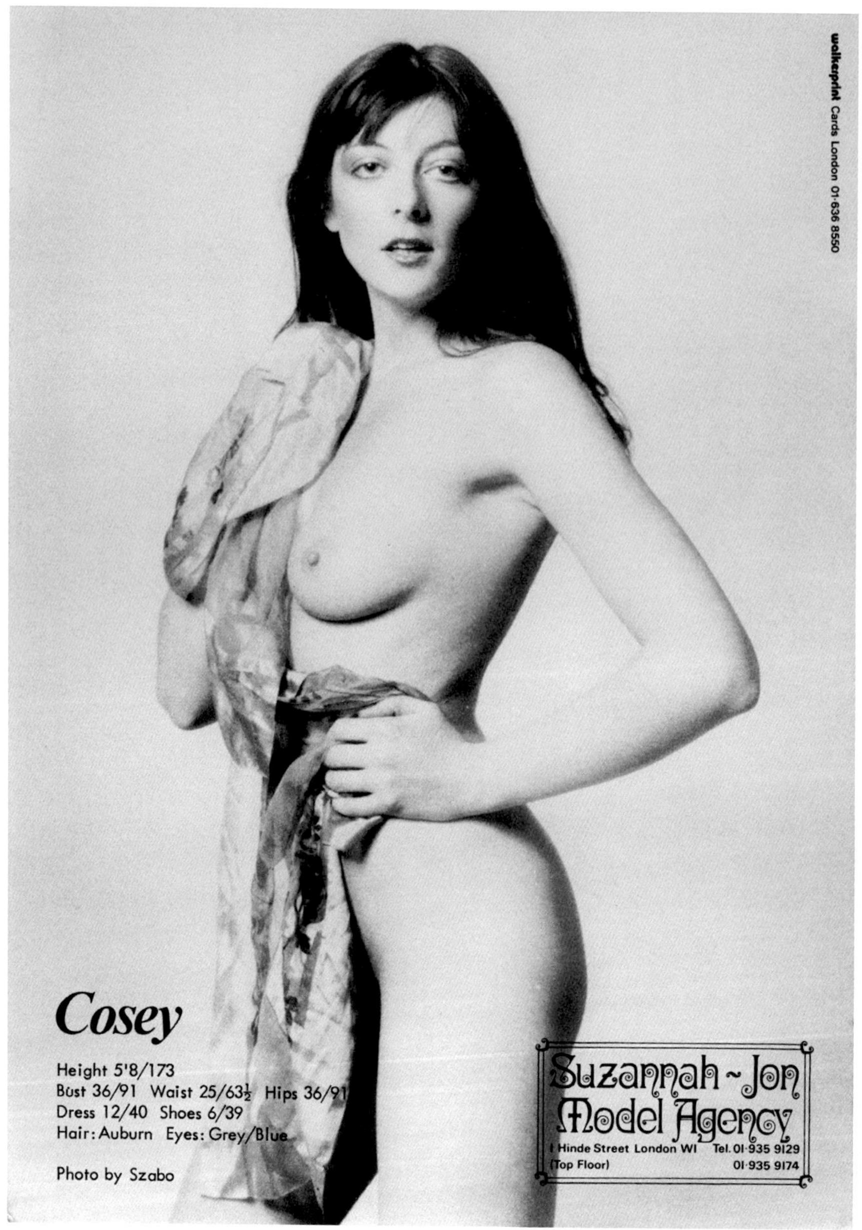

Cosey Fanni Tutti, *Prostitution* exhibition poster, Institute of Contemporary Arts, London 1976

as an artist while procuring work and participating in the shoots as a model. It was only after her images were published that she would source the magazines to display them in a gallery context. Beyond the psychological implications of performing as a picture, Cosey Fanni Tutti's intervention drew attention to the circuit of labour, desire and money at stake in her participation: she was a paid worker, an object of desire, and an artist with a critical overview, simultaneously.

Taking an alternative approach to embedded performance in character, Hong Kong-born artist Tseng Kwong Chi began a self-portrait series, *East Meets West*, also known as the *Expeditionary Series*, in 1978. This sequence of photographs involved Tseng adopting the guise of a Chinese government official or dignitary – dressed in what he called his 'Mao suit' and sunglasses – and photographing himself situated, often emotionlessly, in front of iconic tourist sites in the West. Art historian Amy Brandt has observed that the 'performance allowed Tseng to manoeuvre like a chameleon, insinuating himself with equal poise into nightclubs, art openings, beach parties and posh society galas. Yet in nearly every photograph of these encounters, Tseng's unchanging costume and Asian identity mark him as an outsider.'[52] In this work, the artist assimilates himself to a recognisable cliché by appearing as an 'other' within an American or European landscape, one that points to both his belonging (he is recognisable) and his exclusion (he is different). Tseng's work conflates a queer approach to performing identity with a critical take on the racial US politics of the period.

These select examples of work show how, through the 1970s and into the 1980s, a new space for acting and performing began to be used within the two-dimensional realm of the image. Collapsing their own identity with their mediums, artists began to perform as images. They assumed different identities and even enacted those in different social contexts in order to consider the roles of gender, race, class and social standing in the formation of the self. Questions were posed about how one's identity is contingent upon context, but might actively be manipulated. Fiction became a form of political power. Through a variety of approaches, these works reveal an increasing gap between one's literal bodily presence and one's ability to create one or more personae as a picture that intersects with, and intervenes in, a culture of images.

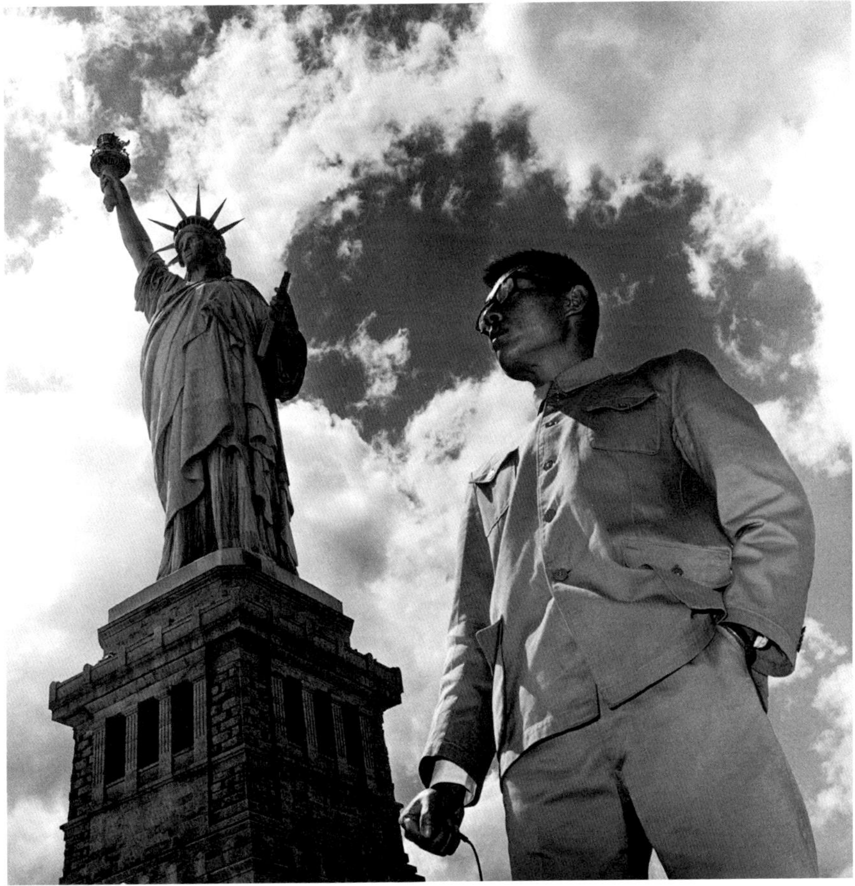

Tseng Kwong Chi, *New York, New York* 1979, silver gelatin print, 91.4 x 91.4, from *East Meets West* self-portrait series 1979–89

Contemporary

I, and Not I

So far, I have described the staging of 'making' in the art of the 1950s, charted a shift towards the naked or 'raw' body as a new medium and marker of authenticity in the 1960s, and thence the manipulation of make-up and costume to invent self-portraits from the 1970s onwards. These approaches represent the basic foundations of self performance in the postwar period, but how do artists perform now, in a contemporary context? How do they stage themselves as subjects (or objects), present their bodies or style themselves as images in the media-saturated and cyber-networked landscape of the twenty-first century? For a so-called post-internet generation, is the idea of individuality, or the presence of the body, still relevant? How are artists pushing beyond the notion of a single, coherent subjectivity to dismantle the presumption of individual autonomy? And, simply, what does it mean, now, to stand up in front of others and perform live in an art context?

If performance is fundamentally to do with the act of showing, of projecting a temporary reality, its immediacy has to be understood, today, against the exponential increase in image distribution within culture at large, and the embeddedness of technology within social relations. Artists negotiate this landscape not only as image producers, but also in terms of how they themselves appear and are visible in circuits of communication. Or, rather, the two realms are increasingly blurred. As theorist Donna Haraway wrote in the late 1980s, arguing against the notion of embodied presence as the only truth, 'we are all chimeras, theorised and fabricated hybrids of machine and organism', or cyborgs.[53] In the twenty-first century, where one's 'Data-Self' has a life independent of one's immediate presence, it seems that the physical body apparently no longer represents an existential limit. Or does it?

In the late twentieth and early twenty-first century, being visible has become an imperative for artists, as well as for workers in the field of cultural production. Taking a cue from Warhol's blurring of product and persona in the 1960s, states of being, making, appearing and acting have become increasingly hard to separate for the millennial generation. We see a key shift taking place in much performance after the 1980s: the search for authenticity during the immediate postwar period and the critique of essentialism that followed it in the 1970s and 1980s have led to an extreme attention to the question of, and demand for, visibility in contemporary practice.

On the one hand, many artists are dealing with the new existential fact that how one appears – one's performance – equals one's worth within the capitalist economy. On the other hand, artists continue to find ways to assert physical or psychological presence as a form of resistance against this kind of alienation, and to the increasing mediation of all aspects of life through images and technology. Artist LaTurbo Avedon, for example, exists only as a virtual presence, an online avatar who is not linked to a person with real-time presence; Liz Magic Laser works with actors to create phantom iterations related to the simulated production of authenticity in political speech-making; while Tino Sehgal's work,

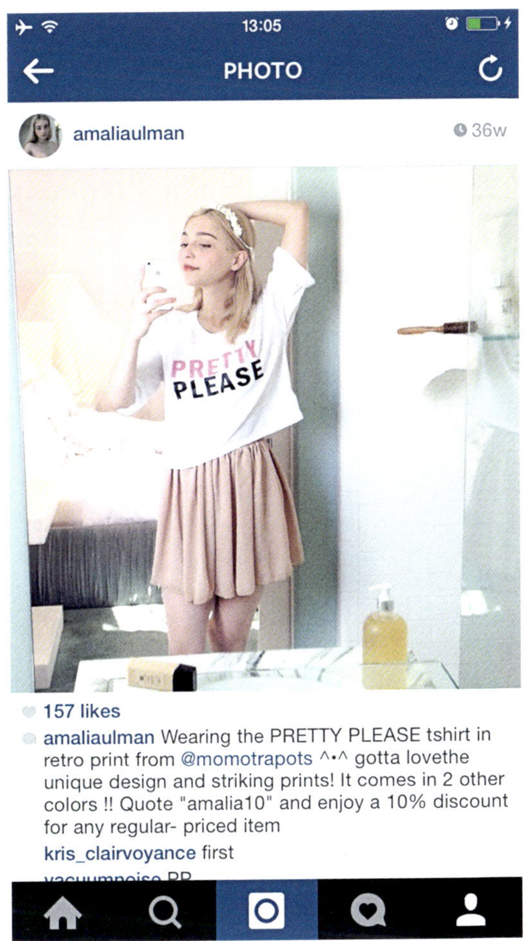

Amalia Ulman, *Excellences and Perfections* (Instagram Update, 1st June 2014), 2015

conversely, is entirely focused upon the staging of enactors' real-time presence and their direct exchanges with viewers, which are nonetheless pre-scripted within uncannily self-contained loops that repeat like basic algorithms.

This section will consider, then, a shift from a sense of self defined by the limits of the physical body, towards its prosthetic extensions via technology and networking. Looking at how artists perform the position of the / since the 1990s – as themselves, as characters or as embodied subjects – notions of passing, colonisation and assimilation to the image become important, and contribute to works where identity and subjectivity are taken apart to depict the 'post-human'. Through select examples, we see how artists have built on the work of the 1970s and 1980s in attempting to negotiate a twenty-first-century culture of image saturation by becoming themselves images. At the same time, a number of artists in the 2000s have bypassed these questions almost entirely by picturing identity as a kind of free-floating shell that might no longer be linked to a human referent in real time and space, namely through an exploration of the avatar. The idea of a performed 'extimacy' – one's subconscious being externalised – is also part of the character of the social media age.[54]

Street and site: the body in context

If, historically, artists have used performance in art to stage new representations of the self, either as real and present, or as constructed characters and images, since the 1990s they have increasingly built upon these newly staked-out positions to highlight the structural contexts that their identities are embedded in and shaped by. In staging the *I*, the recent generation also ask more explicitly what such an assertion potentially excludes, raising questions of alienation and otherness, fluidity and multiplicity.

In a contemporary context of ultra-visibility, there is increasing pressure for contemporary artists – and contemporary subjects more generally – to position themselves in relation to the image; to how they appear. And, yet, the question – or possibility – of the real presence of the body in space and time remains important for some, often as a potential resistance to such pressure. The body continues to be used as a tool to experiment with situations and formats, as well as to signify the humanity of the subject, even while it is reoriented to acknowledge the image plane, and the network in which virtual communications exist.

One of the key figures who persists with working on the body as a physical fact that nevertheless intersects with identity and image in complex ways is African American artist Pope.L. *eRacism*, a project that Pope.L began in the late 1970s, includes over forty endurance-based performances consisting of crawls that he performs himself, varying in length and duration. In *The Great White Way, 22 Miles, 9 Years, 1 Street* 2001–9, Pope.L set himself the marathon task of crawling up the entire length of Broadway, a road traversing Manhattan, New York, on his hands and knees, dressed in a Superman costume with a skateboard strapped to his back. Such a work might be linked directly to the earlier history of body art, representing, as it does, a feat of endurance that involves pain and duration, akin to the work of Pane and Abramović.

But Pope.L's work, being staged as an intervention in the busy city street, moves away from the rarefied intimacy of that side of historical body art, and into a more provocative, catalytic situation that activates a much wider urban context, pulling social dynamics into the frame and being performed for the camera. Like those of Adrian Piper or VALIE EXPORT, Pope. L's actions represent a situated form of body art, in which passers-by are not sure how to take or read the situation with which they are presented. Pope.L has described how, during the making of one performance – *Tompkins Square Crawl*, on 18 July 1991 – he was challenged on being followed by a (white) cameraman, and regarding the politics of the relationship: a crawling older black man, a white man filming. Reportedly, the action 'was stopped after only one block … by a police officer summoned by a black spectator who was dismayed at and confused by what he perceived to be a malicious intent on the part of the artist. Pope.L had asked that he be let alone "to do my work" and offered to talk with him when the piece ended. To no avail.'[55] In this piece, then, Pope.L presented a collision between his physical task and the construction of the image, conceived as a second frame around the action itself. The politics of representation – who is filming whom, for whom – were framed as clearly as the possibility of acting in a pure sense. Pope.L's performance thus situates the so-called authentic body – the artist's physical presence, his blackness, his age – within a constellation of vectors to do with the relative power of doing, acting, appearing and being seen, while performing an extreme act of endurance that tests his basic physical capacities. This work might, then, be connected back to Günter Brus's *Vienna Walk*, in which the artist shocked passers-by on the bourgeois postwar city streets with his face and body thickly painted. In New York's very different contemporary context, Pope.L aggravated questions of racial politics, power hierarchies and age that dug deep into the broader issue of civic conformity, including the problem of mediation.

Guatemalan artist Regina José Galindo often uses her own body as a tool or site of experimentation to underscore her commitment to activism. She puts herself on the line, in carefully designed actions which expose her vulnerability, and that of the victims of political violence with whom she sides. Galindo grew up during Guatemala's decades-long civil war and her practice articulates a personal response to this traumatic history. One of her earliest works is *Who Can Erase the Footprints?* 2003, an action that involved the artist dipping her feet in human blood and walking from Guatemala City's Constitutional Court to the steps on the National Palace, leaving a trail of footsteps that visualised the stains of military history on the country. Galindo has pushed her body to extremes of pain and endurance through rituals she has set herself within. In the performance *Blind Spot* 2010, the artist appeared stripped bare, standing on a plinth, alone in a room where blind people were invited to gather. She submitted herself to being felt by people's searching hands – people who did not understand why she was there, or why she was naked. In the video *Earth* 2013, we see the artist standing, naked, in a green field (p.78). The scene looks idyllic until we hear the sound of noisy machinery. A bulldozer appears in view and begins to dig the earth around

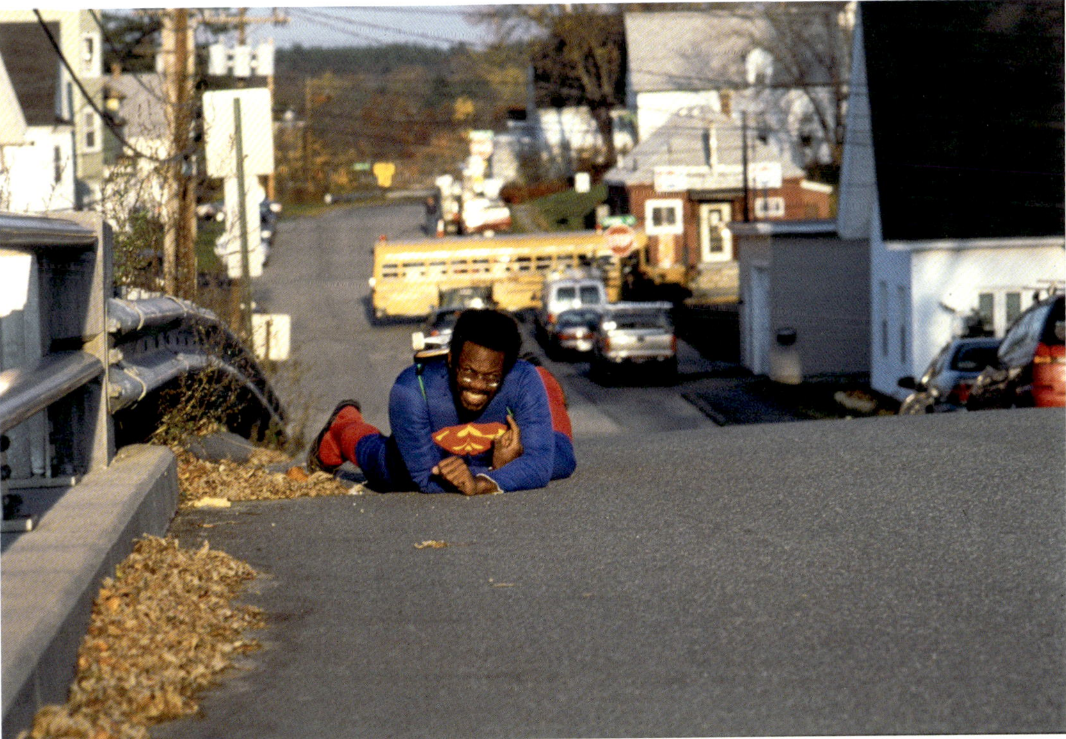

Pope.L., *Training Crawl (For The Great White Way: 22 Miles, 5 Years, 1 Street)* 2001, Lewiston ME

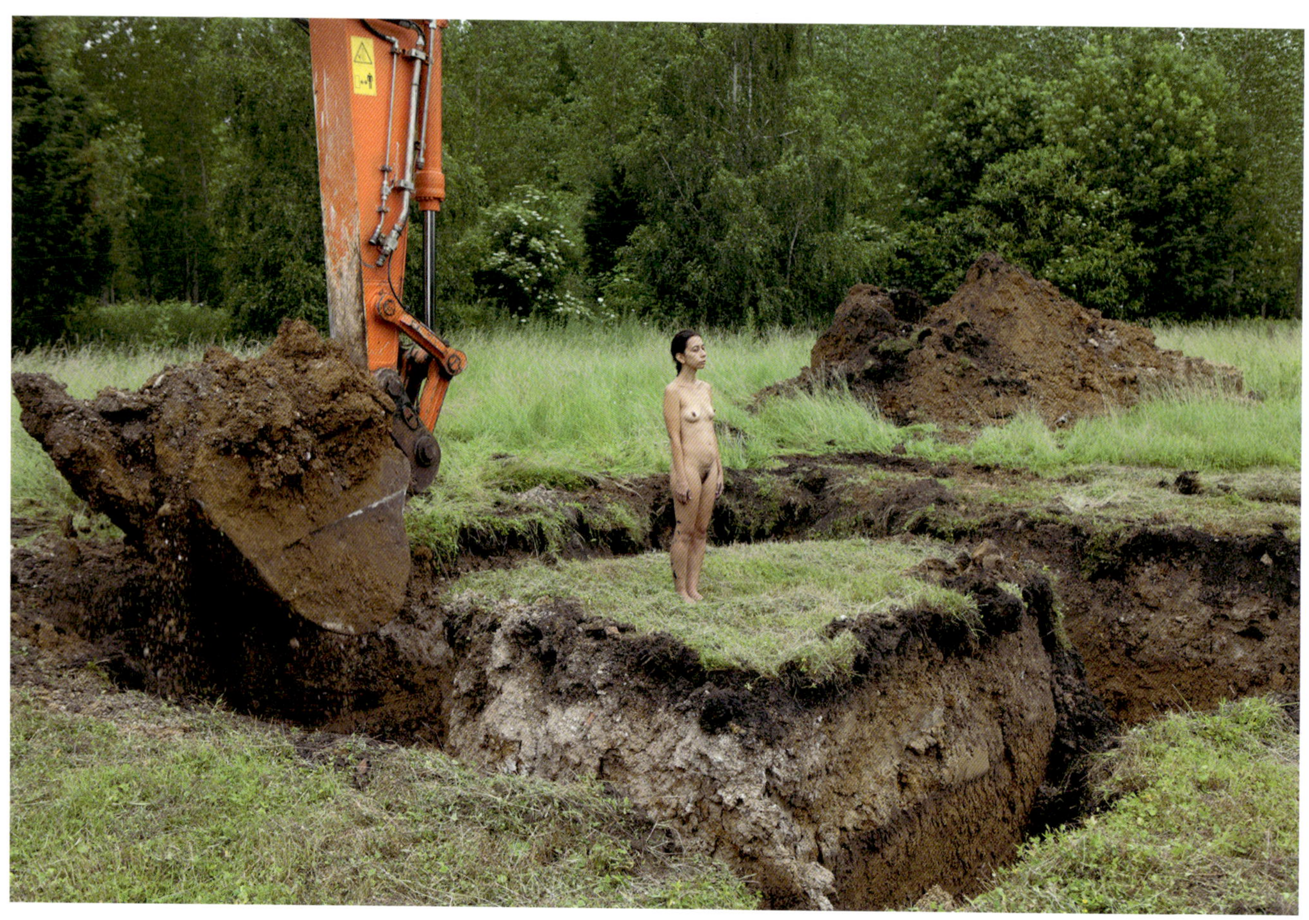

Regina José Galindo, *Tierra* 2013, Les Moulins, Paris

the artist, her slight body remaining still as the surrounding land is excavated, and she is left to stand on a small, isolated patch of turf. The artist intended this action to allude to the murder and burial in a mass grave of innocent civilians under the regime of José Efraín Ríos Montt, charged in 2012 with genocide, and subsequently acquitted.[56]

In her work, then, Galindo lends the body's presence renewed potential as a marker of authenticity, shrugging off the suspicion cast upon it by postmodernism. Though Galindo's brand of body art has been less commonly seen since the 1990s in a Western context, notable figures to which her approach might be compared are the Javanese Muslim artist and activist Arahmaiani, whose ritual body performances, installations and participatory projects with social and religious communities bridge performance and protest against social injustice. Arahmaiani's action *Offerings A to Z* 1996, for example, raises questions about women's rights via a sacrificial self-presentation involving blood, weapons and the burning of pornographic magazines. Equally relevant are Mexican artist Teresa Margolles and Cuban artist Tania Bruguera, who have each – in different ways – made strong body art images with political narratives.

The relationship between art and an understanding of political and social realities is also an important concern in Tania Bruguera's work for the gallery context. *Self-sabotage* 2009, for example, takes the form of a lecture-performance during which the artist plays Russian roulette with a 9mm firearm, taking the staging of the body's vulnerability to an extreme limit. Bruguera sits at a table reading her reflections on political art and the function of artists in the context of art, institutions and society. Twice she pauses in the reading, takes the gun, puts a bullet in it, turns the drum, points at her temple and pulls the trigger. Audience questions are answered when the action finishes. Bruguera has described this work as commenting on the function of artists as catalysts of social change, as well as being concerned with the idea of sacrifice: the sacrifice of oneself in the interest of one's ethical values as an artist. 'This is an exercise in Behaviour Art through self-aggression as a sort of call for a political art taken to its utmost consequences', she has said.[57]

The Chinese artist Zhang Huan made some of the most radical and affecting body actions of recent times in Beijing in the early 1990s, emerging in a context in which, as I have described in the preceding section, the body was manipulated as a form of political resistance. He began his work as part of a small artistic community, known as the Beijing East Village, early in the decade. This group of artists and peers, including Ma Liuming, Zhu Ming and later also others, such as Cang Xin and the female performance artist Duan Yingmei, pioneered a new form of body art in China during the period of political instability following Mao's death in 1976, which culminated in the Tiananmen Square massacre of hundreds of protesters on 4 June 1989. Even in the early 1990s, when the atmosphere was ostensibly more open, Zhang Huan was often in trouble with the authorities for the perceived inappropriateness of his actions, and Ma Liuming and Zhu Ming were arrested and imprisoned for their performance works. For the purposes of the work, the artists often appeared naked, with Zhang Huan occasionally performing masochistic rites of self-harm, such as in the performance *65 Kilograms*, in 1994. His best-known work in this period is titled *12m2* after the size of the public bathroom in which it was staged, also in 1994 (p.81). It is documented in the form of a photograph showing him as 'a naked man, his head half-shaved, sitting in a public toilet in the village. His skin was covered in honey and fish oil and with flies. His face looked blank but tough, as if he were trying to meditate his way through pain.'[58]

In stark contrast to the official channels of art in China at this time, or even the collective actions of avant-garde groups in the late 1970s and early 1980s, Zhang's performances of the 1990s were experimental and impermanent, primarily using his own body as a medium. Unlike in Europe and the US, or Latin America, where ideas of self-expression had long circulated, in China the idea of self-performance only appeared after the end of the Cultural Revolution.[59] Although performance historians Lu Hong and Sun Zhenhua nevertheless described the arrival of performance in Beijing as "premature" in terms of the country's recovery from global isolation.[60] From the mid-80s, according to Thomas Berghuis, artists were moving away from public actions towards performances that focused more on the behavioural aspects of action, often including theatrical performance, expressive painting and early forms of body action.[61] The work of He Yunchang is a paradigmatic example of the latter. In 1999, the artist tried to 'cut a river in half' with a knife, while suspended upside down from a crane, his own blood dripping into the river from the incisions made in his arms (*Dialogue with Water*), and he surgically removed a rib from his own body as part of another performance.[62]

The work of Zhang Huan and He Yunchang demonstrates that in the Chinese context there was a shift in focus from *We* to *I* in the late 1980s and early 1990s, at the same time as many artists in the West turned, instead, from the *I* to the *We*. At that point, the question of *I* was taken very seriously, often at real risk to the artists. Exemplary of this shift was a curious meeting point between the Young British Artists (YBAs) featured in the 1997 Royal Academy exhibition *Sensation* and Chinese performance, with unexpected results. Images of work by Damien Hirst, Marc Quinn, Tracey Emin and others – encountered as pictures, without translation of the accompanying texts – inspired artists to respond to, and build upon, these post-pop representations of slaughter, blood and masochistic self-expression with new, extreme forms of body art. Zhu Yu's photographic series *Eating People* 2000, for example, which was featured in the notorious, Ai Weiwei-curated publication *Fuck Off* (2000) that followed an exhibition in Shanghai with the same title, shows the artist cooking and eating what he alleges is a human foetus. In the Beijing East Village in the 1990s, artists including Ma Liuming and Zhu Ming also created aggressive embodied practices.[63] Other work related to this tendency, but with a more subtle approach, includes Chen Lingyang's *Twelve Flower Months* 1999–2000, a performance series in which the artist recorded her menstrual bleed and framed it, together with the traditional flower of the month, in a self-portrait photograph, and Cui Xiuwen's video *Ladies Room* 2000, which documents the behavioural practices of Beijing prostitutes as they prepare themselves in the restrooms of a karaoke club.

If these artists dramatised the body as fallible flesh and blood by exposing its interiority, the Canadian artist Cassils has worked upon the exterior signifiers of the body to address themes of queer and trans sexuality, and the relationship between physicality and image. In the performance *Becoming an Image* 2012–ongoing, Cassils puts their own bodily presence at the nexus of questions around performance, photography and sculpture. The piece was originally conceived as a site-specific work for the LGBTQ ONE Archives in Los Angeles. In a situation of complete darkness, into which the audience is ushered in by torchlight, Cassils – exposing their muscular physique – violently hits, kicks and punches a two-thousand-pound clay block. The action is only visible via the flashes of light from a photographer's camera. It thus appears as a succession of still 'flashed' images, a sensation at odds with the brute physicality of what is taking place. There is an impression, in witnessing this piece, of sadistically restricted access to seeing the collision between the material fact of the body and this obstinate block of clay – each equally malleable and solid in paradoxical ways. Cassils's work can be seen within a tradition shaped by artists such as Los Angeles-based Ron Athey, who was known for his extreme, queer S&M inflected approach to body art, orginially developed for Club contexts in Los Angeles. His key works include the *Torture Trilogy* and *4 Scenes in a Harsh Life* 1993–6, and later, *Incorruptible Flesh* series 1996–2013 and *Self Obliteration* solos 2008–2011.

Indonesian artist Melati Suryodarmo's *Butter Dance* 2000 (p.82) represents a counterpoint to Cassils's epic confrontation with the clay. Suryodarmo often works with materials – whether butter or charcoal – performing apparently simple tasks as a way of situating her own subjectivity in relation to labour, matter and time. Dressed in a 'feminine' style; black, figure-hugging evening dress and red high heels, the artist walks onto the stage, where, under a spotlight, is a large pat of butter, made of twenty brick-sized blocks. To the sound of low-key drumming, the artist steps onto the butter and balances for a moment, arms outstretched. She moves slowly, sensuously, arms in and out, twisting her feet from side to side

Zhang Huan, *12 Square Meters* 1994, performance, Beijing

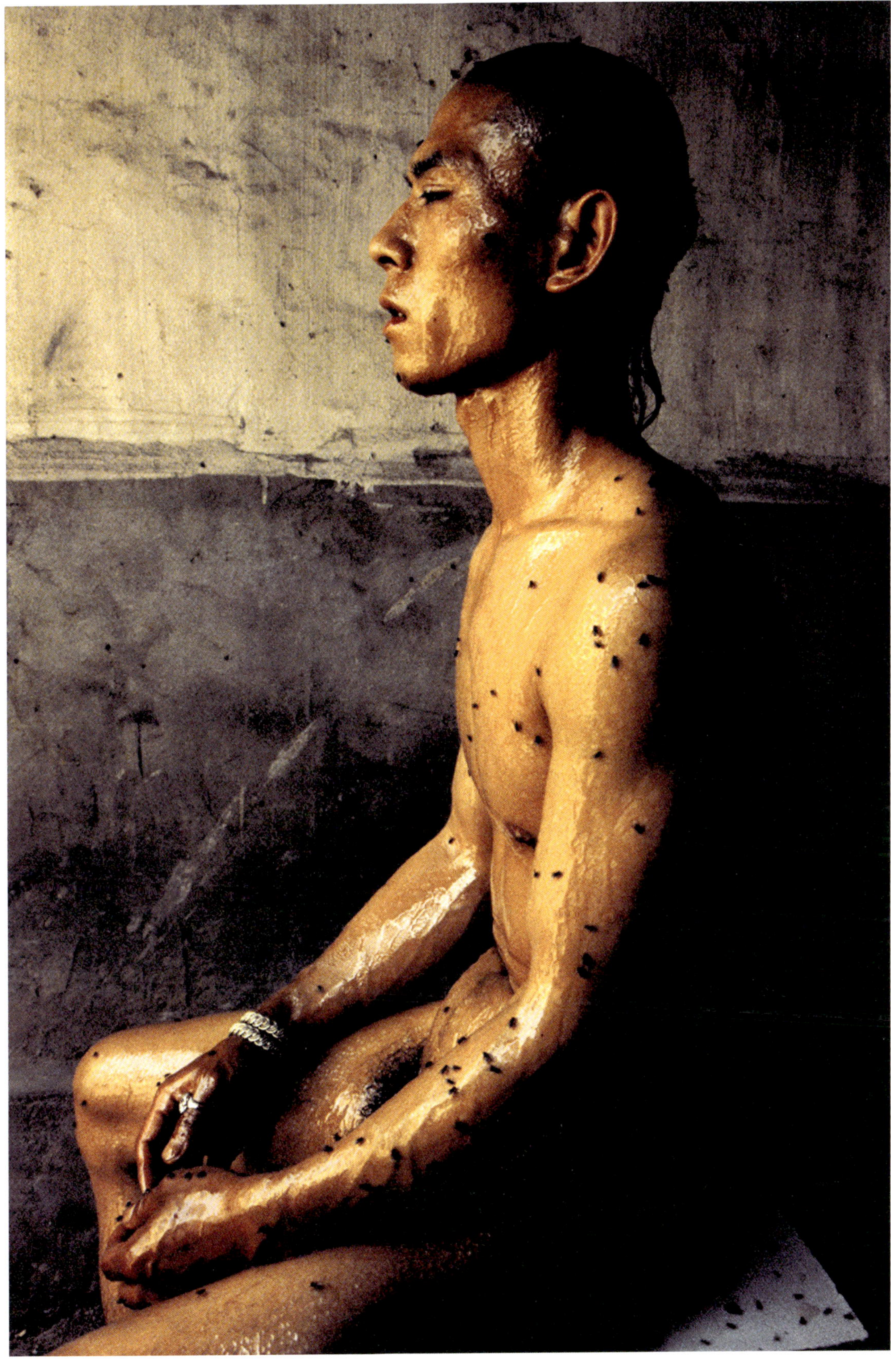

Melati Suryodarmo, *Butter Dance* 2000/ EXERGIE, performed at Videobrasil, São Paolo, 2005, video stills

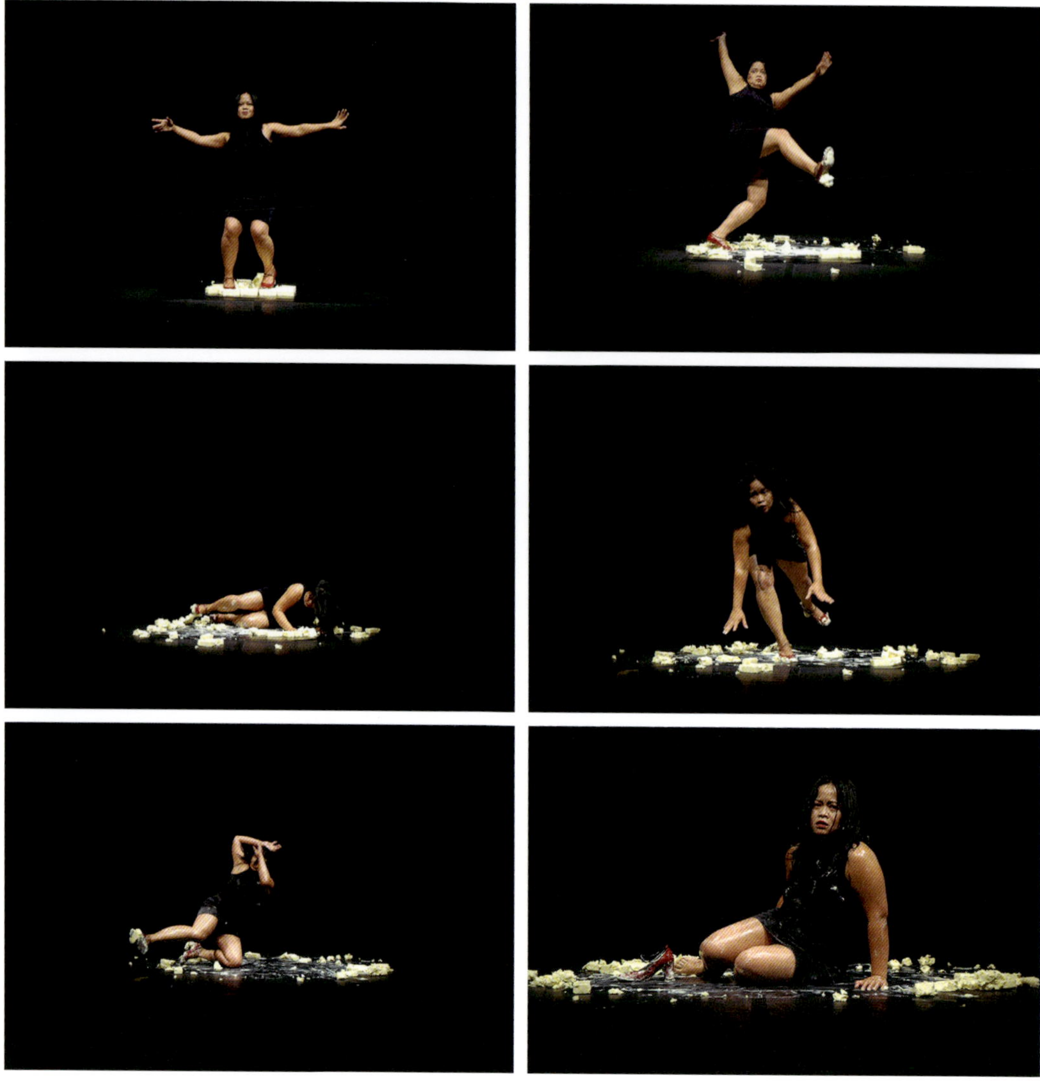

in a slow dance, inspired in part by a traditional Indonesian dance. Her feet slide a little, and then slip as though she is going to fall. She dances some more, a little faster, her feet sliding and smearing the butter which is now also all over her shins and the sides of her dress. As the action continues, resembling in part a strip-club dance, the artist becomes gradually smeared all over in butter. She continuously attempts to continue her dance and continuously falls, crashing down again, the once-neat butter block now a splattered, spread-out mess of lumps and tracks. As the action repeats its failure, the artist's movements become slower again and eventually she gives up, lying horizontally in the butter, the drum-beat gradually slowing down. The work has a Sisyphus-like quality, but, like Cassils's work, does not bring specific political or biographical information to bear on the image we encounter. Rather, it creates an image of struggle that speaks to broader questions of human labour, consumption, endeavour and failure, through the lens of gender. The language of Suryodarmo's work speaks of her combined influences, being mentored by Anzu Furukawa, a Japanese Butoh dancer, and Marina Abramović.

Auto-portraits

If these artists assert their own physical presence as forms of resistance, often in a political context, a different approach to the self as material has appeared in parallel in the 1990s: that is, one with a more plastic, choreographic form, which draws upon autobiographical narrative. The staging of the mind-body relationship has been explored to deconstructive effect in the work of French conceptual choreographer Xavier Le Roy, which is clearly indebted to that of Yvonne Rainer and the Judson Dance Theater, and which, like that of his peers Jérôme Bel, Eszter Salamon or Trajal Harrell, exists both in the context of dance and visual art.

In his influential early work *Self Unfinished* 1998, Le Roy performs wearing a stretchy, black costume with a top and skirt, which mask the head and lower body in the same way. The performer walks or crawls around the stage on all fours, undermining the body's hierarchy and verticality to propose a headless creature that moves in strange ways, even inverting the body altogether, as he scales along the wall upside down. In the lecture-performance *Product of Circumstances* 1999, Le Roy delivers a monologue detailing his own life story, using his background as a researcher in macro-biology – specifically the study of oncogenes in breast cancer – to consider the constitution of his subjectivity via the metaphor of cellular abstraction, among other things. The movements Le Roy

Xavier Le Roy, *Self Unfinished* 1998, by and with Xavier Le Roy, collaboration with Laurent Goldring, music by Diana Ross, 50 min.

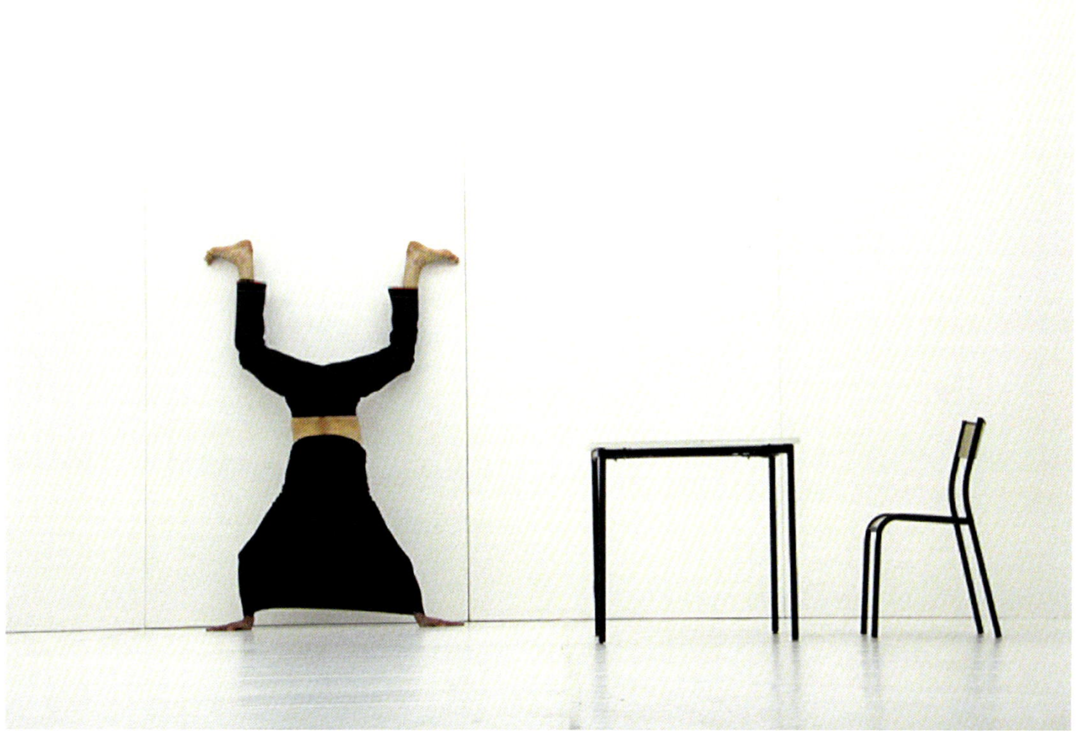

performs as part of this piece extend the cellular metaphor, taking the body's image apart. He stands with his back to the audience, for example, arms wrapped around his torso so that they appear – waggling and slapping his back – as though they might be the arms of someone else grasping him.

Le Roy's defamiliarisation techniques, which play with the orientation of the body and the relation between speaking and doing, recall Rainer's attempt to undermine the dominance of the expressive face in dance by blanking out her features – and at one point painting her face with black paint to match her leotard – whilst performing a version of *Trio A* in the late 1960s. The ordinary dance language of Judson Theater and this fantasy of a body-led-thought, which Rainer encapsulated in the title of her 1968 concert *The Mind Is a Muscle*, has become a central concern for this generation of choreographers emerging in the late 1990s. Nevertheless, Le Roy proposes an alternative perspective on the notion that the body is a vessel for the mind, by focusing on how experience shapes thinking – an idea that resonates with French philosopher Catherine Malabou's concept of plasticity, which relies partly on current scientific thinking on changes to the brain occurring as a result of physical experiences, such as traumatic accidents.[64]

The actions of Polish artist Cezary Bodzianowski, usually staged in public spaces, elaborate the primary language of 1960s body art, too, but within miniature dramas set in everyday situations. Although there is a character of sorts in the deadpan approach that Bodzianowski takes, he performs consistently as a kind of everyman. Bodzianowski's performance space, his stage, is the world at large, and the objects, architectures, behaviours and signs that he encounters become props in this unfolding form of theatre. Extemporising from everyday urban encounters, the artist pursues the latent implications of particular things or scenes ad absurdum.

Bodzianowski is a straight-faced performer with a Charlie Chaplin-like moustache and a sturdy gait. His benign expression – reminiscent of a Watteau clown – amidst such a variety of contexts belies the spontaneity of composition, as he responds to a given situation using his body as material. Improvisation as a theatre technique was developed in the early to mid-twentieth century, firstly in vaudeville comedy, and later by many theatre-makers including Jerzy Grotowski and Peter Brook as a workshop technique that could enable actors to discard stylised conventions of acting in favour of performing in a more creative way.[65] In Bodzianowski's case, however, it is the city itself that triggers the artist's improvisational game: he takes hints or prompts from its structures, signs and facilities. In *Serso* 2008, standing by a set of black metal bollards arranged in line to block cars from a pedestrian street, Bodzianowski hangs back, looks around, and then attempts to throw a rubber ring to circle one, as though it were a game of hoopla. Or, finding a defunct neon sign depicting champagne glasses on top of a Łódź building in *Stuntman* 2007, he climbs onto the roof and proceeds to animate the drink by adding a bubble effect, achieved by repeatedly throwing a hula hoop in the air, its circular silhouette perfectly matching the scale of the neon tubing seen against the pink sky.

Bodzianowski's work seems at first to comment on society (*We*), but reveals the artist to be an idiosyncratic and solipsistic figure, an *I* struggling to connect. In fact, Bodzianowski's apparent compliance only adheres to a set of codes that he has invented for himself, according to his own improvisational game. Instead of adapting to the world, he intuits its potential adaptation to his own imagination

Cezary Bodzianowski,
Serso 2008, Bremen

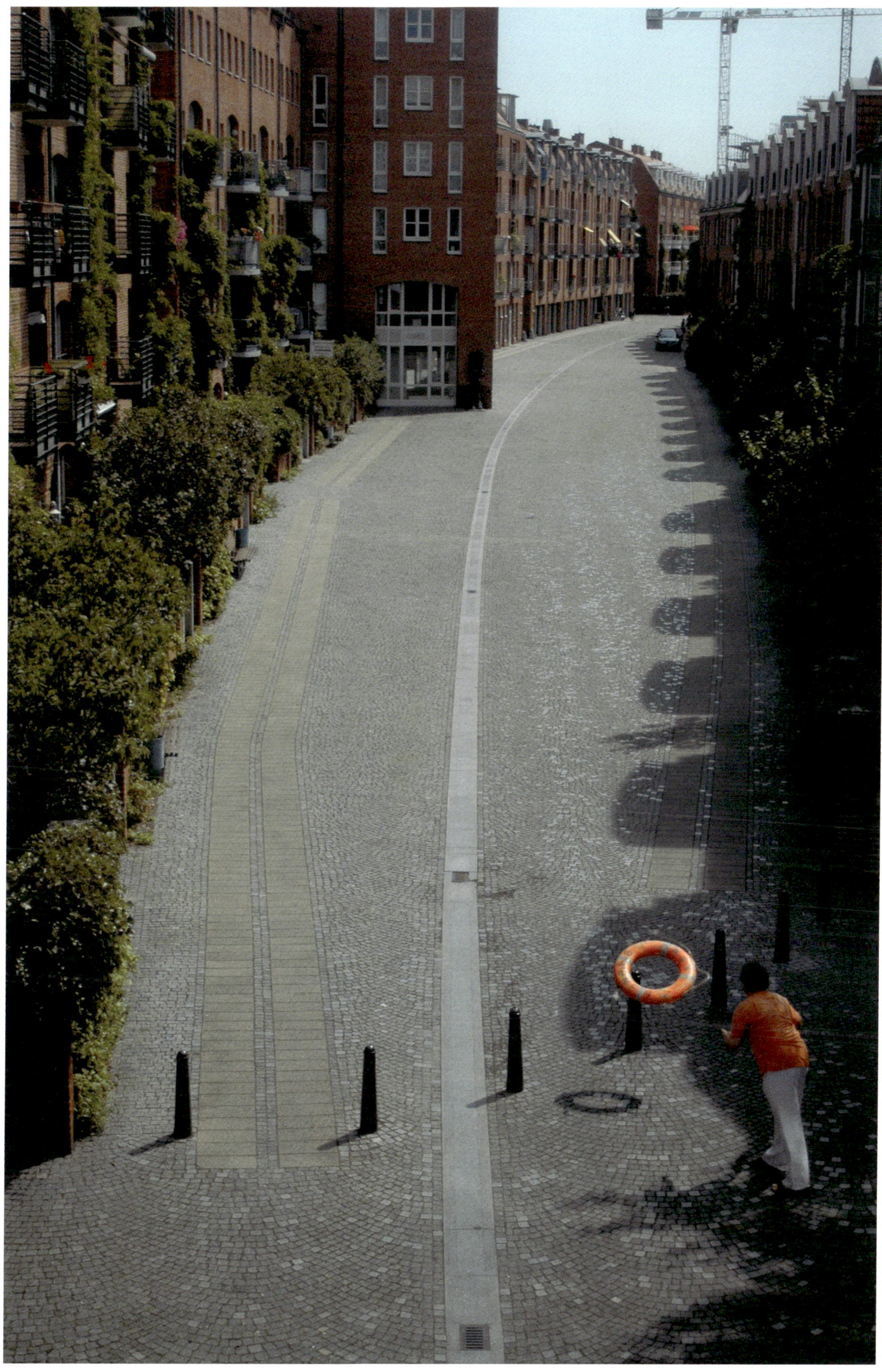

– a child-like reversal that opens up new possibilities, but with an isolationist air of tragedy.

Suggesting formal abstractions and mimed images through the movement of his own body, the Burmese artist Moe Satt performs live, elaborate choreographies. He often focuses specifically on parts of the body, for example his hands and fingers. He has said: 'In performance art, I played mostly with meaningful and meaningless hand positions and actions. I based these on positions of my own body combined with space to challenge and experiment with my body's levels of endurance.'[66] Satt's work plays upon the infinite possibilities for movement and gesture contained in the raw material of the body and its expressive potential.

F n' F (Face and Fingers) 2008–9 is a very slow, charged, ritualistic performance in which Satt removes his long jacket, kneels on the floor, and proceeds to perform a choreography with his hands and fingers to create striking patterns or forms, like masks, across his face and forehead. Occasionally he whistles, tracing his fingers along his eyebrows and making shapes with his hands, such as two fingers pointing up from his head like the horns of a deer. Satt is interested in the ambiguity of the gestures, signs and symbols that he can make by only using his own body as a tool. The artist explains that '*F n' F (Face and Fingers)* is based on how the expressions of the face and fingers can combine to reveal different meanings. If there is only a hand gesture of a gun, that only signifies a gun; when the gun gesture is combined with a facial expression, another meaning is created. I try to communicate with the audience so they can find out the meaning of the sign.'[67]

Satt's nuanced performances create a kind of bodily poetry using the barest tools. Their quietness gives them a mystical quality. Satt stages the self as a communicatory tool, using his body to effect intimate address, while preventing his gestures from being understood in any literal sense. In effect, they stage a kind of signing that is open-ended.

Italian artist Roberto Cuoghi makes installation, sculpture, sound and other theatrical works that deal with perceptual duplicity. Often, his work engages with the idea of metamorphosis, prompting us to look again at what we take for granted. One of his earliest works involves the wearing of a pair of Schmidt-Pechan prisms as goggles: these rotate whatever is seen through them by 180 degrees, temporarily lending the wearer a completely distorted vision of the world and redefining his or her whole sense of orientation. Cuoghi's best-known work (although given its personal nature, there is a question as to whether it can be considered as a 'work' as such) was a performance lasting seven years, from 1998 to 2004, during which he transformed his appearance entirely so as to resemble his now late father. Cuoghi – who, at the time, aged twenty-five, had been self-styled as a punk – dyed his hair white, grew a beard, wore his father's clothes, and adopted his mannerisms and habits, as well as eating the food he ate, causing him to begin to morph beyond his costume and to put on forty-one kilograms in weight. In this way, he transformed himself to resemble a middle-aged man. The critic Luca Cerizza has observed of this action: 'Cuoghi's imitation survived the original, but his body paid a high inheritance tax: when his father passed away, the artist started to reverse the premature ageing, but the stress to which he had subjected himself over the years rendered the process extremely slow and painful.'[68] In this approach to self-experimentation, the question of performance

Moe Satt, *F n' F (Face and Fingers)* 2008–9

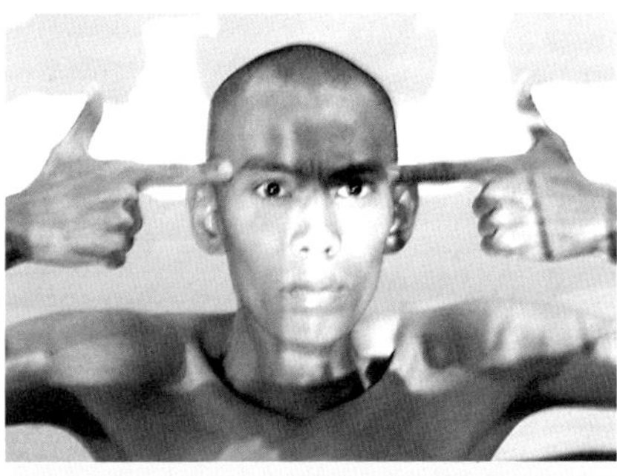

GUN
When you make a gun sign with your hands, it is just a gun. But when you put the gun sign to your face, how does the meaning change?

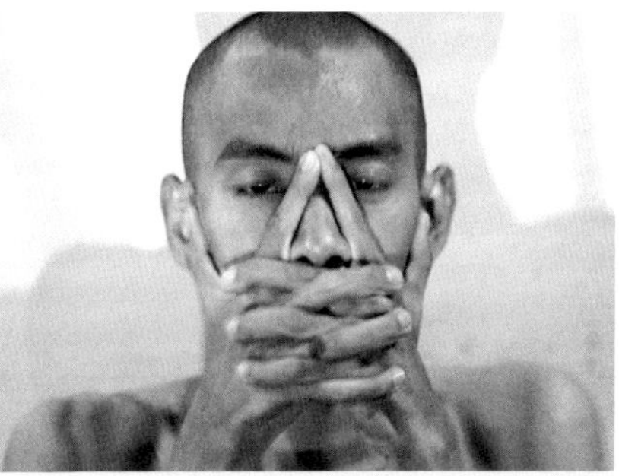

MASK
In this action, your hand cover your face like a mask.

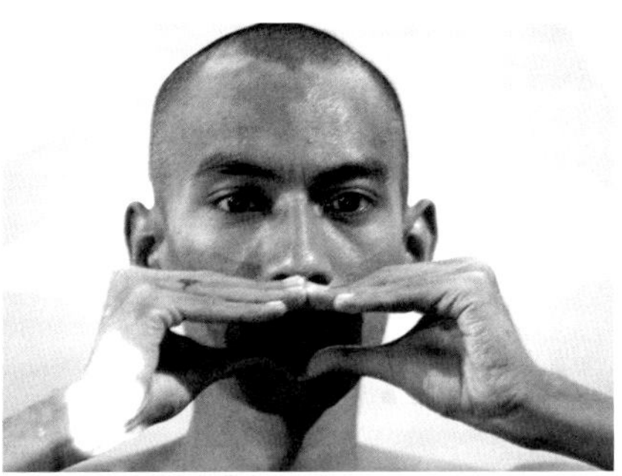

CLOSED SOCIETY
In a closed society, there is a limit to how much you can open your mouth.

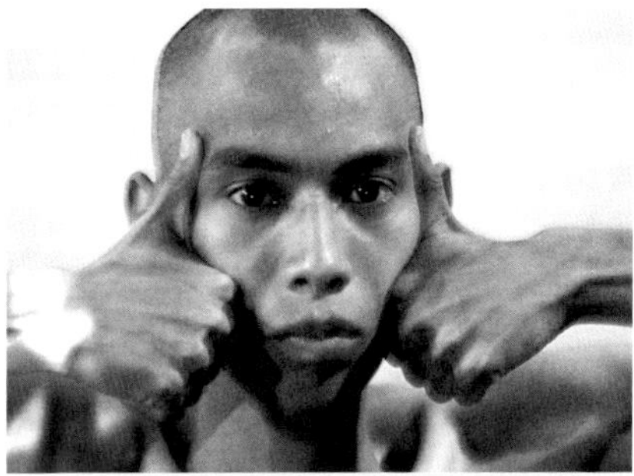

THUMBS UP
This is a play on the "Thumbs-up" sign. Put two thumbs up and rotate them.

is exceeded. Simulation becomes real transformation, confusingly blurring art and life in an extreme process of identification that pushes beyond the question of image and proposes a deeper undertow of behavioural heritage. Cuoghi's action destabilises the idea that we possess ourselves as individuals, and undercuts the idea that we have the freedom to deviate from our social and familial scripts. His sense of self is transformed here into that of his father, undoing the boundary between self and other that is perceived to be a key developmental stage of the infant in psychoanalysis.

Also dealing with his relationship with his family – both his father and his paternal grandmother, the head of a matriarchal clan in the Democratic Republic of the Congo – French artist Paul Maheke has made a series of performances and installations in which he performs, and dances, to assert his own presence, all the while creating layers of erasure and flows between surfaces that point to the permeable boundaries of the subject. In *What Flows Through and Across* 2017 and *Mbu* 2017 (pp.88–9), Maheke's dancing body is obscured by, or veiled between, scrims, screens and projections, moving in cyclical rhythms that present his own, untrained dance practice as a way of finding presence, through time. These works suggest that as human beings we are connected by a flow (of water, or technology) that exceeds the limits demarcated by skin or indeed the idea that 'blood is thicker than water' – an idea that the artist draws from Astrida Neimanis's theory on 'hydrofeminism'.[69]

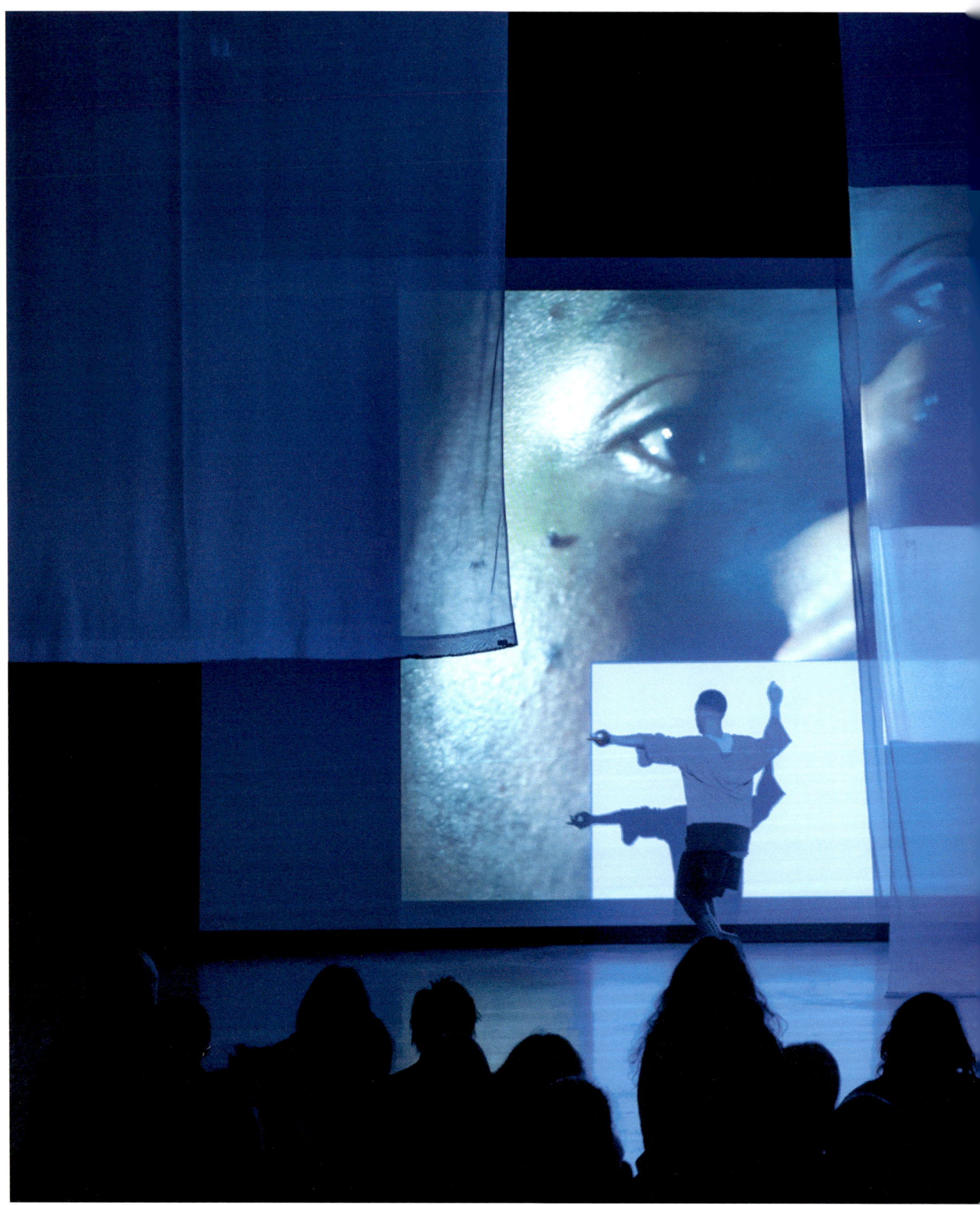

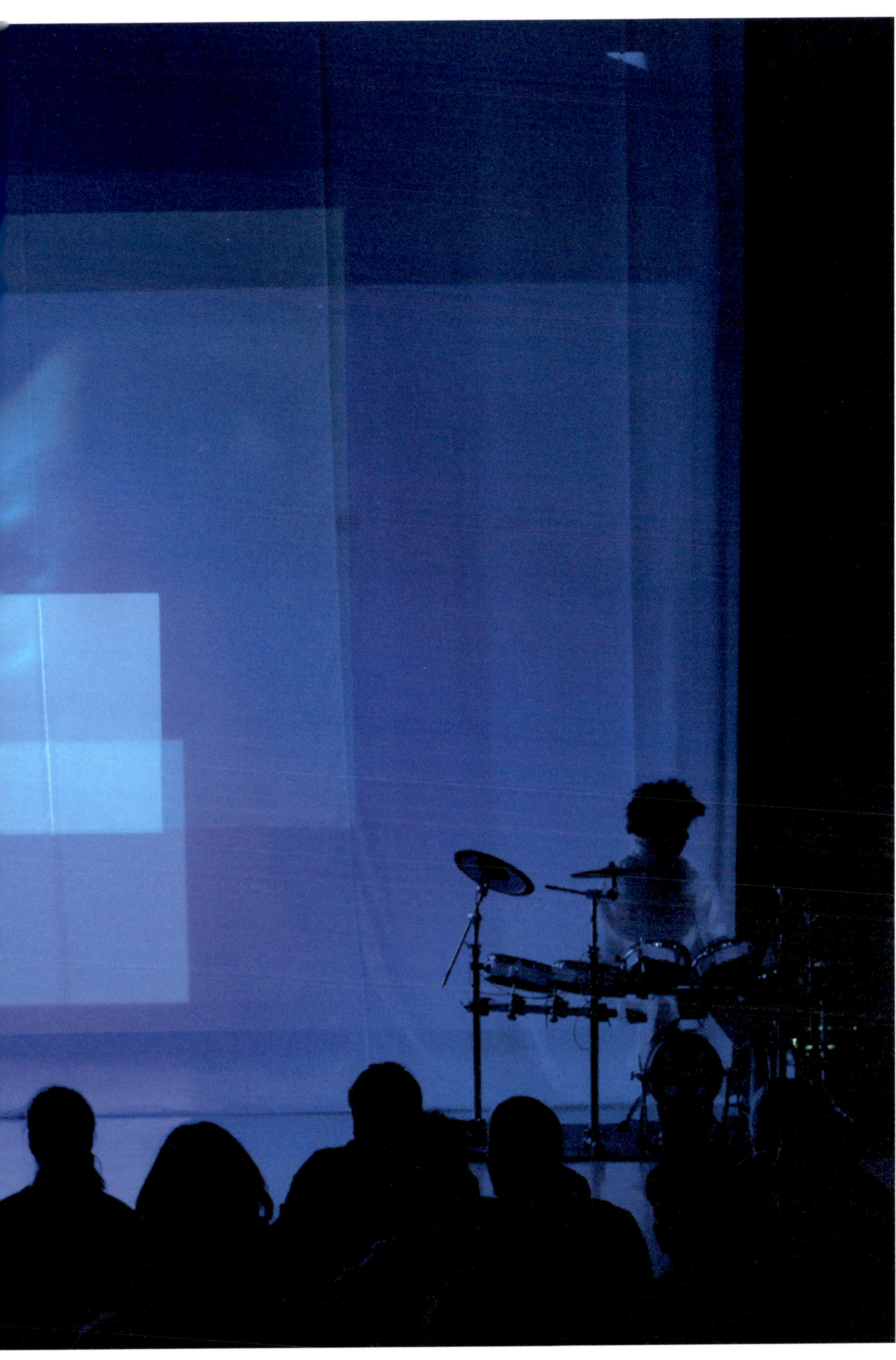

Paul Maheke, *Mbu* performed as part of *Ten Days Six Nights*, with Cedric Fauq on drums, The Tanks, Tate Modern, March 2017

The body as surface

When a new wave of live performance began to appear in the UK, Europe and the US in the late 1990s and early 2000s, it was not so much body art and its concern with authentic, real-time presence that was in the air, but rather broader questions about how lived life relates to, and can be performed within, the dominant logic of the image. The fragmented history of performance was brought into visibility, too, as questions of re-enactment arose afresh. This was not just a fetishistic return – an emergence of 'zombie time',[70] as Hal Foster has decried it – but an attempt to summon and visualise a relevant history for an emerging generation interested in this relatively obscure area. Between 1985–1996 Tania Bruguera made a series of reenactments of the performances of Ana Mendieta. Subsequently, artists such as Monster (formerly Lali and, in 2006–13, Spartacus) Chetwynd have staged historical performances, by Yves Klein as new live tableaux, while others were invited to re-enact performances from the 1960s and 1970s in the context of the project *A Little Bit of History Repeated*, curated by Jens Hoffmann at Kunst-Werke, Berlin, in 2001. Jeremy Deller, on the other hand, convened a group of almost one thousand participants to re-enact the 1984 UK miners' strike protests, as documented in the video *The Battle of Orgreave* (2001). These new iterations of historical performances and events might be likened to the re-enactments that take place within communities who wish to reflect upon significant religious narratives or political events of the past that constitute their community, whether annual Christmas Nativity plays or the re-staging of the Russian revolution in 1917.

Instead of taking for granted a sense of intimacy between artist and audience, as many of the experiments with performance in the 1960s and 1970s had

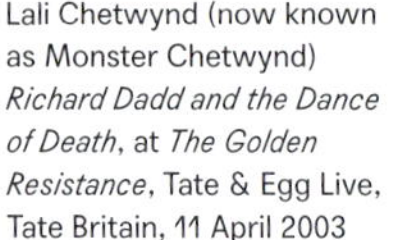

Lali Chetwynd (now known as Monster Chetwynd) *Richard Dadd and the Dance of Death*, at *The Golden Resistance*, Tate & Egg Live, Tate Britain, 11 April 2003

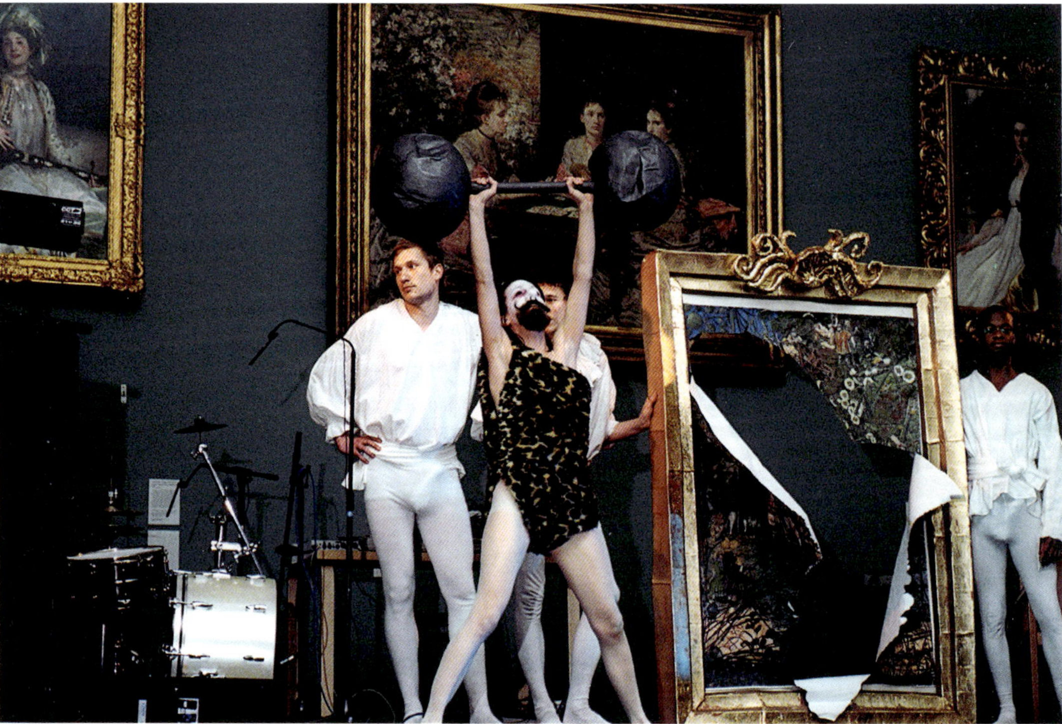

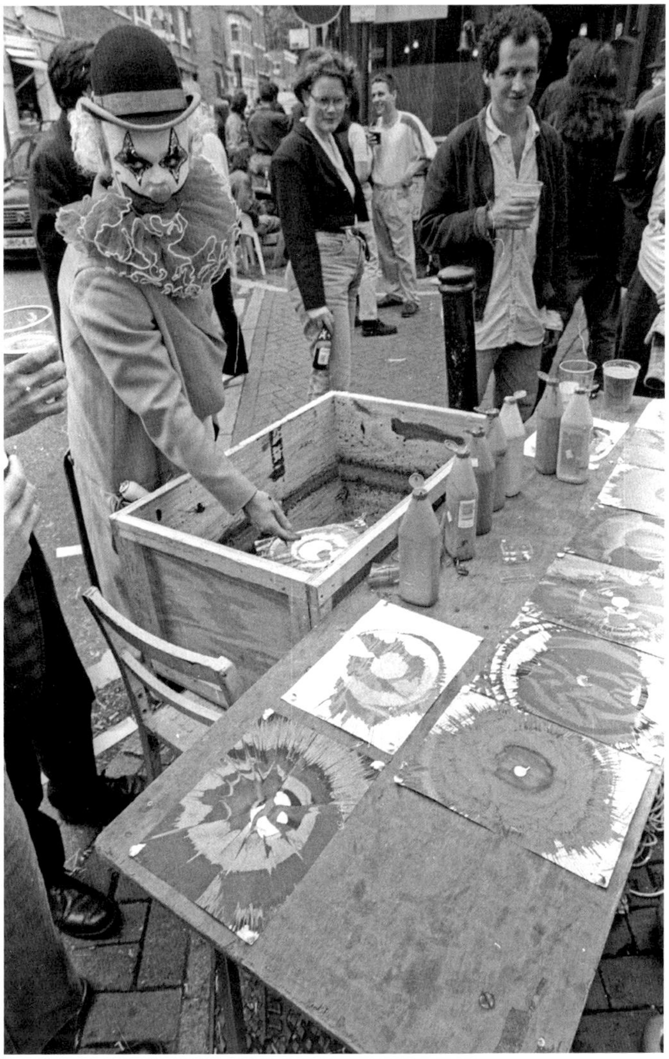

Damien Hirst, *A Fête Worse Than Death*, Hoxton Square, London, 1993

done, performance at the turn of the millennium often navigated the question of mediation. As Guy Debord had anticipated in the 1960s, the space of intersubjectivity – of being together, and being mutually aware – was being increasingly mediated by the spectacle of the image, whether photographic or filmic, broadcast or digital. In a context of accelerating neoliberalism in the UK and the US, in which media corporations gained increasing power, artists began to perform in new ways in relation to the notion of publicity. The so-called YBAs in the UK were emblematic of an early phase of this shift in the late 1980s and early 1990s. This new generation turned its back on the establishment (then dominated by the existentialism of Francis Bacon and Lucian Freud) and embraced an idea of the artist as entrepreneur. In 1993, in London's East End, Tracey Emin and Sarah Lucas performed live as shopkeepers at The Shop, selling homemade badges and postcards, while Damien Hirst and Angus Fairhurst set up a spin art stall at the 1993 artist-led street fair 'A Fête Worse Than Death', 1993, dressed up as a clown. The YBAs' image was partly built upon that of American artist Jeff Koons, who from the mid-1980s had taken a cue from Dalí's cultivated persona,

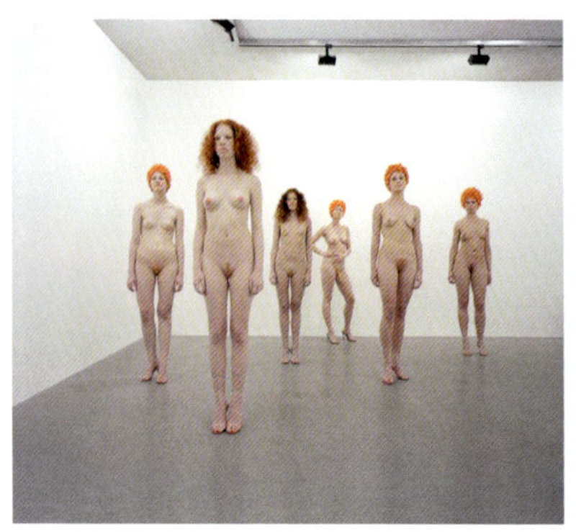
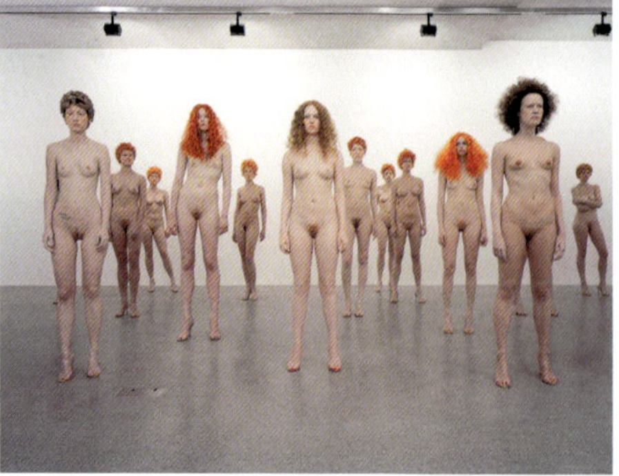
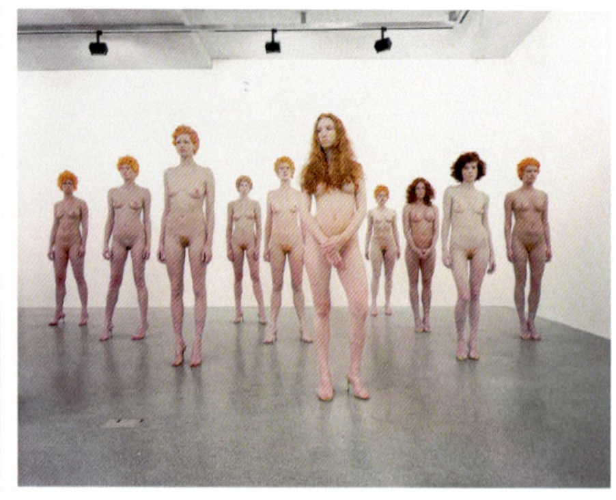

Vanessa Beecroft, *vb43.029.te*, *vb43.069.te*, *vb43.074.te*, triptych, Gagosian Gallery, London, 2000

consistently performed a kind of straight drag as a successful, suit-wearing, white male executive. Arguably only being understood in this performative capacity later on, by the 2000s,[71] Koons fused the roles of the artist-as-maker and artist-as-image into a single, seamless performance without any apparent critical perspective.[72] In Koons, as with German artist Martin Kippenberger, a sense of costume is not visible: no make-up alerts us to his performance as masquerade.

Instead of appearing as outsiders to society, as artist 'bohemians', Koons and Hirst, after Klein or Warhol, foregrounded the commercial aspect of the artist role, proposing a new model of the artist as either market trader (in the case of the YBAs) or executive worker (in the case of Koons). Koons's image was all about the suit, tie, success and luxury: an emphasis on surface to match the highly polished, gleaming and apparently hollow pleasure offered by his *Rabbit* 1986, or his *Balloon Dog* 1994–2000. In different ways, all of these artists were exploring, and performatively inhabiting, a post-pop landscape, and also drawing upon attitudes initiated by queer culture.[73] Instead of assuming authenticity as a baseline, or even drawing attention to the process of masquerade, one's identity could be manipulated as easily as the surface of an image to become a brand – one constructed according to desire and performed in the world as a self-actualised fact. Whether clownish and absurd, or seductive and sleek, this idea of assimilating to the image, and of creating deadpan characters, avatars or clones, gained further currency in the 1990s.

In the late 1990s, New York-based artists such as Vanessa Beecroft and Matthew Barney extended this emphasis on performance as image in a slightly different direction, exploring what we might call cinematic modes of staging the body. Beecroft's live tableaux derived from her earlier drawings that obsessively documented her self-image and her anorexia: an approach linked to important early feminist works dealing with female body image, such as Eleanor Antin's photographic series documenting her weight fluctuations, as if she were a living sculpture (*Carving: A Traditional Sculpture* 1972) and Suzy Lake's parody of making her face up, using pencils (*A Natural Way to Draw* 1975). But, crucially, Beecroft's performances transposed her fantasised self-image onto the bodies of multiple hired models, who were styled as clones in matching flesh-coloured tights, make-up and wigs, and choreographed to stand in inert or listless block formations as living sculptures of sorts. Beecroft's grand tableaux were designed by the artist to create what she described as 'monumental images in the memory',[74] more than to assert her models' real physicality. In fact, her use of cosmetics and accessories had the effect of making her performers less lifelike and more like mannequins. Despite occupying the same gallery spaces as the viewers, they appeared at one remove: otherworldly and uncanny in their image-like-ness. The artist herself was deliberately absent: she was replaced with this corps de ballet of avatars in a substitute self-portrait that emptied the notion of *I* into a distribution of attributes of femininity without any sense of interiority on the part of the models.

Matthew Barney's *DRAWING RESTRAINT* 1987–ongoing offers an exaggeratedly masculine counterpoint to this image of styled femininity. The project began as a series of documented actions that involved the artist performing alone by climbing around his studio using mountain equipment and negotiating various obstacles. The body staged here is founded upon an idea of athletic development (related to Barney's own background as an American football player), in which growth is encouraged through working against restraint. These actions evolved into more complex video presentations in the early 1990s, which began to incorporate narrative, and later into the full-scale cinema of the elaborate *The CREMASTER Cycle* 1994–2002, eventually incorporating mass choreographies within surreal, quasi-mythic scenarios. The physicality of Barney's early actions – testing his body against gravity and negotiating architectural space with his movements, in ways that prioritised the body's reliance on prosthetic extensions and props – was always mediated through video and film, the image plane of the screen becoming essential to the body's co-ordinates. In this sense, Barney's earlier work references, but moves distinctly away from, the body art practice exemplified by Cyprus-born, Australian artist Stelarc, whose works has focused on bodily endurance, and on extending the capabilities of the human body with prosthetics or robotics, since the late 1960s. Stelarc, most well-known for over twenty-five

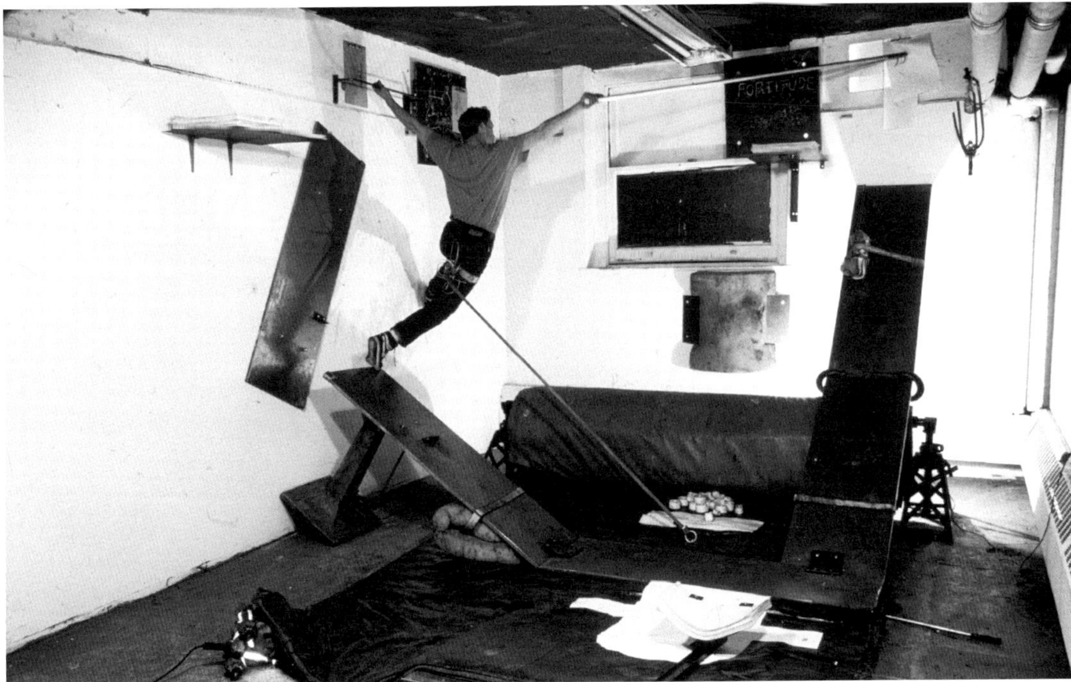

Matthew Barney
Production shot for
DRAWING RESTRAINT 2.
1988, video (black and white, silent), 5 min. 1 sec.

'Suspension' events, in which he has hung his entire body with hooks piercing through his skin, focuses on the body as an individual – albeit networked – entity, whilst Barney situates body action within cinematic narratives.

In the late 1990s and early 2000s, the British artist Mark Leckey put the artist's own presence obliquely at the centre of a constellation of concerns revolving around his relationships with – or his 'colonisation by' – images.[75] Leckey, however, deliberately eluded the idea of building his own brand by making work that was fugitive and chameleon-like. In the live events that he made in the early 2000s, such as his performances as part of the band donAteller, Leckey offered a distinct alternative to the staging of presence in performance art of the post war period: he presented himself less as a maker, and less still as an authentic subject, than as a conduit through which pop culture was passing and being digested, assimilated and registered. Little Richard, Brandy or David Bowie offered him templates, rather than Burden or Abramović. donAteller performed and sang in ways that harnessed the seduction of pop music and imagery – an approach that was flagrantly, and almost shockingly, inflected by the entertainment industry, albeit with a deliberate degree of dishevelment.

Leckey's film *Parade* 2003 likewise presented a fantasy of his self as seamless, feminised image, seen in relation to a succession of pictures of women in pop culture, interrupted occasionally by the fact of his real flesh and blood as the camera zooms in on a hand, or the side of his face. Leckey's work registers a struggle to negotiate his self-understanding as image in relation to a world of images. His use of these close-ups, or of recordings of his own voice, hints at a sense of depth or real presence, which is inaccessible via the screen. Leckey's work poses the question as to whether there is a subject behind the image, or whether the subject is inevitably stuck, in its striving to identify with the image's perfection – and so the grubby physicality of the real body is repeatedly brought forth and denied, creating a psychological schism. Rather than presenting a coherent identity, *Parade* proposes the contemporary subject to be lost in a struggle to distinguish between interiority and surface, attempting to camouflage himself as an image. Like much of Leckey's work, it succinctly articulates a conflicted desire for the performing subject to both create and inhabit the image, to be two- and three-dimensional: complicit and resistant.

Lebanese artist Rabih Mroué also plots his subjectivity within a complex matrix of images, albeit to very different ends. Mroué began making work in Beirut's theatre scene in the 1990s, but, not fitting easily in that context, since the 2000s has been invited to present his autobiographical performances in visual art institutions as well as cross-arts festivals. Mroué scripts and performs in the work, which often takes a lecture-cum-storytelling format. He interweaves the recounting and analysis of political events in Lebanon and the wider region with stories from his own life, invoking critical pathos and humour, and drawing upon projected images – both personal and media-generated. In the performance *Make Me Stop Smoking* 2003, Mroué draws upon his personal archive of what he calls 'worthless things' – personal documents, videos, newspaper clippings, photos – to piece together a meandering story of the Lebanese civil war (1975–90) from a personal perspective. As he speaks, the artist casts doubt on the veracity and cogency of the archival documents we see, voicing his suspicion that they may be mere props, and foregrounding contradiction and hesitation in the attempt to construct any such narrative memory.

Rabih Mroué, *Make Me Stop Smoking* 2006, lecture-performance, Beirut 2007

Mroué's later work *The Pixelated Revolution* 2012 is a lecture-performance about the impact of mobile phones and social media in the Syrian uprising of 2011, which plays upon his own use of video in relation to the subject about which he speaks. Mroué's work creates a curious space of intimacy through his spoken revelations that is nevertheless continuously undermined by his exposure of fakery and construction. Rather than positioning himself as an objective observer of political reality, he exposes the messier truth of his implicated and partial perspective as part of it. Mroué appears, live, in his work, which might appear to anchor his stories and recollections to his authentic real-time presence, but he stages his own embeddedness in layers of representation and networks of information that unsettle our seemingly direct access to him as a figure onstage. Who is he? Who are they? What is the truth? His installation of *The Pixelated Revolution* at Documenta 13, Kassel, in 2012, drew a line between the smartphone camera's eye and the barrel of a sniper's gun. Mroué seems to fantasise a singular and palpable connection between the photographic shot and the gun shot, based on their shared indexicality, as though this connection might mark a real place for the human subject that is not contested by the malleability of the image.

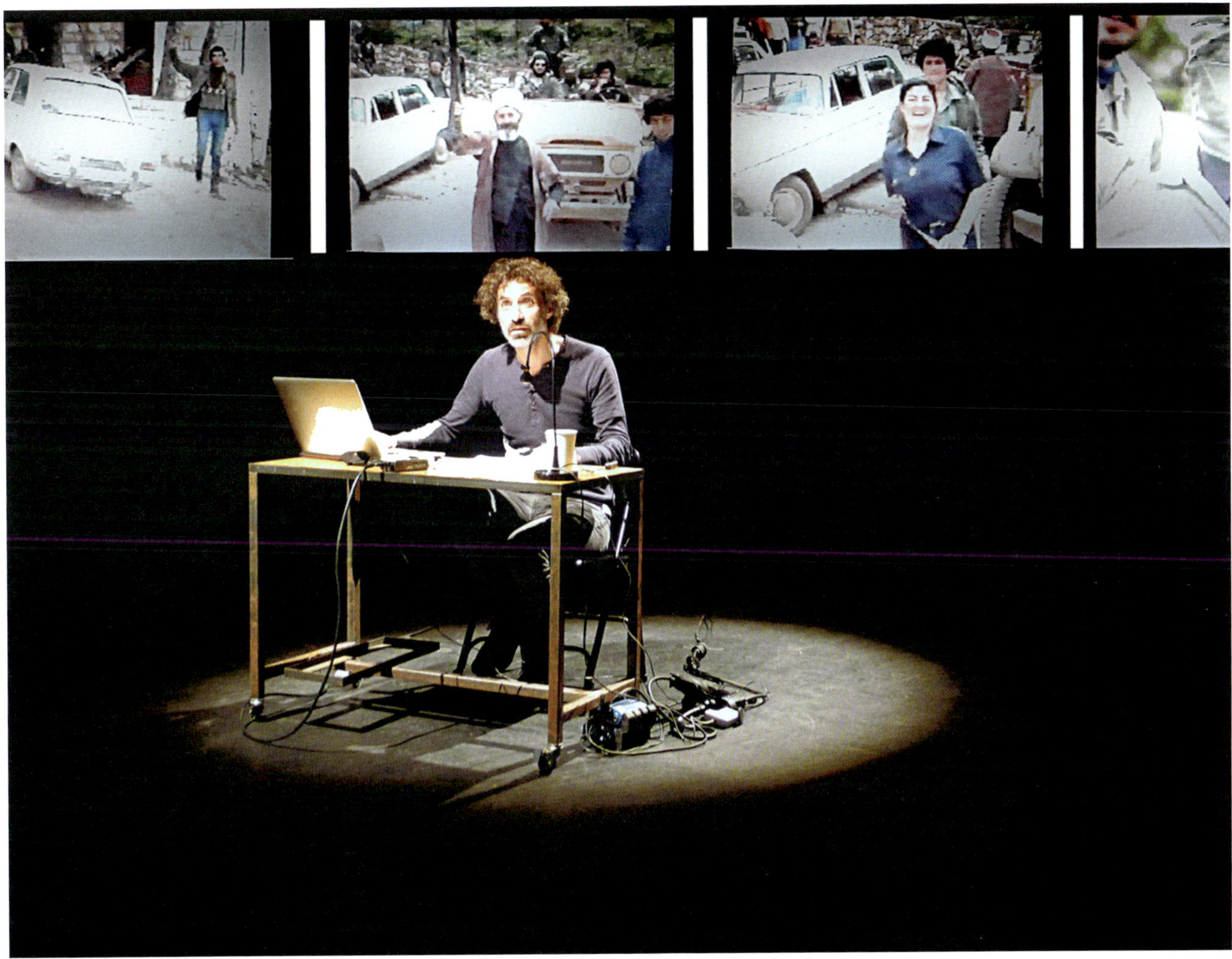

Painted scenes

If Mroué and Leckey negotiate a relationship to the image via media and technology, other artists such as Paulina Ołowska perform within the frame of traditional media, specifically painting and drawing. Such work is less about revealing the process of making (as in action painting or Gutai) and more about a way of considering the painted image as a projection of the individual subject's imagination: either creating a world that the artist can step into, or extending its logic towards the body as a canvas. Emblematic of a generation of artists who move freely across media, Ołowska's approach draws a continuum between painterly composition, her self-fashioned lifestyle and being a woman, whether invoking female artists from the Bauhaus and Socialist Realism, dress patterns, vintage fashion magazines, or other pointers towards femininity. The handmade image-space of representational painting seems to offer her, as well as her past collaborators, Lucy McKenzie and Mathilde Rosier, an alternative habitation. Painting offers a theatrical space for performing, a visibly provisional and constructed one, in contrast with the ubiquitous lens-based image technology of daily life. In these ways, Ołowska connects herself to a selective history summoned from a female perspective, building a foundation towards who she is or might want to be.

Indeed, Ołowska embraces anachronism, and has chosen to perform the role of 'the painter' as a bohemian figure. In a portrait photograph taken for an invitation card – for the 2001 exhibition *Heavy Duty* at Inverleith House, Edinburgh – she is pictured with McKenzie. Ołowska stands as though painting at an easel, poised with brush in hand, while her collaborator lounges on the floor wearing a leotard (a nod to a series of paintings of Olympic gymnasts made by McKenzie). They pose as artists, but also deliberately as women whose mode is, according to Ołowska, 'feminine' as much as feminist.[76] This photograph is typical of Ołowska's frequent dramatisation of the act of painting itself, which she relates to her own body in sensual and physical terms: 'In painting, I jump from large scale to small, just because it takes you away from stretching your body into a hunched-back position with a tiny brush. I love using my body in painting and physicality in painting – treating the canvas like it is made of clay or almost as in cooking, smearing, spraying, washing the paint.'[77]

For her 2011 exhibition *The Revenge of the Wise-Woman*, at Foksal Gallery Foundation in Warsaw, Ołowska placed Suzy Lake's video *A Natural Way to Draw* alongside her own paintings. The video shows a woman's face in close-up, covered in white make-up. As a male narrator reads aloud from a drawing manual by Kimon Nicolaïdes, the woman first draws black lines onto her face, then proceeds to shade and texture it with black pencil. She subsequently applies mascara to her eyelashes, focusing the viewer's attention on the parallel between the making of a drawing and the social implication of make-up. Ołowska, similarly, recognises that such experiments, by women artists who had learned conventional painting skills at art school, erased the medium's associations with an essentially masculine, heroic tradition and shifted it towards a reinvention of an age-old feminine practice. Between the gestural traces of the artist's body and the masquerading surfaces of the tightly painted simulations of fashion images, the outer parentheses of Ołowska's world as a painter are marked: at one extreme, drag-like pictorial illusion, and at the other, a tangible, primary space to be lived in – a kind of theatre set.

Lucy McKenzie
and Paulina Olowska,
Heavy Duty 2001

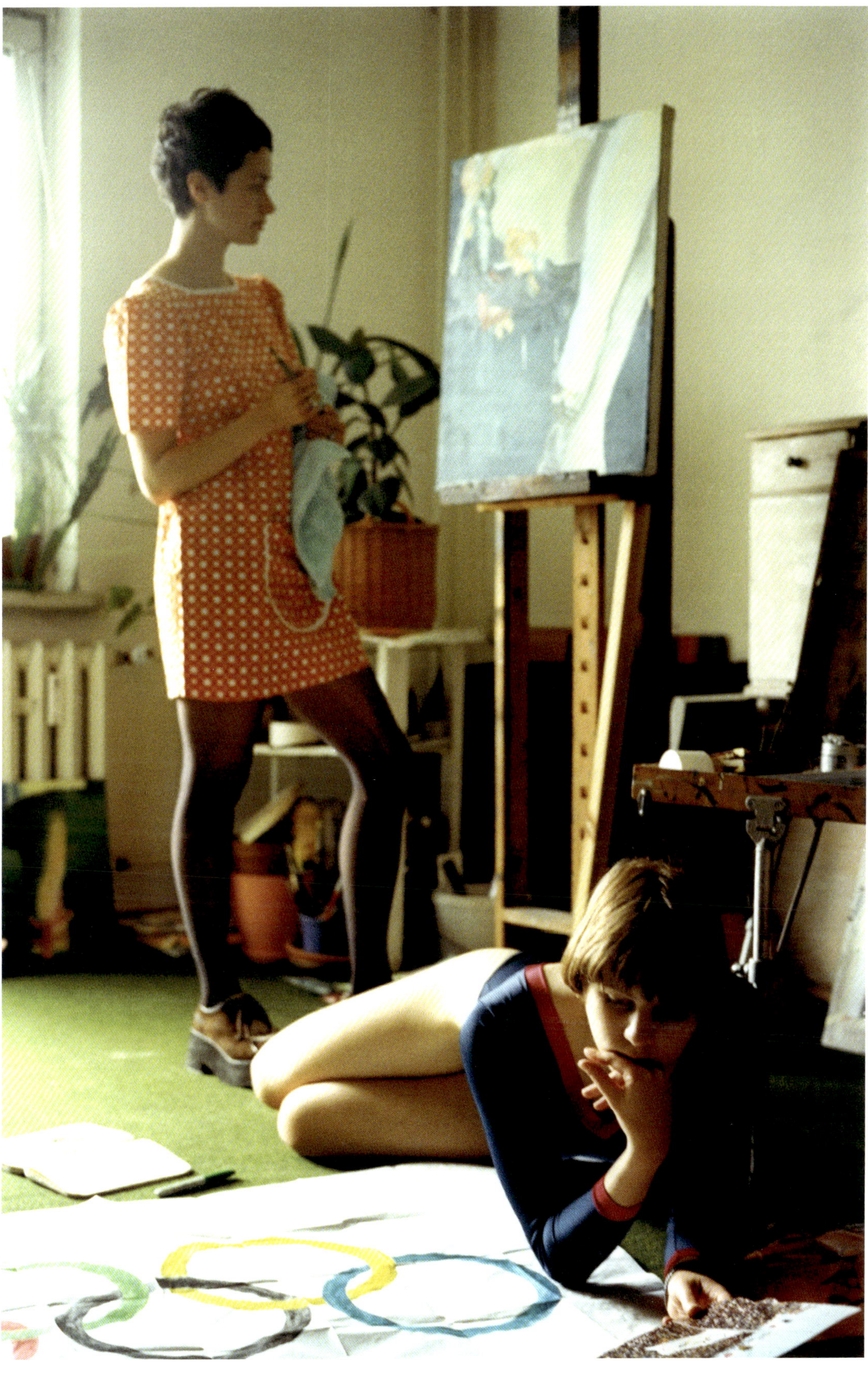

If Ołowska can be said to inhabit an image-world of her own devising, performing fictionalised versions of herself and her autobiography that foreground her Polish identity and her gender, the Indian artist Nikhil Chopra works within the space of drawing to perform as different characters who reflect on his own subjectivity and personal history, with a more explicitly political dimension. Chopra's practice combines narrative theatre and a kind of live installation within which he performs, whether as Yog Raj Chitrakar, a dandyish late nineteenth-century draughtsman, explorer and landscape painter, as 'The Queen' in a hooped skirt, or as Sir Raha, a nineteenth-century maharaja.

Chopra produces a visual context for the emergence of these fictional personae, or alter egos, using drawing to create both recordings of his characters' memories and a theatrical backdrop against which he performs his stories. The characters that he plays are a way to look at himself: to think about how his own subjectivity has been historically constituted, both through his family history and through the broader history of colonialism in India, as well as to shift his gendered appearance through forms of period costume and drag. Yog Raj Chitrakar, for example, is a dandy figure dressed in cream a suit with headdress and jewellery, and a carefully manicured moustache. The character is loosely based on the artist's grandfather, Yog Raj Chopra, who 'spent his early college years in England and Germany in the 1930s, and who was in his later life a passionate, yet inconsequential, landscape painter who spent his fifties and sixties in Kashmir'.[78] Through this character, Chopra considers a particular kind of post-colonial Indian subject who is both nostalgic for the British Empire and energised by India's relatively recent liberation. Chopra describes his grandfather's paintings as 'windows' into 'a time when I spent the summers with my grandparents in their cottage by a stream

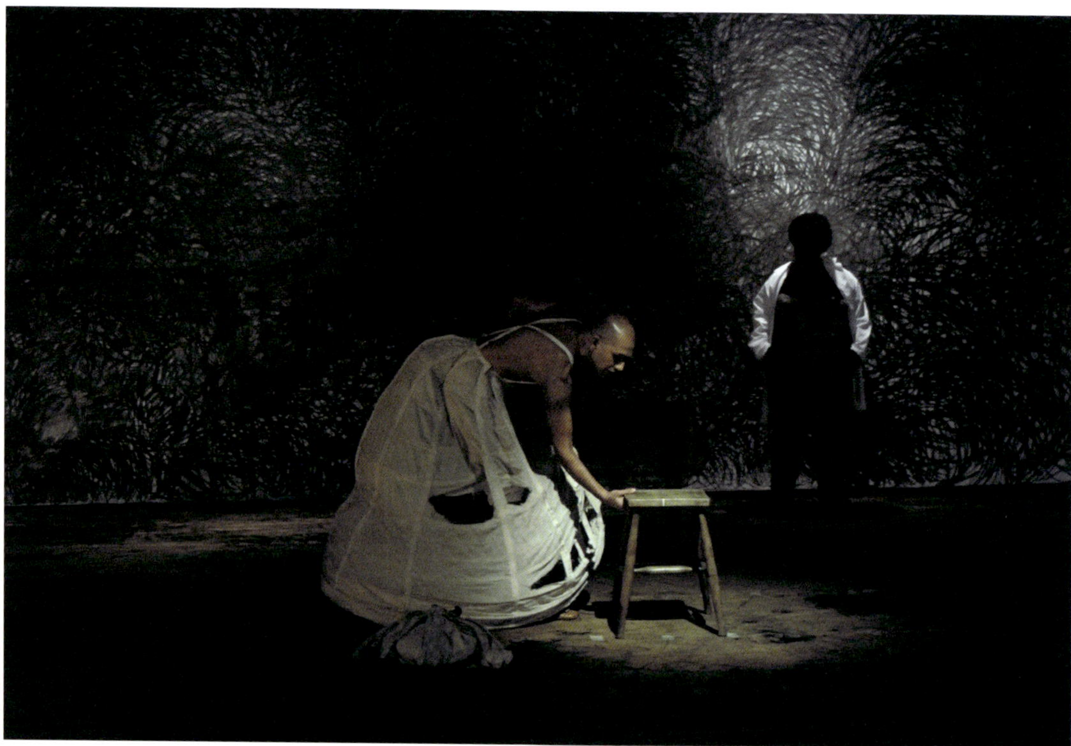

Nikhil Chopra, *Yog Raj Chitrakar: Memory Drawing VIII* 2009, Manchester International Festival, Whitworth Gallery. Costumes Tabasheer Zutshi

flanked on all sides by pristine Himalayan Mountains'.[79] In his performances, the artist conjures a real-time equivalent for the evocative space of those paintings, becoming the image of his grandfather in the past, as a way to dramatise his own identity in the present. Yet, if the performing of a character seems to be associated with conventional theatre, by isolating character from a narrative script or context, and by playing multiple characters within single performances, Chopra inserts the potentially disruptive energy of this fiction into other situations. His live installations are often testing in their duration, blurring the line between enacting and actually living as his character. In this way, the artist metamorphoses into characters that reiterate elements of his own autobiography, allowing familial relationships and histories that constitute his own identity as a subject to emerge, for him to play-act in drag, and to critically deconstruct his own autonomy in the process. If drag emerged in recent history as a form of comedy whereby straight male actors would perform as women in European pantomime (the 'dame') or vaudeville theatre, it developed after the early twentieth century as a queer entertainment subculture among the LGBTQ community. In the 1980s, queer and transgender African American and Latino communities – as documented in the film *Paris Is Burning* (1990) – staged elaborate masquerading performances, in which they enacted various drag characters, from glamorous divas to sharp businessmen. Chopra's mode of dressing up invokes the queer subversion of drag, while appearing as period 'role play' – an activity that might be defined as enacting a specific character within a context of make-believe, perhaps within a form of improvised theatre, or a game.

Assimilation: role play

Since the late 1980s, Andrea Fraser has developed a significant, performative critique of art's institutional and behavioural structures. She makes interventions into ideological circuits by performing as characters that bring into relief the wider set-up in which they exist. Her work foregrounds the role of the individual in the constitution of societal structures, demonstrating how each shapes the other in turn. Over the last three decades, Fraser has inhabited the roles of curator, visitor, dealer, collector, critic, art historian and artist. In her influential work *Museum Highlights: A Gallery Talk* 1989, she plays a museum tour guide called Jane Castleton, who articulates and gestures in such a way as to draw attention to the details, set-up and hitherto unseen hierarchies of value within the museum (p.100). As she tours imaginary visitors around the galleries, she points not to the art but to the donor panels, the water fountain, and the glosses and pretensions of institutional etiquette. Against a backdrop of institutional critique by artists such as Hans Haacke, Daniel Buren and Michael Asher, whose work of the 1970s revealed the power structures hidden behind the museum's supposedly neutral fabric and architecture in a variety of formal ways, Fraser put her own subjectivity and presence into the frame. In her videos and performances, she often identifies with her characters' apparently innocent compliance with a system that – like Roberto Cuoghi's prismatic glasses – has totally skewed our orientation in terms of the values that we expect to find endorsed by the museum.

Fraser, who began as a critic, has said that she thought of these tours as 'art criticism in action'.[80] Fraser's early approach built upon her participation from 1986 to 1996 in the feminist performance group The V-Girls, who re-performed art-world mannerisms, such as the convoluted theoretical language used in

Andrea Fraser, *Museum Highlights: A Gallery Talk* 1989

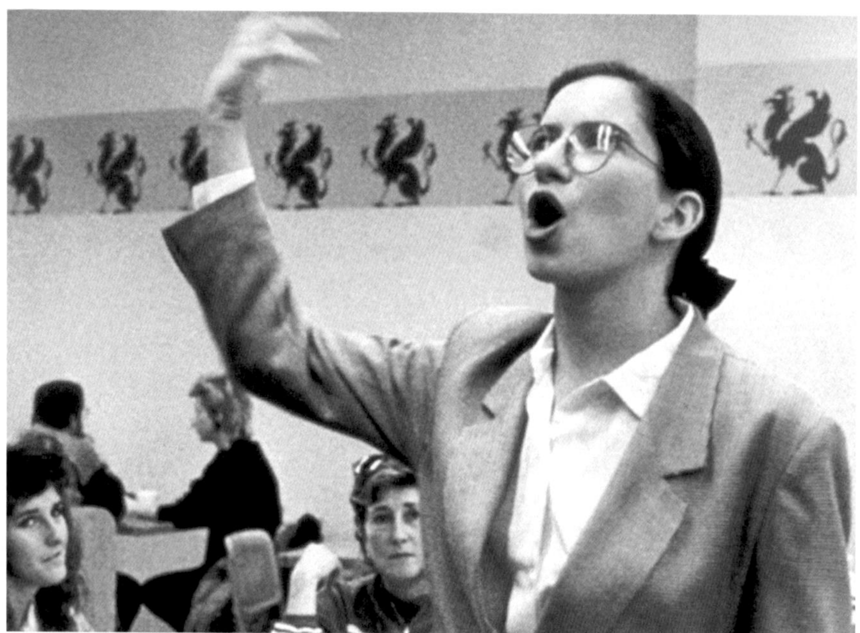

panel discussions, to satirical effect. This approach was extended in subsequent works such as the film *Little Frank and his Carp* 2001, in which she responds to the spectacular architecture of the Guggenheim Museum Bilbao in overly sexualised ways, or *Art Must Hang* 2001, in which she performs the script from a drunken after-dinner speech given by the late artist-provocateur Martin Kippenberger. In the latter work, Fraser creates a visible schism between her own position as an artist and the studied re-delivery of the behaviour of this legendary artist figure, with his punk machismo and camaraderie with male peers, to unsettling parodic effect. Fraser stages the self as a series of ready-made attitudes based on acute observation and mimicry, born of the context in which they operate.

South African artist Tracey Rose assumes the appearance of different characters to create a typology internal to her practice, and reflective of her socio-political context: post-apartheid South Africa. A significant early series of carefully composed self-portraits involves the artist dressing up and performing as different racial, ethnic and gendered stereotypes in South African culture – as a 'white woman', a 'black woman', a 'hottentot', and so on. Rose extends Cindy Sherman's approach to self-styling, pushing this towards specific critical commentary about the legislative context of identity politics in the country in which she lives; showing, in an apparently playful yet bitingly critical manner, not only that the image-surface is a malleable veneer, but also that the racial criteria upon which recent South African history was founded are changeable and irrelevant.

In Rose's *Ciao Bella* 2001, a feminist parody of Leonardo da Vinci's *Last Supper* 1495–8, the three-channel projection shows the artist performing multiple roles in an exaggerated manner. Some represent fictional characters, such as Vladimir Nabokov's Lolita; others have 'mythical' status, but are grounded in historical fact, such as Marie Antoinette and Jeff Koons's former wife, Ilona 'Cicciolina' Staller (his collaborator in his infamous *Made in Heaven* series from 1989). While much of this work concerns the manipulation of the artist's appearance through costume and make-up, in one of her earliest videos, *Untitled* 1998, Rose used surveillance cameras to film herself shaving off all of her bodily hair. Rose described this act as both emasculating and de-feminising her body, in that she was shaving off her masculine and feminine hair simultaneously. Rose's work appears to deal with the surface presentation of the self – self-image – but carries with it a threat of violence as it hints towards the deeper implications of these appearances and how she is manipulating them. Her work opens up the possibility of existing within the gap between the modes of identity offered by the labels that language gives us.

Mumbai-based artist Tejal Shah's work operates at the intersection of body art, choreography and activism. Shah investigates gender, sexuality and the question of 'contact' through sculptural body-actions, as well as through photographic portraits, in which either the artist herself or others are invited to inhabit the image. *Hijra Fantasy Series* is part of the installation *What are you?* 2006, which investigates the construction of gender. In producing this work, Shah formed a relationship with members of the hijra community, a community of transgender people as well as intersex and eunuchs in India. Hijras are reportedly viewed with a mixture of curiosity and fear in Indian society: partly revered because of perceived mythical powers, and partly shunned, often living together in marginalised communities because of social and familial ostracism. For this work,

Tracey Rose, *Venus Baartman* 2001

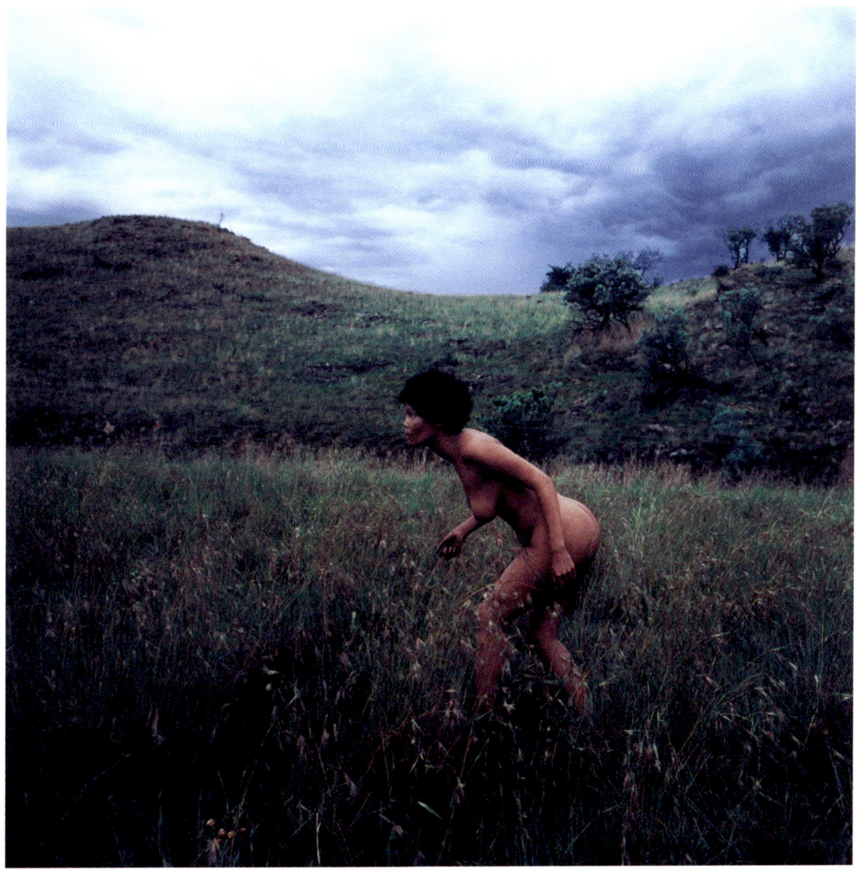

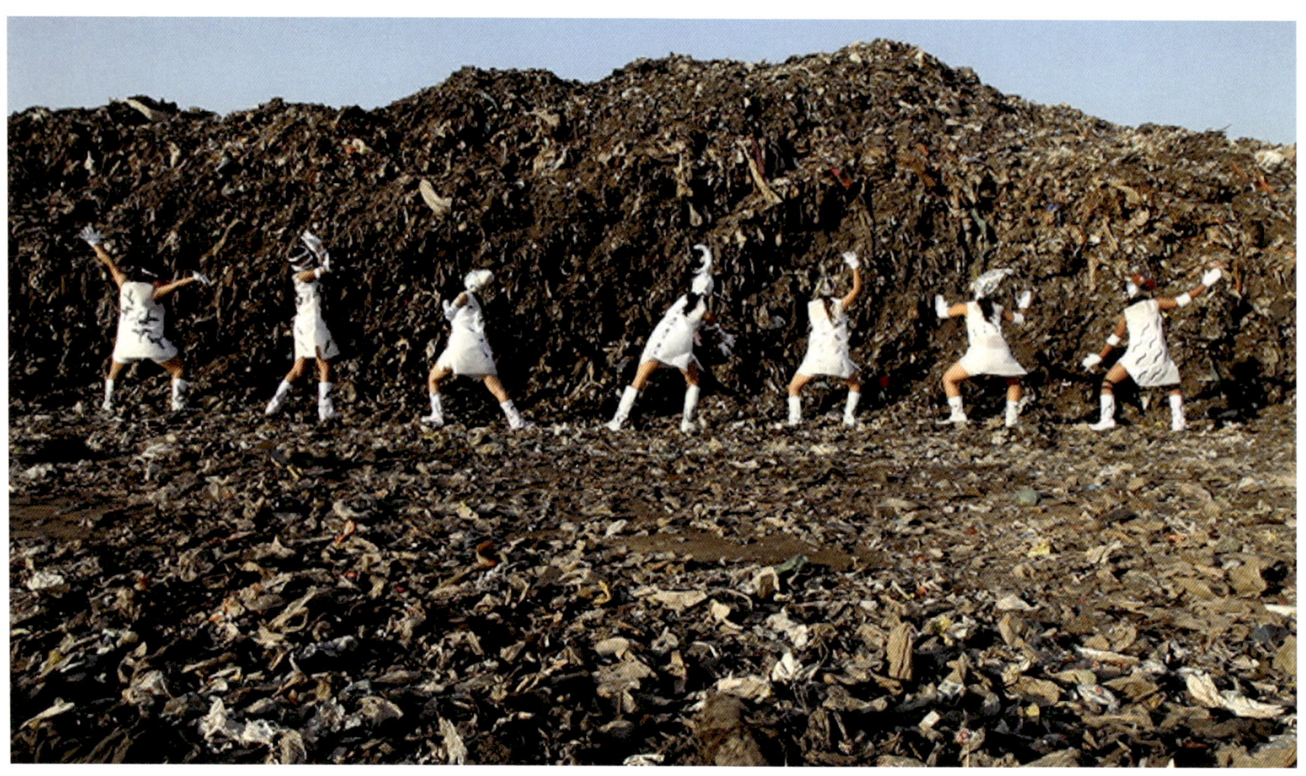

Tejal Shah, *Landfill Dance (Channel II, Between the Waves)*, video still, HD, 2012

Shah performed a series of constructions, for the camera, of the fantasies of three hijra performers, as relayed to the artist. An active member of the LGBTQ community in India, Shah espouses a queer radical politics and in this respect identifies with her subjects. Observing that the secret desires of hijras and, more generally, a queer perspective on fantasy would rarely be open for discussion in India, Shah asked her subjects how they would like to be photographed and – to some degree – incorporated their wishes into her own creative process. Initially, Shah had imagined her subjects' innermost desires would be ambitious for careers in the law, medicine or politics. 'Instead, she was made aware of her own assumptions and stereotypes when her subjects articulated hyper-feminine fantasies – of being Cleopatra, a mother and a South Indian film star', as they are subsequently depicted.[81]

In other works, such as *The Stinging Kiss* 2000, *Trans-* 2004–5 and *Women Like Us* 2010, Shah focuses on the social and biological constructs of gender; and in the five-channel video installation *Between the Waves* 2012, she and other performers who appear as fictitious 'humanimals' play and interact, sometimes in erotic ways. In this way, Shah weaves a story about the origin of a forgotten, or perhaps future species, elaborating a grand metaphorical narrative that highlights the politics of gender in an allusive way. Shah's work pictures new forms of relationship, new possibilities for identity, fantasy and communication outside of habitual societal scripts.[82]

The manipulation of identity permitted by new technology is taken to an extreme in the work of Argentine-born, US-based artist Amalia Ulman. Her project *Excellences and Perfections* 2014 was her first, five-month-long performance on Instagram, in which the artist inhabited the character of a pretty, blonde female who shape-shifted from 'cute girl' to 'sugar baby' to 'life goddess' – the female roles that she perceived as being most popular on social media. Ulman fabricated a narrative, through these postings; a virtual life in character that centred around a certain kind of lifestyle. Her blonde persona was seen enjoying 'girly' experiences such as a spa or a breakfast table with flowers and decorative touches to the food, and also having cosmetic procedures such as breast augmentation surgery. The posts solicited both sympathy and admiration from Instagram users, as she posted a stream that mixed found images with manipulated shots of her own body. Ulman amassed a huge following. Many of these followers were outraged when, months later, the reality of what she had presented was exposed, by the artist, as being faked.

Ulman's project emptied the presumed intimacy of social media, exploiting the colonisation of its users' peripheral vision, so as to build a story that grew 'at the back of their consciousness', as the artist sees it.[83] Ulman understands the performative nature of her medium as having a power to blur art and life that comes from the almost incidental nature of the encounter with the images. Even if her posts are only occasionally glimpsed, her fiction becomes somehow lodged in the imagination, embedded in people's daily lives. The 'real' Amalia Ulman lurks behind it. Questions of trust have been disturbed by this work, via the manner in which the artist has used online self-disclosure to imply authenticity (about having cosmetic surgery, or, in a recent series, an apparent pregnancy) and subsequently exposed the images as artistic constructions.

Born digital

As part of this striving towards visibility and self-representation, the increasing availability of digital image processing tools and networked computers as means of communication gave rise, in the early 2000s, to artists beginning to work with the avatar: a digital body or figure that stands in for us when we communicate online. Today our identities are often highly mediatised, filtered through technological prostheses, whether smartphones, Skype or social media. The extent to which one's outer appearance connects with one's interior becomes, for this generation of artists, ever more unstable. The question of appearance is no longer only about gender or race, but concerned with the pervasive demand for visibility 24/7, as Jonathan Crary has put it, to which the itinerant twenty-first-century worker is subjected.[84] If the relationship between appearance and interior has been troubled by artists performing the image since the 1970s, the digital native proposes a new *I* that is ghost-like, and potentially disconnected from interiority. This image-subject model masks and colonises the unconscious to the extent that it creates an uncanny image even if seemingly familiar in surface appearance.

The above artists work on questions of image and presence in different ways that imagine a persistent possibility of a coherent subject; at least, one in which name, appearance and bodily presence cohere. Le Roy, Rose or Leckey begin to pull these elements apart; to criticise this fantasy and open up new potential for acting within its given limits. Today, many contemporary artists work in and on the increasing gap between the things that constitute the subject as a perceived whole. Appearance, physical presence and specific aspects of personality become materials for this work, often appearing simulated, mediated or refracted through technology. Liveness extends from being a human or organic quality towards the myriad activities of our digital prostheses.

Pierre Huyghe and Philippe Parreno, *A Smile without a Cat (Celebration of Annlee's Vanishing)* 2002, fireworks display at the inauguration of Art Basel Miami Beach

Leaving aside, for now, the question of the 'object-actor' (since I shall return to it in the third section), the idea of the post-human has gained increasing currency since Donna Haraway wrote her 'Cyborg Manifesto' in 1983, in an attempt, from a feminist point of view, to break away from both Christian determinism and the patriarchal implications of familial origin, and to reposition the subject as a potentially self-constituting, self-determining being. 'A cyborg is a cybernetic organism, a hybrid of machine and organism, a creature of social reality as well as a creature of fiction. Social reality is lived social relations, our most important political construction, a world-changing fiction', she wrote.[85]

Artists have worked on this idea from both critical and exploratory perspectives, asking how one's identity might be imagined as emanating from points of origin not determined by genealogy or biology; how one's sense of self is mediated by technology; how one's supposedly unique or personal qualities become externalised; and, conversely, how digital bodies are able to simulate human qualities. In this early twenty-first-century context, performing – as both acting and showing – can take on a life of its own. If performance is everything, and everything is performance, it leaves us to question the substance of reality.

In 1999, Pierre Huyghe and Philippe Parreno found the image of a female character – an 11-year-old girl – in the catalogue of a Japanese agency that develops manga figures for cartoon films, comics, advertising and video games. These images are priced according to how complex their character traits are, and this one was simple and cheap ($428), so they bought her, apparently rescuing her from a short life in a cartoon and placing her within an artwork. Parreno and Huyghe named the cipher AnnLee, redesigned her to improve her appearance and set up a video animation facility in which she could be 'used' however one wanted. Imagining her as an avatar with no soul, whom they were 'liberating from the realm of representation', they lent (pimped out?) AnnLee to other artists, free of charge, and they commissioned them to build on her 'skeleton' form however they liked, just as they had done.[86]

The resulting work – a collection of video animations, paintings, posters, books, neon works and sculptures by artists including Liam Gillick, Dominique Gonzalez-Foerster and Melik Ohanian, titled *No Ghost Just a Shell* (after Mamoru Oshii's 1995 Japanese animated film *Ghost in the Shell*, based on the original manga by Masamune Shirow) – shows a bland, commercially produced cartoon drawing of a wide-eyed, prepubescent girl who represents a kind of latent, blank potentiality. By buying her and sharing her with others to generate new appearances and identities from her basic existence, Huyghe and Parreno explored the idea that through this 'rescue' she would have new experiences beyond those that she was intended or designed for. AnnLee would become 'somebody', and would live on beyond her expiry date. After three years of experimentation with animating AnnLee, Huyghe and Parreno decided to close the loop of their project, and her extended life, by creating a certificate giving AnnLee 'back to herself'.[87] The legal document which transfers AnnLee's copyright to a foundation that belongs solely

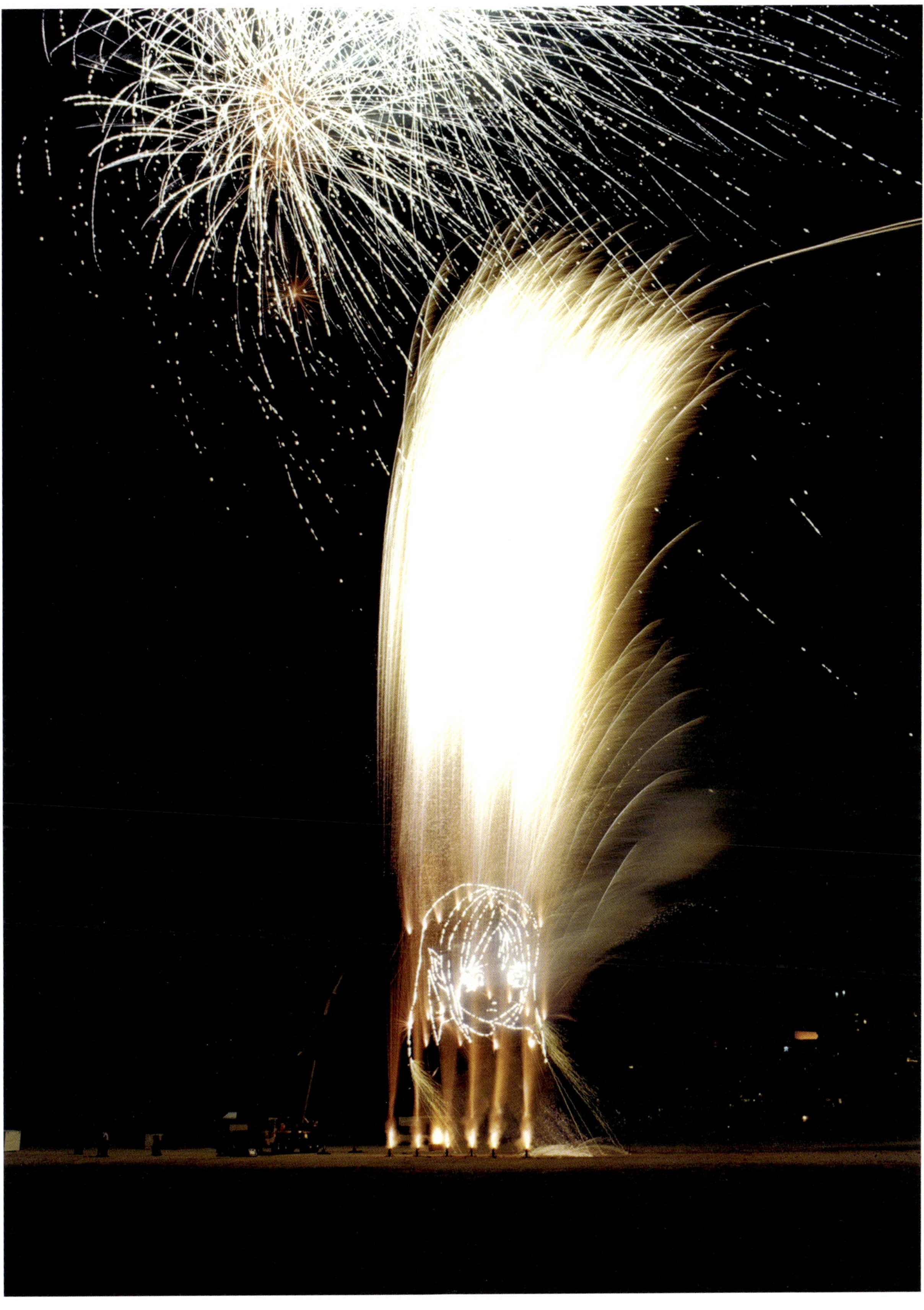

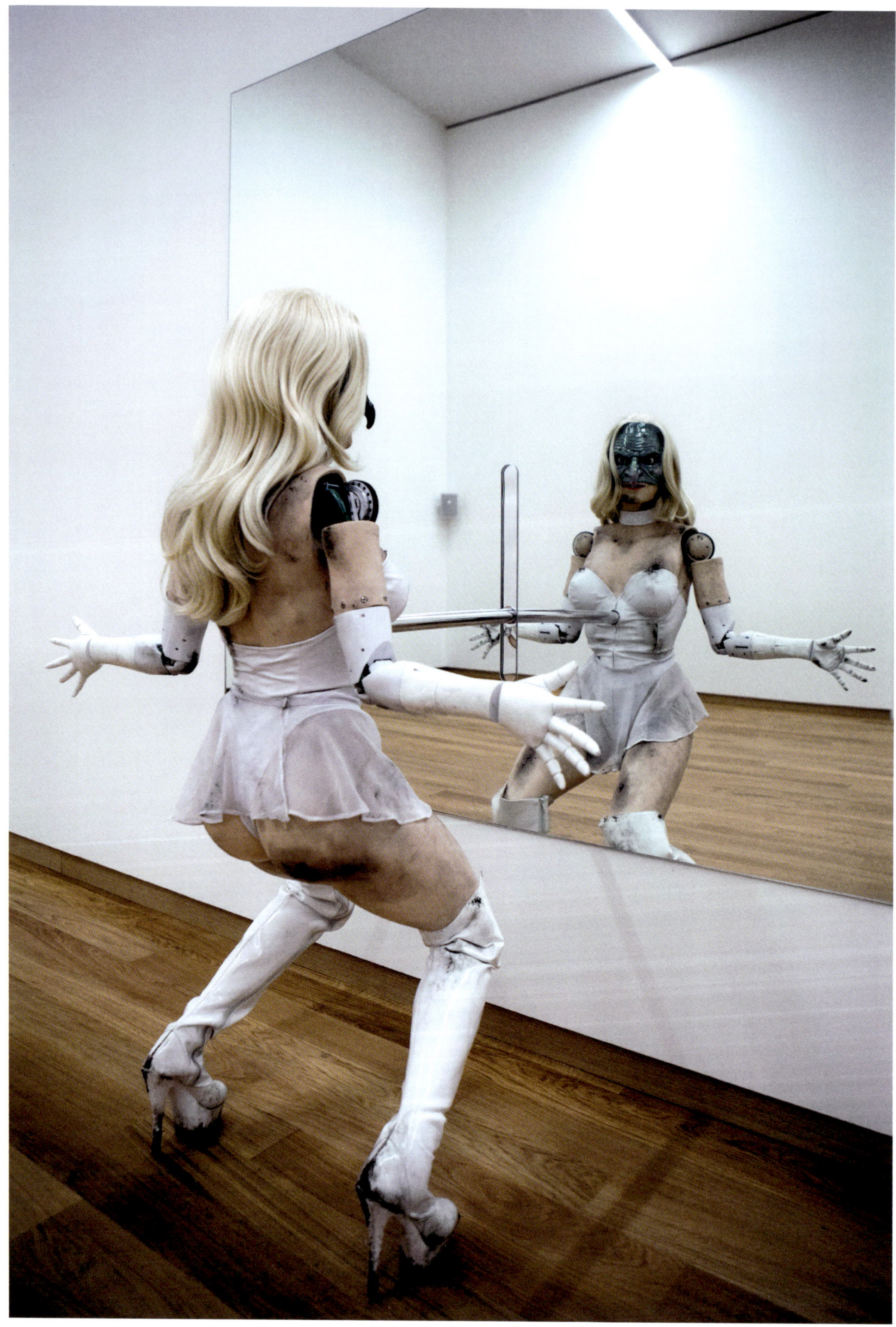

Jordon Wolfson, *Female Figure* 2014, installation view at MANIC / LOVE / TRUTH / LOVE, Part 2, Stedelijk Museum, Amsterdam, 26 November 2016 – 22 April 2017

to her – she, being a character without agency within the real-world legal arena – is, simultaneously, her freedom and an impossible state of inaction that effects her death. Nevertheless, for *11 Rooms* at Manchester International Festival in 2011, Tino Sehgal made a live work played by a young girl who performs as AnnLee in real time, her slow, slightly stilted movements mimicking those that a computerised animation might make.

AnnLee might be seen, then, as a digital performance whereby a character who is very much not related to the real-life identities of the two artists who created her – rather, in fact, a kind of obvious projection of their assumed desires, or of a generic kind of consumer desire, and a familiar gendered relation of passive female to active male – exists as a ghost-performer in another realm. AnnLee a celebrity performer manipulated by artists, prostituted by and performing for them, and because of them, but not identical with them. The piece taps into the fantasy of living a second life as an avatar, with all its deeply unsettling associations of control and manipulation. The project of Japanese artist Mariko Mori, who in the 1990s styled herself as a kind of living cartoon-cum-robotic character and appeared in elaborate videos such as *Play With Me* 1994, costumed with metallic and plastic body parts, could be seen as a precursorand counterpart from a feminist perspective, in which the artist inhabits the image of the erotic avatar on her own terms.

The artist Jordan Wolfson has pushed the uncanny separation at stake in AnnLee to an extreme, if also cruder, conclusion in his *Female Figure* 2014, and more recent animated puppet, *Coloured Sculpture* 2016. For *Female Figure*, Wolfson worked with engineers and special-effects experts in Los Angeles to create a sophisticated animatronic female robot attached to a mirror by a pole. Masked and bewigged, 'she' simulates sexually provocative dance movements to the tune of Lady Gaga's 'Applause', as she looks at her own reflection. The degree of convincing simulation of human movement is extraordinary: the robot disturbingly alternates between gyrating and pausing to make soft, detailed hand movements. She swirls back and forth, looking spectators in the eyes through her ornate Venetian carnival mask. Yet, despite her blonde wig and voluptuous figure – cheap signifiers of 'woman' added to the machine – the robot's body is dirty and abject, showing its mechanisms bluntly. The deeply uncanny effect of this performance is that we can see exactly how she (it) works, but cannot help being seduced, if simultaneously horrified, by its lifelikeness. She is a simulacrum, an animatronic cyborg made flesh, but clearly a machine. The more recent *Coloured Sculpture* consists of a Pinocchio-like puppet, manipulated by clinking metal chains, that performs a cycle of abuse and entertainment, as the cables yank the puppet's limbs to make him dance. In these works, Wolfson creates extreme images of performance detached from human agency. These works show performance as an end in itself, with an unsettling dimension that taps into common fears about the encroachment of automation, coupled with suspicion about the spectacular nature contemporary art.

The making of female avatars or robots by male artists builds upon a direction evident in surrealism (the dolls of Hans Bellmer, for example) or even in E.T.A. Hoffmann's Gothic stories of male infatuations with a mechanical doll, Coppelia, which propose that the suggestion of female attributes is enough to convince us of an object's liveness: a short-hand sketch of femininity as (subdued) subjecthood. Critical questions hang in the air as to the gender relations at play here. But an emergent wave of young artists, often female, have gone beyond the staging of such feminised avatars as 'others' and have worked in ways that identify with the avatar as a stand-in for themselves, or employed avatars as a critical way of exploring how the image itself performs, as well as moulds and shapes subjectivity.

British artist Kate Cooper makes high-definition films of female bodies and faces in which it is impossible to distinguish what might be real photographic images from what is constructed pixel by pixel. Realism of this kind has a suffocating quality, with no sense of a reality horizon, of any 'outside'. Cooper is influenced by other artists operating in this realm, including LaTurbo Avedon: an artist who appears only as an online avatar, keeping their real identity unknown, but who promotes and creates their web art using the screen name 'LaTurbo Avedon'. This avatar is actively involved in most popular social media networks and exists as a sort of ongoing performance piece/persona cultivated by the artist. The relationship between their online and offline personalities is unknown and difficult to trace.

In Cooper's video work, there is little sense of where the artist is situated in relation to the image plane, whether physically (no trace of the hand) or psychologically (how she, as a female artist, positions her presentation of these airbrushed bodies and faces). Going beyond Huyghe and Parreno's idea of setting something in motion, creating a performative reality that is digitally constructed, Cooper presents her female subjects as being entirely complicit with, composed of, and continuous with the surface of the digital screen. In Cooper's world, Debord's spectacle, as a screen, is no longer mediating a prior reality. Instead, subjects exist in a state of pure alienation that becomes so detached from reality that it is almost transcendent; it defies the existing boundaries of the subject. Her characterisation of this fetishised surface choking out the subject could be understood with reference to French theoretical collective Tiqqun, who have written about the ubiquitous feminisation of the image in capitalism as a desire-producing mechanism: the subjection of all image-making to the 'theory of the young-girl'.[88]

In parallel, Ed Atkins, also a British artist, works with hyperreal, high-definition video to create simulations of life: these are typically male avatars – talking heads, body parts, animations – that reflect back on our own embodied experience as viewers. In the touring 'live exhibition' after Manchester International Festival's 2011 project, *14 rooms* 2014, Atkins staged a live character – an actor – against a projection of a high-definition avatar. On a large, flat-screen TV, a 1:1 scale 3D head, shaved and tattooed, appears and tries to convince us of its humanity. Atkins has said, 'I think of an expansion of the term "performance", to include the processing power of a computer, the ways in which something succeeds at being "real", at being convincing.'[89] The speaking voices, singing and movements of the avatars are those of the artist himself, onto which digital features have been mapped. He uses these avatar figures to appeal to, act for, prey upon the emotions of the viewer 'demanding empathy and violent identification'.[90] Atkins has described the male protagonist of *Ribbons* 2014 as 'a character that is literally a model, is demonstrably empty – a surrogate and a vessel'.[91] His avatars suggest a masculine and emotional counterpoint to Cooper's blank, feminised image. But despite the emotive music and poetic syntax of the protagonists, their emptiness serves to remind the three-dimensional, 'warm-bodied' viewers of their own physicality.

Auto Italia (Kate Cooper, Marianne Forrest, Andrew Kerton, and Jess Wiesner), MY SKIN IS AT WAR WITH A WORLD OF DATA, 2012

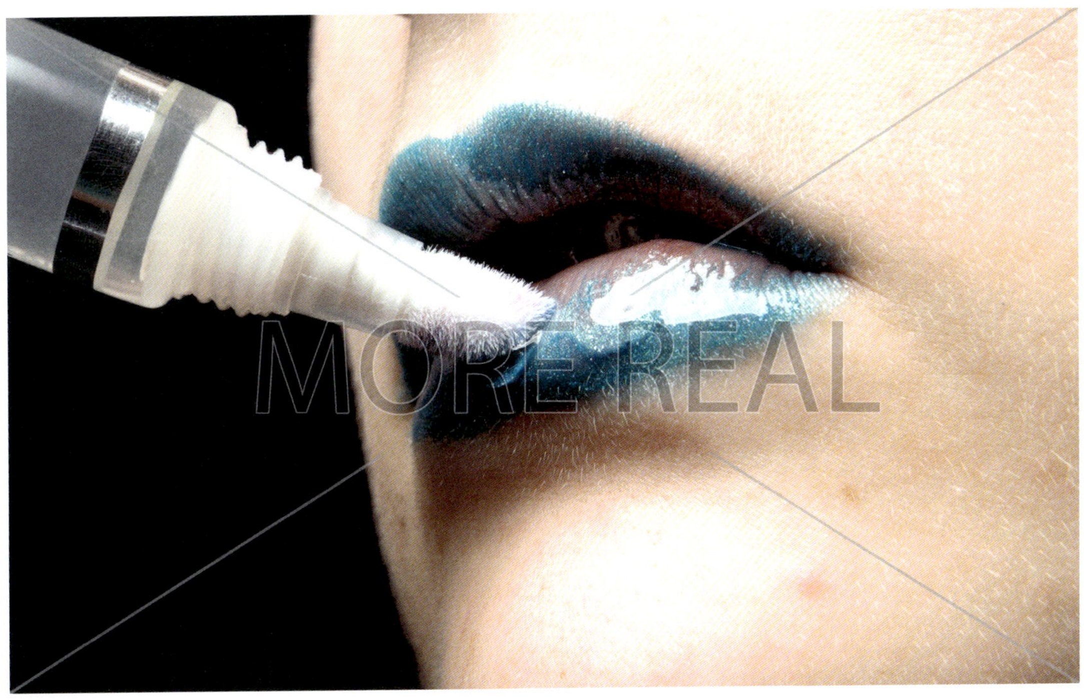

In a similar vein, the Danish artist Sidsel Meineche Hansen works on the emotional components of subjectivity. Her work investigates nervousness as a form of institutional critique, in the sense that nervousness is a failure of the body, marking an irruption of authentic subjectivity that undermines the projection of a coherent self through confident performance in public situations. Meineche Hansen's 2014 exhibition at Cubitt in London, *INSIDER*, showed a body of work reflecting on ideas of self-destruction and mutation. 'Using violence and tenderness as a strategy', the high-definition video and CGI animation *Seroquel®* 2014, which was at the centre of the exhibition, presents the behaviour-altering qualities of psycho-pharmaceutical drugs as a kind of 'internalised, institutional structure' of normalised psychology.[92] The body, in this work, is subjected to both chemical and digital prosthetic alteration, at the same time as elements of personality and subjectivity are externalised and objectified.

Since 2014, Meineche Hansen has worked with the same female avatar, EVA v.3.0, purchased online from a digital platform geared towards the gaming and pornographic industries. This character represents a figure who is empty of any sense of self altogether: figure as vessel. The artist mines such sources where 'she' can be built to spec (selecting the type of hair, breasts, vulva, skin, movement and other attributes) to depict a fragmented entity where classical ideas of the flesh-and-blood body, the soul and the mind are contaminated or disintegrating. Yet, at the same time, Meineche Hansen draws attention to how the authentic, 'unperforming' body appears as a comparative failure in this complex and demanding environment. The living body is positioned less as an autonomous agent and more – after the writings of theorist Bernard Stiegler, to which the artist Cally Spooner also refers – as being propped up, inflected and impacted upon by the prosthetic supplements that constitute our contemporary technological environment. These factors reorient twentieth-century notions of what it means to be human.[93]

South Korean artist Geumhyung Jeong is an artist of the same generation, whose work registers this digital-native attitude, but expresses it in a post-digital form – making live performances in which she appears, with real objects, in real time. Using props including gym equipment, household appliances, robots, dummies and machines, Jeong has developed a kind of performance-puppetry. In pieces such as *CPR Practice* 2013 and *Rehab Training* 2015, we see her invest inanimate, usually masculine, representations of figures, or therapeutic fitness equipment, with intimate meaning. Jeong poses these plastic avatars, and this machinery, as curious extensions of her own body or physical capacity, and also as bizarre and fantasised erotic counterparts to her own presence. Her work pictures a human subject who cannot distinguish between projected fantasy and palpable reality, or between subjects and objects. In this way, Jeong offers up a vision of online fantasy made plastic: a world of entangled humans, dolls and machines in which questions of coercion, control and intimacy are at its disconcerting boundaries.

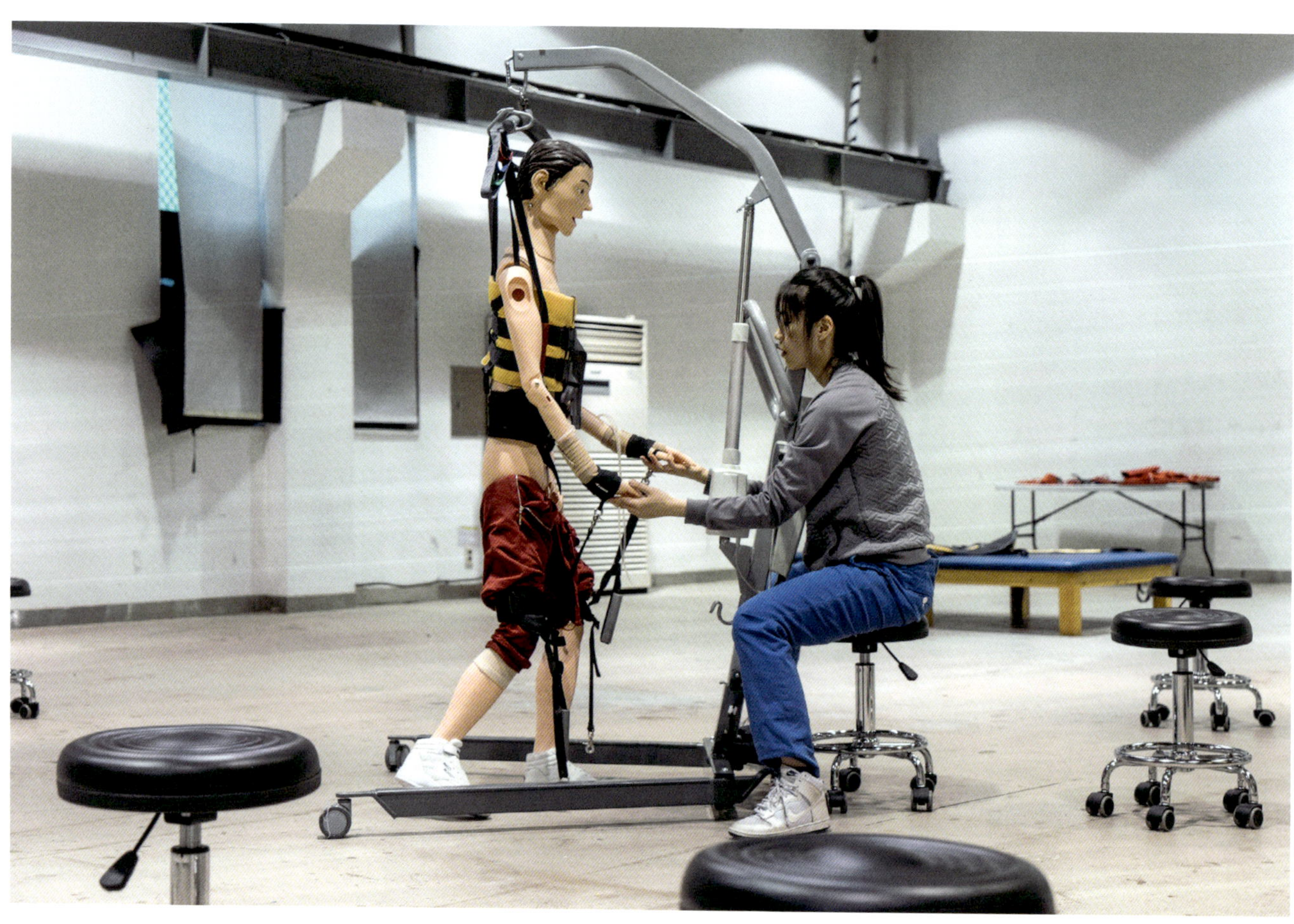

Geumhyung Jeong, *Rehab Training*, Seoul, December 2015

Summary

If within the flesh-and-blood experiments of body-art practitioners, the presentation of one's individuality was a marker of authenticity that attempted to peel the subject away from socially constructed habits and scripts, what does it, or can it, signify now? Where are the individual subject's boundaries in the early twenty-first century?

Peggy Phelan's assertion that performance happens in the present tense – that it cannot be reiterated, that its immediacy and one-off status is its essential characteristic – is difficult to maintain in an age when liveness is underwritten by dissemination via the digital.[94] What relevance does a 1970s construction of characters through rudimentary means (wigs and make-up) have now, in an age of almost infinite potential to manipulate the surfaces of images, to construct appearances digitally, and to engender human equivalents in virtual space? How does the notion of performance dig at existential questions in this hall-of-mirrors refraction of real-time presence within the contemporary technological landscape?

We have, here, dealt with the performance of individual subjectivity and the presence of the body in performance; how the activity of art-making, the physical and psychological dimensions of being, and the construction of identity have been staged by artists. We have also considered the ways in which the boundaries of the subject have become less clear through its prosthetic extension via technology, and the increasingly nuanced interplay between people and machines. And we have looked at how this has been explored in recent art: in some cases, detaching the interiority of a psychological subject from the performing image, and in others, investing objects with the capacity to perform as animated beings. Defining the boundaries of the performing subject – *I* – is as complex as determining the limits of the artwork in the early twenty-first century, and the two questions are certainly interrelated. Just as the physical and communicatory capacity of the body is extended by prosthetic technology, meaning that the skin of the physical body does not represent a limit, so too the art object is acknowledged to be situated: in architecture, in language, in networks, but also among other people. The dissolution of the boundaries of the self in this way necessarily leads to a consideration of the notion of the *We*, with which I shall deal in the next chapter.

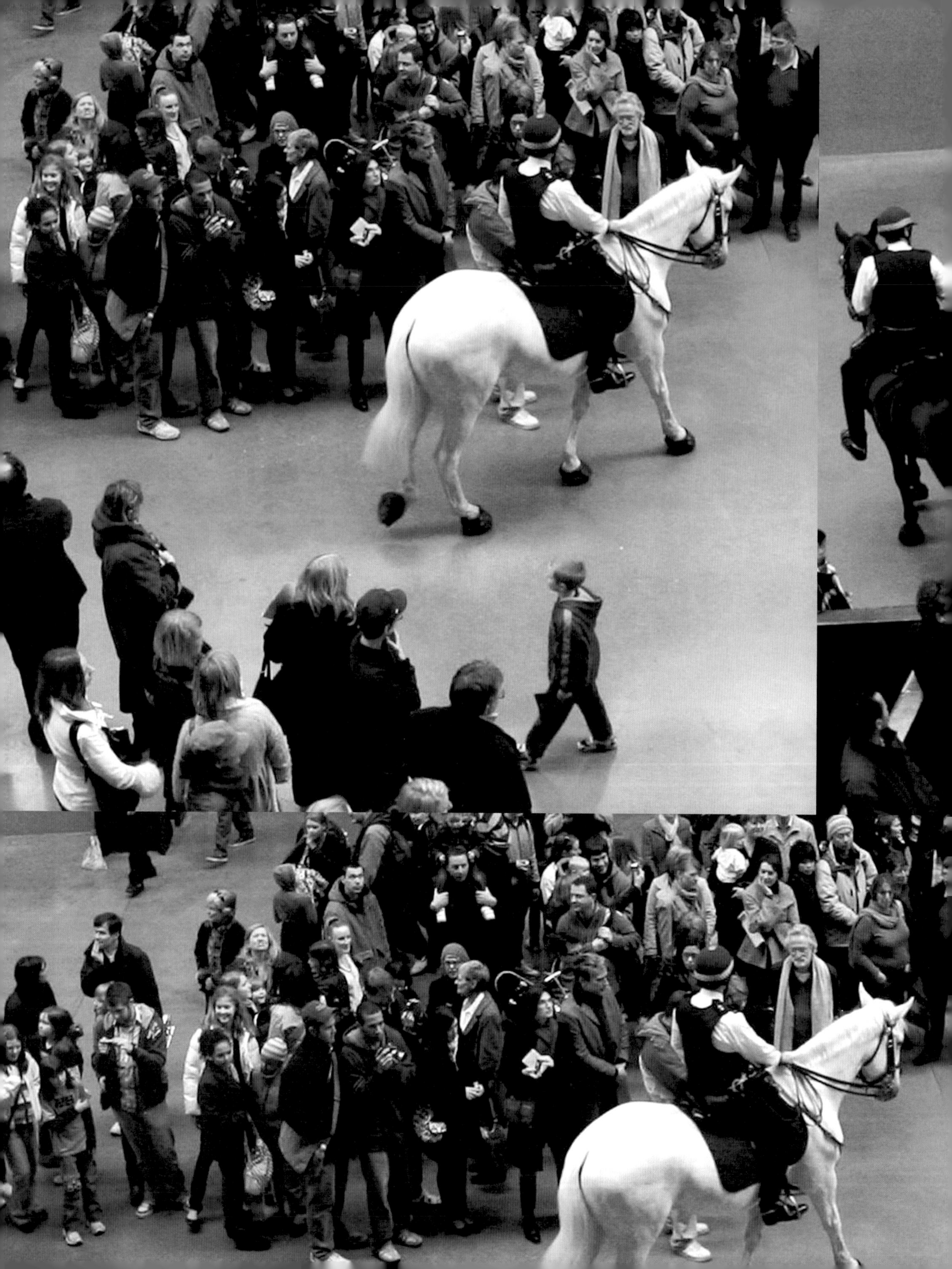

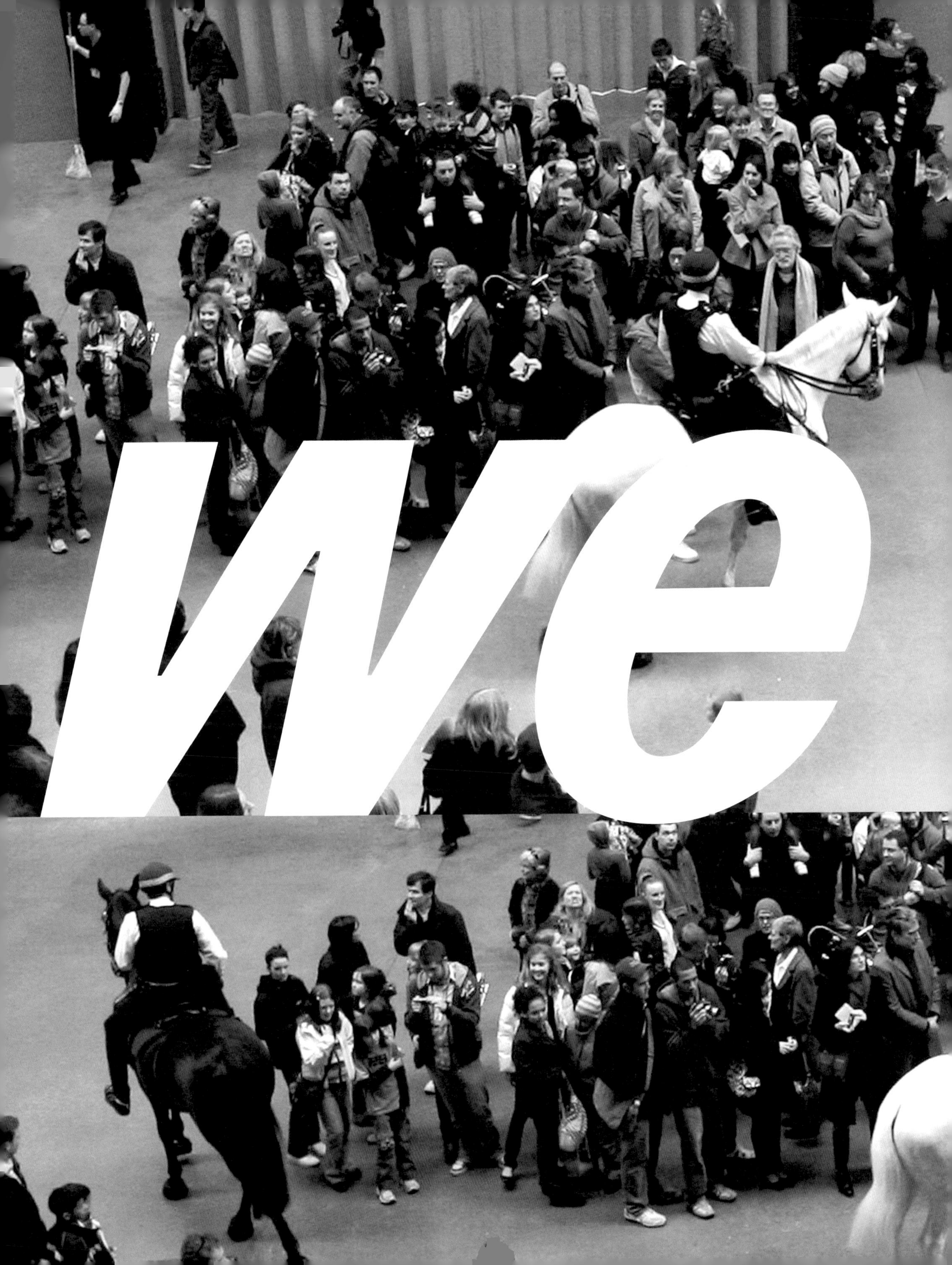
we

Social sculpture

Approaching the German Pavilion at the Venice Biennale opening in 2017, guests were confronted by barking dogs, wire fences and a black-clad, sniper-like figure balanced stealthily on top of its neoclassical façade, before being shunted around to a side entrance by security attendants. Anne Imhof, representing Germany, had worked on both the outside and the inside of the national pavilion to create her work, *Faust*. The interior had been transformed, with glass partitions and precariously high plinths for her performers, as a stage-set for her choreographic installation therein. Imhof's work represents, and is performed by, a group of people with a languid, alienated presence, more theatrical in spirit than participatory, but her treatment of the entire situation brought the politics of social dynamics into play. Her 2016 project *Angst*, presented at Kunsthalle Basel and the Hamburger Bahnhof in Berlin, had comprised a rolling score of choreographic gestures (at times spectacular: in Berlin, Michelangelo's Sistine Chapel ceiling came to mind as two figures met across a high-wire and tenderly touched hands), with the use of drones and live electronic music. As an audience there, in the vast atrium of the Hamburger Bahnhof, we were included in the performance, if not directly addressed, by our very acts of witnessing and moving in groups around the action. In Venice, Imhof dared us to stand and participate in her vision of a sweet, but somehow sick, protection zone: in the bright lighting, her performers were on show, but always just out of reach. The pavilion effected a sadistic state of hyper-visibility without contact, buttressed by the glass architecture. Critically activating the symbolic status of the commission, the artist seemed at one level to overidentify with the idea of nationalistic identity and power in a way that drew attention to Germany's position within a contemporary context grappling with the assertion of European borders, but also to our own privileged position as a visitor in relation to that of the contemporary subject as a worker-performer who has to be seen to succeed. At the same time, Imhof's performers held our attention through their exquisite rendering of carefully choreographed gestures, tableaux and movement passages, set to a composed electronic soundscape and melancholic live singing.

Imhof's work has come to wider visibility a decade after Tino Sehgal's choreography, which had occupied the German Pavilion in 2005. If Imhof's commission connected up the theatre – inside – with the wider choreography of the biennial – outside – in a confrontational and critical way, Sehgal's work has been responsible for drawing attention to the choreography that underpins the inner workings of the art institution: sculpting relations between museum and gallery staff, visitors and planted 'interpreters', as he likes to call his performers.

For three months during the summer of 2012, sixty people dressed in casual clothes massed in the Turbine Hall at Tate Modern daily. Under flat lighting that occasionally darkened or flickered, they continuously moved around: walking, running, moving in swirling patterns, occasionally as a swarm, then at times slowly chanting in unison the word 'electricity', before breaking off to approach visitors individually and engage them in conversation. 'I was coming here on the train,' one woman told me, 'and I saw a rough-looking man with two small children, asleep, who looked out of place. I felt sure they did not belong to him. I don't know why, I had a bad feeling about it, so I alerted the station guard, but he said that since there was no obvious evidence of distress, he couldn't do anything.' I was just digesting this potentially traumatic story, sympathising with her feelings

Eliza Douglas and audience in Anne Imhof's *Faust* 2017, German Pavilion, Venice Biennale 2017

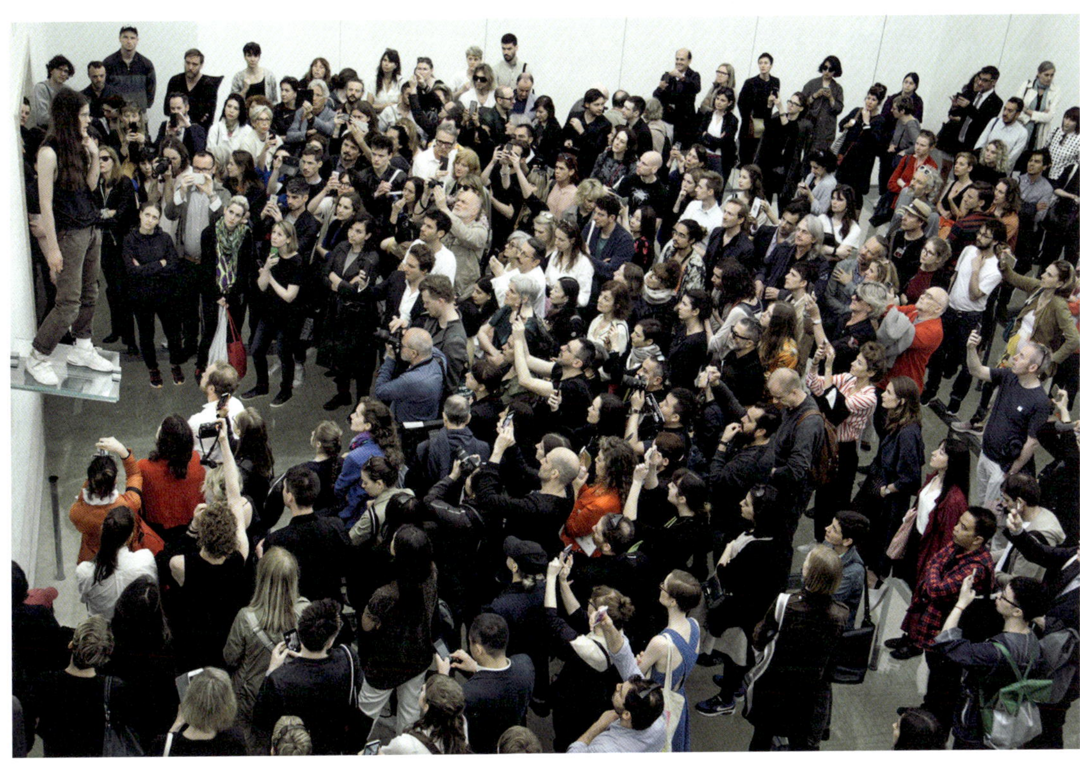

of anxiety and helplessness, when the woman moved off, disappearing into the crowd and leaving me with a feeling of passing, shallow intimacy: a reflection of urban life's alienating anonymity, made up of glimpsed narratives, just like the one she had described.

This was part of Tino Sehgal's commission *These Associations*, his most ambitious constructed situation to date. As is characteristic of his work since the early 2000s, he used movement, speech and interaction by and with people in space – no objects as such – to create a live artwork (though one *not* to be labelled a 'performance', according to the artist).[1] The word 'associations' in the title appears to reference Bruno Latour's analysis of social networks and how connections, relations and ties are invented and can be remade.[2] Sehgal's attitude to sculpting live action is significant because of his insistence that the situations he creates are staged throughout the gallery's regular opening hours, giving them a presence equivalent to exhibited objects, but disallowing any photographic record thereof. These situations are then sold as editions with no material trace, thus theatricalising the rehearsal of a legal contract as a live situation.

Sehgal's work is exemplary of a tendency in contemporary performance to make art out of people's movement, speech and physical presence only, and to invite dialogue with – and/or the reciprocal actions of – the viewer. Sehgal is influenced by the South African-born conceptual artist Ian Wilson, whose practice since the late 1960s has consisted in initiating 'discussions' on such subjects as 'time' and the 'pure awareness of the absolute', which take place only as live moments of direct conversation for small groups of participants. Similarly, in the past decade, Sehgal's work has enacted situations of radical objectlessness in place of artworks that are made by transforming physical materials. He prohibits the capture of his work through film or photography to guard against its potential fetishisation in the form of document-relics.

Sehgal himself doesn't talk so much about 'the social' as about 'subjectivity', but subjectivity as it is shaped by interaction with others.[3] Like his peers Roman Ondak, Tania Bruguera and Elmgreen & Dragset, he takes the realm of social interaction – between his interpreters and visitors – as one that can be shaped, formalised or intervened in, to aesthetic and political effect. The group of artists who came to prominence just before Sehgal, labelled by French critic and curator Nicolas Bourriaud as 'relational' (including Olafur Eliasson, Rirkrit Tiravanija and Carsten Höller), staged the social – or the sociable – using different forms of installation that would serve as familiar, often domestic, prompts to behaviour and interaction. But what is striking about the mode of art-making proposed by Sehgal and others in the early 2000s is its denial of the material object or prop altogether and its emphasis on gestures as forms in themselves. It is significant that Sehgal himself had a background in dance and choreography.

In the 1970s, Joseph Beuys conceived of 'social sculpture' as a means to extend his assertion that 'everyone is an artist' in an activist direction; the idea that if everybody engaged in creative action, the world could be changed. This approach to making art went further than the idea of blurring art and life by considering art's potential utility via direct action. By the 1970s, Beuys was deeply involved with politics. In 1972, he founded the Committee for a Free University and was working with the Organisation for Direct Democracy through Referendum, which had been formed the previous year. In 1982, for his *7,000 Oaks: City Forestation Instead of City Administration* project, Beuys planted seven thousand oak trees over several years in Kassel, Germany, with the help of volunteers: each one was placed with an accompanying basalt stone.

Beuys, somewhat paradoxically, imagined his audience as a creative mass of individuals. One of his key works declares: *We Are the Revolution* 1972. Images of Beuys lecturing and performing frequently show him surrounded by people, and his cult of personality was both an inspiration and a contradiction, in terms of his political views. In his *Information Action* at Tate Britain in 1972, Beuys was challenged by other artists (including Gustav Metzger and Richard Hamilton) about the taking of authority that his holding the microphone implied. And yet when the audience voted on what should happen, they wished for him to continue.[4]

Beuys conceived of social sculpture in the 1970s as a way in which human action could impact upon and shape society – an important notion linking politics and aesthetics. A significant direction in contemporary art since 2000 concerns how artists have sculpted movement and social behaviour in a more concentrated, choreographic way, frequently inside the museum, but also in off-site contexts. Performance art may have begun as an alternative to the kinds of art found inside institutions, but it has increasingly found a place within them. Still, it continues to press both the museum and the market to change to accommodate it, if not to remake them in more fundamental ways.

How did art take this turn towards making social activity visible, and aestheticising it? After the Second World War, two kinds of social and economic organisation were being pitched against each other in propaganda wars across the world: capitalism and communism – a competition that intensified as the Cold War raged

Joseph Beuys, *Information Action*, part of *Seven Exhibitions*, Tate Gallery, London, 24 February – 23 March 1972

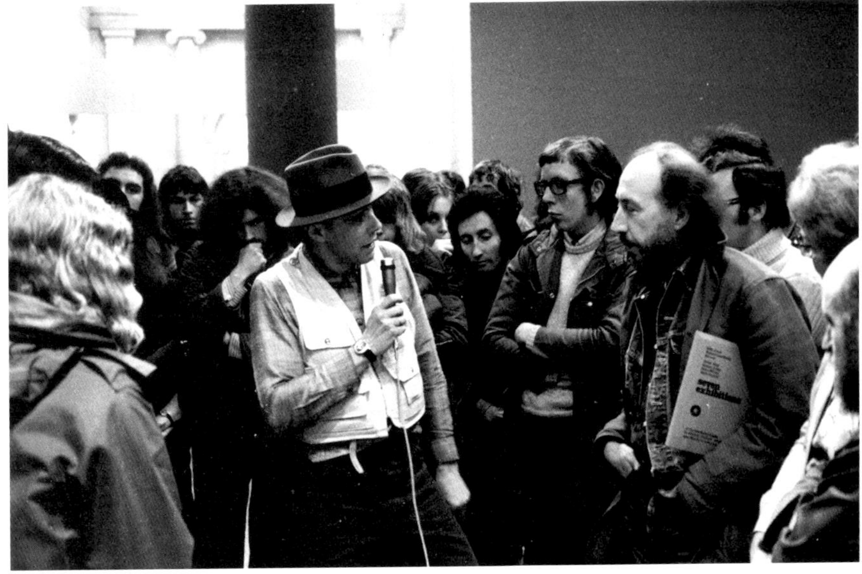

from the 1950s to the 1980s. Big questions were thus being asked about how the world is shaped by social structures, and how it might be reshaped, or imagined differently. In the 1950s, a new interdisciplinary science called 'cybernetics' began to explore the potential benefits of automation to society by asking how humans and machines might communicate. One of its most important proponents, Norbert Wiener, argued that society could be understood through a study of the analogous communication structures of human beings and machines, which he conceived of in terms of feedback systems. These ideas were discussed in a series of conferences held in New York in 1946–53, popularly known as the Macy conferences, which advanced new thinking on the relational and communicational patterns of human society, imagining new lines of contact between living beings, machines and cultural artefacts. Presciently, participants warned that 'experience would not return directly to the inner self but would instead surface as external layers and lines that could be … modelled'.[5] Human networks began to take on a new significance, and to challenge the idea of autonomous individuality.

It was during this period of upheaval and change that many artists began to make work that considered the meaning and formation of art and culture in a different way from body art, which had focused primarily on individual subjectivity. Artists began to create new social situations whereby microcosmic images of society were enacted in provisional ways. The idea that art would be encountered within the conventional viewing set-up of a gallery was fundamentally challenged as part of this, leading artists to invent new kinds of encounters: outdoor mass action, imagined by Beuys as social sculpture; immersive live environments, called 'happenings', by Allan Kaprow, Marta Minujín and others; sensuous spaces in which the whole body was addressed, by Hélio Oiticica amongst others; interventions in public spaces intended to be glimpsed by passers-by, by artists such as Jiří Kovanda; abstract choreographies that undid conventional dance partnering and patterns, by Merce Cunningham or Anna Halprin; and interventions into socio-economic structures to make labour patterns visible, for example, in the 1970s *Maintenance Art* of Mierle Laderman Ukeles. In 1974, the American artist

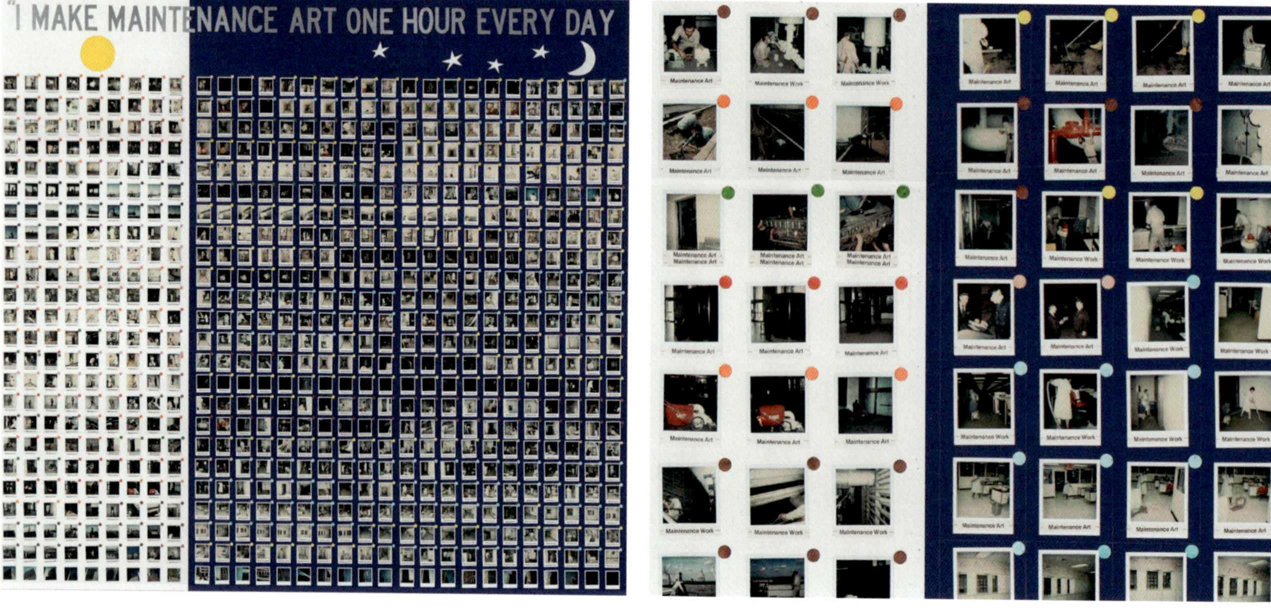

Letter distributed to 300 maintenance personnel

MAINTENANCE **ART** WORKS ©

MIERLE LADERMAN UKELES

"I MAKE MAINTENANCE ART ONE HOUR EVERY DAY"
55 Water Street

Dear Friend Worker:

I want to invite you to join with me in creating a living Maintenance Art work. This art work will take place all throughout the 55 Water Street Building from September 16 to October 20, 1976. Your supervisors have already O.K.'d it. It is part of an exhibition during this time at the Whitney Museum on the 2nd floor of the building called "ART⇄WORLD".

I am a maintenance artist. My work is called Maintenance Art Works. I use my "artistic freedom" to call "maintenance" -- the work that you do, and the work that I do -- "art." Part of the time I do private maintenance at home taking care of my family; and part of the time I do public maintenance in museums and galleries to show people my ideas. Like this Maintenance Art work I'm writing you about now.

I want people to know about and to see the kinds of jobs you do. Because this whole huge building NEEDS your work. Your work keeps this building going. Without your work, the whole building would not work. Then all the people who do office work and bank work and business work etc. couldn't continue their jobs here. In a way, it is your daily support work that keeps this whole building up just as much as the steel and marble and glass.

"I MAKE MAINTENANCE ART ONE HOUR EVERY DAY" 55 Water Street -2

Your part is very easy. It will not take one minute of extra time or effort. You will not have to do anything different from the way you always do. Really, it will take place inside your head -- in your imagination.

This is how it goes: It's like a game you play with me. I ask you to take my idea of art for yourself! Pick one hour each day, any working hour, during all the days from Sept. 16 to Oct. 20 (5 weeks) and think during that one hour that your same regular work is Art. You do not have to tell anyone about it while you do it, or you can if you want to -- that is your business. You continue to do your work as usual -- just imagine in your head that your regular work from, say for example, 9 to 10 is Art.

I am asking you to do that. Also, at the end of every day, when you punch your timecard OUT, I will leave a form paper for you to sign -- very simple -- you write your name and the hour when you chose to do maintenance art that day, what kind of job (for example, floor washing, window cleaning, elevator repair, dusting, security, etc.) and any comments you might want to share. I will pick these forms up every day and put them in the museum on the 2nd floor so visitors can look at them.

Two more things. 1) I have a button to give you to please wear everyday on your uniform, so people in the building and visitors to the museum will know you're doing this Maintenance Art work with me. 2) I will be in the building every day during these 5 weeks,

"I MAKE MAINTENANCE ART ONE HOUR EVERY DAY" 55 Water Street -3

going around and taking some photographs of all the different maintenance and security work. I will show these photographs in the museum so visitors can get an idea -- for their own imaginations -- of how much human labor is going on around them every day and night to keep this building going in the world: your work. I won't bother you; I won't disturb your work -- but you'll get used to seeing me around.

Please help! Everybody is cooperating:
1. choose any one hour for imagining your regular work as Art . . . . DAILY
2. wear your button . . . . DAILY
3. sign your forms . . . . DAILY
4. I'll take my pictures . . . . DAILY

Together, we'll make a true picture of 55 Water Street, New York City.

Thank you.

Mierle Laderman Ukeles

MAINTENANCE ART SAYING:

If you don't know who's keeping you up
You don't know what's flying.

Mierle Laderman Ukeles, *I Make Maintenance Art One Hour Every Day*, 16 September – 20 October 1976, Whitney Museum, New York

Bonnie Sherk and co-founder Jack Wickert created one of the most ambitious social projects in art of this period: the Crossroads Community, known as The Farm, on seven acres of disused land located partially underneath and adjacent to a motorway interchange in San Francisco. With the help of the community and collaborators, they turned two warehouses, abandoned concrete and open land into a site-specific sculpture, farm, community center, school, and human and animal theatre, and took residence there. Sherk described her approach as the creation of a 'life frame'.[6]

However, the question of interpersonal dynamics also had a more intimate nature. 'I started making performance because I was lonely', Vitaly Komar, of Russian art duo Komar and Melamid, has reflected in recent years.[7] Having been making painting and sculpture in the studio, he was looking – in his early actions of the 1970s – to create situations in which the making and the presentation of his work could be shared. His early actions with Melamid, such as *A Catalogue of Superobjects: Supercomfort for Superpeople* 1977, a photographic series in which a model is seen interacting with objects made by the artists designed to enhance social prestige, mark a shift from the notionally private space of the studio towards a practice founded on collaboration.

Komar and Melamid were working in the Soviet Union at a moment when the ideological battle between socialist propaganda and Western consumerism was at a peak. They parodied both systems. Rather than siding with either ideology, they proposed images of collaboration with a spirit of playful, critical camaraderie between them. Their dual process was partly a way of deconstructing the bourgeois model of the lone artist, but Komar's statement also points to a psychological (or emotional) need for reciprocal acknowledgement.

In the past decade, Czech artist Kateřina Šedá has worked on the issue of loneliness in a direct and expanded way, intervening in and shaping real-life social relationships. In projects such as *There is Nothing There* 2003, she dreamed up a game, a kind of applied Fluxus score, for the three hundred inhabitants of a small Czech village – Ponětovice – to participate in or play together, based on their ordinary daily activities. Seda persuaded villagers, with the help of their Mayor, to join in, asking them to perform their ordinary Saturday activities, but according to a fixed timetable posted on the village noticeboard. In this way, Šedá cultivated the growth of new community relations. Everyone, for one day, shopped, rode

Kateřina Šedá, *There is Nothing There (Game for an unlimited number of players)* 2003

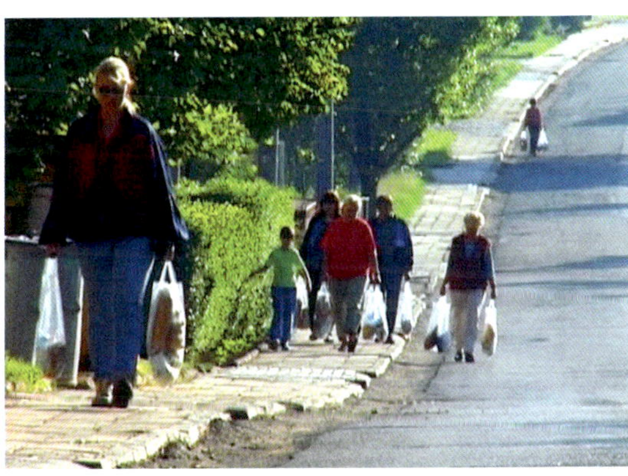

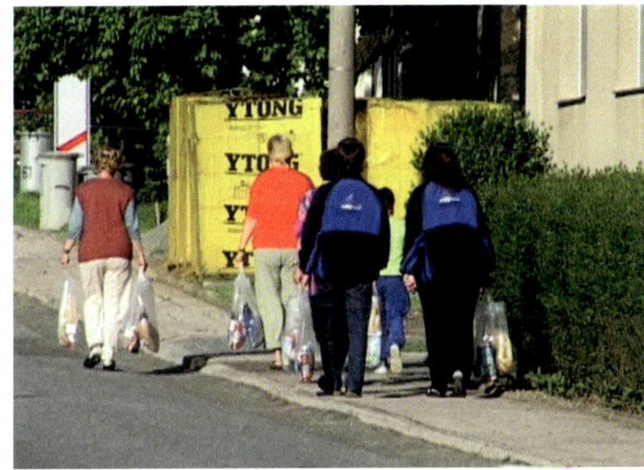

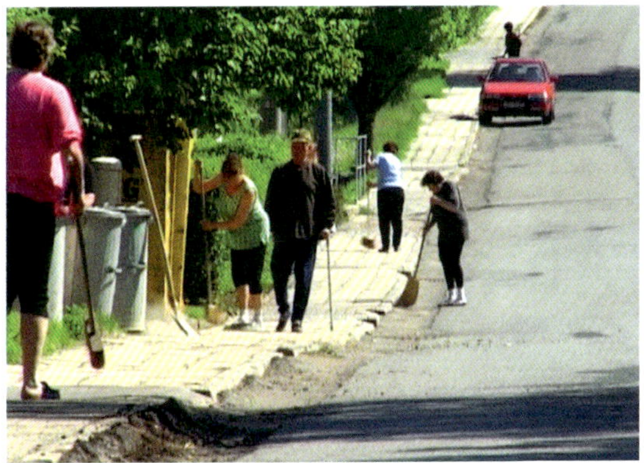

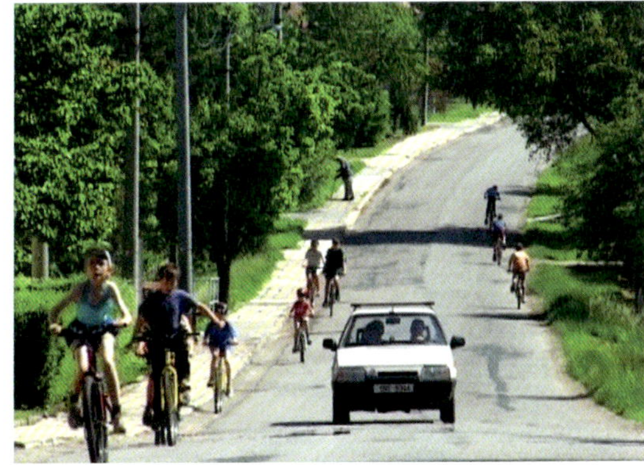

bicycles or drank beer at the same time, encountering each other afresh and creating an informal mass choreography of behavioural patterns.

How are these historical moments, which suggest the possibility of a social basis of performance, connected? How do they relate to Tino Sehgal's radical proposition that art could be made only of gestures and relations, with no objects at all? I have, so far, considered the basic condition of performance from the point of view of a spectator looking at a figure who somehow acts. From here, working back from the examples of Šedá and Sehgal, I will consider how artists have elaborated this impulse towards staging all kinds of live, social situations of reciprocal attention, looking at its different forms and formats: as a duet, a circle, a group, a workshop, a mass, a network or an intervention into an anonymous crowd, or mimicking a corporation even.

If, in the first section of this book, I dealt with existential questions about the self and its boundaries, here I will consider how intersubjectivity and communality have been worked on performatively in the postwar period and in a contemporary context. I will suggest that the social dimension of performance has run in three parallel tracks since the 1950s: firstly, the shaping of 'social sculpture' built upon the basic idea that a performer needs a witness, or an interlocutor, to stage an act; secondly, certain artists' attempts (exemplified in the work of the Russian group Collective Actions in the 1970s) to blur the line between performer and witness, by making work among and for themselves as groups; and thirdly, the invention of new ways of framing social relations, founded on the realisation that society is itself built of behavioural patterns and institutions. Useful writings on these themes can be found in Andrew Hewitt's book *Social Choreography* (2005), which tracks how social dances both reinforce and produce social relations, and Judith Butler's *Towards a Performative Theory of Assembly* (2015), in which she considers the political act of gathering with reference to the Occupy movement as a 'pre-ideological' mass protest whose power was simply in the act of assembling.[8]

Post-1950

Reciprocity

Evolving from studio-based painting and sculpture, much historic performance made in a visual art context has a solipsistic feel to it, and often a deadpan refusal to engage the audience via theatrical strategies of entertainment or narrative: for example, rejecting tactics that would pace the encounter pleasurably through time, in order to disrupt expectations. In this sense, Komar and Melamid's desire for company might seem surprising: performance in art rarely seems to care. But the need for a witness – a basic condition of reciprocity – nevertheless underwrites our understanding of it, even if that role is not clearly prescribed, or is couched in the anonymity of online experience. Whether or not it appears to be actively solicited, being watched lends meaning to action, and is, of course, an essential part of performance's psychology. Theatre director Peter Brook famously wrote in *The Empty Space* (1968), that the basic conditions for theatre to emerge are simple: 'I can take any empty space and call it a bare stage. A man walks across this empty space whilst someone else is watching him, and this is all that is needed for an act of theatre to be engaged.'[9] But within the field of visual art, other artists, spectators or the audience as a mass tend to be staged as participants, too, even as material components or active players of the work, rather than simply as witnesses. In this way, the social situation of performance in art is about much more than the presentation of acts for an audience. Arguably, it opens up new spaces: a kind of soft architecture formed of positions and attention. The choreography of performance within the field of visual art has a social dimension that is considered formally, and frequently extends off the designated stage.

In *The Politics of Aesthetics* (2004), Jacques Rancière suggests a relationship between the aesthetic and political spheres that is to do with how the 'sensible' (what is perceivable) is distributed and shared amongst a community, and how this might be altered through intervention. Fundamental, for him, is the question of what democracy means, and how much it is founded upon the taking of positions, in relation to each other, and to the locus of power. Rancière analyses the relationship between art and life by considering the community of human relations and activities as a dynamic field, whose patterns depend upon prescribed inclusions and exclusions that might – and, in a democracy, should – be challenged politically.[10] American artist Emily Roysdon observes that 'to take a position is both choreographic and discursive': a point that links Rancière's theory to histories of performance and conceptualism quite literally.[11]

Images of performance art often appear retrospectively, in archives and art history books, almost as solo portraits. Yet if the camera had panned back from the image of that performing figure, a bigger picture would have become visible that includes the audience as its essential frame. What is the artist's fundamental relationship to the assembled spectators? Why make work in this way, and for whom? Who is watching? Where and how is the audience placed: standing or seated? What shape does this temporary community take? And what kind of mobility or agency does the audience have? How are performances positioned in networks of witnessing, dialogue, collaboration and other kinds of reciprocity, and how have these relations been acted in and on, or shaped within art? If these questions began to be dealt with in the art of the 1970s, they are increasingly essential to work made in the past decade.

At a basic level, then, it is impossible to think of performance without imagining a recipient of the performed act. As Lea Vergine has observed, this is essentially a structure of recognition, because, in this relationship 'the artist has found an "other" who is willing to give him reassurance in the fantasy or utopianising world that he is attempting to make visible'.[12] Within a theatre set-up such a dynamic is assumed to be obvious: the architecture usually presupposes the audience's position as receiver in relation to the act, in the arrangement of seating. Choreographer Jérôme Bel, who has made some of the most significant choreography since the 1990s that works in and on the dynamics of a conventional theatre situation, states: 'There is a continuous reciprocal relationship during performance, and that is what my work has been about since the beginning. What is the relation of the people sitting in the darkness to the people standing in the light in front of them?'[13]

In the arena of performance within an art context, broadly speaking, we cannot take for granted being directed to look by the arrangement of seating to stage,

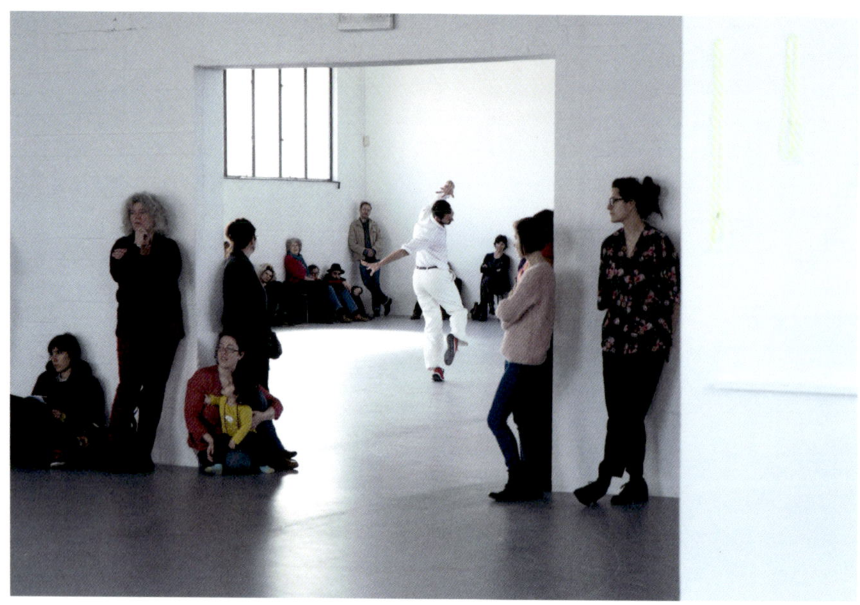

Anne Teresa De Keersmaeker , *Work/Travail/Arbeid*, WIELS – Contemporary Art Centre, Brussels, 2015

nor darkness to light. Such boundaries are less defined, or even open to being continuously rearranged. Choreographer Anne Teresa de Keersmaeker observes, of the shift from the theatre stage to working in the museum, 'everyone can decide individually … and organize his or her time and space. As a performer, you see the people that are watching you. This is nice: the museum is in liquid space and liquid time.'[14] In the museum or gallery, we are often directed to look at the act of witnessing itself. Collective presence is frequently staged as part of the work, as may be the technical or architectural elements of support for the performance situation. Indeed, John Cage's seating plans for *Theater Piece no.1* at Black Mountain College in 1952 – a foundation for our understanding of performance in art – created a four-section arrangement of triangular blocks of seats, converging in a central stage so that the audience could not only see the action happening within that centre but could also see each other and, importantly, see themselves as a collective body. Subsequent artists have paid attention to this self-awareness of the act of witnessing. As Cage wrote: 'The audience could see itself, which is, of course, the advantage of any theatre-in-the-round.'[15]

Relatedly, the Jikken Kōbō (Experimental Workshop) – which was founded in Tokyo in 1951 – was an interdisciplinary group of fourteen artists, musicians, choreographers and poets whose members worked individually or in groups. Active for about seven years, and to a degree influenced by the ideas of John Cage, they operated mostly in cafés or theatres and attempted, through collaboration, to create an egalitarian space of representation 'in the lived space of present time', and a sense of sharing work as it was produced with a live audience.[16] In their work, the entire mechanics of the set-up was theatricalised so as to reveal the social substrate underlying the production of aesthetic effects: the lighting, set design or music, and production thereof, were as integral as any danced or performed action, and the café context could be seen as an early nod to ideas of the relational situation. Art historian Miwako Tezuka notes Katsuhiro Yamaguchi's reflection that the most memorable scene, highly applauded, was that in which the dancers disappeared from the stage entirely, 'leaving the set illuminated by a chromatic play of light accompanied by a pre-recorded score of musique concrète that combined the repetitive mechanical sounds of a metronome with [Kuniharu] Akiyama's reading'.[17]

In the primary crucible of performance relations, then, the physical set-up between performer and audience, as well as the architecture of the theatre's technical set-up, are as essential to our understanding of the work as what is purportedly enacted in its choreography. But the psychological relationship is equally significant. To return for a moment to the image of Yoko Ono's *Cut Piece*, with which I began the previous chapter: whereas, seen retrospectively in photographs, the work seems to focus on the figure of Ono passively performing before a crowd, in reality it was a live test of the boundaries of interpersonal space, inviting a degree of active participation from the audience, bordering on aggression. It brought the question of reciprocity into relief in a surprising way. Chris Burden's *Shoot*, equally, might seem concerned with the expressive staging of the self, but in fact the artist said that audience members 'were implicated in his self-inflicted act of violence through their failure to intervene'.[18] Similarly, without – or with! – certain intervention from the audience, Marina Abramović's *Rhythm 0* could have turned out very differently. In these works, the conflicted capacity of the audience to watch or act is what constitutes the work.

Yet, other key works in performance history highlight the audience's role in even more deliberate choreographic or sculptural ways. The focus of Yves Klein's *Anthropometries*, as discussed in the previous chapter, was not just on their body-painting spectacle, but on their framing of the audience within the performance's picture: the spectators' gold chairs, evening dress and cocktail drinking appeared as a deliberate, ritual readymade. Similarly reflexive, if quite different in spirit, Yvonne Rainer's work has sometimes deliberately represented spectatorship within the frame: in *Terrain* 1962, for example, she directed resting dancers to remain visible, sitting on the stage instead of disappearing, and actively watching others perform solos.

Moving on from the primary experiments of the 1960s, the analogue set-up of Dan Graham's experiments with the staging of relations between artist, audience and intermediary object in *Performer/Audience/Mirror* 1975 (p.124) serves as an important, founding template for the increasingly complicated state of self-aware mediation in which we find ourselves in the twenty-first century. During this performance, the artist stands before an audience that is seated in front of a large-scale mirror and can thus see itself reflected as a collective body. Graham faces the mirror in turn, and proceeds to narrate what he observes in the reflection: his own appearance and movements, as well as those of his viewers.[19]

Performer/Audience/Mirror created a prescient, early visualisation of the constructions of making, seeing and being seen, which have a host of new connotations in a post-internet era. Indeed, Graham also experimented with rudimentary video feedback loops at this time, using video's capacities for delayed transmission to jolt our sense of technology's reciprocation of our action and make it disconcerting. *Performer/Audience/Mirror* deliberately blurred the line between the performer (ostensibly the artist, who stands up speaking) and the audience (who are reflected in the mirror, and talked about in detail, so as to appear onstage). A study of fractured relations between performing and passivity was dramatised in this piece. In the subsequent generation, the giant ceiling mirror within Olafur Eliasson's 2003 Unilever commission at Tate Modern, *The Weather*

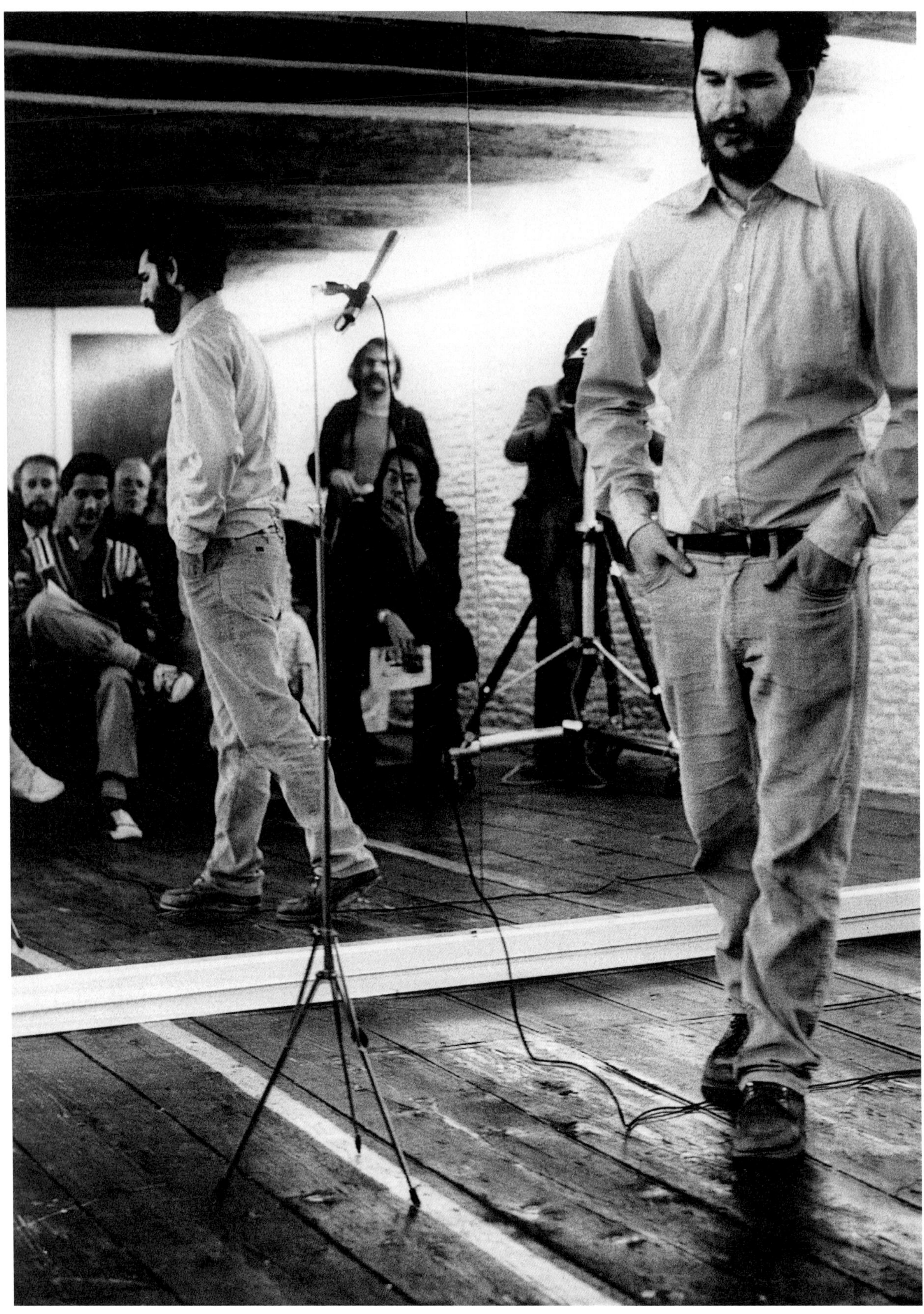

Dan Graham, *Performer / Audience / Mirror* 1975; this image from the second performance at PS1 NY, 1977

Project, marked a turning point whereby the museum audience, reflected in it, recognised itself as a collective body: visitors quickly deduced that in order to see oneself, one had to bond with others to make larger patterns or shapes, or indeed that it provided a spectacular space in which to stage protests. It was also an early example of a work refracted and disseminated on social media.

If individual artists have used bodily gestures and actions in either expressive or formal ways to perform versions of themselves, the social dimension of performance is located in how points of connection between participants are made visible. Form and meaning are found in the taking of positions, the choreographing of relations, the initiation of interactions. But what does it mean to highlight the very act of watching by incorporating the audience within art's frame? This approach is far from high modernism's pure optical engagement with a work of art – a work whose meaning is assumed to be internal to its form. It locates the art experience explicitly among people, rather than in a separate, transcendent sphere. It is, perhaps, exactly what art critic Michael Fried complained about when he said that 'theatrical', minimalist works such as Robert Morris's human-scaled plywood boxes seemed to be 'lying in wait' for him in the gallery.[20] Morris's activation of the total gallery situation, influenced by the theories of embodied perception in Maurice Merleau-Ponty's writing on phenomenology, meant that the viewer could not disappear into imaginative communion with the work simply by looking at it, but was always inevitably staged as a physical presence. This kind of artwork could never be grasped in a pure form but only ever from a partial, contingent, embodied perspective, pushing back from a notionally private space of contemplation towards a situatedness in space and time; an inevitable relation to things, and to others. What Fried saw as a problem is precisely what many artists after minimalism have chosen to work with and on, from both political and perceptual perspectives.

In the 1960s and 1970s, artists experimented freely with different ways of working in groups and networks, as well as intervening directly in the fabric of social life, to aesthetic ends. If what is seen as 'performance art' proper had its foundations in body art, its expanded counterpoint, emerging a little earlier, would be what came to be known as happenings: cross-disciplinary actions including both installation and social elements. The term was coined and popularised by Allan Kaprow in New York in the late 1950s but was also pioneered by artists internationally, including Jean-Jacques Lebel in France, Marta Minujín in Argentina, Milan Knížák in the former Czechoslovakia, Adrian Henri in the UK and Frog King (Kwok Mang Ho) in Hong Kong.

Happenings represented a radical experiment with the art encounter by drawing participants' attention to its total situation, and rearranging its expected co-ordinates. They emphasised action and liveness over fixity and permanence, and undid conventional hierarchies between viewers' experiences of space, time, materials and movement. Happenings often included discrete objects (Claes Oldenburg's soft sculptures, Kaprow's painting-screens, Minujín's labyrinthine constructions) but shifted emphasis away from these objects as artworks, or even from the artist as a central authorial figure, towards a more democratic configuration in which it was imagined that spectators would make their own way through the work as an experiential totality, inventing new pathways of interaction. Kaprow is the most well-known proponent of the happenings, especially through his critical writing on performance from the late 1950s, collected in his *Essays on the Blurring of Art and Life* (1993). He also proposed, presciently, that disciplinary

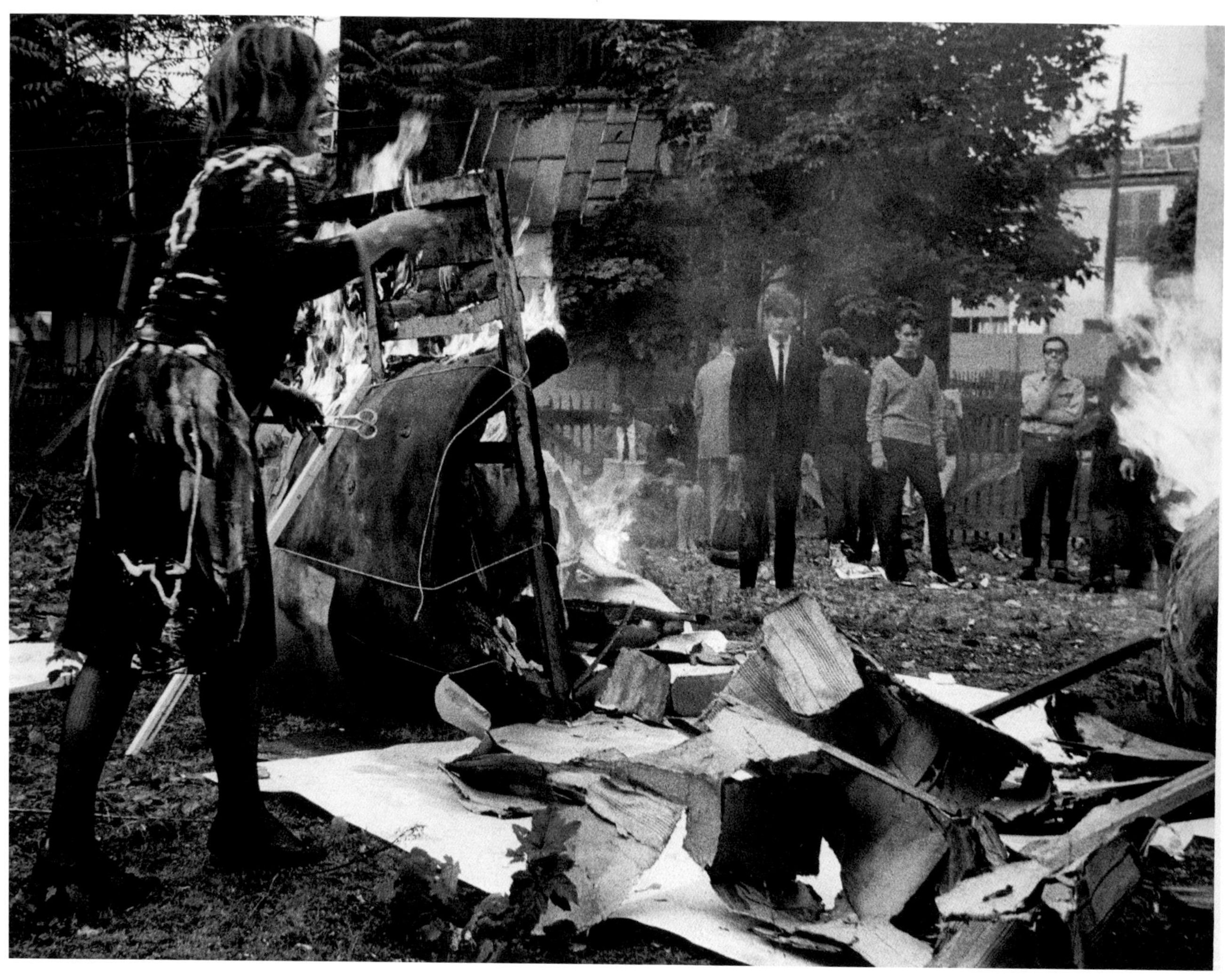

Marta Minujín exhibition and happening, *La Destrucción (The Destruction)*, Impasse Ronsin, Paris, 6 June 1963

boundaries (between dance, poetry, music, visual art) would become increasingly blurred for the emerging artists of his time.

Minujín also began to make more ambitious pop-inflected happenings after leaving Paris in 1963, where she had lived for a couple of years on a scholarship. One of her earliest works, *Roll around and Live!* 1964, invited audience members to release their inhibitions by rolling around on hand-painted mattresses. Her most well-known piece in this vein, *Mayhem*, which she conceived with other artists including David Lamelas, was staged at the Di Tella Institute in Buenos Aires in 1965. Participants made their way through sixteen rooms of her specially built installation, through which they would encounter immersive installations: television sets playing, couples having sex in bed, a staffed beauty counter, a walk-in freezer with sculptures resembling pieces of meat, and a mirrored room with ultra-violet lighting and confetti. The installation, its own architecture in the shape of a body, was designed to appeal to all the senses, including smell. In the former Czechoslovakia, at the beginning of the 1960s, where under Soviet Bloc restrictions artists often relied on contact with international peers less through travel and more through mail art networks, Knížák began to create happenings, ceremonies, installations and various environments on the streets and in the public spaces of Prague, such as *A Walk around Novy Svět* (a part of old Prague that is called 'New World') and the *Demonstration for Oneself*, both made in 1964. Acknowledging the international reach of these practices, in 1965 George Macuinas named Knížák Director of Fluxus East.

The notion of the happening spread widely globally and was interpreted in various ways in different contexts. For example, around 1970, Bombay- and Baroda-based painter Bhupen Khakhar began to integrate happenings, reminiscent of pop art and nouveau réalisme, into his artistic practice. In 1971 he staged an opening of his painting exhibition to mimic the rites of an Indian marriage procession and a government inauguration. 'Poking fun at the overblown excessiveness of wedding celebrations and at the formality of official public ceremonies,' Beth Citron has observed, 'the event generated polemical media publicity that questioned the role of the professional artist in post-independence India.'[21] In casting his artist friends, like Vivan Sundaram and Nasreen Mohamedi, as participants in the event, Khakhar radically challenged the conventional interaction between artist and audience as it had been experienced in an Indian context to date.

In parallel with happenings, artists were also using both game structures and choreography to either initiate or demonstrate ideas of participation. These kinds of works were often initiated by female artists, with an evolving feminist sensibility through the 1970s and into the 1980s. Such work found its prototypes in the choreography of Yvonne Rainer, Simone Forti and others at the Judson Dance Theater in New York; performances by Rose English in the UK; actions by Graciela Carnevale in Argentina; and events by Lygia Pape in Brazil, among many others.

Alongside fellow dance-makers including Steve Paxton, Deborah Hay, Trisha Brown, David Gordon and Lucinda Childs, Yvonne Rainer played a central role at the Judson Dance Theater in the early to mid-1960s by taking part in, and then leading, dance workshops in the space and making performances. The Judson was a place where the spirit of social engagement was very much in the air, and its aesthetic was implicitly related to a democratic attitude, characteristic of the free spirit of the Greenwich Village scene at the time.

The Mind Is a Muscle 1968, Rainer's most significant work from this period, was presented as a succession of individual and group tableaux showing people performing simple movements, negotiating or manipulating objects, interacting with each other in primary, physical ways, and dancing her signature piece, *Trio A* (p.13). The way that Rainer, and some of her Judson peers,[22] directed movement proposed that choreography might be a kind of ready-made aesthetic to be found in the city streets. *The Mind Is a Muscle* staged a shift away from the notion that meaning comes about through individual expression of interiority and instead proposed a form of meaning that could be generated collectively and was readable at surface level. In works such as *Diagonal* 1964, Rainer's dancers performed gestures and interactions according to game-like scores, which evolved through numerical rules with tacit consensus on how to play them.

Rainer's dance combined images of co-operation between men and women (which prioritised the texture of relationships as the substance of the work, over and above outcomes or objects) and presentations of the body-as-object (either as heavy weight to be lifted or as mannequin-style automaton). It is precisely by virtue of its capacity to create images of a radical literalness that *The Mind Is a Muscle* presents itself as an intervention into the dominant patterns of action and consumption in the then-emerging context of capitalism in the US.

What we could term an 'applied' and directly activist approach to social choreography and performance was developed in the subsequent decade by feminist artists such as Suzanne Lacy, whose work emerged out of West Coast practices, such as the performances of Paul McCarthy, the media interventions of the activist group Ant Farm, and the feminist work of Judy Chicago and Miriam Schapiro. In 1972, Chicago and Schapiro, co-founders of the CalArts Feminist Art Program, created the exhibition and installation space *Womanhouse* in an abandoned Victorian house in Los Angeles. Involving both their students and local women artists, this project was dedicated to the creation of installation and performance works focusing on framing life rituals such as domestic labour. *Womanhouse* set an important precedent for artists who, like Lacy, were interested in blurring the boundaries between symbolic and political action. Through the 1980s and 1990s, her work would further these questions substantially.

Staged on Mother's Day, 10 May 1987, in the Crystal Court shopping centre in Minneapolis, Lacy's major mass performance work, *The Crystal Quilt*, consisted of a one-hour action that was broadcast live on television: 430 women aged over sixty were seated at tables, each manipulating coloured and shaped cloths placed upon their own table to form the effect of large-scale quilt patterns devised after a design by Schapiro. The action was accompanied by a music composition by Susan Stone that included the women's recorded voices. With this work, Lacy wanted to create a powerful image of older women, who were often invisible in terms of mainstream media representation in the US. The work resulted in an archive of film, photography and sound, but it was underwritten by the foundation of her longer-term, less visible, groundwork: the *Whisper* project 1985–87. Activities generated by the *Whisper* project and feeding into the *Crystal Quilt* included workshops, conversations, lectures, leadership seminars and dialogue with and through the mass media, so that the work extended radically backwards, and forwards, from the moment of its visualisation as an action in 1987. Its significant community outreach activities set a precedent for 1990s relational aesthetics and beyond. Lacy's body of work has persistently crossed the line between direct and symbolic action, investigating rape and violence against women, prostitution and ageing as its themes and utilising community-building strategies to go beyond creating images of political issues, choosing instead to intervene in social reality and foster deeper relationships and communication with the communities with which she engages. However, Lacy – distinct from Tania Bruguera, who cites her as an influential role model – never set out to lead a political party as such, nor to engage in pure activism. Her attention to the filmic nature of the actions she produces asserts their status as artworks. She makes passing but powerful images embedded in life that temporarily mobilise a community around an important idea.

Although I have discussed Marina Abramović's practice in terms of the performance of the self, her work was also part of an important feminist trajectory that considered intimacy and personal relations as the shapers of society: the notion that 'the personal is political'.[23] Her staging of collective action and responsibility in *Rhythm 0* served as an antagonistic precursor to experiments

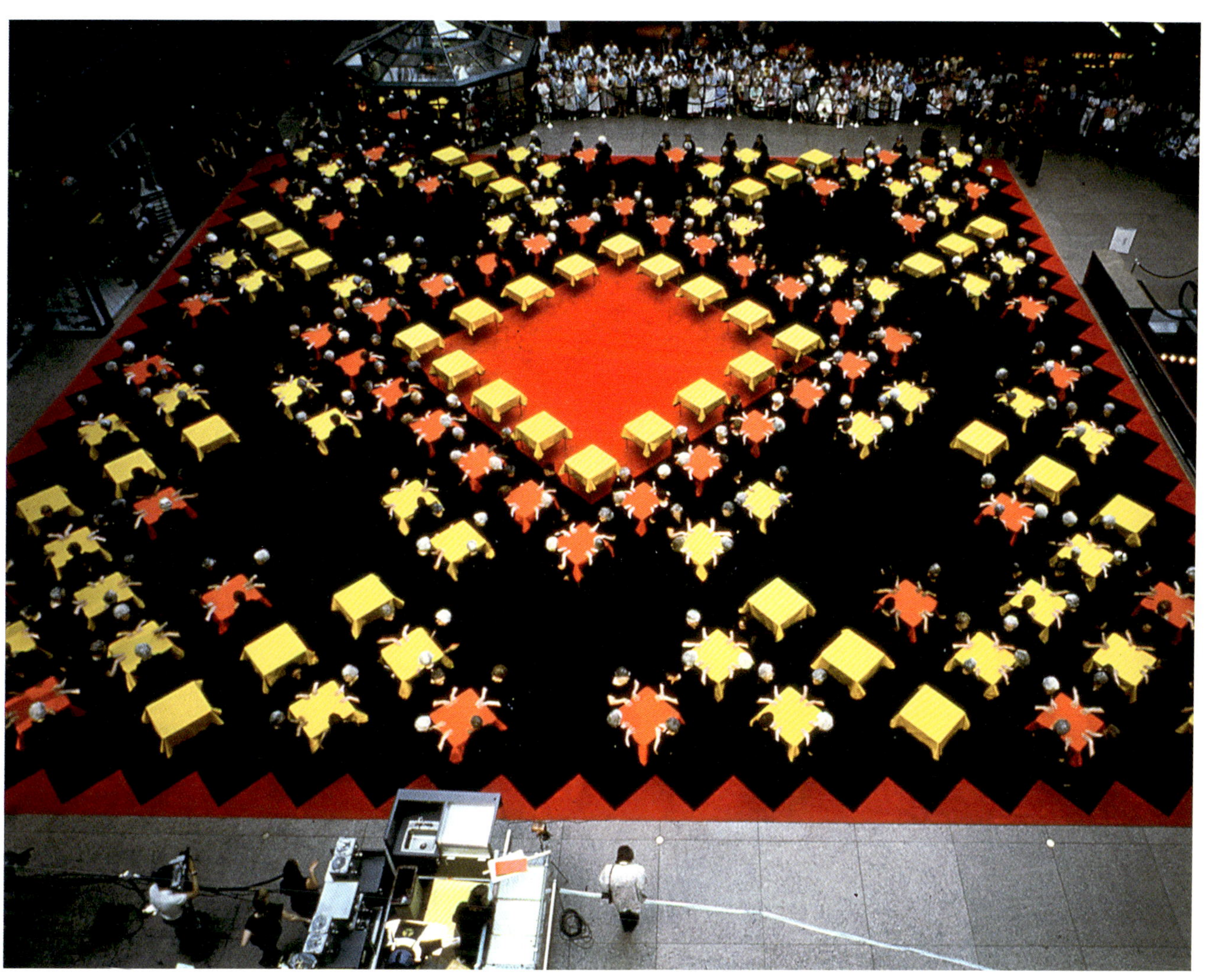

Suzanne Lacy, *The Crystal Quilt*, Minneapolis, 1985–7

with these issues in the 1990s and early 2000s. The aggressive live installations and video documents of Spanish artist Santiago Sierra during this period, which represent a key example, dramatised the dynamics of extreme inequality by paying participants to undertake potentially humiliating acts in exchange for money, and to make these exchanges visible as art, in self-explanatory pieces such as *160cm Line Tattooed on 4 People. El Gallo Arte Contemporáneo. Salamanca, Spain. December 2000*; *133 Persons Paid to Have their Hair Dyed Blond. Arsenale. Venice, Italy. June 2001*; and *Workers who cannot be paid, remunerated to remain inside cardboard boxes. Kunst Werke. Berlin, Germany. September 2000*. Sierra's work might be understood as a form of symbolic activism, but his approach has been controversial in its delegation of those body-art markers of authentic endurance and pain to enactor-workers in need of income.

Collectives and networks

Happenings, then, were a collective name for informal actions carried out in a spirit of public exhibition and participation, often connected to the ethos of Fluxus and linking artists internationally as an informal movement. At the same time, other artist groups, such as Gorgona in Croatia, Collective Actions in Russia, Jikken Kōbō in Japan or the movement known as Open Form in Poland, approached collective production in ways that made the *We* both the subject and the means through which a private community came together in a common search for meaning, posing alternatives to official institutions. Such groups and micro-communities became testing grounds for art to challenge social contexts. But these groups often also problematised the idea of collective practice or of identifying under any banner – not wishing to replicate aspects of the prevailing system – and thus questioned the group's form and limits. Other artists such as Jiří Kovanda or Isidoro Valcárcel Medina made absurd, poetic actions embedded in the social fabric, on the street, in order to both disrupt and draw attention to behavioural norms and codes, and simply to find moments of expressive freedom amid urban anonymity. All of these prefigure the ways in which artists have begun to work in networked ways in the early twenty-first century.

The Gorgona Group, for example (named after the mythological creature, the Gorgon), was an avant-garde art group which operated along the lines of anti-art in Zagreb between 1959 and 1966.[24] The group declared themselves as such, but, hesitant to institutionalise collective activity in a communist context, they did not in fact perform as a group, aside from talking and going for walks informally. They each worked in their own medium and style individually, and members proposed different concepts and forms of artistic communication, as well as running a gallery and publishing the 'anti-magazine' *Gorgona*. Each issue featured one artist's work, including that of Dieter Roth and Julije Knifer.

Gorgona Group's emphasis on creating communal space, and initiating artistic discussion as a primary motivation that did not make the art object of central importance, was shared by Collective Actions Group, a Russian group founded by Andrei Monastyrski in 1976.[25] This group's actions took place both outside the city, in fields, forests or rivers, and in indoor spaces. Their work progressed from early, extremely minimal events – one involved spectators being given documents evidencing their participation in the event of an alarm bell sounding that had been buried in the snow, and which continued to ring after they had left – towards more complex actions.

An important characteristic of the work was that there was usually no distinction between artist, performer and participant: all those present were both makers and witnesses. An essential early work was *Appearance*, staged on 13 March 1976 and involving thirty audience members. Upon arriving in a field outside the city, at Izmaylovskoe, the group was instructed to wait and watch. After some time, two of the organisers appeared on the horizon, in what Monastyrski refers to as the 'zone of indistinguishability', which he defines as the moment when one can tell that something is happening but the figures are too far away for one to understand who they are and what exactly is taking place. The two people then met the group and gave them certification of having participated in the

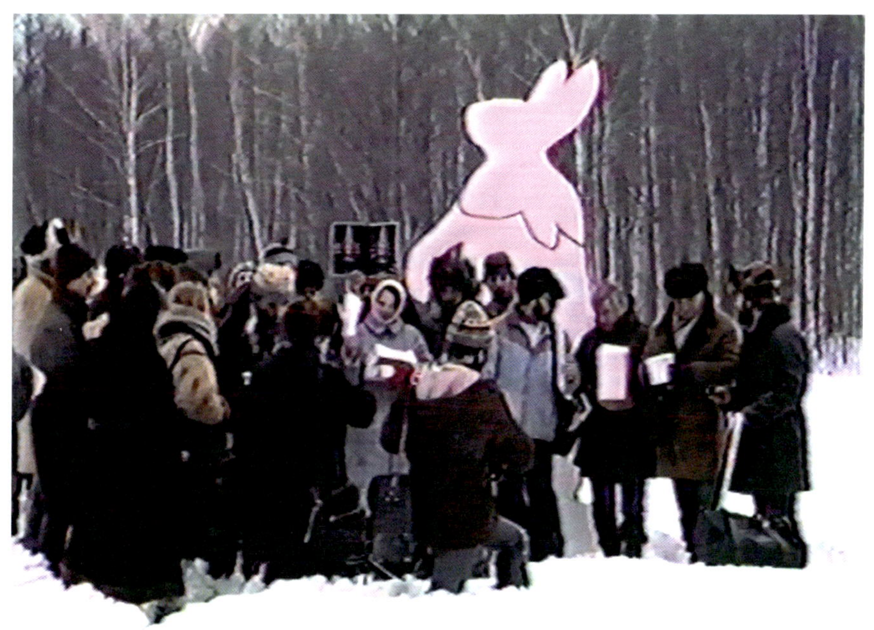

Collective Actions/Sabine Haensgen, *RUSSIAN WORLD* 1985

work. Monastyrski's interpretation of their intentions in this piece was not that the organisers had appeared for the audience, but the reverse: the audience had appeared for them. Art historian Claire Bishop observes that the audience's role in waiting was not seen to be 'as a prelude to some more specific action, but as the main event'.[26]

For Collective Actions Group, the experience of immediate events was less important than the group discussion and analysis that ensued, considering what had taken place. In Monastyrski's words, the mythological or symbolic content of the action is 'used only as an instrument to create that "inner" level of perception in the viewer', with the idea that this altered perception could be carried into the world at large.[27] The secondary materials, such as the commentary texts and photographs, were seen not just as documentation, but as a basis for the creation of what Monastyrski described as a distinct 'factographic space'. He stated: 'The documenting through photography, slides, etc. ... [exists] not to record the fragments of the event and its stages for future reference, but in order that in the process of subsequent discourses, new textual and conceptual spaces would emerge.'[28] The witnessing of such actions was, here, a prompt to a different kind of analytical conversation between artists and participants.

No-Grupo (Non Group) was a Mexican group active between 1977 and 1983, which comprised four core artists – Maris Bustamante, Melquiades Herrera, Alfredo Núñez and Rubén Valencia – and several associated members. There was no leader. Their first work was an unsolicited action within the context of the 1977 Paris Biennial, for which they sent masks made from photographs of themselves to be worn by the biennial audience, effectively representing both themselves and their work in a tongue-in-cheek way. No-Grupo often used a similar strategy of distributing texts and props to the audience to create critical, and fun, participation. They set out to counter the art world's fetishisation of objects by instead creating unstable events which they called 'montages of plastic moments'.[29] Self-financing their work, and meeting once a week to decide on projects, the members of the group were not organised around a central figure, nor did they call themselves a 'collective'. Instead, they were individually credited for their works in film, mail art, drawings and actions, which were based on shared themes and presented together as a joint 'montage'. In 1979, when given a lunch-time slot at the First Salon of Experimentation at the National Institute of the Fine Arts in Mexico City, they responded by creating 'lunch boxes' for the audience, which contained what they described as 'artistic food'. Herrera, for example, added a tag to a Coca-Cola bottle, 'describing that Andy Warhol had taken this well-known beverage out of mass circulation and turned it into art. If the person wanted to maintain the status of the bottle as art, he or she was not to drink it; but those who wanted to return the beverage to mass circulation were to drink it.'[30] As well as a print with a portrait of Marcel Duchamp dispensing sweets labelled as 'vitamins', made by Valencia, and a powdered milk sachet by Núñez, each lunch box was accompanied by a text outlining the group's critique of institutional funding structures, which they claimed forced artists to compete for survival. This work was typical of No-Grupo's satirical sense of humour.

In an emerging context for contemporary art in China in the 1980s, broadly speaking, group work was more often the norm than in other parallel art contexts. This was because artists were often attempting to gather together and create spaces that did not exist within official institutions, or through organised groups or unions, outside of state-sanctioned possibilities for showing art. The group Xiamen Dada was formed in September 1986, in southern China, by ten artists including Huang Yong Ping, Lin Jiahua, Jia Yaoming, Yu Xiaogang and Xu Chengdou.

Xiamen Dada were inspired by the relationship between European Dada and Chan Buddhism, and embraced absurdity as a principle. They were particularly interested in the concept of chance, using it to determine the making of the artworks. The group first came to prominence in 1983 with a controversial

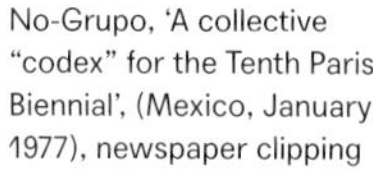
No-Grupo, 'A collective "codex" for the Tenth Paris Biennial', (Mexico, January 1977), newspaper clipping

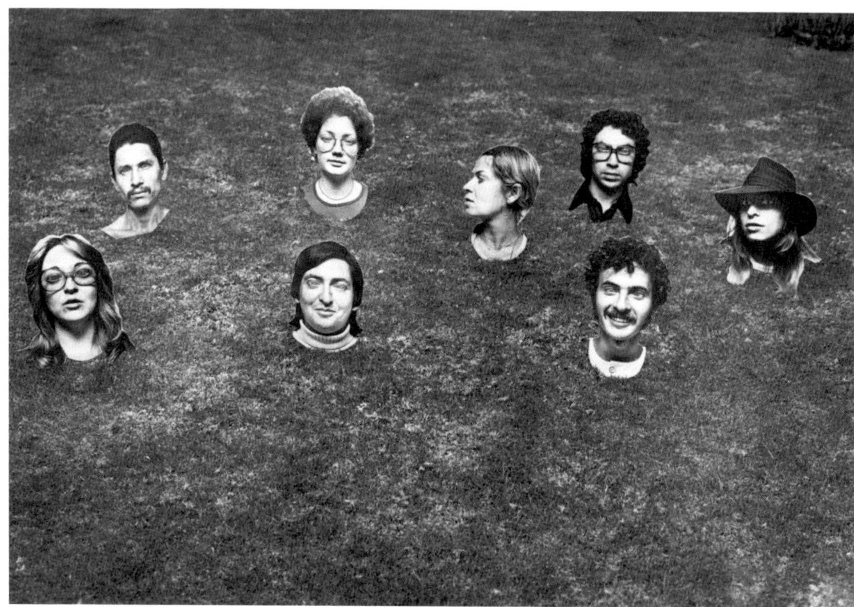

exhibition, held at the Cultural Palace in Xiamen, featuring assemblages and paintings. In early October 1986, in a public action known as *Burning Event*, the artists famously took sixty works from a large group show that was just closing and burned them while painting various slogans in white paint on the ground, including 'Dada is dead!' (p.134). This resulted in the group being banned from mounting any further public art exhibitions. In a recent interview, Huang Yong Ping recalls how collectivity was a strategy for creating a space in which to exist as an artist: 'When I returned to [the town of] Xiamen, I started off as a middle school art teacher. Back then … we didn't think of ourselves as "artists" per se. This concept wasn't presented to us in any formal manner. At the time, it was hard doing things on one's own or finding a way to exhibit on one's own, which is why we first began to collaborate.'[31]

Founded in 1988 and reorganised in late 1989, the New Measurement Group (Xin Kedu) was a group formed by three artists – Gu Dexin, Wang Luyan and Chen Shaoping – which evolved the idea of collective practice conceptually. This was an art collective that was less involved in performance action and more concerned with exploring ideas of a collaborative studio practice as an alternative to the model of the lone artist. Their work was first seen in the 1989 groundbreaking exhibition *China Avant-Garde* at the China Art Gallery in Beijing. Carol Linghua Yu describes how, 'meeting on a regular basis, the three [artists] would adopt rules agreed upon by majority with the goal of regulating every aspect of artistic creation, from the type of drawing tools to working procedures'.[32] The result of this process was an apparent elimination of any trace of individuality in the resulting artwork.

Between 1990 and 1995, the group produced five books that registered their working process in the form of graph drawings titled *Analyst I–V*. However, 'in the autumn of 1995, in view of the conflicts created between its radical founding principles – i.e. to deconstruct the legitimacy of the collective institutional system by creating an institution of its own – and the unavoidable sanctioning process of the artistic system', the group called its final meeting and decided to destroy all documents and drawings heretofore produced.[33] Such a project, even if it might be considered as having failed, represents an extreme experiment with ideas of communication and systems that positions notions of imagination, creativity, collaboration and the artist's role in society radically differently.

Embedded

If the above artists asserted collective identities, be it to protect a free space in which to make individual art or to collaborate more fully, other artists in this period drew attention to collective norms and behaviours via interventions among crowds.

In the 1970s, artists such as Jiří Kovanda in Prague, and Isidoro Valcárcel Medina in Spain, performed actions that were more or less invisible, only glimpsed by a photographer planted by the artist, or maybe a handful of friends who had been advised that a work would happen at this place and time. In this kind of art, slightly different from the actions of Cezary Bodzianowski, the emphasis is on the social field as a whole, with the artist as interventionist. The crowd on the street was within the frame, but just as a ready-made cover for these artists' covert actions,

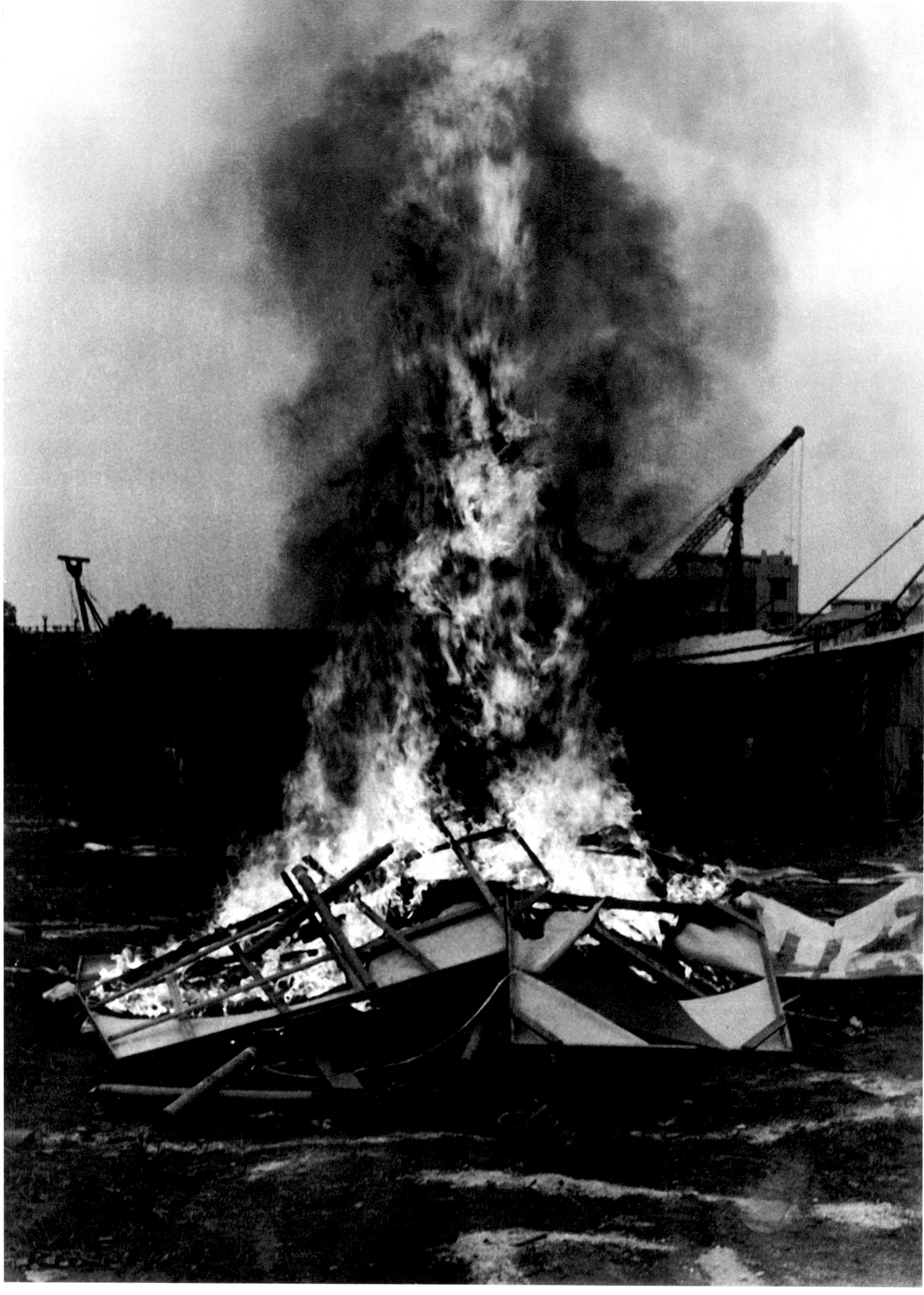

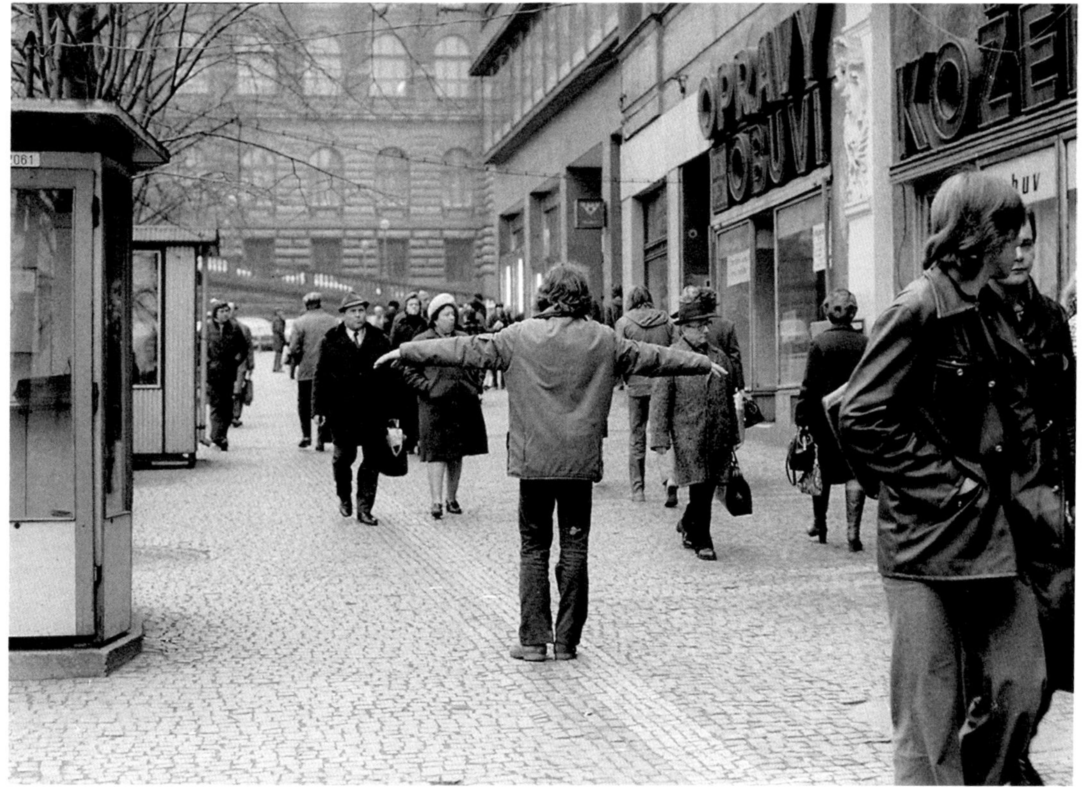

Left: Xiamen Dada, *The Art Event of Burning the Exhibited Works of Xiamen Dada*, Xiamen, November 1986

Right: Jiří Kovanda, *Untitled*, 19 November 1976, Vaclavské namesti, Prague

which would blend in among other everyday activities, while at the same time bringing into relief the social patterns of the city. As well as discreetly placing small objects in the city as temporary public sculptures, Kovanda would enact gestures that were almost imperceptible as art: standing in the street with his arms temporarily stretched outwards towards the oncoming flow of pedestrians (*Untitled* 1976); staring strangers in the eye as they walked past, or deliberately bumping into them (*Contact* 1977); standing the wrong way on an escalator (*Untitled (On an escalator … turning around, I look into the eyes of the person standing behind me …)* 1977); or sitting next to a telephone and waiting (*Untitled (Waiting for someone to call me …)* 1976).

Within the context of communist Czechoslovakia, at a time when political obedience and conformity were demanded of citizens, making non-official art was a risk. Kovanda, today, describes the actions that he carried out as 'non-political', in the sense that they were neither propagandist for the party nor directly agitating – against it.[34] But from a contemporary perspective, we might infer a political intention in these independent acts of disobeying civil norms, to do with asserting individual freedom, and initiating illicit networks of mutual understanding.

Isidoro Valcárcel Medina was working in a similarly repressive context in early 1970s Spain, under Franco. Initially, he was engaged in public actions using sculptural objects such as *Tubular Structures* 1972: scaffolding pieces that he would make spaces with, in which he would stand, walk, sit or lie in the street. José Díaz Cuyás observes that 'placing those iron structures amidst the flow and transit of the city had a profound effect' on the artist, who later reflected: 'I presented a work that could be called "plastic" but soon realised that it was an exclusively social work.'[35] From here, Valcárcel Medina decided to 'abandon himself to the city', working 'in order to offer a precise description of the system of rules and regulations that govern the city, in order to give an account of what happens in a public place'.[36] He went on to make works such as *12 Measuring Exercises about the City of Córdoba* 1974, which consisted of a series of physical and symbolic measurements of the environment and traffic of that city, performed by the artist using his own rudimentary equipment.

Graciela Carnevale was a member of the late 1960s Argentinian collective Grupo de Arte de Vanguardia de Rosario (Rosario Avant-Garde Art Group). Together with a group of artists from Buenos Aires, they carried out the now-legendary artistic and political happening *Tucumán Is Burning*, a project conceived in collaboration with a national trade union, for which they orchestrated a significant intervention in the national media. The group generated different forms of counter-information opposing the official reports being circulated by the dictatorship, following the closure of sugar factories in Tucumán. Within the First Biennial of Avant-Garde Art, this group of artists staged an exhibition at the union headquarters in Rosario, including photographs documenting the plight of the Tucumán workers, and created an ambitious publicity campaign, which included fly-posting posters simply reading 'Tucumán' across the city, and organising travel to Tucumán for the biennial's artists and visitors. Seeing art as a potential instrument for social change, the artists controversially utilised the situation of public exposure offered by the biennial to bring the social conditions of Tucumán to the attention of a large public, using the symbolic power of the space of art to gain visibility for pressing political issues.

On 8 October 1968, Carnevale took part in the *Experimental Art Cycle*, organised by the same group, making her now-notorious *Confinement Action*. For this work, the public attending the exhibition opening were locked into the gallery that they had just entered, without prior notice or explanation, for more than an hour. Carnevale has said that she was attempting to unleash a form of 'exemplary violence' for participants, as they would be forced to find a way to break out.[37] The artist understood this action as a metaphor for the power struggle in the capitalist system, closely following Frantz Fanon's idea that the experience of violence could ignite revolution, as he put it in *The Wretched of the Earth* (1961), a key text for her generation. Although in the event the participants were helped to escape by a passer-by, Carnevale's practice at the time combined an awareness of the political agency of art with a kind of metaphorical activism: choreographed actions as rehearsals for the revolution.

In parallel, Brazilian theatre director and activist Augusto Boal engaged in a more directly political form of performance embedded within social reality. From the 1960s, he developed a specific theatrical form, known as the Theatre of the Oppressed, whose audience is often captive, in the sense that observers believe themselves to be witnessing a real interaction. Boal explained that he saw revolutionary potential in applying the drama of theatre to real life. He wrote, 'in the beginning the theatre was the dithyrambic song: free people singing in the open air. The carnival. The feast. Later the ruling classes took possession of the theatre and built their dividing walls. First they divided the people, separating actors from spectators: people who act and people who watch – the party is over! [...] The walls must be torn down! First: the spectator starts acting again:

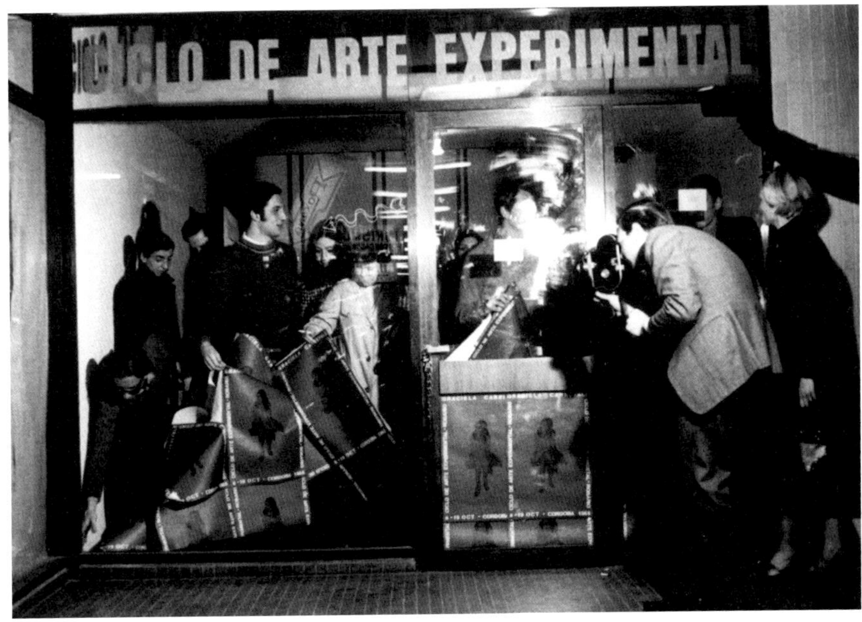

Acción del Encierro [Confinement Action], 'Ciclo de Arte Experimental', Rosario, Argentina, 1968

invisible theatre, forum theatre, image theatre ... people [must] reassume their protagonistic function in the theatre and in society.'[38]

Boal would plant scenarios – pieces of 'invisible theatre' – in everyday situations that would draw attention to a social injustice, or inequality.[39] For example, in a big hotel restaurant in Chiclayo, Peru, he instructed actors to sit at different tables. The actors spoke loudly enquiring about the price of food on the menu, ordered expensive dishes from the barbecue and ate it. When they were presented with the bill, one actor expressed his dismay that he could not pay for it. Upon being challenged, he stated that he would pay for the food 'with labour power' and sparked a discussion in the restaurant, which other customers joined in, about the rates of pay for the different jobs – waiting tables, cooking, washing up, collecting the garbage – and how many hours of labour would be required to pay for the quickly consumed meal.[40] According to Boal, the discussion (which included a collection of money to pay for the meal, and the invocation of solidarity with the waiters) went on 'into the night'.[41] The actors never revealed themselves as such in this scenario.

What is important about Boal's example, although it falls outside of a strictly visual art context, is that no distinction is made between actors and witnesses, thereby abolishing the dichotomy of activity/passivity that, in Boal's view, is detrimental to performance (understood here in a conventional theatrical sense). Boal's practice is relevant to the work of artists such as Paweł Althamer, Roman Ondak and Tino Sehgal, which also engages with ideas of embedded, invisible theatre, albeit to different ends: where Boal sought a covert method of disturbing social relations to intervene in political reality, these artists insert fictional behaviour into the real in ways that effect a different kind of disturbance of relations, with a pervasive and sometimes absurdist sense of mistrust towards apparent reality. Addressing similar issues to Boal by using a different strategy, US-based artist Mierle Laderman Ukeles herself took on the role of a worker performing low-wage or unpaid labour

First Supper (after a Major Riot) 1974, performance by ASCO (left to right) Patssi Valdez, Humberto Sandoval, Willie Herrón and Gronk, 24 December 1974 during rush hour on a traffic island at Arizona Street and Whittier Boulevard, Los Angeles

– what she called 'maintenance work' – from an activist perspective. In 1969, following the birth of her first child, she wrote the 'Maintenance Art Manifesto', which addressed both domestic labour and other forms of manual labour.
In the late 1960s and 1970s, she performed as a cleaner in museums and galleries, for example at the Wadsworth Atheneum in Hartford, Connecticut, and since 1977 has been what she terms an artist in residence at the New York City Department of Sanitation.

ASCO were a core group of four Chicano artists from Los Angeles (Harry Gamboa, Jr., Glugio 'Gronk' Nicandro, Willie Herrón and Patssi Valdez) who began making work in the early 1970s. The group wanted to rethink how art could be produced, distributed, experienced and exhibited. They used public performance to respond to the social and political upheavals in Los Angeles at this time, for example, by creating tableaux that they called 'live murals' in the streets as a form of aesthetic activism. In the first of these actions, titled *Stations of the Cross*, which was performed on Christmas Eve 1971, ASCO transformed the Mexican Catholic tradition into a ritual that was designed to acknowledge, and protest, deaths in the Vietnam War, as well as to prevent Chicano students from enlisting. The artists wore garish costumes and make-up and carried a large, brightly coloured cardboard cross, as they marched along Whittier Boulevard in a procession.
In *First Supper (After a Major Riot)* 1974, the artists occupied a traffic island at Arizona Street and Whittier Boulevard in East Los Angeles, a site of rioting in 1973.

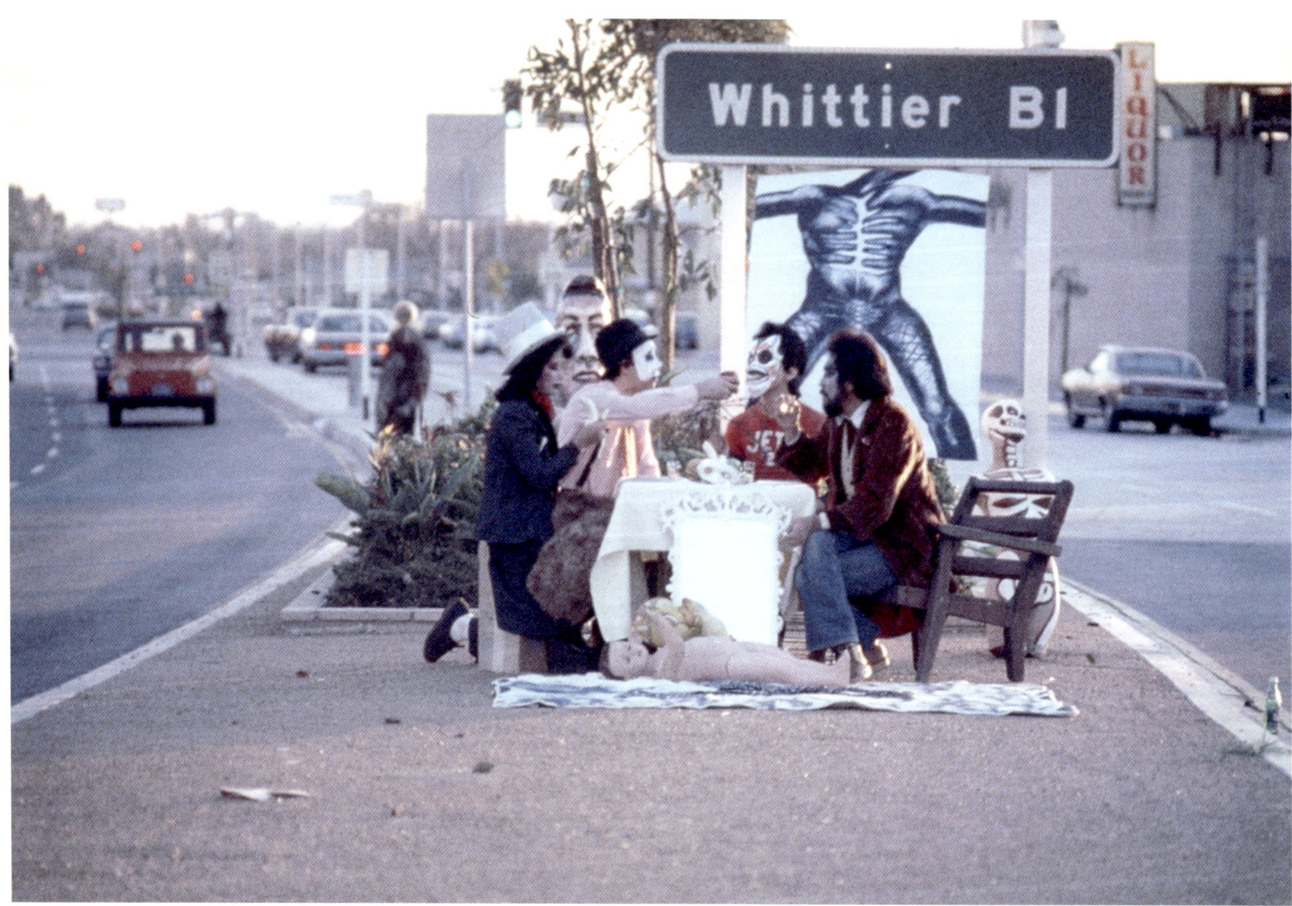

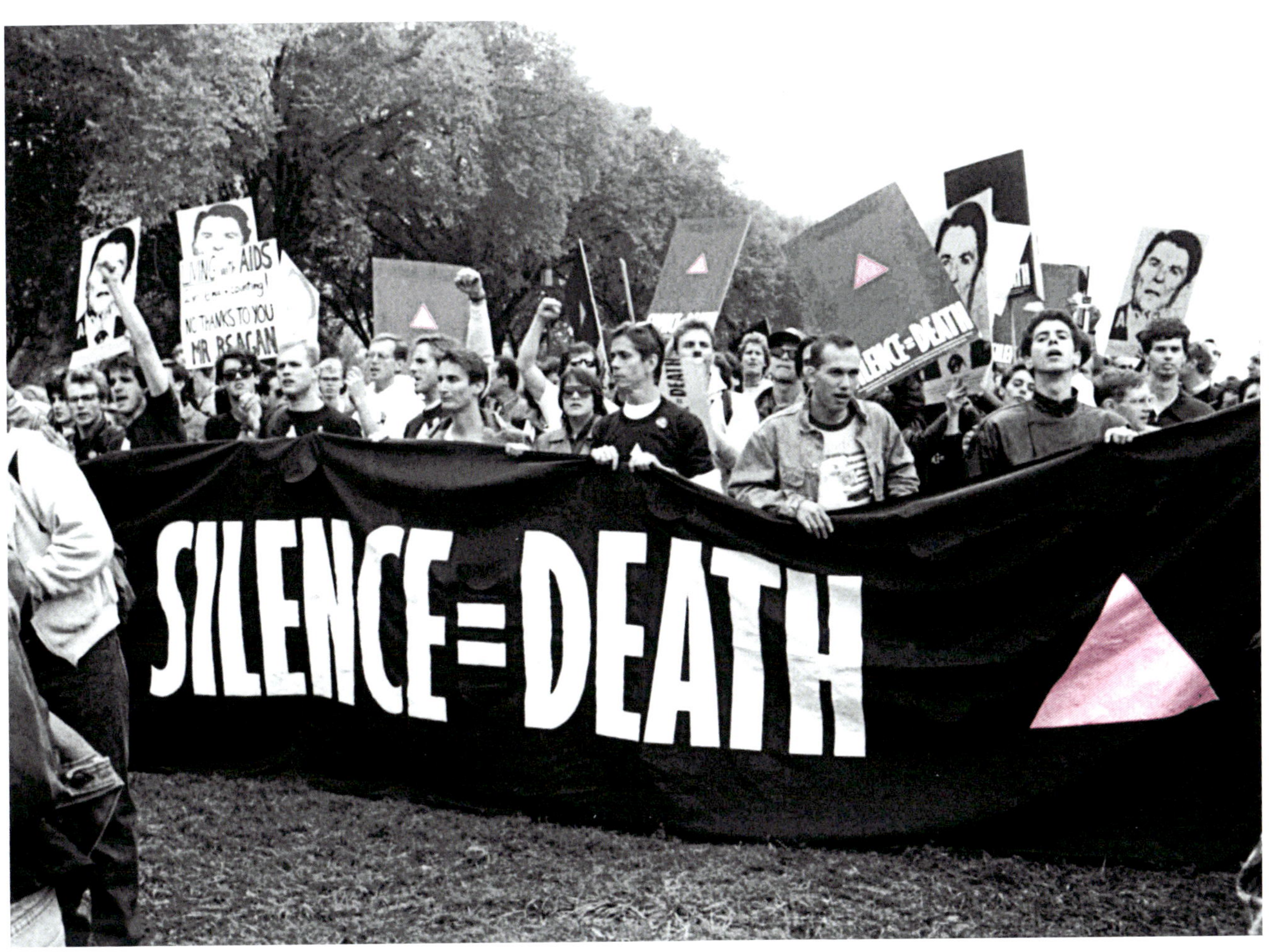

With HIV/AIDS rapidly spreading and killing, protests were numerous at the Second National March on Washington for Lesbian and Gay Rights in 1987. ACT-UP (AIDS Coalition to Unleash Power) made a strong statement about governmental policies on the disease. The AIDS Quilt was also on display at the march.

In a 'symbolic attempt to thwart the onset of historical amnesia', the group used this site for a 'macabre re-staging of the Last Supper' that included elements of Day of the Dead celebrations.[42] ASCO combined religious ritual with the language of advertising (billboards), painting (murals) and movie-making, familiar in Los Angeles, to create a new form of street theatre with a political message. These various forms of embedded direct or symbolic action activate, in different ways, the entire field of social relations in which they happen, beyond the delimited action that takes place.

In New York, the work of AIDS activists ACT UP, founded 1987, has been reconsidered in the past decade as a form of collective art practice. ACT UP utilised posters, slogans and live visual demonstrations in public spaces to challenge government policy and the behaviour of pharmaceutical companies related to the treatment of AIDS. Posters bearing the slogan Silence = Death, television material, vox pop videos and fake vox pop videos and fake 100 dollar bills distributed at rallies were exhibited in a retrospective at the Carpenter Center for the Visual Arts (Harvard Art Museums), Boston in 2009–10: this clearly acknowledged the visual strategies devised by ACT UP and indicated a shift in the perceived dividing line between art and politics or activism.

Performing formats: institutions and games

If in the 1960s and 1970s, performance art was often imagined to be cross-disciplinary and anti- or extra-institutional, since the late 1980s artists have begun to understand institutions as settings for enacted behaviours that can be challenged through re-imagining or re-playing. The rules of specific disciplinary formats and institutional structures are more and more often invoked performatively by artists to test out different patterns for articulating social contact (bonds, agreements or simply ways of interacting). Ready-made formats of games and entertainment are employed similarly.

These new attitudes bloomed fully in the 1990s, a decade marked by the emergence of so-called 'relational' situations in art, within which communal activity could take place: some co-operative and convivial, some choreographic, some – as art historian Claire Bishop has described them in her writing on 'relational antagonism' – deliberately divisive or contradictory in nature.[43] In his 1998 book *Relational Aesthetics*, Nicolas Bourriaud defined this type of work as 'a set of artistic practices which take as their theoretical and practical point of departure the whole of human relations and their social context, rather than an independent and private space'.[44] He cited Carsten Höller, Dominique Gonzalez-Foerster, Gillian Wearing, Philippe Parreno, Douglas Gordon, Rirkrit

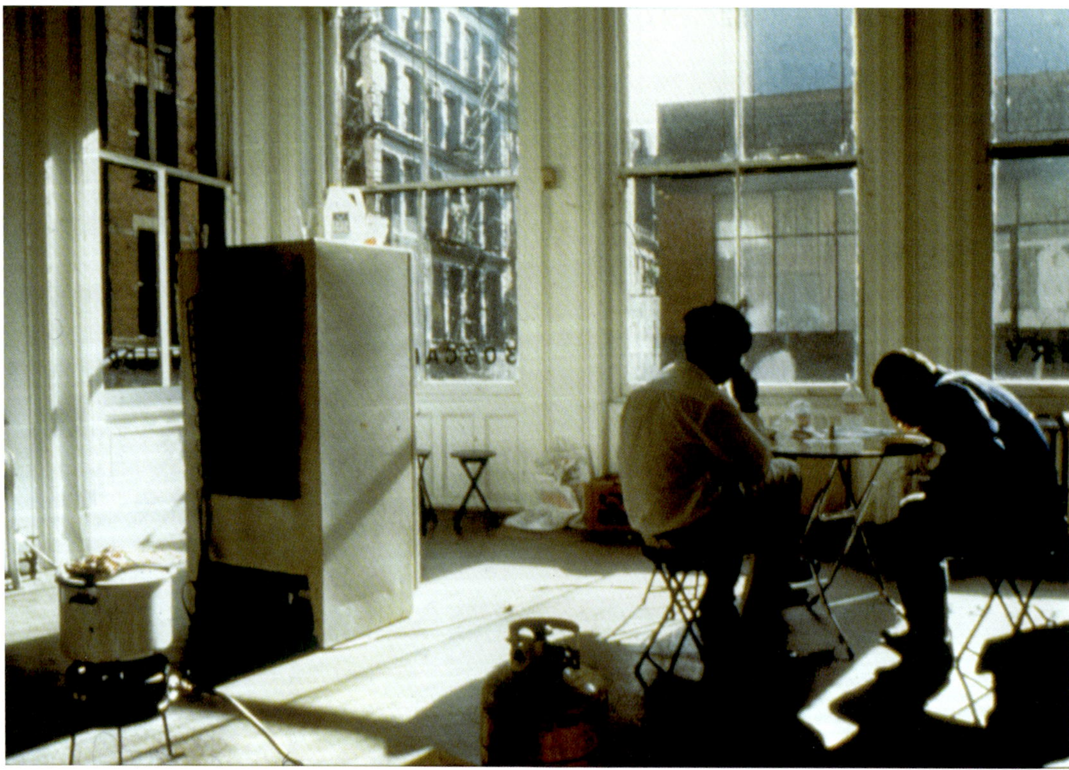

Rirkrit Tiravanija, *Untitled (Free)*, 1992; installation view, 303 Gallery

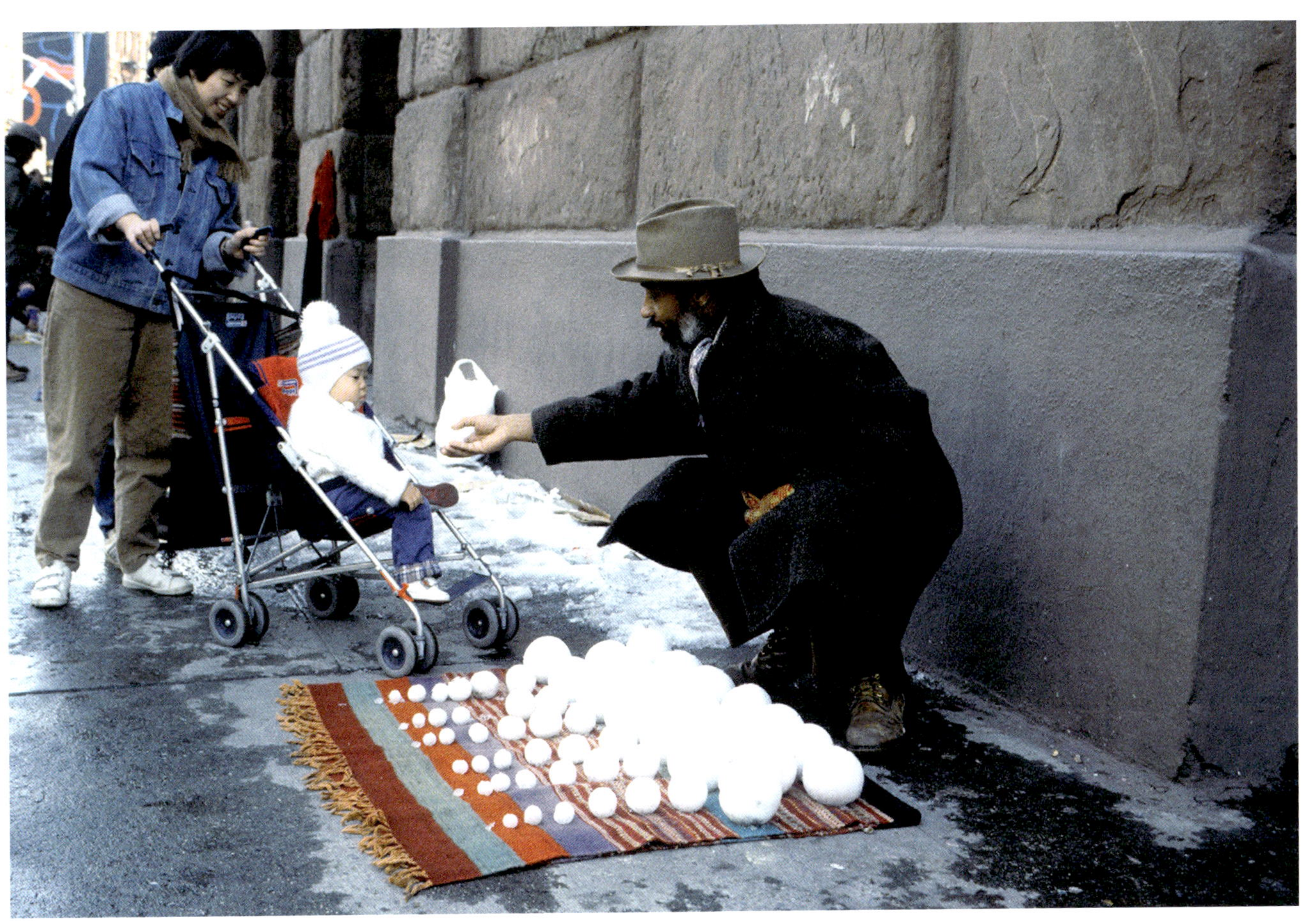

David Hammons,
Bliz-aard Ball Sale 1983

Tiravanija and Liam Gillick as artists who work to this agenda. Primary examples include Höller's interactive sensory environments, which invite viewers to take part in quasi-scientific experiments, and Gillick's interior architecture invoking the contemporary office. Rather than proposing societal revolution, Bourriaud observed, this work would create 'microtopias' within existing reality.[45]

Identifying this tendency was a controversial but important move, even if the territory was much more complex and evolving than that which was charted in Bourriaud's essay. The concept of the 'relational' was originally used, in the 1960s, to think about formal sculptural relations of part to whole, for example in the proto-minimalist work of British sculptor Anthony Caro and his assemblages of found industrial materials. In the hands of Bourriaud, it offered a new way of considering forms of live or participatory art as being less about a performer per se, and more to do with all the actors taking part in the aesthetic encounter, including the artist, the installation or object and the viewer – in relation to each other, as it were. But in the past twenty years, artists have explored the idea of sharing art in many more diverse and experimental situations than this particular group of artists have. Among other things, artists have borrowed from the ready-made formats of theatre and dance, extended the use of games, rethought institutions such as schools or museums from a performance perspective, engaged in activism, created fictional interventions through acting, and worked in ways that mimic trade corporate brands and networks.

In 1983, the African American artist David Hammons set up a table, alongside other street vendors, selling snowballs of various sizes (from XS to XL) in the street in downtown Manhattan. He titled the event *The Bliz-aard Ball Sale* (p.141). By assigning value to and appearing to seek profit from an object made of ephemeral material, usually used for play, Hammons's work drew attention to, and parodied, the arbitrary value system of the art market. His action also highlighted the precarious financial conditions of many working-class New Yorkers, and drew attention to the snowballs as a form of 'whiteness' for sale. In his work since the 1970s, Hammons has consistently and deliberately disregarded the given boundaries between spaces for art and everyday life. A few years after making T*he Bliz-aard Ball Sale*, in a rare interview, Hammons detailed his objection to the gallery-visiting public. He asserted that the audience was 'overly educated, it's conservative, it's out to criticise and not to understand, and it never has any fun. Why should I spend my time playing to that audience?'[46]

As well as literally taking his art out into the street, Hammons has shown a long-term commitment to issues of civil rights and the Black Power movement, and his art has consistently sought ways to make societal structures that create oppression visible, as well as commenting on capitalist logics of value. For a show at a gallery called L&M Arts in January 2007, apparently chosen by the artist as an emblem of a particular Upper East Side culture of privilege, Hammons, in collaboration with his wife Chie, draped luxurious fur coats – including mink, sable, chinchilla and fox – on dress dummies, as a display. Upon closer inspection, the coats had, variously, been splattered with coloured paint, or burned through with a blowtorch. *A Brooklyn Rail* journalist described how the gallery assistant insisted that Hammons had said visitors must think of them as 'just paintings', provocatively suggesting that an erasure of the combined slaughter and vandalism on display could remain unquestioned within the formal concerns of 'high art' for sale. Hammons is notorious for refusing to 'play along' with the art world as it is, and his own performance of the role of the artist 'includes a constant flirtation with notions of the illicit and the fraudulent – the ever-present suggestion that the whole business might be a scam.'[47] In his work, and in how he performs his role as an artist, Hammons refuses the given rules of art's game.

One of the most ambitious social performance projects in the past fifty years, and one that also refuses to acknowledge a defined arena for art, confusingly blurring the lines between real politics and representation, is that devised in Slovenia in the early 1980s by a group of artists, musicians and theatre-makers who formed Neue Slowenische Kunst (NSK). Influenced by the late 1960s and early 1970s Slovenian collective OHO Group, who had asserted new forms of exhibition space outside of official art by making interventions in the landscape, NSK moved beyond existing models of institutional critique by constructing a grand, multi-part social institution of their own – a virtual territory as a composite of four different artist collectives as micro-organisations. The group's attitude drew on the member band Laibach, whose industrial rock shows performed an extreme identification with the militarised apparatus of the Yugoslavian state and the lingering threat of the Soviet Bloc. In addition to Laibach, NSK came to comprise three more groups: the painting collective IRWIN, the theatre group Scipion Nasice Sisters and the design group New Collectivism. Their work addressed the social and political situation in Slovenia in the turbulent period leading up to its split from

IRWIN, *Black Square on Red Square*, Moscow, 1992/2004

Yugoslavia in 1991. The group's name is the German translation of 'New Slovenian Art', pointing to its interest in the complex relationship between culture and national identity in Slovenia, given that it has been repeatedly occupied by foreign powers, including Nazi Germany, Fascist Italy and Hungary during the Second World War. Conceived as a form of Gesamtkunstwerk, the work of NSK manifests an evolution of the notion of appropriation in art. In the early 1990s, philosopher Slavoj Žižek characterised their attitude as one of provocative overidentification with the repressed 'obscene superego' of the state, since the group performatively inhabited structures of power – be they gestures of military authority, canonical aesthetics or political propaganda.[48] Using an array of media – from painting to television – NSK reflected upon the construction of the systems they infiltrated or adapted to their purposes. In the early 1990s, NSK evolved further into a 'conceptual territory', a 'state in time', with its own 'passport' and 'embassy', that has thousands of members, or 'citizens', internationally. As a 'state', NSK now exists as a kind of social and political potentiality whose future direction is openly debated by its citizens at regular congress meetings, the first of which was held in Berlin in 2010.

In quite a different spirit, but in parallel, the all-women group the Neo Naturists (Christine and Jennifer Binnie, and Wilma Johnson) emerged in the UK in the 1980s from a post-punk, New Romantic subculture that included artists such as Leigh Bowery, Michael Clark, John Maybury, Grayson Perry and Cerith Wyn Evans.

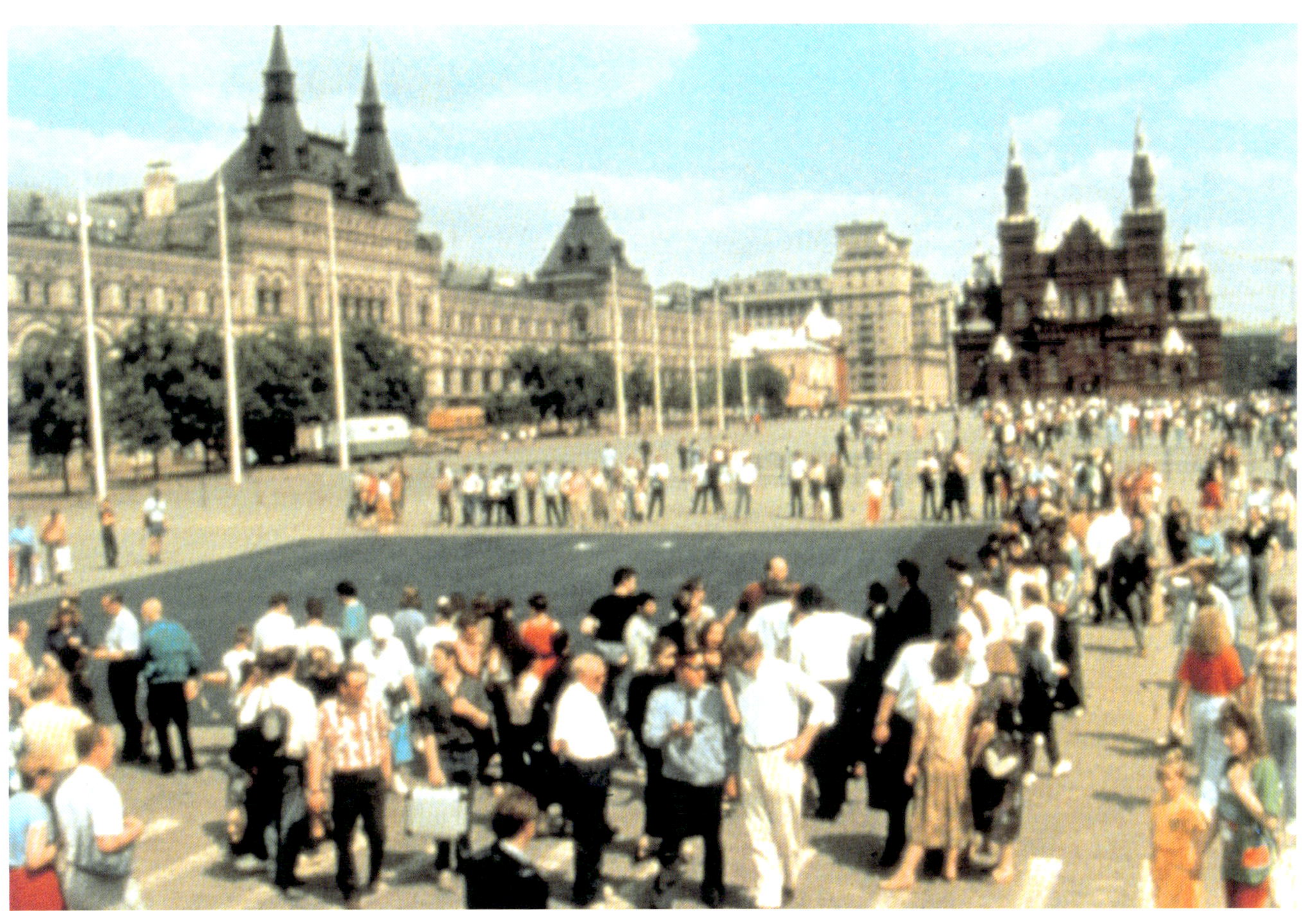

The Neo Naturists came from backgrounds in ceramics and painting, but shared a desire to resituate visual art in a ritualised, lived context, and to reclaim painting from a feminist perspective. Reacting against the abstract expressionist style that was still prevalent among tutors at Central Saint Martins in London (where Johnson studied), they proposed their own bodies as canvases for a primal form of painting, drawing upon English paganism and the use of blue woad pigment as body paint in Roman Britain, as well as the decorative, applied painting of the English modernists, such as the Bloomsbury Group at Charleston Farmhouse in Sussex. In their performances in nightclubs such as the Blitz club and the Fridge, as well as in the street, the Neo Naturists proposed the female body as a voluptuous form to be celebrated and decorated, nude. For *Flashing in the British Museum* 1982, the artists made unannounced appearances, temporarily uncovered from their fur coats, among the Egyptian statuary in the British Museum's galleries. *Sexist Crabs*, debuting at the Zap club in Brighton in 1983, involved the artists combining body-painting with costumes made of real seafood (crabs, clams and squid) and the giving out of food as a form of quasi-communion. The dancer Michael Clark invited the artists to perform with him at his first production in Riverside Studios in London and for this iteration of *Sexist Crabs* 'the group painted scales onto their legs and sellotaped themselves together, transforming themselves into mermaids', while 'Clark danced around them with prawns stuffed into his fishnet tights'.[49] While the idea of self-transformation using make-up had been common among feminist and queer artists since the 1970s, appearing as a collective gave the Neo Naturists the confidence to assert this bold approach to painting and their live, naked bodies publicly.[50]

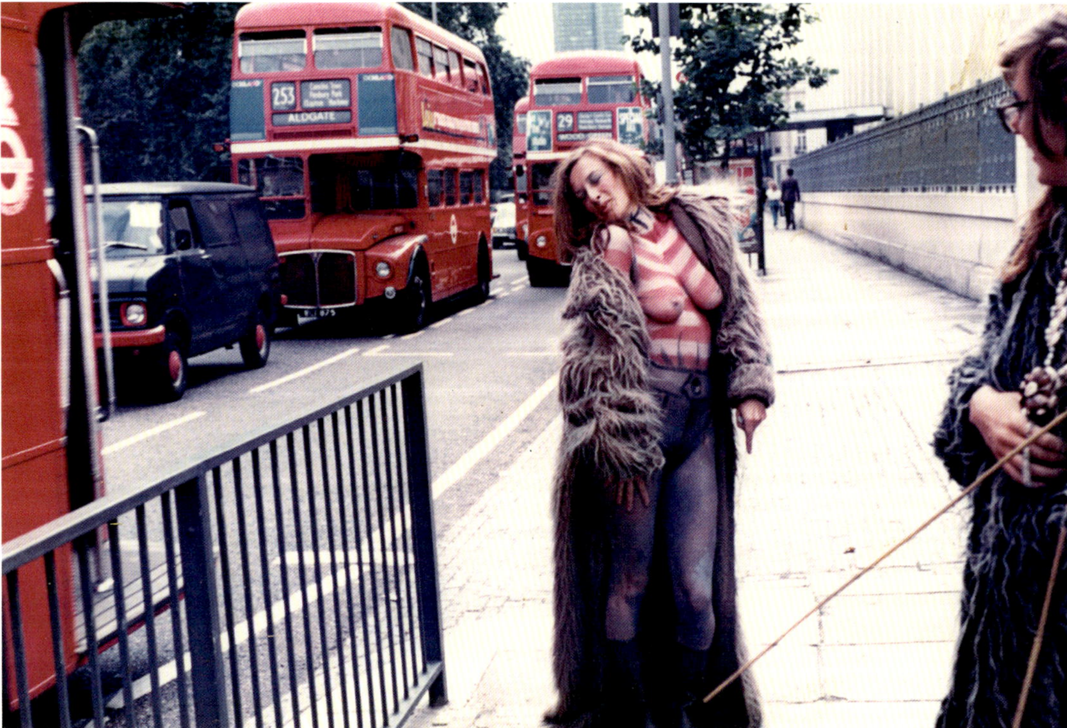

Neo Naturists, *Swimming and Walking Experiment*, Centre Point Fountains, Tottenham Court Road, London, August 1984

Francis Alÿs, *When Faith Moves Mountains* 2002, Lima; in collaboration with Cuauhtémoc Medina and Rafael Ortega, video 36 min., and photographic documentation of an action

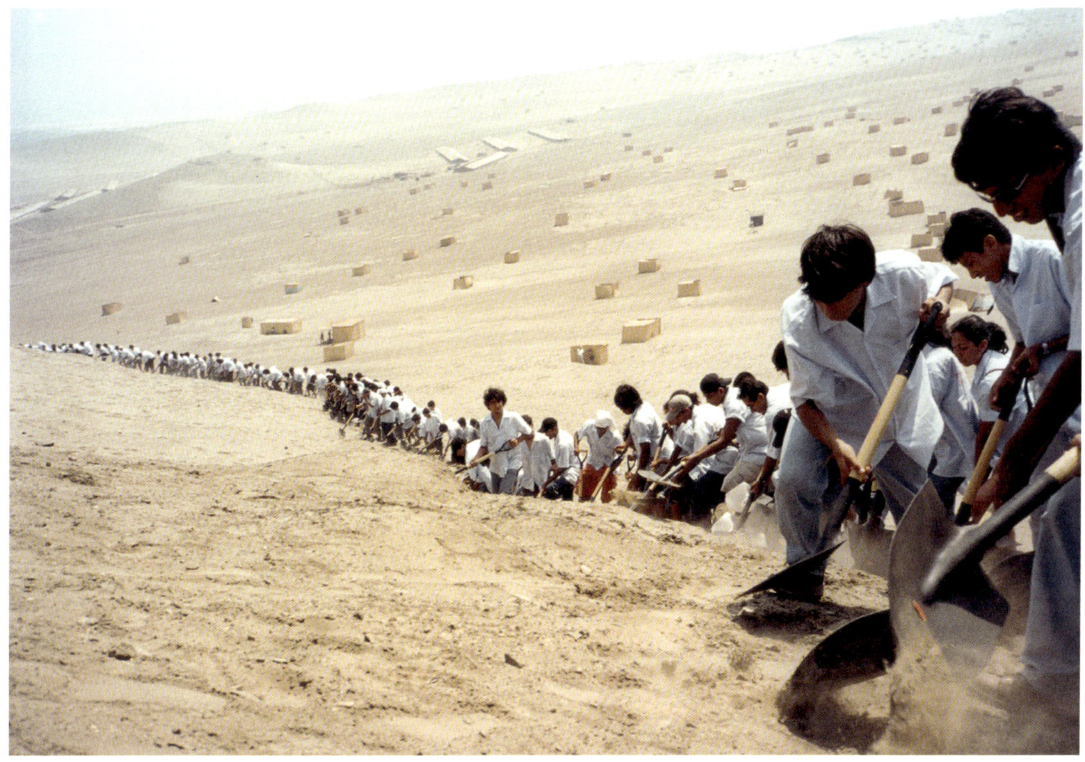

Contemporary

Situations

In the consumption-driven twenty-first century, Tino Sehgal's insistence on the objectlessness of his work appears to be utopian: replacing the fetishised material thing with so-called immaterial movement; purging aesthetic experience of stuff in favour of pure doing, being and saying. How does performance's emphasis on sociality tie in with today's experience economy? How does this work both sculpt and exploit social relations, or dramatise a state of alienation?

The live quality of Sehgal's work rests on the fact that we are invited to interact and exchange with his enactors. But, as viewers, our understanding of the controlled nature of his part-scripted, part-improvised dialogues becomes increasingly heightened as the conversation unfolds. There is a sense, when engaging in *These Associations*, that the enactor and I are almost touching, breathing the same air, and yet separated by the stylised nature of my interlocutor's scored behaviour. Sehgal's work addresses the viewer individually, but its effect, and affect, instigate a far from feel-good relationality. When the enactors talk to us, tell us stories, trade intimacy, history or confession, we experience them without dissolving ourselves into the suspended disbelief that we would take to a theatre play. Rather, we are self-conscious of being in an artwork, and we feel ourselves somehow solidify into an object, too, within this exchange. It is our own subjectivity that is also on display.

The action staged in Francis Alÿs's *When Faith Moves Mountains* 2002 might be linked more directly to the Beuysian idea of social sculpture, but it adapts this for the media age. Alÿs created a spectacular choreography of some five hundred volunteer participants, dressed in matching white shirts, who took shovels and literally moved the peak of a sand dune, located outside Lima, by several centimetres. The project's actual movement of earth was a feat, and it was documented in photographs and video. But the artist was specifically interested in its legacy as a rumour – a collective action founded upon belief rather than its material efficacy, which remained elusive.

As Alÿs often put it, his intention was to create a 'social allegory'.[51] For the artist, such a collaborative act is a metaphor for the capacity of participative action to take on mythical and even religious features in its heroic confrontation with the monumentality of nature. The work is about the power of collective action to alter nature, and yet, at the same time, it represents an ephemeral and senseless gesture. The movement of ten centimetres of sand on a dune that is two hundred metres wide is not perceptible in reality. But it is the participants' investment in collaborating on this work, rather than the result, that the piece documents. Alÿs's action was intended as a kind of myth that would be transmitted between people over time and across distance. The titular question of faith – both among the participants, and in the idea that this myth might inspire it – is the real subject of the work.

Zhang Huan's later work with collective action, such as *To Raise the Water Level in a Fish Pond* 1997, is related in spirit to Alÿs's action. The piece involved a group of about forty migrant workers standing still, spread out across the diameter of

Zhang Huan, *To Raise the Water Level in a Fishpond* 1997, performance, Beijing

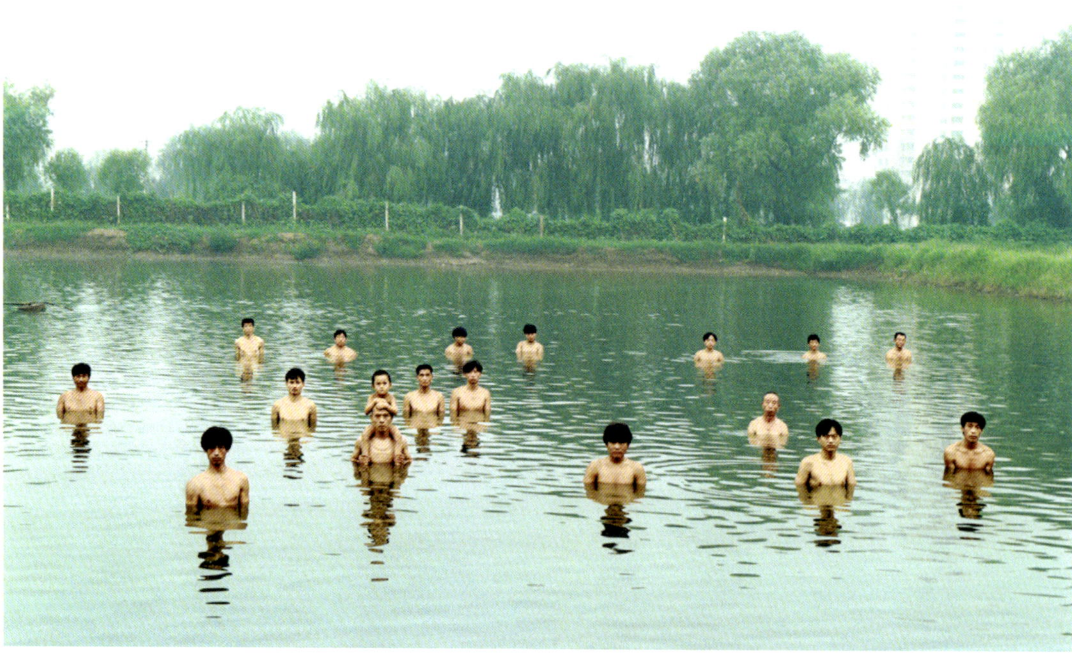

a large pond, in order to create a slight rise in the surface level of the water. The artist notes the symbolic associations of the landscape setting in this seemingly arbitrary action: 'In the Chinese tradition, fish is the symbol of sex while water is the source of life. This work expresses, in fact, one kind of understanding and explanation of water. That the water in the pond was raised one metre higher is an action of no avail.'[52] Typical of Zhang's later work, instead of focusing on masochism and pain as a register of brutal reality, this piece considers the capacity of collective action to change it, even in this apparently purposeless action.

Kateřina Šedá has also initiated actions that give shape to forms of collectivity. In her long-term project *For Every Dog a Different Master* 2007, Šedá sent packages to tenants of a large housing estate in her hometown – Brno, in the Czech Republic – which appeared to come from neighbouring tenants, whom the artist had secretly paired. She then organised a social event so that they could meet, stimulating the creation of new relationships among approximately two hundred, previously anonymous neighbours, most of whom had been displaced to modern housing from smaller villages. In her subsequent work, *Over and Over* 2008, Šedá spent months approaching and negotiating with members of each household in Brno to ask them to build steps going over their garden fence so that she could run through their properties in an uninterrupted circle she had plotted through the neighbourhood, documenting the process with a video camera.

Šedá brings to life what Andrew Hewitt has defined in terms of social choreography: an aesthetic practice that can actively intervene in the ways that people relate and interact with each other.[53] Looking at social dance history from the waltz onwards, Hewitt argues that dance is an art form that is neither simply mimetic nor just decorative, but most intricately woven into the ideology of society itself insofar as it represents forms and enacts them at the same time. In other words, its doubling up as representation and participation has played a key part in bringing new social patterns into being, rather than merely displaying them. The significance of Hewitt's observations extend beyond dance itself, applying to more pedestrian aspects of social choreography. It is often these apparently ordinary patterns of interaction and behaviour that artists have manipulated in order to initiate alternative encounters between participants in their work.

Chinese artist and activist Ai Weiwei's project for Documenta 12 in Kassel, *Fairytale* 2007, is perhaps the grandest example yet of a tendency in the past decade to envisage large-scale, utopian projects involving the participation of a mass of people – either as performers or witnesses, or both simultaneously (p.148). Though it was a 'live' work, it is not entirely appropriate to label this work as a performance. The participants in the project – the 1,001 Chinese people that Ai Weiwei arranged to travel to Kassel, and for whom he provided food, lodging and free passes to the exhibition – were never 'on show' for the exhibition audience, although they may have been glimpsed going about their daily business by the people of Kassel and the art tourists alike, who might even have enjoyed chance encounters with them. In this respect, the dynamics of spectatorship relating to the traditional artwork were inherently – and necessarily, from social and ethical points of view – challenged. As visitors to Documenta, the 'work' was more or less beyond our grasp altogether. Or rather, to grasp it one had to change one's expectations and open one's mind.

On one level, in this piece Ai Weiwei created a spectacular, panoramic image: the mental image of 1,001 Chinese visitors arriving in Kassel at once. On another level, *Fairytale* creates a unique experience for each of the individual participants: it creates opportunity, arguably, as well as opening up a dramatic shift in perspective. But these aspects of the work deal with 'us' (as viewers) and 'them' (as participants) and not with what such grand gestures or actions signify within the field of art. Do we see these projects, after Beuys, as grand new forms of social sculpture orchestrated by a central shaman-like artist figure? Or does such an approach speak of more problematic notions – especially for an artist working in post-communist conditions, such as Ai Weiwei – of 'social organisation' and 'social engineering', albeit put to the service of a fantasy or a dream? What are the dynamics of performing here? Does Ai's action activate a performative awareness of Documenta's meta-structure, more than it being about individuals presenting the 'doing' of something?

Like Šedá and others, Ai works in what sociologist Pierre Bourdieu described as the 'social field', that is, a structured social space with its own rules, power balances, legitimacy and so on: a space in which human agents act.[54] These artists' projects stir up the potential energy that is latent but settled into habit within a specific social field (the European art world) by cross-contaminating it with other spheres. Ai's work, in particular, uses the cultural and financial capital afforded to him by the art field, which reportedly enabled him to raise three million euros, in order to disturb the apparently settled nature of other social fields within different regions of China, within the arena of art-world tourism and within the town of Kassel: in other words, to enable people who may never have been able

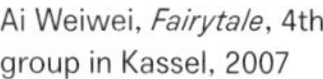
Ai Weiwei, *Fairytale*, 4th group in Kassel, 2007

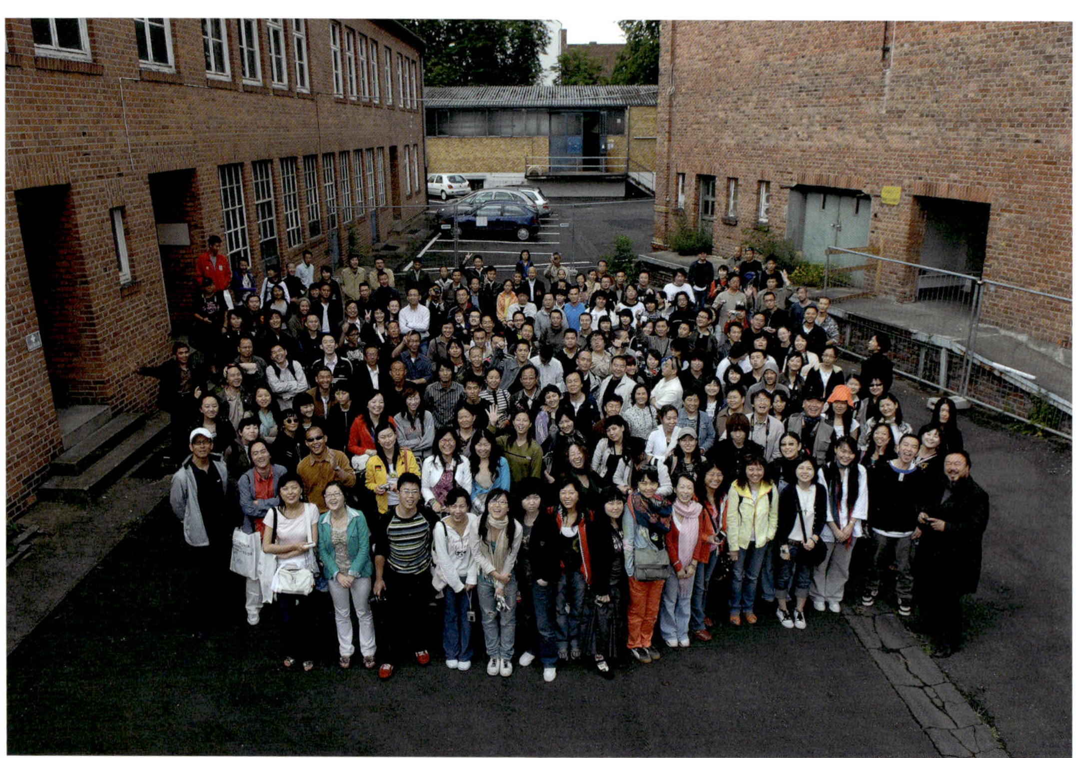

to travel from their own region within China, let alone across the world to Europe, to come to Documenta. And similarly, to initiate the temporary migration of a new community into the German city.[55]

Ai Weiwei was vocal in condemning the 2008 Beijing Olympics opening ceremony, with its massed performance of perfectly synchronised, uniform citizens.[56] He understands perhaps, too, that this is part of what a Western audience expects of China. In contrast, in *Fairytale*, the mass of people signifies a latent potentiality for action: a new social base with a transnational sense of mobility and possibility (even if, in practice, they were subjected to the customary border controls). Like NSK's 'state in time', this artwork opens up the capacity for a new kind of citizen of the world to exist, temporarily, between states and ideologies, in an interval in which no particular kind of behaviour or action is expected. By cross-contaminating and disturbing the common beliefs of the social fields that the work touches upon, it creates a new kind of common humanity that registers, if only perhaps for a fraction of time, the potential to not be determined by given circumstances – to exist within the pause between these states; just to be. The question, however, remains as to whether this fantasy takes us back to a notion of authenticity in the pause between identities; an identity unmarked by society.

Collectives and networks after the internet

I have explored the legacy of Joseph Beuys's social sculpture in fairly concrete terms: the idea of people doing things together in real space and time. But the dominant characteristic of the contemporary field, socially and artistically, is that of our increased connectivity. Being networked online has shifted our understanding of what being a collective might mean – both for art and for politics, as witnessed in the 2010 so-called Arab Spring uprisings in the Middle East that were facilitated by social media. Online collaboration has also opened up new collective formats for direct action ('clicktivism', as it has been referred to). The line between activism and critical experimentation has been productively blurred by a number of artist groups in the past decade.

The collective Chto Delat (Russian for 'What is to be done?') was founded in 2003 in St Petersburg by a group of artists, critics, philosophers and writers based in Russia, with a shared interest in self-education and self-organisation. Their aim was to combine research, political theory, art and activism to look back on socialism and to consider its present and future. The name of the group is taken from the title of a late nineteenth-century novel by the writer Nikolay Chernyshevsky, and is intended to bring to mind the first self-organised socialist workers' groups in Russia, instigated by Lenin after the publication of his pamphlet of the same title in 1902. Taking a term commonly used for online activity, Chto Delat sees itself as 'a self-organised platform for a variety of cultural activities intent on politicising "knowledge production" through redefinitions of an engaged autonomy for cultural practice today'.[57]

In the video *Builders* 2005 (p.151), one of their earliest works, the artists created a performative re-staging of a well-known Soviet painting – Viktor Popkov's *Builders of Bratsk* 1960–1 – in which four men and one woman take a break from

a break from their labour: a depiction of idealised work typical of social realism. The figures are portrayed from a low angle, appearing strong and dominant, against the backdrop of an industrial town. In the video, the artists in Chto Delat re-stage this static pose to create a sequence of still photographs that begin with a similar set-up, but progress as a kind of *photo-roman* sequence, set to a voice-over dialogue that discusses the meaning of labour and community in today's post-communist reality.

Critic Agata Pyzik argues that Chto Delat 'treats history like a living organism, not a fossil, in order to take on old conflicts that are still toxic in the present'. She highlights their use of re-enactments to bring the past to bear on the present, in works such as *Activist Club* 2007: 'a temporary space that relived the experience both of Alexander Rodchenko's Worker's Club (1925) and of the widespread self-organising workers' clubs of Soviet Russia'.[58] The group also publishes a bilingual English and Russian newspaper on activist issues, setting Russian culture and politics in an international context. A potential paradox within the group's agitational stance lies in the fact that political difficulties and complete lack of institutional support in Russia makes Chto Delat dependent on the international art scene and its grants: using frameworks offered by the art world, their newspapers and actions are usually produced in the context of exhibitions and conferences taking place outside Russia. Still, their approach has set an important template for the merging of art and activism in an international context in the past decade.

Mumbai-based group CAMP – an acronym for Critical Art and Media Practice – describes itself not as an artist collective but as a 'collaborative studio'. Founded in 2007 by Shaina Anand, Sanjay Bhangar and Ashok Sukumaran, the group often creates analogue artworks that draw upon the spirit of open-source communities on the internet. Working with people involved in various infrastructures, including the provision of water, electricity, cable TV and the internet, CAMP have developed temporary TV and radio stations, websites and annotated film archives. An early project working with electrical circuits as social metaphors involved setting up an electrical switch in the street outside their studio, its supply drawn from an apartment above. The public was able to flick the switch to activate lights up in the building block, and the electrical supply was also shared by an ice-cream vendor in the street. As a collaborative studio, CAMP attempts to open up new democratic spaces for art production, thinking outside of common binaries that separate art from non-art, commodities from so-called free culture, or individuals from institutions. The artists state that they wish to find ways of working that test the boundaries between private and public ownership, and to reconsider who has power to act within the world. They actively engage with questions around infrastructure in terms of drawing attention to its tools and materials. According to the group, 'this means working directly with such things as electricity, transport, trade, archives, video, radio and the internet; developing ways to think about these as integrated with human life, and beyond the "network" as thought-model'. This also entails re-thinking channels of distribution and, quite simply, being 'hospitable to ideas and to people'.[59]

Also working with the idea of the online network and its anonymity, but taking it in a radically different direction, Goldin+Senneby describe themselves as a 'framework for collaboration', set up by artists Simon Goldin and Jakob Senneby in 2004.[60] The artists use the performative space of virtuality, and the permission it affords, to explore legal, economic and spatial constructions from a critical point of view, using a complex form of fabulation. In their body of work titled

Chto Delat, *Builders* 2005
video, colour, sound,
8 min. 16 sec.

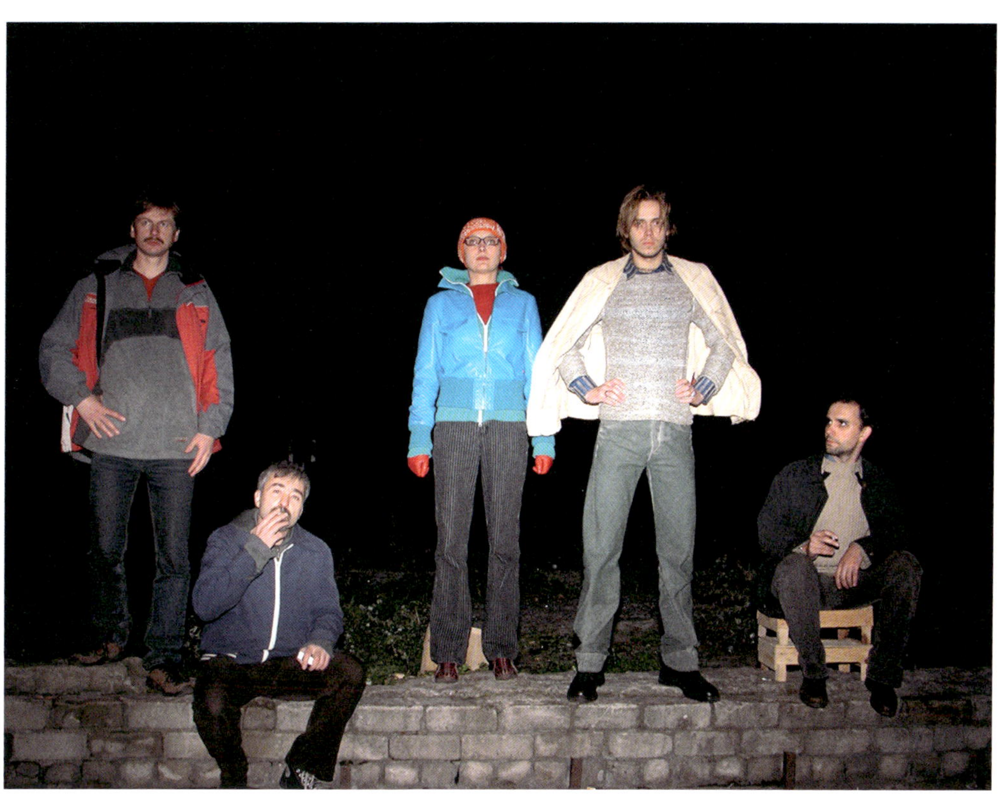

Ashok Sukumaran (CAMP),
Glow Positioning System,
Mumbai, 2005

Headless, begun in 2007, Goldin+Senneby have looked at the sphere of offshore finance, and how it produces virtual space through loops in legislation. For this work, the artists identified and traced an offshore company based in the Bahamas, called Headless Ltd, and examined the peculiar loophole status of this kind of post-colonial tax haven, and the potential for invisibility and withdrawal from social norms that it implies. They have used this company, extrapolating from it in fictional ways, as the basis for an ongoing speculative exploration of the mechanics of narrative. Goldin+Senneby mimic and perform corporate strategies on this fictional construction, effecting a doubling of the immaterial content and form of the work.

Typical of their approach to outsourcing artistic labour, they employed a detective to find out more about Headless Ltd and commissioned a ghost-written detective novel, which is used as a vehicle for narrating their investigations. When they are invited to participate in public programmes, they arrange for an actor to do staged readings of the novel, posing as its author, while a spokesperson conducts interviews on their behalf. For their exhibition at the Power Plant in Toronto in 2008, Goldin+Senneby even commissioned documentary filmmakers to interview an investigative journalist about how to make a documentary about investigating Headless Ltd, and hired a curator and a set designer to devise a didactic display introducing viewers to the characters of the novel *Looking for Headless*.[61] In these ways, the artists play with the logic of the virtual in the real world – whether the status of the avatar, here substituted with an actor in real time, or the loops in legal and digital code that permit fictional transgressions with real effects. At the same time, *Headless* represents a model of anti-social or anti-relational practice: a flat continuum of information that is being shaped by different interests, but without an apparent singular driver or lead.

Interventions

If these artists draw attention to social and virtual networks, and create images thereof, others turn to the kind of social performance initiated by Augusto Boal, which highlights the existing *mise en scène* of the social fabric in which it is embedded. Slovakian artist Roman Ondak's work investigates social codes, conventions, rituals and forms of exchange, in an effort to stimulate the collective imagination. He has created simple group exercises in which participants mark their respective heights on the gallery wall (*Measuring the Universe* 2007) or trade personal objects on a display plinth (*Swap* 2011) in order to create forms of comparative, collective portraiture. But he also makes more stealthy interventions into given situations.

Good Feelings in Good Times 2003 is an artificially created queue that is intended to be staged inside the museum, but can also be adapted to other spaces. The enacted queue moves around the environment in which it is staged, but is deliberately placed somewhere where it would make sense for a queue to form, or where it might almost appear to make sense but not quite, exaggerating its absurd effect. The length of the queue varies, but obeys precise rules, which state that it can be enacted indoors by a minimum of seven and a maximum of twelve people, or outdoors with a maximum of fifteen people. Participants in *Good Feelings in Good Times* are either volunteers or actors hired by the museum. A variety of people are recruited for the piece but there are no specific restrictions

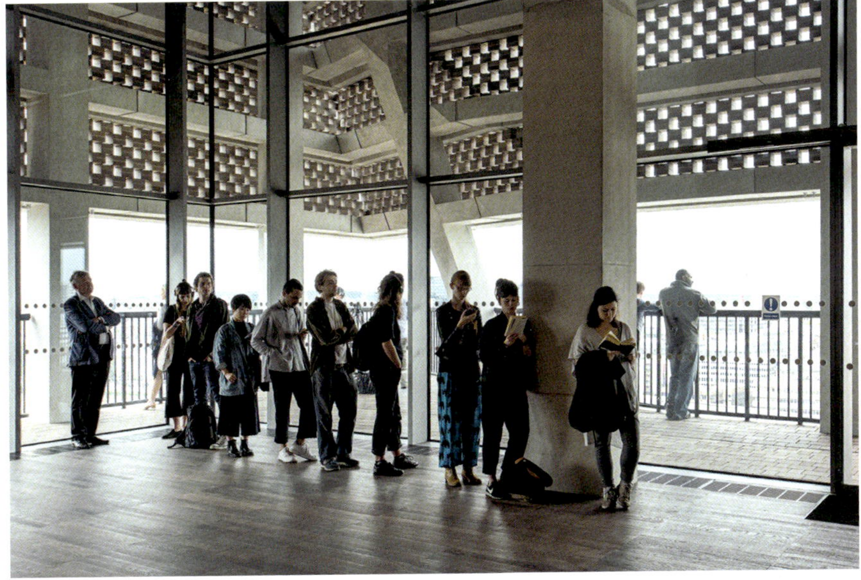

Roman Ondak, *Good Feelings in Good Times* 2003, Tate Modern, 17 June – 3 July 2016

on age or gender, and there is no costume as such; they are only required to dress in a way that will assimilate to the ordinary context of the work, and to hold props (such as a newspaper, or a walking stick) that might be typical of people waiting in a queue. If questioned by onlookers, the enactors – like those in Tino Sehgal's work – are requested not to divulge anything about the performance; they are instead encouraged to improvise as if they were in a real-life situation. Inspired by the artist's own memories of the long lines formed outside grocery shops in his native Slovakia during the communist era, the queue takes on different connotations in different contexts. The artist plants it as prompt to interaction or altered behaviour (people join the queue, observe and query what the queue is for, or simply avoid it), but also to point to the social choreography of the museum at large – a kind of frill of ordinary behaviour inserted decoratively. Ondak is also interested in what happens psychologically when we are waiting to see something, especially within a museum space geared to the idea of looking at and encountering art. He has said, 'On your own you think about your time – what I call "real time" – which has its own value; but when you go in the queue, you slow down and the time is different.'[62] This collective sharing of apparent non-experience might in fact offer a subtle form of enhanced contemplation.

The Finnish artist Pilvi Takala has also made work looking at the values that are shared by participants within different social and institutional structures, but unlike Ondak she works outside art institutions, by embedding herself within everyday situations as a rogue participant. She has, variously, infiltrated and performed within the contexts of a boarding school (*Drive with Care* 2013); the European Parliament (*Broad Sense* 2011); a Finnish dancing club (*Wallflower* 2006); and a shop (*The Angels* 2008), where she performed 'acts of kindness' that – being unprompted – look suspicious. In the performance *The Real Snow White* 2000, staged at Disneyland Paris, Takala documents the process by which she is barred from going into the park dressed as Snow White, because the children might think she is the 'real' Snow White (p.154). The guard tells her that she cannot dress like this, as an adult, because she might be going in to 'do something bad'. If she is in

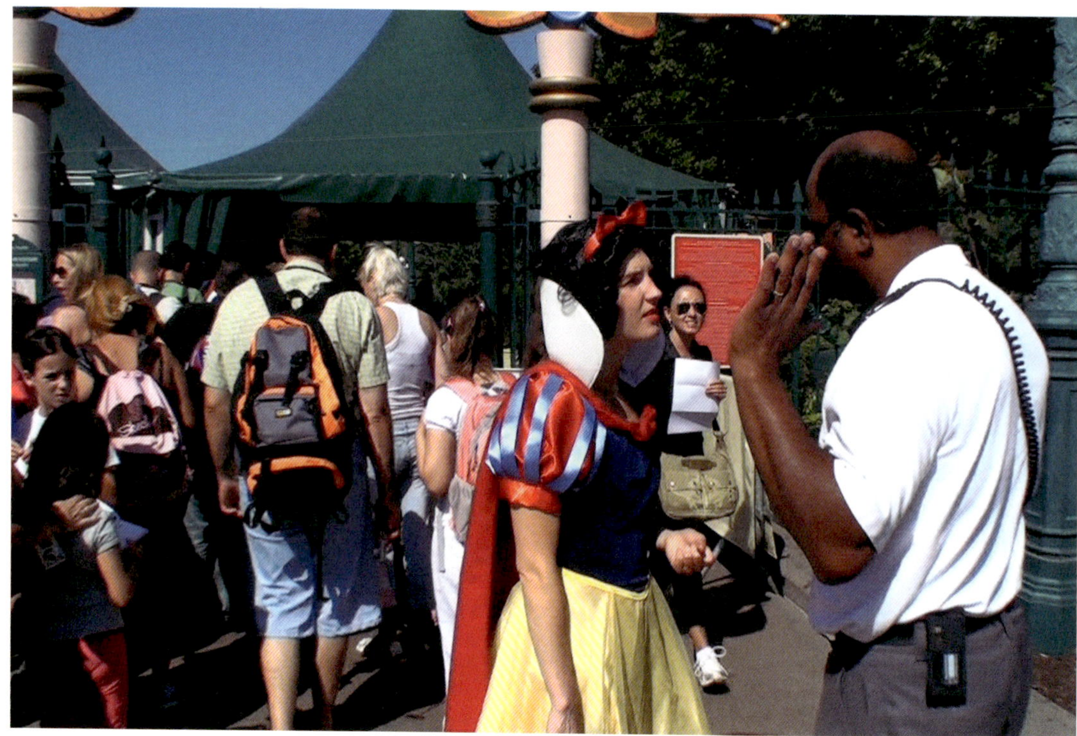

Pilvi Takala, *Real Snow White* 2009, video still

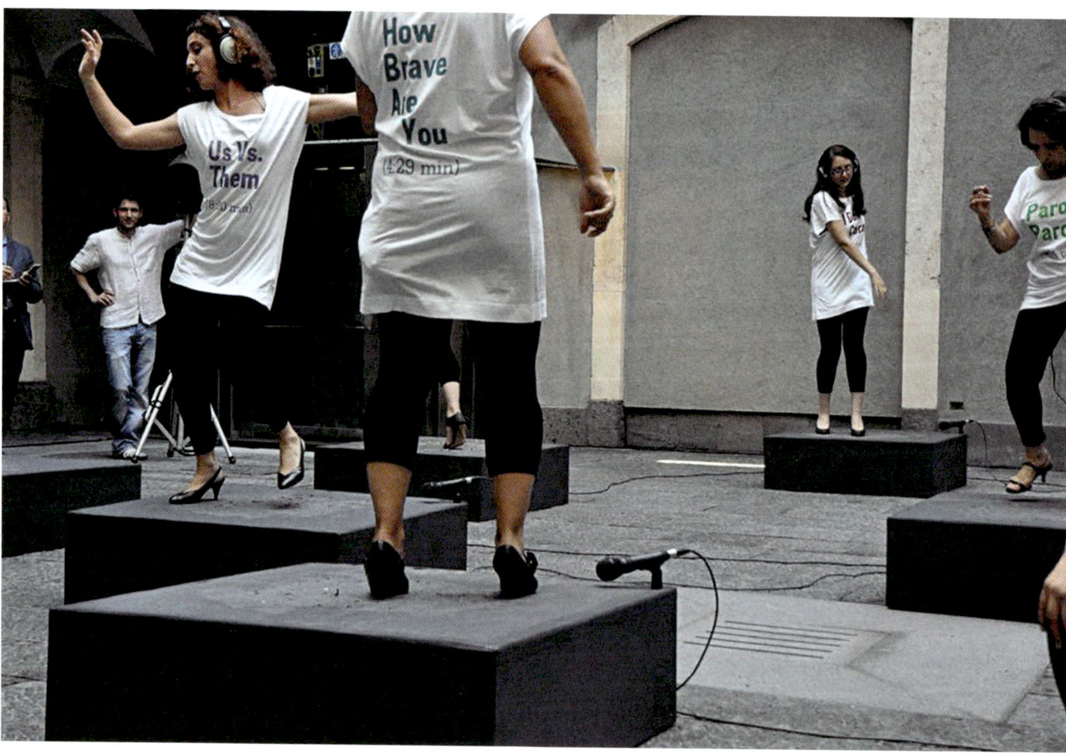

Nevin Aladağ, *Raise The Roof (Catania)* 2010. Others, Palazzo Valle, Catania 2010, 8 min. 30 sec.

costume, she becomes continuous with the cartoon environment of Disney: to appear as part of it, her behaviour must be regulated in accordance with Disney policy, so that the children can interact freely with her in 'Disney Realness' without there being a rupture (of wrong behaviour, or bad behaviour). At one point the guard tells her 'there is a real Snow White in the park'. In Takala's work, as in Andrea Fraser's, the artist does not perform as herself but assumes a character in order to call attention to the social norms within her chosen environment. Her embedded masquerade critically comments on the codes of a given environment and what is at stake in accepting its rules, exposing the degree to which participation in social structures relies on a suspension of disbelief.

Nevin Aladağ works with performance and film to explore social environments and issues of cultural translation, or mistranslation. Aladağ draws upon her experiences of growing up in Germany, as a person with Turkish and Kurdish origins, and becoming highly conscious of cultural differences and implicit hierarchies. In her performance *Raise the Roof* 2007, which is documented on video, a group of women dance on top of an industrial building situated on the former border between East and West Berlin. Each woman listens to music on her own headphones, and wears stiletto heels which form a kind of percussion as they punch holes in and tear up the tarmac roofing. The rooftop had once been part of a patrol route for GDR soldiers, and Aladağ reimagines an echo of their marching boots in the sound born of this surreal action, which for the artist represents the women 'tearing through their limits',[63] and transforming the urban landscape, in the process, into a stage for action.

Non-professional dancers also perform in Aladağ's *Occupation* series 2009–ongoing. At exhibition openings, the artist plants performers passing for ordinary visitors, who, one by one, begin to sway and dance. The instigation of this action nudges others, and, with a sense of permission lent by those who are dancing, even those who are not part of the artist's planted action begin to dance: its first iteration was in 2009 at Berlin's Temporäre Kunsthalle, where forty dancers were planted, with infectious results for the gathering's mood. In different ways, these artists both instigate and frame social behaviours, the work operating from an embedded position inside the scene that is brought to visibility.

Entertainment as readymade

In a visual art context, distinct from a theatre, the fact that there aren't set positions for performers and audiences lends a distinct freedom to the process of making performance (albeit a freedom tempered by lack of infrastructure and equipment!). In an extension of the conceptual gesture effected by the Duchampian readymade, contemporary performance also opens up the possibility of cannibalising other disciplinary formats and social institutions, whether theatre, sport or entertainment. This means that if its conceptual standpoint is not made explicit, art performance can look like something else in another discipline. One of the most famous examples of this within the relational tendency of the 1990s was Thai artist Rirkrit Tiravanija's appropriation of cooking, as he would often prepare a meal inside the gallery space and share it with visitors. The idea of a shared meal as artwork has a representational precedent in Judy Chicago's *The Dinner Party* 1974–9, in which thirty-nine place settings were arranged around a triangular table, each dedicated to a famous woman, either mythical or historical, though no actual food was prepared or consumed. Tiravanija's straightforward approach to cooking and sharing food – sometimes within the context of his reconstructed apartment, as was the case of an exhibition at Gavin Brown's Enterprise in New York in 1999 – was radical in its displacement of such a primary activity into the gallery, without apparent aesthetic transformation.

Ei Arakawa's work, discussed in the introduction, often borrows from entertainment culture, whether the nightclub, the musical or the holiday resort, to create participatory events or share stories. Though collaborative, the artist himself often acts as a catalyst. In one sense, the events he instigates derive from the immediacy and provisional structure of 1960s happenings. Yet Arakawa's approach is emblematic of a generation of artists who create hybrid scenarios merging cultural forms and reinventing their mood. Alongside appropriating the nightclub format of a singles event, he has staged performances and talks within a bar (titled *Stonewall*, after one of his invited speakers, who had participated in the Stonewall riot of 1969), and organised a ritualised procession within the 'free', though highly formal, outdoor space of Regent's Park during Frieze Art Fair. These are sites on the cusp of high culture and abject pickup scenes, charged political histories and shopping-mall ennui.

Arakawa's collaborative situations might be linked in form and in strategy to the way in which postwar Japanese performance – both Gutai and Jikken Kōbō – contested the notion of a core individual interiority in favour of exploring the dispersed agency of the group. For Arakawa, coming from this fundamentally collaborative approach, any authentic claim to a unified interior self seems, if not impossible, then largely irrelevant. Arakawa appears to be enacting an understanding of the self that cannot stand alone, one that is irrevocably tied to new forms of collectivity. Naming a significant tendency for the networked contemporary generation, the New York-based artist has said that he approaches the conception of the subject 'from the outside'. He sees his work as building 'a kind of architecture of subjectivity that is externalised, but also has a fictional capacity'.[64] Japanese curator Yuko Hasegawa asserts that while emphasis on individuality has always been less important within Japanese culture, a young generation of Japanese artists, after the Fukushima incident in 2011, to which Arakawa is also linked, are increasingly interested in forms of communal work and activism.[65]

Israeli born artist Keren Cytter's practice consistently involves working with other people: her films and theatre pieces are made with multiple actors, and she stages relationships, conversations and choreographies in the work. But she explores how individual vision meets collective production: her interest is in representing group dynamics, according to a script written by her, rather than experimenting with others in the process of making the work. *History in the Making, or the Secret Diaries of Linda Schultz* 2009, for example, is an hour-long take on the idea of total theatre that combines spoken text with a variety of gestures, movements and music. The actors' performances range from mime to a rudimentary form of sign language, to a semblance of contemporary choreography, with bursts of pure dance-entertainment thrown in. The piece is set to a pleasing electronic score composed by the artist.

In Cytter's film work, the authentically imperfect detail of her found settings and the ready-made cast, drawn from her circle of friends, exaggerate the provisional quality of her productions. But transposed into theatre, that verisimilitude is outed

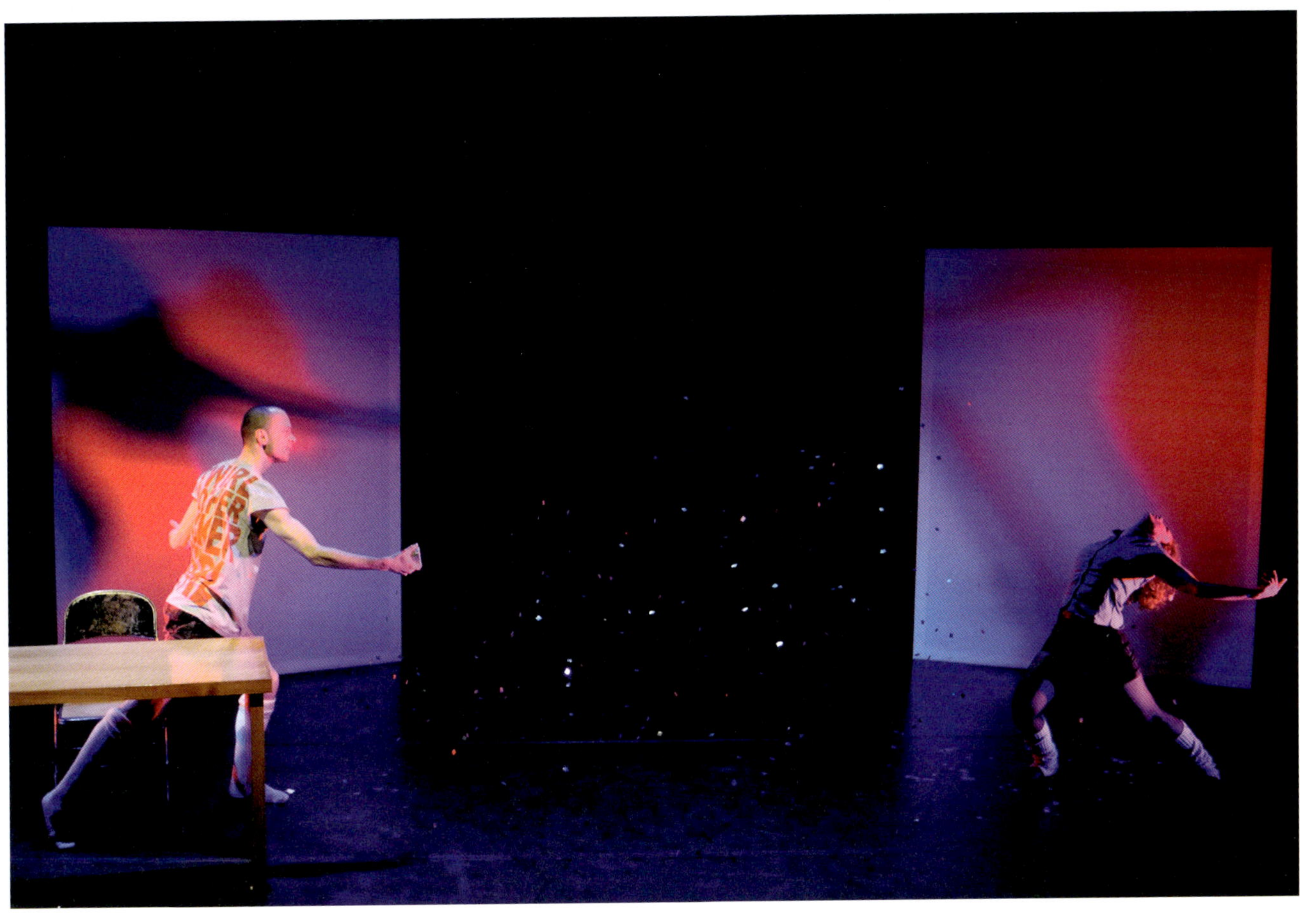

Keren Cytter & D.I.E. Now, *The True Story Of John Webber And His Endless Struggle With The Table Of Content*, 19 and 20 March 2010, Plaza Futura Theatre in collaboration with the Van Abbemuseum, Eindhoven; commissioned by If I Can't Dance, I Don't Want To Be Part of Your Revolution, Amsterdam; produced with Hebbel am Ufer, Berlin, Performa, New York, and Tate Modern, London

as a form of masquerade. Even the moment when one of the actors messes up, as he appears to stumble with his lines and apologises for having to start again, turns out to be obviously scripted. Process is seemingly revealed, but in fact it has all been planned beforehand. In *History in the Making*, Cytter uses the necessarily artificial frame of theatre to depict a world in which there is no longer any authentic sense of private, inner self. Behaviour is everything. The revolution that occurs in the work's story – in which everybody changes gender – exaggerates this proposition. In conflating the acting onstage with this gender switch via a suspension of disbelief, Cytter projects an absurdist literalisation of Judith Butler's ideas about performativity and gender construction.

This is so much the case that her making of dance appears rather as dance in parentheses. It's somehow an idea of dance that is deliberately acted out, set within an *idea* of theatre. Both are treated as exotic clichés, with a heightened sense of their irrelevance. Indeed, the slight gap between speech and gesture that Cytter's work often incorporates lends her live production an echoing quality, as though the whole thing were a fantasised scenario played out in someone's head. Cytter is a prolific writer, of novels as well as scripts, and that is evident within this thought-led acting out, which points to an extreme self-consciousness. In this

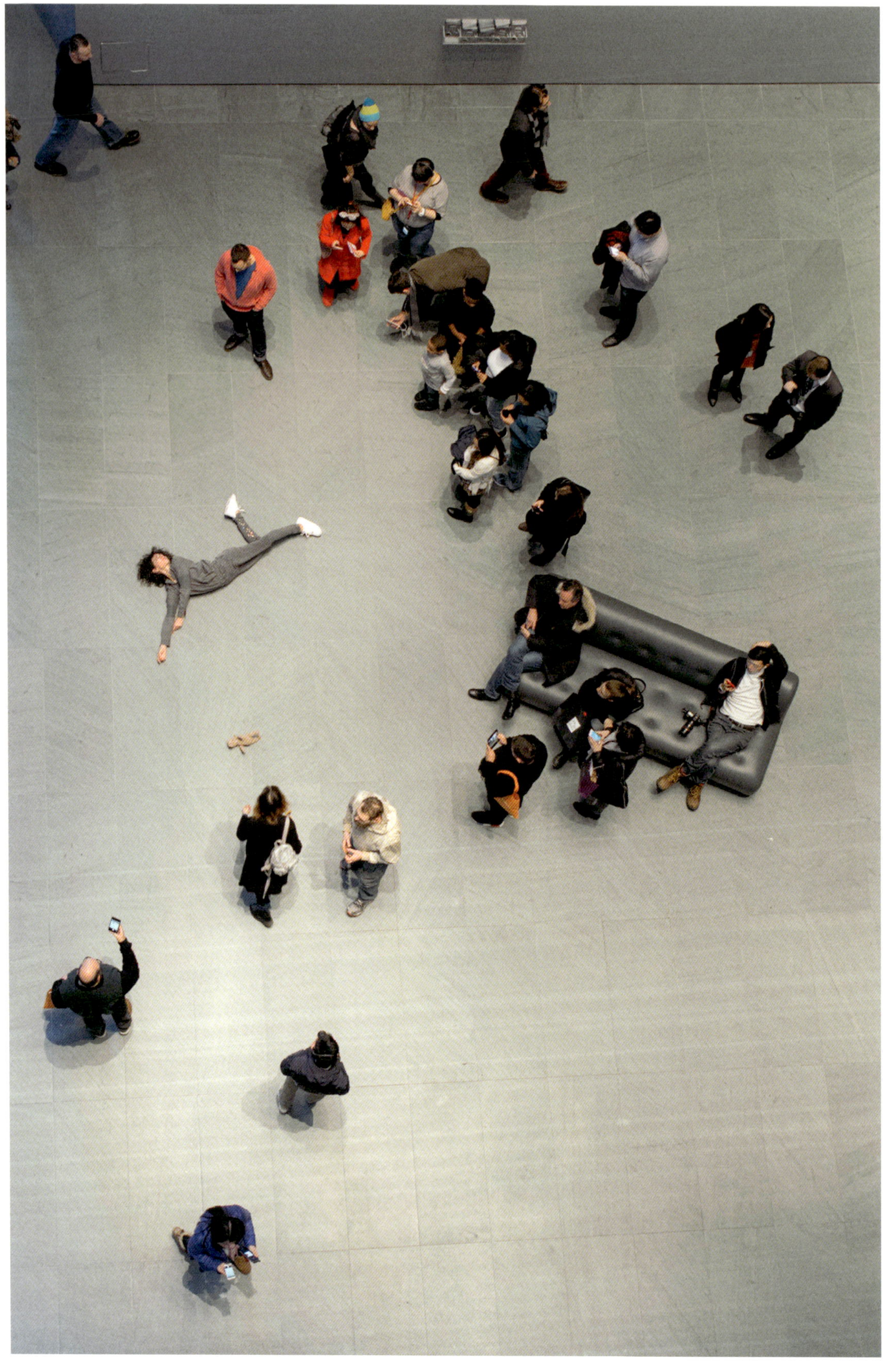

Maria Hassabi, PLASTIC, 2015–16. Installation view, Museum of Modern Art, New York, 21 February – 20 March 2016, performed at The Donald B. and Catherine C. Marron Atrium

sense, Cytter makes visible the paradoxically solipsistic quality of the 'social' in the social media mindset.

Artist and choreographer Maria Hassabi moves between working in theatre and gallery contexts, as well as in public space, underscoring the different protocols of behaviour therein. Her choreographies often have an exaggeratedly slow pace, drawn out with durational poses. For example, her work *Intermission*, presented in the shared Cypriot and Lithuanian pavilion at the Venice Biennale in 2013, involved Hassabi and two other dancers performing continuously to create an ongoing sculptural tableau of sorts, as they moved on and around the stepped sides of an arena-like gym space that was also host to sculpture and installation by other artists, and to visitors walking around, and up and down the steps.

Much of Hassabi's work explores the question of display as it plays out in both exhibitions and theatre, elaborating on the conventions of both formats. Hassabi's *PREMIERE* 2013, for example, addresses the expectations of viewership by foregrounding beginnings and endings in performance-based work. *PREMIERE* staged the seated audience's state of passive attention against the spectacle of five dancers performing a slowly rotating turn. This could be seen as an excruciatingly slowed-down version of Yvonne Rainer's task-like activity: the length of the work – 83 minutes – was determined by the time it took the performers to turn 180 degrees so as to face the audience, creating an elongated ritual of observance and revelation that fetishises the roles of performers and viewers to an absurd degree. In this performance, Hassabi also emphasises the lighting, which becomes very present as a material, almost a body in itself: both heating and showing, then hiding, what is happening onstage, and also marking a transition from the working-out space of the studio to the exposure onstage, from process to product. Hassabi observes: 'what I'm dealing with in *PREMIERE* is ... what the expectation of a work of art is'.[66]

In 2015, Hassabi made a performance for the Hammer Museum in Los Angeles, which responded to the relaxed conventions of display of the gallery context, in comparison with those within the performing arts. In the ensuing work, *PLASTIC*, a group of performers enacted a continuous live installation based on a looped, four-hour solo, both inside the galleries and in the spaces outside the museum. Moving with exquisite control at a glacial pace, the luxurious drag of time on the dancers' visibility while in movement threw the whole situation into sharper view. In another iteration of the same work at MoMA, dancers moving at a barely perceptible pace slid across the museum's floors and melted down its staircases. With no apparent beginning or end, Hassabi's work maximises the tensions at play between live bodies and the gallery as a context designed for object presentation, to absorbing and charged effect.

Dominican-born, Berlin-based artist Isabel Lewis creates spaces that might be likened to Arakawa's appropriation of social formats, but she extends the idea of the nightclub as a space of encounter to meet the quirkier territory of the amateur gardening club. Lewis, too, plays the role of host and considers the space of her work as a temporary site for extending hospitality to her audience, whose participation is integral to the dynamic of her performance situations (p.160). For Frieze Projects 2014, Lewis used the rough open space above the department store Selfridges in London to create one of her 'occasions': a situation set out with a jungle of potted palms, low lighting sprinkled with the glitter of mirror balls, and hosts and hostesses handing out crates of beer and trays of snacks, as well

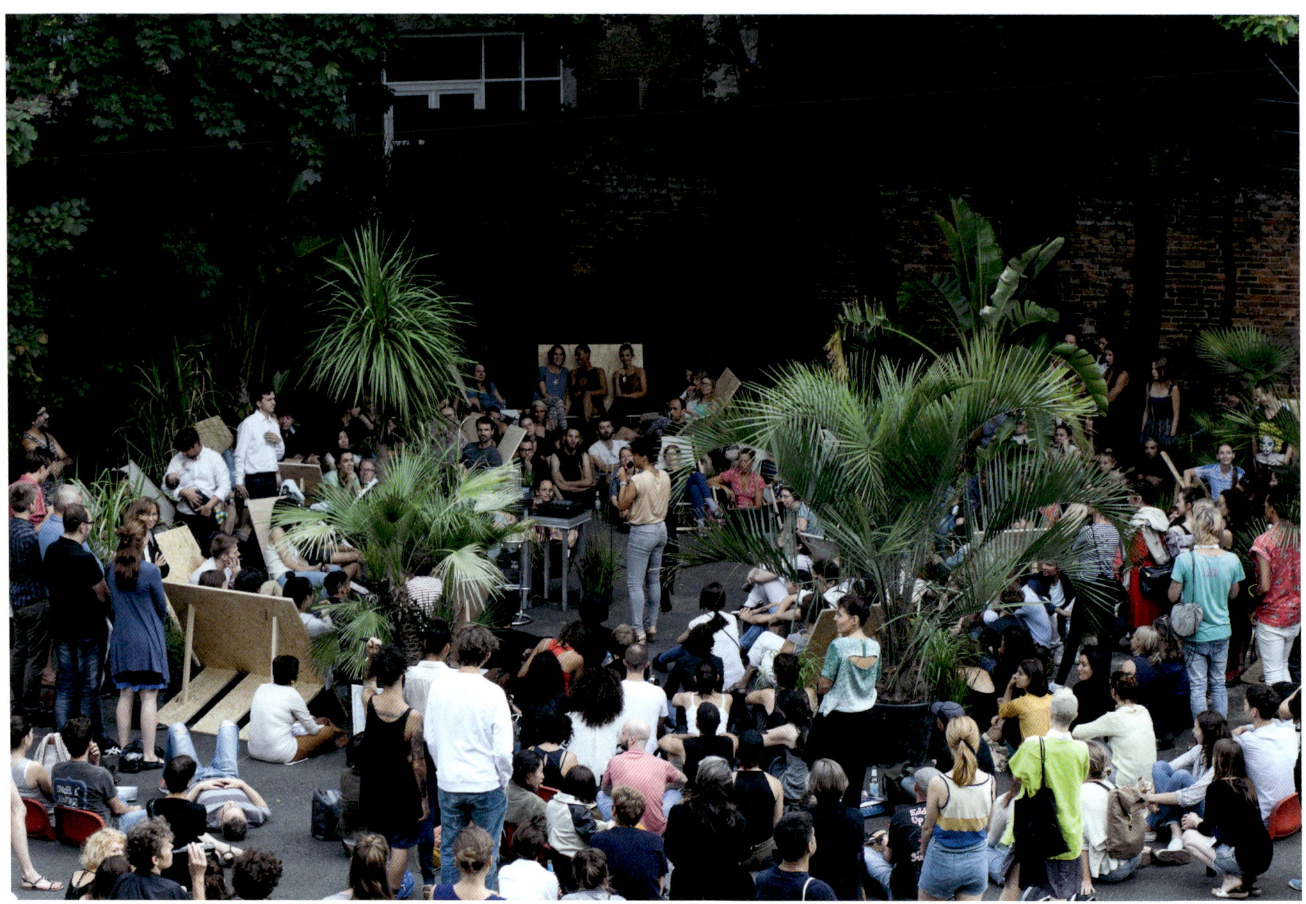

Isabel Lewis, *Occasion*, Tanz im August, HAU Hebbel am Ufer, Berlin, 2015

as comfortable sofas and ambient music played by invited DJs. Within this set-up, Lewis addressed the lounging audience with philosophical theories about gardening, sex, love, friendship and culture, with references to Plato and Max Weber.

With a distinct nod to Hélio Oiticica's sensory environments of the late 1960s and early 1970s, Lewis's art takes a different starting point from the clean-cut white cube. She aims to conjure a state of 'noise' or 'interference' – as organic life has been described by the philosopher Michel Serres in his writing on Work[67] – which acts as a backdrop for an art experience or a conversation about art, over and above the usual idea of neutrality associated with the blank gallery. Lewis makes work that deliberately appeals to the body as a totality, to communality, and to all the senses. In her practice, the work of art is an organic activity woven into the mess and earthly pleasure of real life, rather than a transcendent sphere.

Lewis's approach, then, envisages discourse as embedded in life experience, rather than as content to be transmitted. Her ambient atmosphere can be seen as a pun on the 'consumption' of ideas. A merging of performance, entertainment and discursive space, these 'occasions' not only generate peripheral conversation but also make it feel newly valuable as an informal and relaxed experience of sharing. Lewis imagines her choreographing of such situations in terms of a collage of materials, ideas and experiences. 'Choreography is bringing things into relation in time,' she says, 'and that can be human bodies, plant bodies, object bodies, all different kinds of bodies. [...] Choreography can give us ways to access strategies of reading and composing situations in all of their multiform and ever-changing complexity.'[68] Different from exhibition or theatre formats which create a space of distanced observation, or entertainment, Lewis's 'occasions' address the entire human sensorium, wherein seeing is only one aspect among others, and wherein she is not only performer but also 'host': a role drawn from a specifically feminist trajectory, as one often enacted in a domestic realm by women.

Italian artist Marinella Senatore uses the protracted process of film production as a score to make large-scale collaborative works. Senatore sees her role as an artist working with people as one of 'catalysing processes',[69] and she thinks of the audience not as a homogeneous body but as a set of individuals with their own stories, skills and perspectives. She begins each project from scratch by listening to their ideas and views, and then works from these individual positions to initiate dialogues between histories, cultures and social structures.

Having studied music, Senatore applies ideas of structure gained from playing in an orchestra, but also those involved in the collaborative process of filmmaking. One of Senatore's early significant projects is *Nui Simu* ('That's us', in Sicilian dialect). In the former mining town of Enna in Sicily, she met some of the retired miners who had worked in the sulphur mines until they were decommissioned in the 1970s, and did extensive research on the area. She was especially interested in the ways in which the workers had, historically, banded together to form unions, social groups and mutual aid societies.

In Enna, Senatore set about creating a kind of oral history project, but one filtered through the proposition of making a film. She met with former miners to do screen tests, where they would speak about their past experiences and, working with volunteer participants from the art school, she began to use the miners' stories as the basis for a co-written script: they became the screenwriters. Many other members of the local community, including taxi drivers and workers in the local services industry, also contributed. The resulting film both tells the stories of the retired miners and that of the film's own production, so that the artist operates both inside and outside the object that is ostensibly produced, and undermines the processes of inclusion and exclusion ordinarily initiated by an audition process.

Senatore's approach to the idea of mass community participation and storytelling is indebted to the kind of social practice work made by Suzanne Lacy and her peers, and, more recently, has elements in common with that of Jeremy Deller. Alongside re-enacting the UK miners' strikes in *The Battle of Orgreave*, Deller has made artworks that take the form of community events, rooted in his fascination with the traditions of late nineteenth-century pageants, parades and festivals. In 2004, as part of Manifesta 5, he organised a work titled *A Social Parade* in San Sebastián, Spain, to celebrate its diverse community. Deller subverted the nature of such a public procession by collaborating with the city's underground youth groups and associations, rather than municipal authorities. Similarly, as part of Manchester International Festival in 2009, the artist created a live ritual titled *Procession*: a parade composed of different self-identified groups in the city, from the Boy Scouts to trade unions, and from a pipe band to gay rights activists, all of whom created floats or staged appearances as the procession advanced through the city centre.

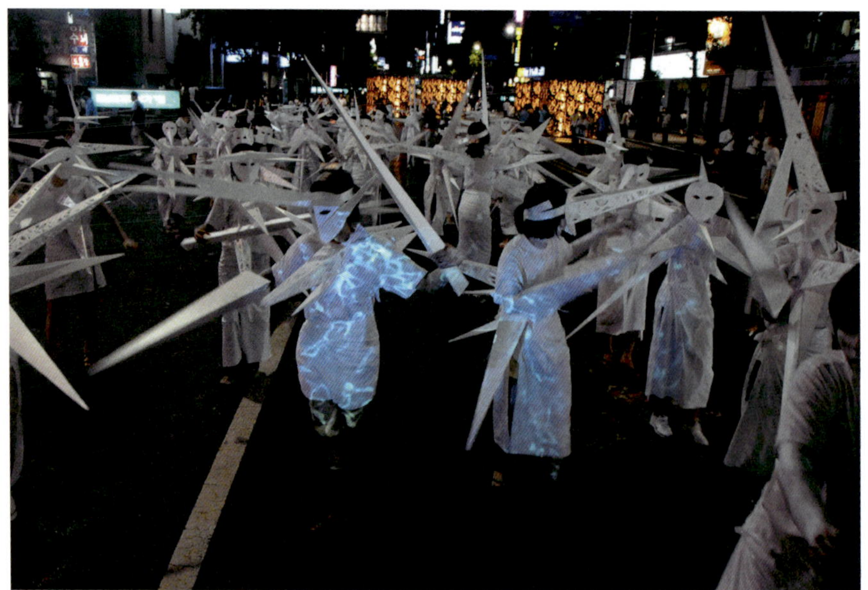

SPRING, 90-minute processional performance curated for the 7th Gwangju Biennale, curated by Claire Tancons. Pictured: Marlon Griffith, RUNAWAY/REACTION (foreground), Mario Benjamin, Le Banquet (background). Geumnamro, May 18 Democratic Square, 5 September 2008

Curator and art historian Claire Tancons, who has worked with Deller, has written extensively on the subject of the parade and carnival as forms of 'processional performance'.[70] Tancons situates this work more broadly in the context of the street, used thus, as an alternative kind of exhibition space that is especially important from the point of view of black diasporic history, given its contribution to the development of spaces for the production and display of art by a community for whom such opportunities did not exist, and of shared aesthetic experience outside of official institutions. Key figures in her research include Peter Minshall, a Trinidadian artist whose carnival work is conceived as a form of sculpture in movement – Mas – with an activist dimension that looks at issues such as nuclear weapons and AIDS, or Marlon Griffith, who combines his training as a traditional 'masman' with a contemporary art practice.

Game-changing: activist strategies and invented institutions

While game-like strategies for participation have been a common approach among artists since the 1960s, the Mexican artist Carlos Amorales has deliberately proposed the mass spectacle of sport as a late capitalist perversion of the idea of participation. In the early 2000s, Amorales staged a series of Mexican wrestling matches in contemporary art galleries and museums, which involved real sports practitioners. For his 2003 performance at Tate Modern, *Amorales vs Amorales*, the artist himself and four fighters from Mexico, performing as the characters Satánico, Ultimo Guerrero (The Ultimate Fighter), Olympico and Rey Bucanero (The Pirate King), dressed in Lycra costumes designed by the artist and wearing brightly coloured masks. As they descended the stairs in the centre of the Turbine Hall to music and a live commentary, the dispersed crowds of visitors circulating through the public spaces of Tate Modern transformed into a vast and temporarily unified cheering mass. The insertion of the masked fighters' compelling image in the museum – in the same period, the piece appeared at SFMoMA, the Walker Art Center and the Centre Pompidou, alongside Tate Modern – inevitably reconfigured audience attitudes and their patterns of attention.

Amorales considers the activation of the audience, brought together in this temporary constellation, to be as important as the presentation of a quasi-self-portrait woven by the wrestling match itself (two fighters bore the same name and mask: that of the artist, Amorales). In this view, then, the performance is less an image to be viewed, and more a catalyst that disrupts and reorganises people's positions and attention; in this case, borrowing from the ready-made format of the live sports arena. In bringing a populist form of entertainment into the cathedral-like space of the gallery, Amorales takes an unexpected route to the self-reflexivity of the avant-garde: the audience seeing-themselves-seeing. Alternatively, his action could be read as a prescient unmasking of the contemporary art museum as a typically neoliberal entertainment complex. Amorales is one of an emergent generation of artists whose work dramatises the tension between collective activity, understood as a way of imagining and engaging with alterity, and massification, as art historian and theorist Sven Lütticken describes it: performance in the museum as a product of late capitalist expansion of the cultural complex, which stages active participation as a spectacle, rather than as a space of solidarity.[71]

Tania Bruguera's work is founded upon what she terms 'behaviour art': the idea that art is a sphere through which civic action might be transformed.[72] For Bruguera, art is a means of enacting social change instead of representing social and political issues. She takes advantage of the cultural capital afforded

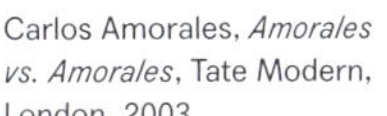
Carlos Amorales, *Amorales vs. Amorales*, Tate Modern, London, 2003

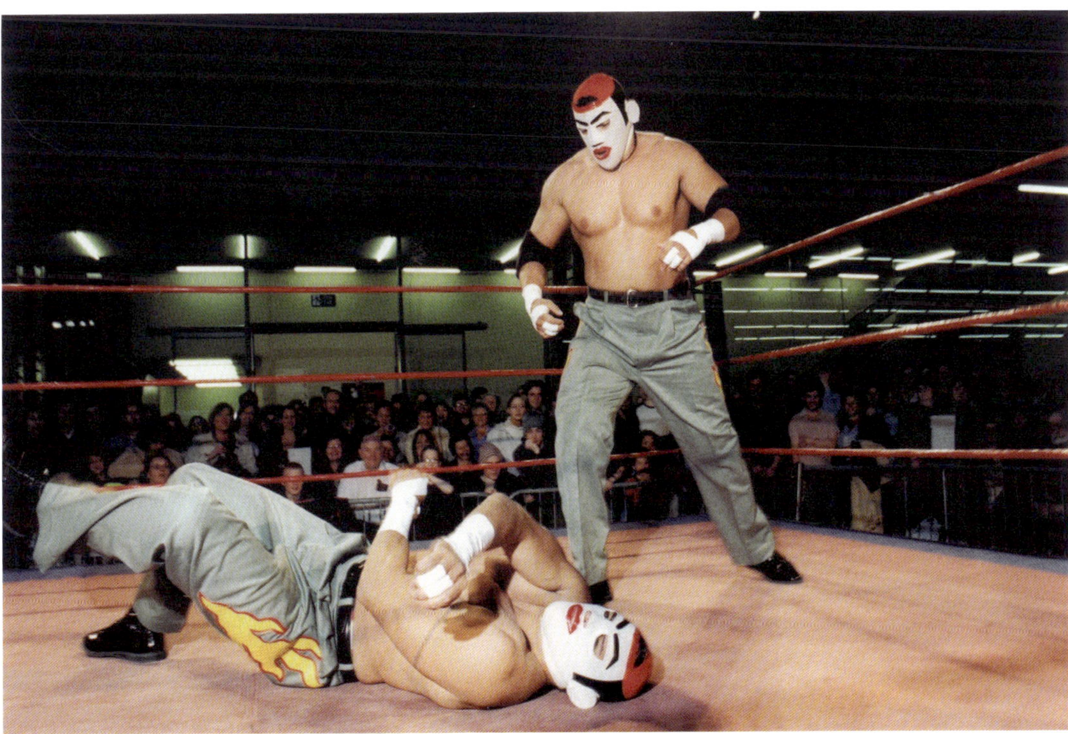

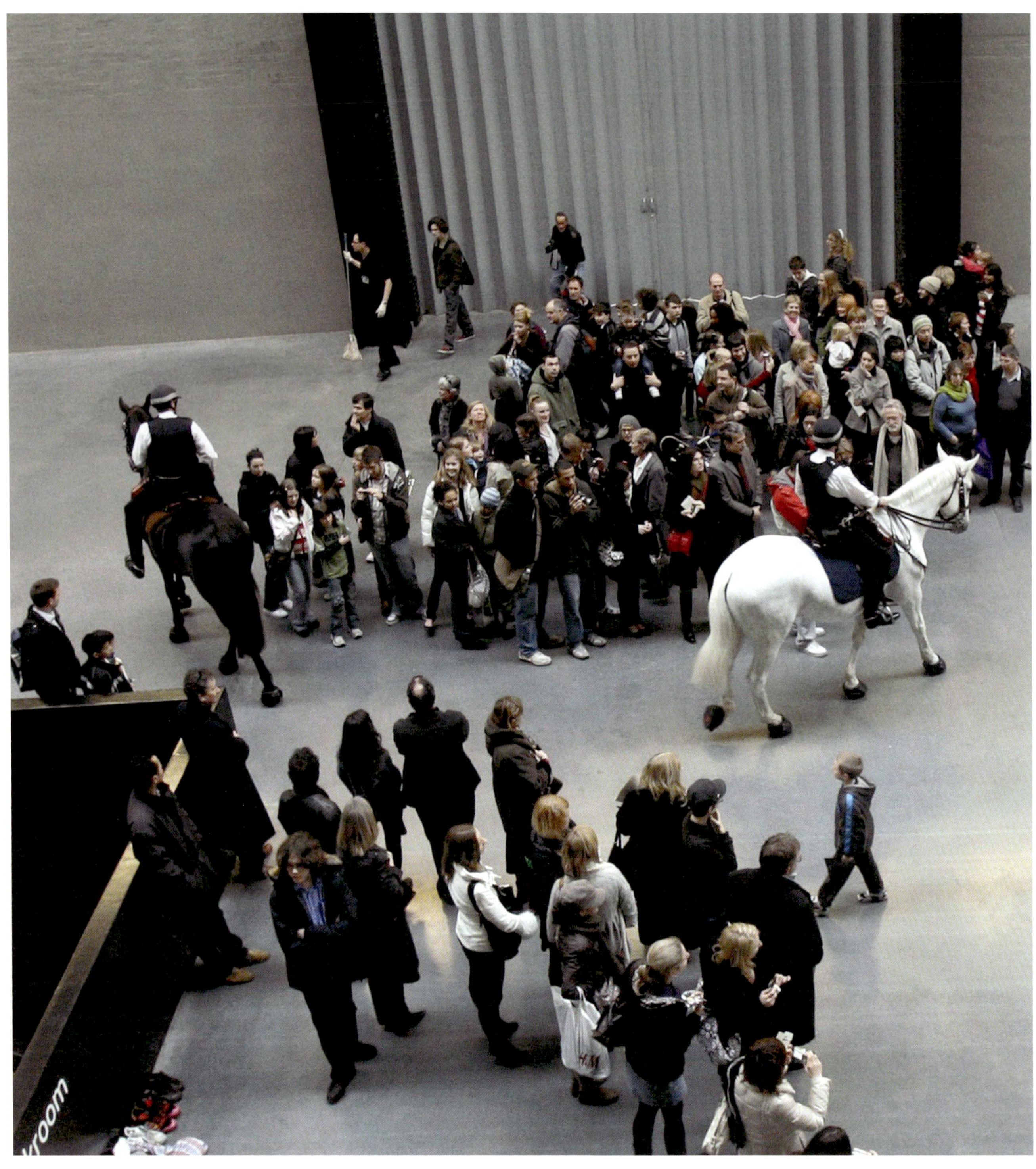

Tania Bruguera, *Tatlin's Whisper #5*, [*El susurro de Tatlin #5*], Tate Modern, London, 2008

to her by art institutions to build frames and containers for political action, and has pushed the creation of social situations and institutions as artworks perhaps furthest among her peers. Influenced by Lacy's work, among other artists of the preceding generation, Bruguera has blurred the lines between direct and symbolic action to an extreme degree.

Bruguera describes her work as consisting of both 'short-term' and 'long-term' actions.[73] One of her most significant works in the first category, *Tatlin's Whisper #5* 2008, involves a patrol of mounted police who continuously shift crowds of visitors around a museum or gallery space, exerting power but to no apparent end. The piece can be performed in any location where there has been a state of civil unrest, or an incident involving this kind of crowd-control policing, within recent memory, and it entails engaging that country's mounted police or equivalent. On one level, *Tatlin's Whisper #5* is a choreographic spectacle that is quasi-participatory – one can choose to watch or to stand within the crowd that is being moved – but in fact the piece stages an imbalance of power that is ultimately founded upon a forced complicity with the apparently free space of the contemporary museum. On another level, Bruguera slyly doubles the critical power of the piece by staging the museum's own complicity with the apparatus of the state, and with military or police power more specifically, by asking the institution to create arrangements for the police to participate, relying on official networks and cooperative favours. State and cultural power are visibly merged in this action. It is a demonstration of how the artist might hack or occupy the museum.

Since 2011, Bruguera has run the project Immigrant Movement International in New York, a paradigmatic example of a long-term action. The artist began the project by spending a year running a community space in Queens, where the movement was first headquartered. During this time, she lived in an apartment shared with migrant women and their children. Engaging both local and international communities, as well as working with social services, politicians and artists focused on immigration reform, Bruguera attempts to find ways of addressing questions about the social conditions facing immigrants, and their political representation. The challenge inherent in Bruguera's practice, in her being both part of the community she supports and part of the art world, and servicing both communities at once, lies at the crux of debates about art's place in the world, and whether its status as a removed activity negates its potential to produce real political effects.

Bruguera's approach is exemplary of how an expanded idea of performance has fed into the development of contemporary art, by encouraging artists to build spaces where none exist, or what exists is not adequate. By taking a performative approach and imaginatively constructing a fictional space, artists have begun to create new narratives that have the potential to become new realities to act within. Benin-based artist Meschac Gaba's *Museum of Contemporary African Art* offers another example of such tendency, in terms specific to the museum (p.166). Akin to the approach of IRWIN, of NSK, in setting out the history of Eastern and Central European art in their project *East Art Map* 2001–6, the *Museum of Contemporary African Art* is essentially a provocation, calling on the art establishment to pay attention to contemporary African art, but also to question why the boundaries between Western and African art exist in the first place. Gaba came up with the idea in the late 1990s, during a residency at the Rijksakademie in Amsterdam. He describes his impression of 'another reality' when visiting

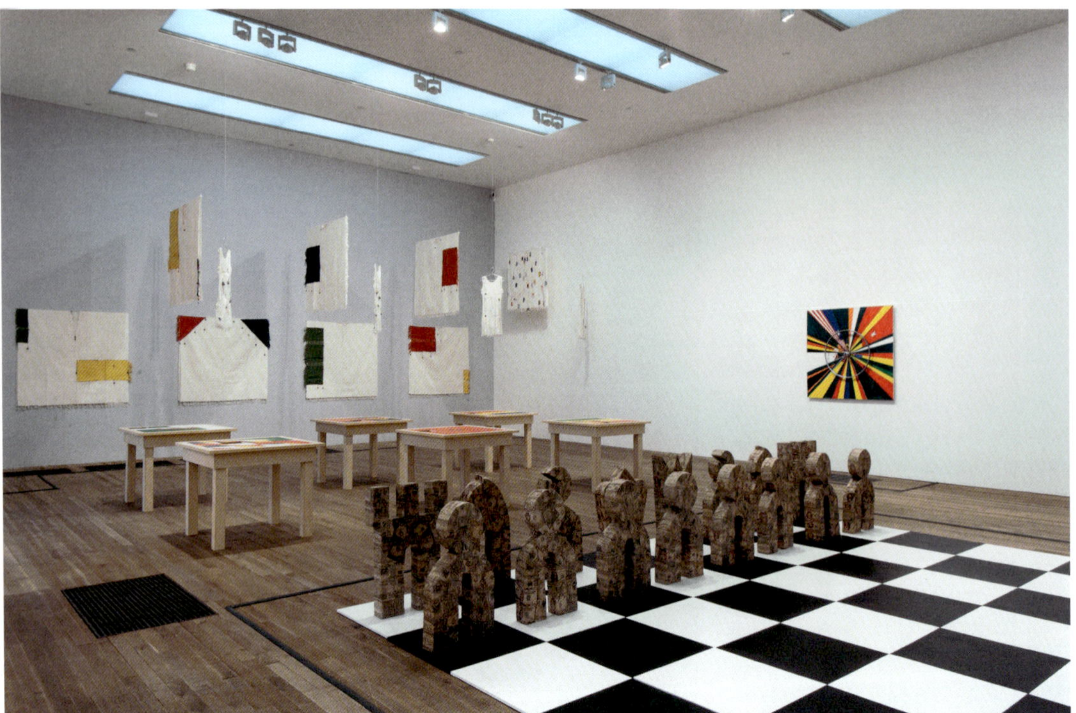

Meschac Gaba, *'Game Room',* from *Museum of Contemporary African Art* 1997–2002, Tate Modern, London, 3 July – 22 September 2013

museums in Europe, in which his own work could not fit in. 'I needed a space for my work, because this did not exist,' he has said. Gaba has claimed that the *Museum of Contemporary African Art* is a 'question', a conceptual space more than a physical one.[74]

The *Museum of Contemporary African Art* comprises twelve sections, or rooms: the Draft Room, the Architecture Room, the Museum Shop, the Game Room, the Summer Collection, the Museum Restaurant, the Music Room, Art and Religion, the Marriage Room, the Library, the Salon and the Humanist Space. The first part of the project, the *Draft Room*, was conceived in 1997, and contained an unusual assortment of handmade, found and altered objects, including decommissioned banknotes and ceramic food. Subsequent rooms were developed, one at a time, appearing in exhibitions and museums internationally, each presenting a playful selection that mixes the functional with the traditional, and precious artefacts with everyday objects.

Certain rooms, such as the Library, Museum Restaurant and Museum Shop, are familiar elements of most contemporary art museums. By placing these apparently non-aesthetic, social activities on a par with the artwork on view, Gaba doubles his challenge to the Western museum. He not only organises African material displays, but also calls into question the nature and function of the museum and our relationship to it, theatricalising it as a social structure. Gaba's museum is a relational space, not just for the contemplation of objects, but for sociability, study and play, resembling sometimes a market stall or common room, and at other times a valuable display of sacred relics. The role of viewers in this work shifts with its fluctuating formats: we may be cast as consumers, witnesses, viewers, players or worshippers. But first and foremost it is the work's broader fiction, its instatement of one kind of museum within the space and conditions of another, that puts into play a kind of critical theatre in which we can participate in new ways.

French choreographer and dancer Boris Charmatz has approached the notion of the museum with a similar interest in building a space that did not yet exist. Charmatz's practice, rooted in dialogue with visual art, is heterogeneous and frequently collaborative. From a choreographic point of view, he has made duets, group works and installations, all of which reconsider figural relations in dance through imagining reciprocity and movement in fresh ways. But in addition to this, he has also initiated a 'nomadic' school (Bocal, 2003–4) and a museum (Musée de la danse in Rennes, since 2009).[75] The work of his peer, French choreographer Jérôme Bel, represents an important parallel, albeit with a different emphasis. Bel's work concentrates on the theatre stage, but his attitude resonates clearly with conceptual art in a deconstructive approach: in 2000, he delegated the creation of a piece titled *Xavier Le Roy* to Xavier Le Roy himself. Bel has a quasi-anthropological eye, and has consistently investigated the notion of community, for example with twenty dancers responding to shared pop songs (*The Show Must Go On* 2001), deconstructing the corps de ballet by making a solo portrait of one of the usually anonymous dancers (*Véronique Doisneau* 2004), or working with a disabled theatre group (*Disabled Theatre* 2012). Bel's work foregrounds the individuality of his performers, but always by raising awareness of the social framework through which we encounter them.

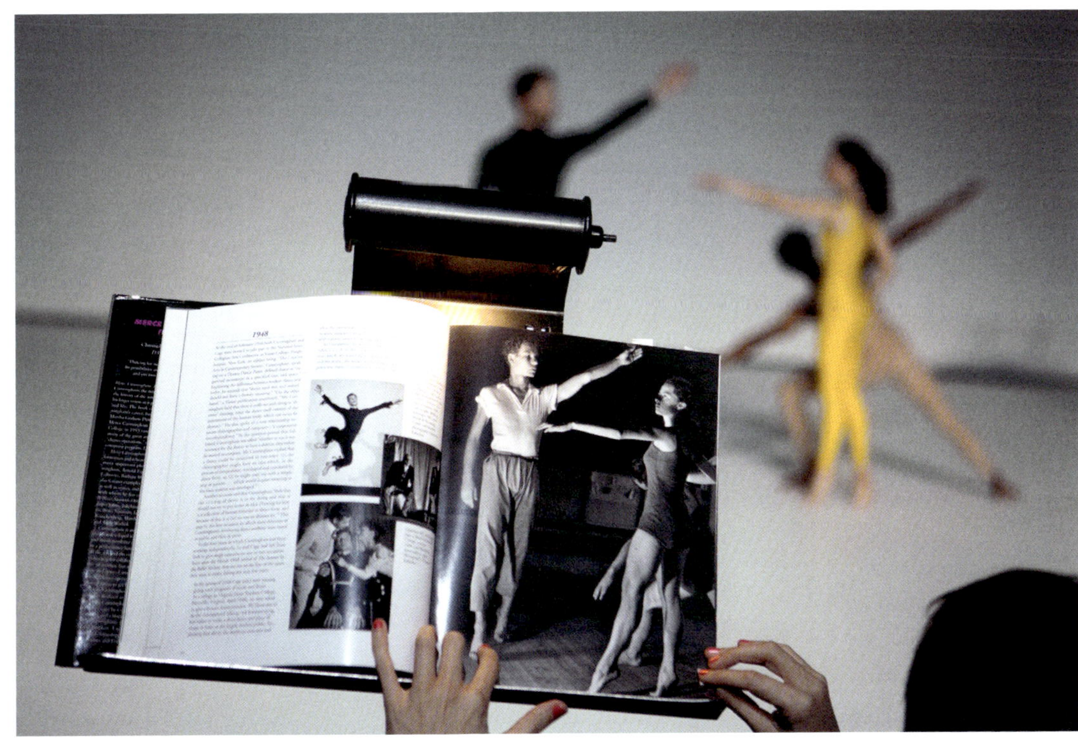

Flip Book, conception Boris Charmatz; with Boris Charmatz, Ashley Chen, Raphaëlle Delaunay, Christophe Ives, Lénio Kaklea, Mani Mungai; the work is based on free interpretation from the photographs of David Vaughan's book *Merce Cunningham, un demi-siecle de danse*, directed by Melissa Harris, and Ed Plume, 1997; presented at The Museum of Modern Art, New York, November 2018

Charmatz's work asks, slightly differently, how might choreographic explorations of the body, and bodies together, determine the foundations of an alternative kind of architecture for dance? In reorienting the body's own hierarchy, Charmatz also opens up new possibilities for acting, as well as new points of contact between figures and behaviours. Working on the body, he organises patterns of practice that do not necessarily fit into describable relationships or codes of interaction. In *herses (a slow introduction)* 1997, for example, two male-female pairs (performed by dancers who are partners in real life) move with, on and in relation to each other in ways that conjure a different sense of the 'relationship' as a contract or a space for movement. Another of Charmatz's early works, *Aatt enen tionon* 1996, set on a three-tier stage that isolates its three dancers, already represents a substantial reorganisation of the coordinates of dance's theatrical set-up. The dance architecture he has developed is a bricolage of grander, borrowed institutional frameworks – hence the incorporation of the 'school' and the 'museum' alongside the 'theatre'.

In 2009, Charmatz took on the directorship of one of France's national dance institutions – the Centre chorégraphique national de Rennes et de Bretagne – and renamed it Musée de la danse, or Museum of Dance. He gave its working principle in a manifesto: 'We must first of all forget the image of a traditional museum, because our space is firstly a mental one.'[76] Charmatz envisions the possibilities for the institution by imagining its structures as performed acts, and enacting them from the point of view of the nuanced movement of the dancer: a means of opening up the medium with an activist dimension. Though these frames are often institutional, Charmatz's work is not a form of institutional critique. Instead, like Gaba or Bruguera, he uses institutional formats as ready-made structures to cannibalise, and from which to productively build. Performance theorist Shannon Jackson observes, in this vein, that it is necessary to qualify the art world's 'critical impulses to equate radicality and progressivism with "anti-state" or "anti-institutional" resistance. [...] If our critical language only values agency when it is resisting state structure,' she writes, 'then we can find ourselves in an awkward position when we also want to call for the renewal of public institutions' – that is, the spaces that form the often-underplayed basis of support connecting art with social and political life.[77]

Two works that imagine the convention of the 'collection' in immaterial form propose alternative performances of the body as museum. *Public Collection* by Romanian artists Manuel Pelmuş and Alexandra Pirici – who have a background in dance – is an ongoing project, developed since 2013, that addresses the context of the public museum and the question of ownership. This work takes the form of a succession of artworks being acted out by five interpreters, akin to a looped game of charades. Critically reflecting on the museum's role as it archives, historicises, collects and reflects on society, shaping expectations as to what is valued, the artists possess or reclaim these objects of value by enacting them. Each work is carefully represented in its imaginative transformation from material to gestural forms. By incorporating a wide range of different artworks in the piece, taken from different museum collections – from a stripe painting by Daniel Buren to a body action by Ana Mendieta, and even Da Vinci's *Mona Lisa* 1503 – Pirici and Pelmuş play upon the audience's own mental repertoires and shared experiences of art, which are brought to bear upon the inferred meaning of the performed gestures.

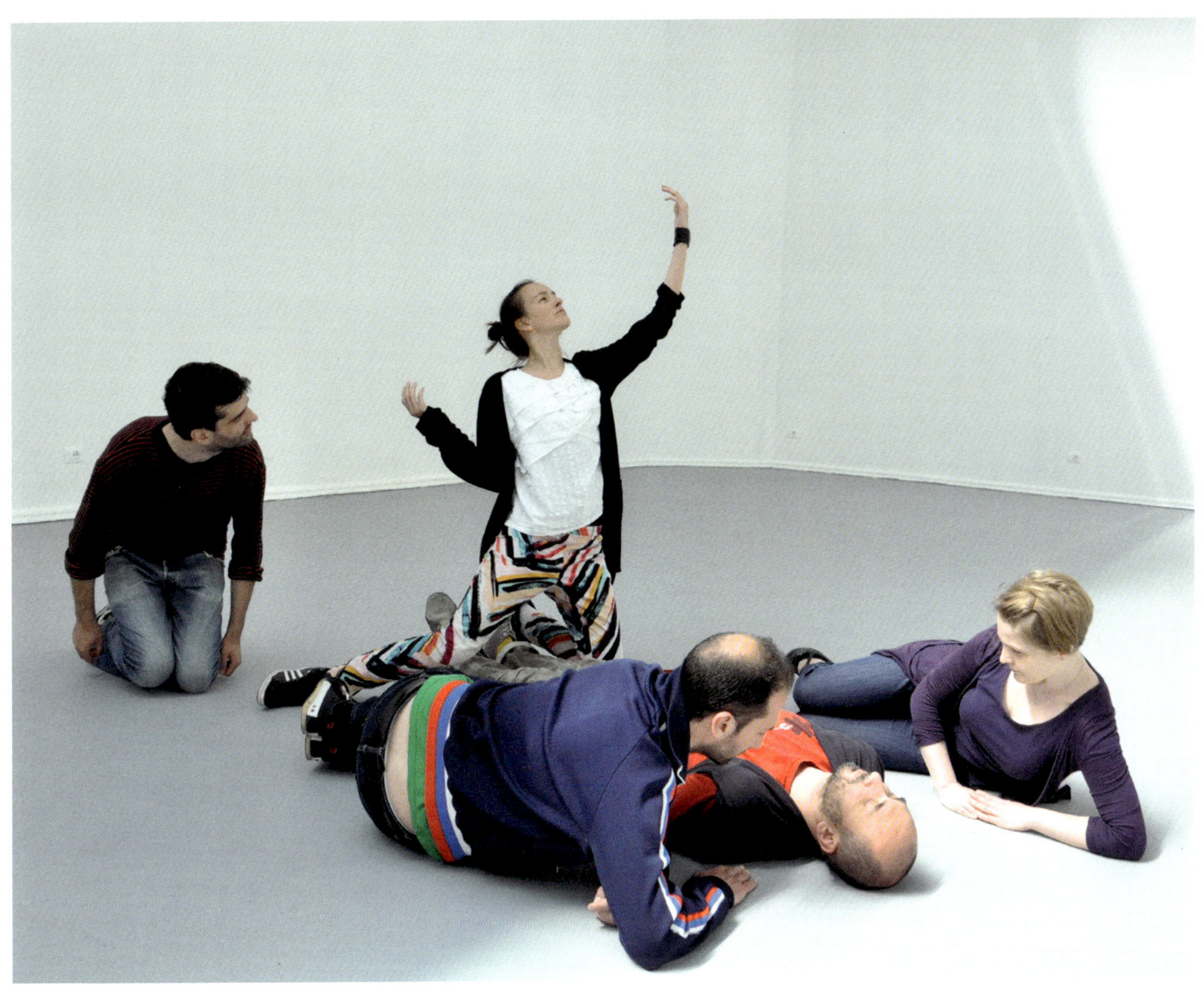

Alexandra Pirici and Manuel Pelmuş, *An Immaterial Retrospective of the Venice Biennale*, 2013. Enactment of 'Supreme Meeting', painting by Giacomo Grosso, 1st International Art Exhibition of the City of Venice, 1895

Public Collection uses similar strategies to previous works, such as the *Immaterial Retrospective of the Venice Biennale* 2013 and *Just Pompidou it: A Retrospective of the Centre Pompidou* 2014. In the former, a group of performers depicted the history of the Venice Biennale in an empty pavilion; in the latter, histories of French protest and political action were intertwined with iterations of artworks. Enactment is used as a strategy to scale down, or de-monumentalise, history, while simultaneously actualising significant artworks and events using the 'poor' means of only human bodies. An alternative canon founded on collective memory and the transformative potential of action is suggested by the work.

The founders of the Living Dance Studio at CCD Workstation in Beijing, Wen Hui and Wu Wenguang, set up an important space for supporting new cross-disciplinary practice in the city in 2005. And yet they recognised the need to underwrite innovation with foundations drawn from their locality, exploring similar interests in terms of how the living bodies of dancers carry history and might

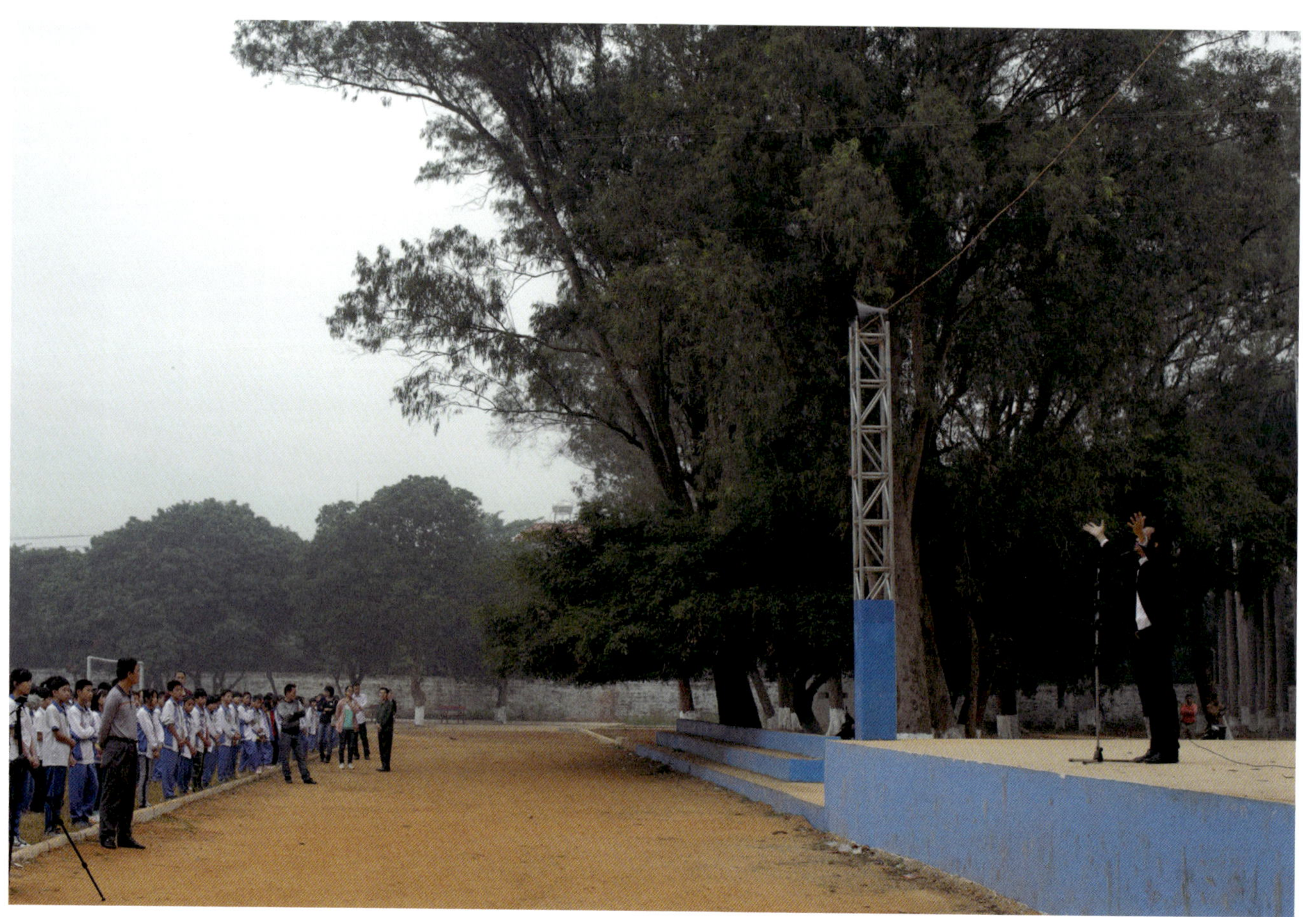

Hu Xiangqian, *Speech at the Edge of the World*, 2014, 12 min. 30 sec., video still

enact collective memory – from where the contemporary might emerge. One so-called 'documentary theatre' piece, *Red* 2016, drew from the 1964 celebration of socialism during the Cultural Revolution, a narrative ballet called *The Red Detachment of Women*. The Living Dance Studio worked with older dancers in their sixties who had performed in these ballets, and interviewed original members of the audience, as a way to ask questions about what is retained in their shared history in this bodily memory. The Living Dance Studio understand their role as being to create a bridge between past and present; a present which has not been readily accessible for a young generation, but might be accessed in this oblique way, often to emotional effect.

In his work *Xiangqian's Museum* 2010, Chinese artist Hu Xiangqian, like Pelmuş and Pirici, mimes a series of artworks he has 'collected' in his mind. The artist is fascinated by the absurdity of this idea, of trying to communicate their myriad complexities through the body alone, and the work is funny. But it also contains a disdain for the exclusive, ownership-based collection system of the conventional museum. Instead, his work proposes a portable institution that can be carried in the artist's own body. He states: 'Everyone is born to be empty. We need materials and non-materials to fill ourselves. A museum fills itself with materials, but … in my performance, these museums and artworks are represented through my body to the audience. I think the best thing about art is we can carry it wherever we go.'[78]

In a subsequent video work, *Speech at the Edge of the World* 2014, Hu performs as a school leader delivering a speech via a megaphone to an audience of two thousand school students. The pupils are assembled in a mass on the outdoor sports ground of the artist's old school in Leizhou, a small village in Guangdong Province. For the speech, lasting just under ten minutes, Hu borrows techniques from the motivational speech format used by business and political leaders: an authoritative tone of voice, emphatic gestures, dramatic pauses, and so on. The content of the speech draws upon his own personal experience growing up in this area, but is filtered through a corporate format that renders it somewhat absurd. This work, like the museum piece, finds a way to stage the artist's autobiography through a matrix of fictional and formal ready-made elements borrowed from social convention. Both works dramatise the negotiation of individual subjectivity in relation to passing through or encountering collectively built institutions. If Hu's work borrows these institutional frames as containers through which he might examine his autobiography, Gaba, Charmatz, and Pirici and Pelmuş treat them as opportunities to enable what dance theorist André Lepecki has described, within theatre, as the 'co-imagining' of a new temporary reality. Extended in time through the permission offered within the frame of art, such non-existent spaces (whether the portable museum or the *Museum of Contemporary African Art*) are called into being via an act of collective witnessing.

Arahmaiani is an artist and activist, born in Indonesia, who makes performance, painting, sculpture and installation. As an artist who openly expresses her Muslim faith, she has nevertheless protested orthodoxies of religion, as well as issues around class and violence against women. Since the early 1980s Arahmaiani's works have provoked certain Islamic community leaders and political authorities and she was imprisoned for a short period in 1983. In a performance titled *Dayang Sumbi Menolak Status Quo (Dayang Sumbi Rejects the Status Quo)* 1999, the artist appeared in a traditional red costume and – whilst humming a devotional Islamic song (shalawat) – invited the audience, which included men, to participate, and even write on her body: a transgression of sociocultural norms of a Muslim-majority Indonesian society. Her work titled, *Offerings from A–Z* 1996, comprised a series of performances that took place in Chiangmai, Thailand as part of the Chiang Mai Social Installation. Arahmaiani first lay down on a white cloth surrounded by objects including guns pointed towards her, then positioned her body – in a sacrificial manner – on a stone table used for washing corpses, around which she had pasted black and white erotic photographs of heterosexual couples. She distributed these pages, from pornographic magazines, to the audience and set them on fire as a type of ritual offering, in such a way as to disturb the distinction between sacred ritual and secular art practice. The last part of the performance involved the artist lying on the floor and covering herself with white sheets stained with blood, apparently symbolising both violence and female fertility. In the past decade Arahmaiani has spent time working with communities around the world on environmental issues using non-violent methods and aimed towards fostering unity between potentially conflicting groups. One of these works, *Parangtritis*, involves a workshop that results in a community procession bearing flags that are fabricated by participants, and carrying messages of anti-corruption. Her work consistently attempts to speak to common human concerns – love, spirituality, truth – in the intervals between institutionalised religion or political affiliation.

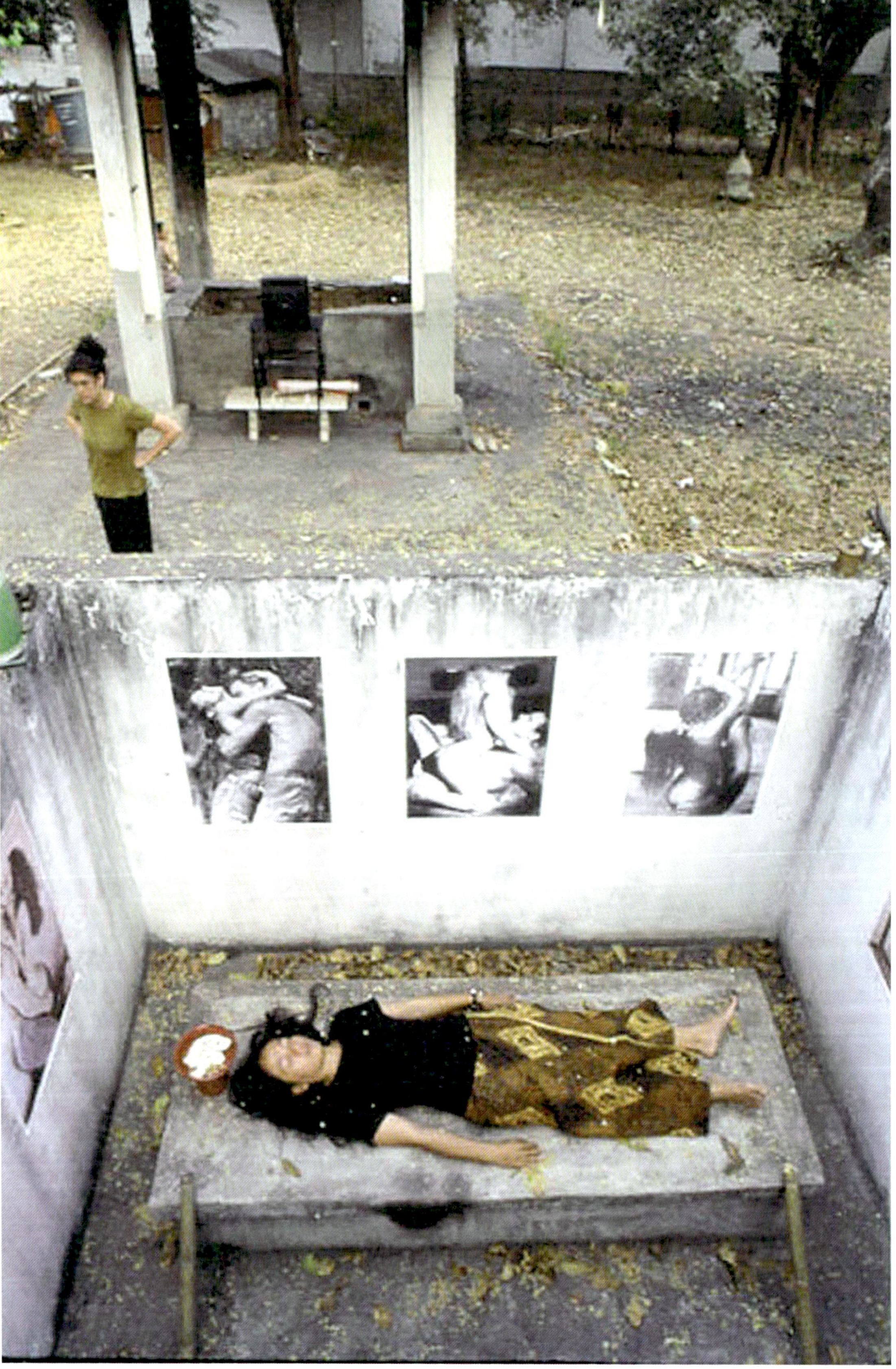

Arahmaiani, *Offerings from A to Z* 1996, performance view, Padaeng Crematorium, Chiang Mai, Thailand

Summary

If art, in its broadest sense, offers a way for us to look at ourselves and reflect on our time – a kind of symbolic mirror – then performance within art stages us in the act of observing ourselves: it produces a two-way mirror. As these diverse examples make manifest, however, the question of who *We* are is contingent and fractured – often more an aspiration, a utopian desire, than a coherent reality. *We* might be a temporary gathering, more than a permanent identity. *We* opens up the possibility of community in real time, or through virtual networks. But *We* – with its implied inclusions and exclusions – is something that is, and has been, perpetually in question. Performance in art has often sought to transfer the focus of aesthetic attention from the discrete object or action towards the broader social frame. It is mostly employed by artists because of its promise to reach beyond representation and allow us to see ourselves as collective shapers of a space in which we give our attention to something, whether beautiful, agitational, co-operative or transcendent. Performance frequently dramatises the unresolvable questions around how the collective basis of *We* is defined by proposing temporary configurations of being together.

While expanded sculpture and painting, or installation art, also situate the viewer explicitly within space and time, the live situation adds a condition of mutual awareness between people. Diffracted through the multiple image-screens of contemporary living, the acts of performing and bearing witness, seeing and being seen, become increasingly complex. At the same time, the assertion of collective presence in real time gathers new charge in a context of technological mediation: whether the procession, the parade, the protest or the performance per se. Beyond the notion of participation, the very act of gathering, and the act of assembling, become inherently political acts because of their raw sense of potential for further action.

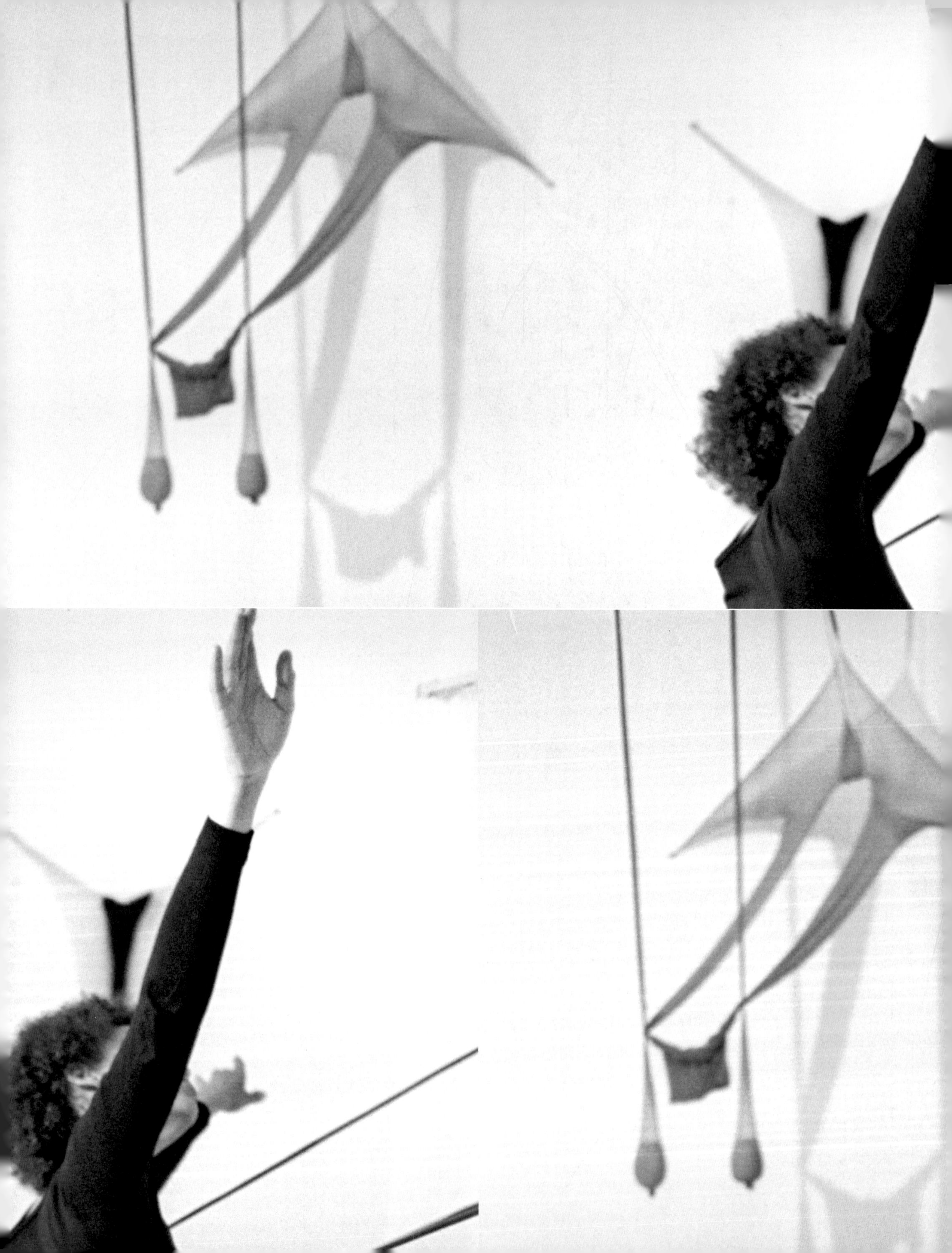

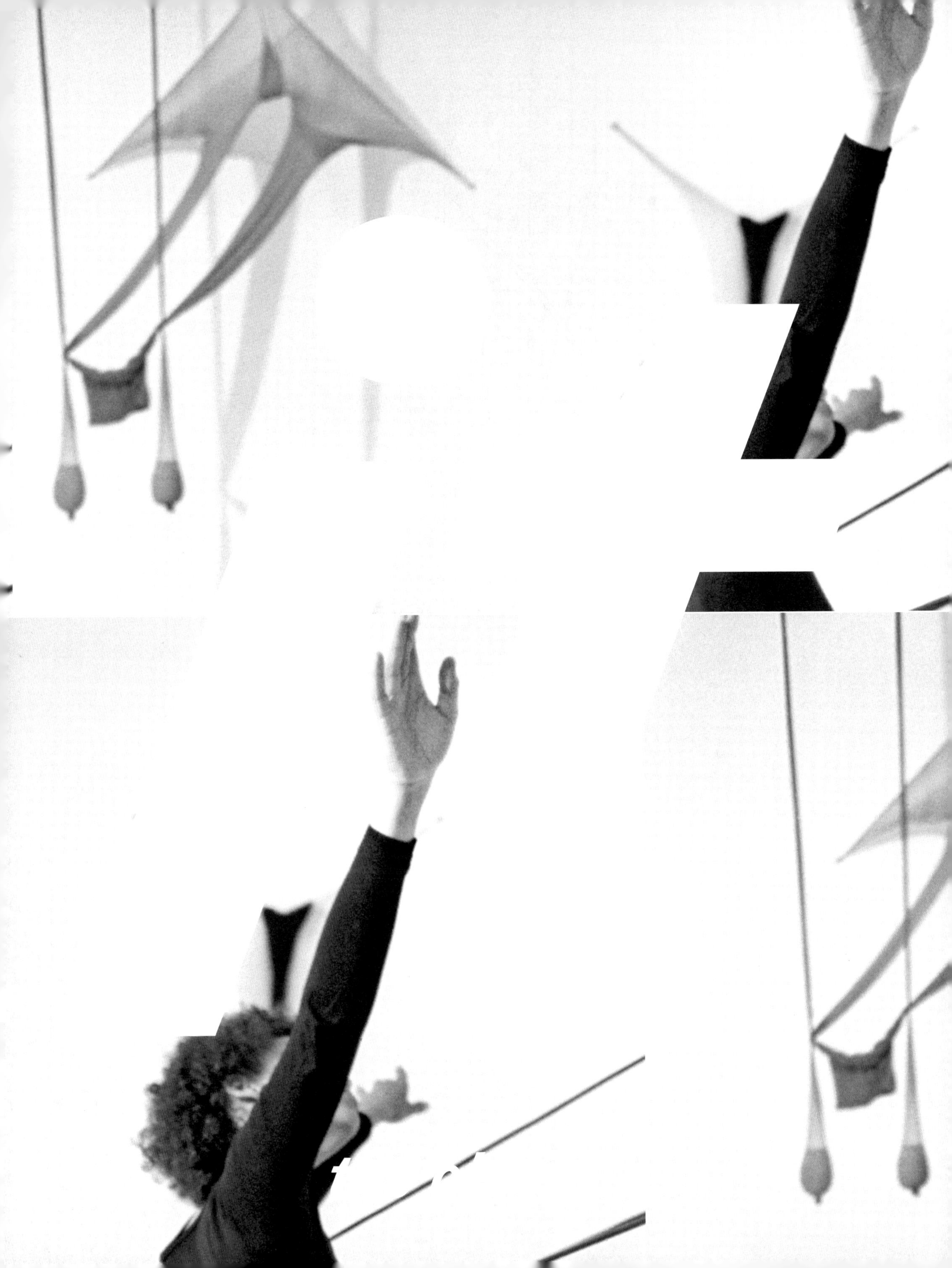

Living Sculpture

In 2003, Mark Leckey made a performance at Tate Britain, for which he requested the loan of a well-known sculpture from Tate's collection, Jacob Epstein's *Jacob and the Angel* 1940–1. He installed the alabaster sculpture in the central atrium of the museum, placing it opposite, and in conversation with, a sound system that he had had made for this event: a large speaker stack, whose form was derived from those used in the Jamaican sound-system culture to stage music and dance gatherings, primarily outdoors, often involving sound clashes confronting two or more sound producers. The sound system's proportions were approximated to those of the blocky statue, and Leckey requested a grey Tate plinth – equivalent to that used on the base of the Epstein – to be made for the speakers. The two objects were placed underneath the domed octagon roof in the heart of Tate Britain, facing each other.

The event was staged after the museum's closing time, so that, aside from this lit area, the galleries were dark and empty. An audience of approximately three hundred people stood in a broad circle around the two sculptures. Leckey had invited a group of fellow artists – Enrico David, Bonnie Camplin, Edwin Burdis (then Ed Laliq) and Lucy McKenzie – to perform the piece with him, which comprised a three-section sound composition, played live, that moved from attack to serenade, and then to synthesis. It included Leckey and Laliq's own voices, cuts of recorded Dada poetry, the end of Handel's *Messiah*, live flute and sampled electronic dance music.

Leckey's treatment of the museum space, an artwork in the Tate collection, and the audience itself, assembled in this late night gathering, created a significant experiential shift in my understanding – and in the understanding of many of those present – of how we could be in the museum and be a part of it at the same time: it redefined what the encounter with an artwork could look and feel like. The museum's atmosphere of apparent timelessness and the object's autonomous presence were transformed, via this action, into a place and a thing that were in the audience's possession within a certain period of time only. The event being staged after hours in an otherwise deserted building lent a certain atmosphere of it being illicit, which inflected this sense of 'occupation' and temporary possession.

Through Leckey's attention to – or, rather, his conversation with – Epstein's sculpture, its hand-carved texture as well as its narrative content, sensuousness and drama were brought out in an extraordinary new way. This first iteration of Leckey's performance, *BigBoxStatueAction* 2003–11, created a script for a cultural ritual, which somehow enacted his love for the artwork, caressed it, in such a way that it could be experienced collectively, and shared. His action transformed the high modernist idea that the encounter with the artwork is a suspended moment of grace outside of time, and rewrote it as a public situation. And yet this was not the theatrical space-time of minimalist literalism either.

BigBoxStatueAction proposed how we might encounter that which has been conventionally defined as 'the artwork' differently: neither as a singular, fixed point to be looked at, or even glanced at and walked around in a matter of seconds, nor as an object to be encountered from different perceptual viewpoints, phenomenologically. Instead, Leckey approached the work obliquely, imagining

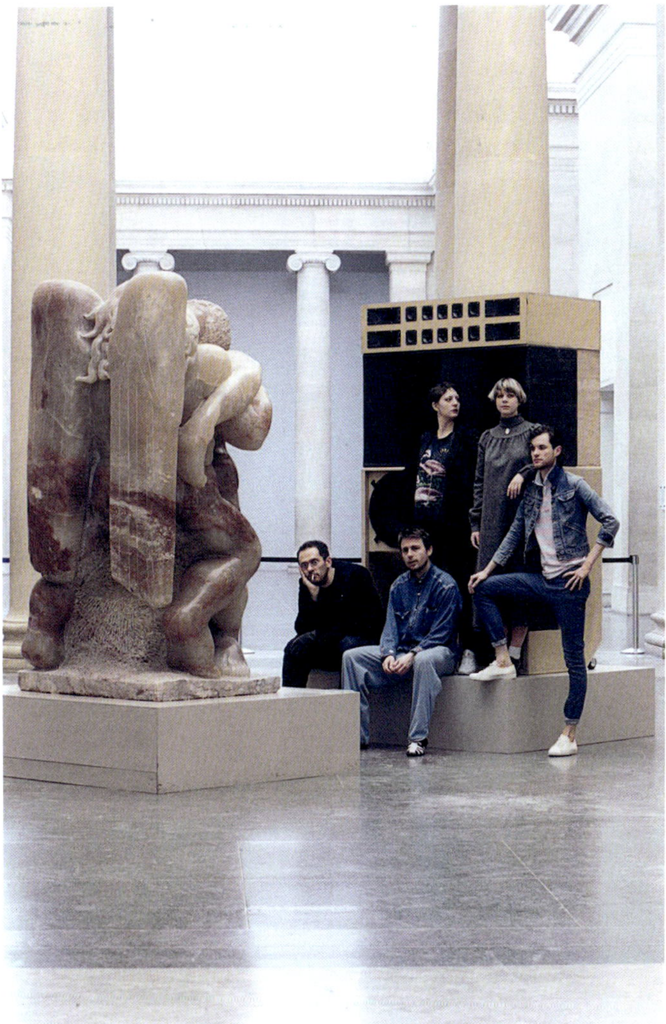

Mark Leckey, *Big Box Statue Action*, Tate Britain, London, 2003, performance in the Duveen Galleries, Tate Britain, 1 February 2003

it as a focus of gradually unfolding concentration. This approach somehow enabled us to enter the historical time of the sculpture – both in terms of its made-ness and its dramatisation of a Biblical narrative – and at the same time drew attention to our here-and-now presence in a shared collective event: he wove the museum artefact into his own narrative. A finely modulated composition of temporal densities, *BigBoxStatueAction* allowed for the coexistence of such differences, and such qualities of experience. It part-beautifully, part-aggressively asserted a thinking-feeling-experiential space as 'our' museum, and brought the Epstein to life.

In this piece, Leckey shows us a way to dig into our own archives of cultural memory and, taking a cue from internet navigation, dissolve their solid, fixed states as relics into a new reciprocal fluidity that elaborates unexpected and boundless conversations. Instead of challenging the idea of the museum as a site for the rationalised display and conservation of objects, Leckey works in this context to make it more like what it is: more fetishised, more mysterious, more enchanting. Things affect each other and things affect us. We are bound together and to things. In this context, we are forced to rethink how we, as viewer-consumers, are situated in relation to objects in such conversations.

A book on performance in contemporary art such as this one might be assumed to exclude art objects entirely in favour of actions. Indeed, ideas that art might evolve towards objectlessness have been in the air since at least the late 1960s, when Lucy R. Lippard and John Chandler's writing on the 'dematerialisation of the art object' identified a broad shift from 'art as product to art as idea'.[1] Such reconsideration of the status of the object in art has accelerated in the past decade, for example through the ephemeral actions of artists such as Tino Sehgal, whose work featured in the previous chapter.

Even so, the art object, or the idea of the artwork as an object, underpins much of the performance work discussed thus far. We have seen how the enactment of the process of making art, often in traditional media, posited the action of painting as an early form of performance that nevertheless resulted in an enduring object distinct from the action itself. And it is clear that certain histories of performance, such as the exhibition *Out of Actions*, place an emphasis on live action as an experimental phase in practice that gives rise to the creation of new objects whose fixed form is retained (and can thus be canonised within a museum collection). However, objects and performances have much more complicated relationships than these attitudes suggest.

Beyond the emergence of performance as a medium, art history encompasses what could be termed a secret history of performance, formed by the traces of actions, exchanges and verbal propositions that have historically seeped through

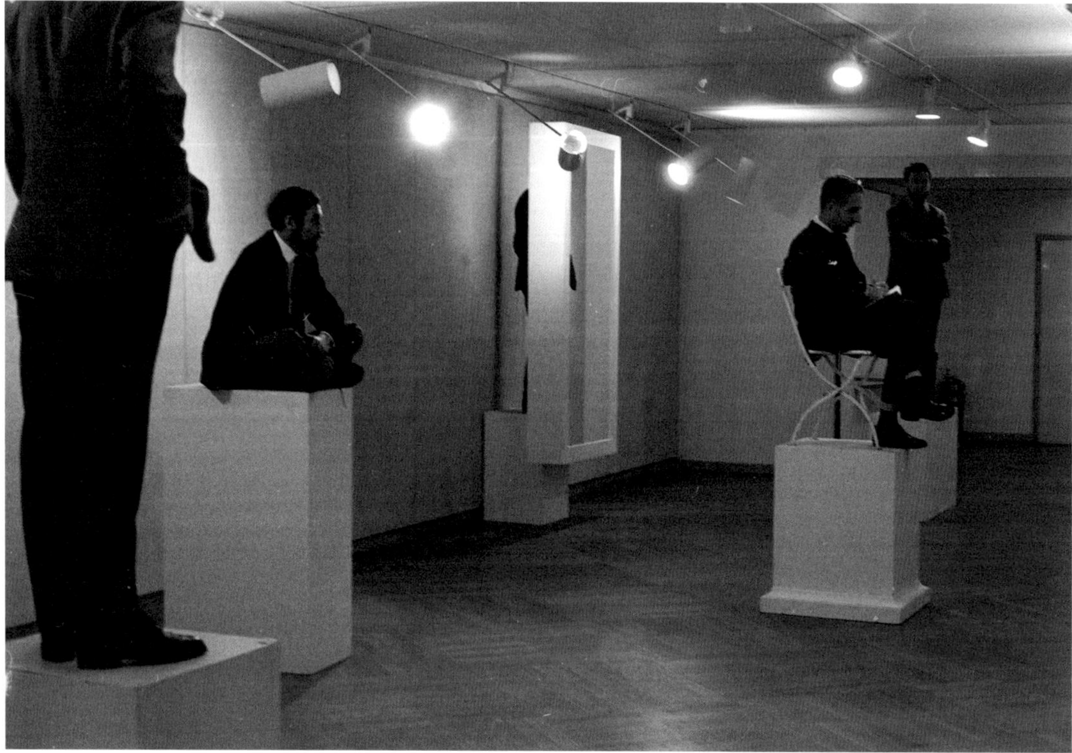

Pi Lind, *Living Sculptures* at the Moderna Museet, Stockholm, 1967

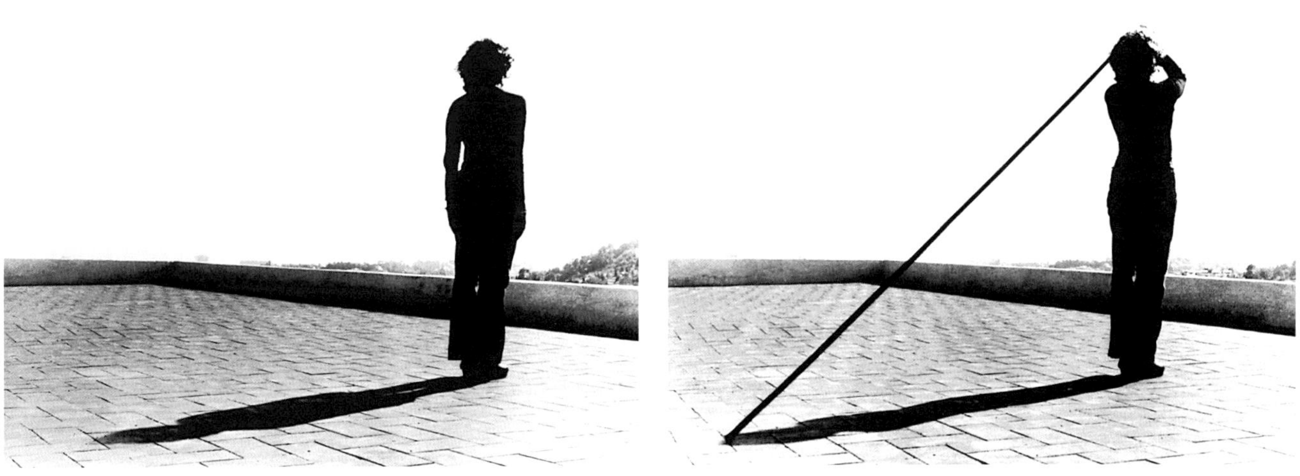

Àngels Ribé, *3 punts 2* [*3 Points 2*] 1972

object-based art. In parallel with the development of body art and happenings, certain artists in the 1960s and 1970s performed *as* traditional media. In 1967, the Swedish artist Pi Lind presented a piece called *Living Sculptures* at the Moderna Museet in Stockholm, in which he staged twenty different social types on plinths for nine hours a day during a five-day 'sociological exhibition' – an idea with shades of August Sander's use of photography, in the 1920s, as a taxonomic tool. In *The Singing Sculpture* 1969, Gilbert & George painted themselves gold and stood on a plinth while singing 'Underneath the Arches' – a camp riposte to the truth-to-materials of their Central Saint Martins' tutor, modernist sculptor Anthony Caro. From the early 1970s, the pair went so far as to conceive of their daily lives as an extended living sculpture performance: they dressed in matching suits and ties, carried walking sticks and posed for photographs for their work. Around the same time, Catalan conceptual artist Àngels Ribé made simple, sculptural actions balancing her body against material elements. In her photographic series *3 Points* 1970–3, triangular figures are created by the artist's staging of her body in tension with lengths of fabric, in this sense appearing related to the minimal action-sculptures of German artist Franz Erhard Walther. His *First Work Set* 1963–9, for example, comprises a series of canvas objects that invite and support specific choreographed interactions. Activations by participants consist of them wearing, holding or being joined by the cloth, creating living sculptural arrangements.

In the 1980s, shifting the idea of living sculpture in a surreal direction, Brazilian artist Tunga created works such as *Xipopaga Capilares Entre Nos* 1984, in which prepubescent twin girls appeared bound together by a wig that connected their long hair – a work relating to his plaited floor sculptures in copper wire or lead, such as *Untitled (Braids)* 1981. In 1991, five years before he died of AIDS, Cuban-born artist Felix Gonzales-Torres's *Untitled (Go-Go Dancing Platform)* updated and explicitly queered these earlier takes on living sculpture. The artist cast a dancer to appear on his light-bulb-edged podium sculpture at intermittent intervals – a figure whose erotic and fun connotations presented at odds with with the melancholy of dancing alone, wearing headphones.

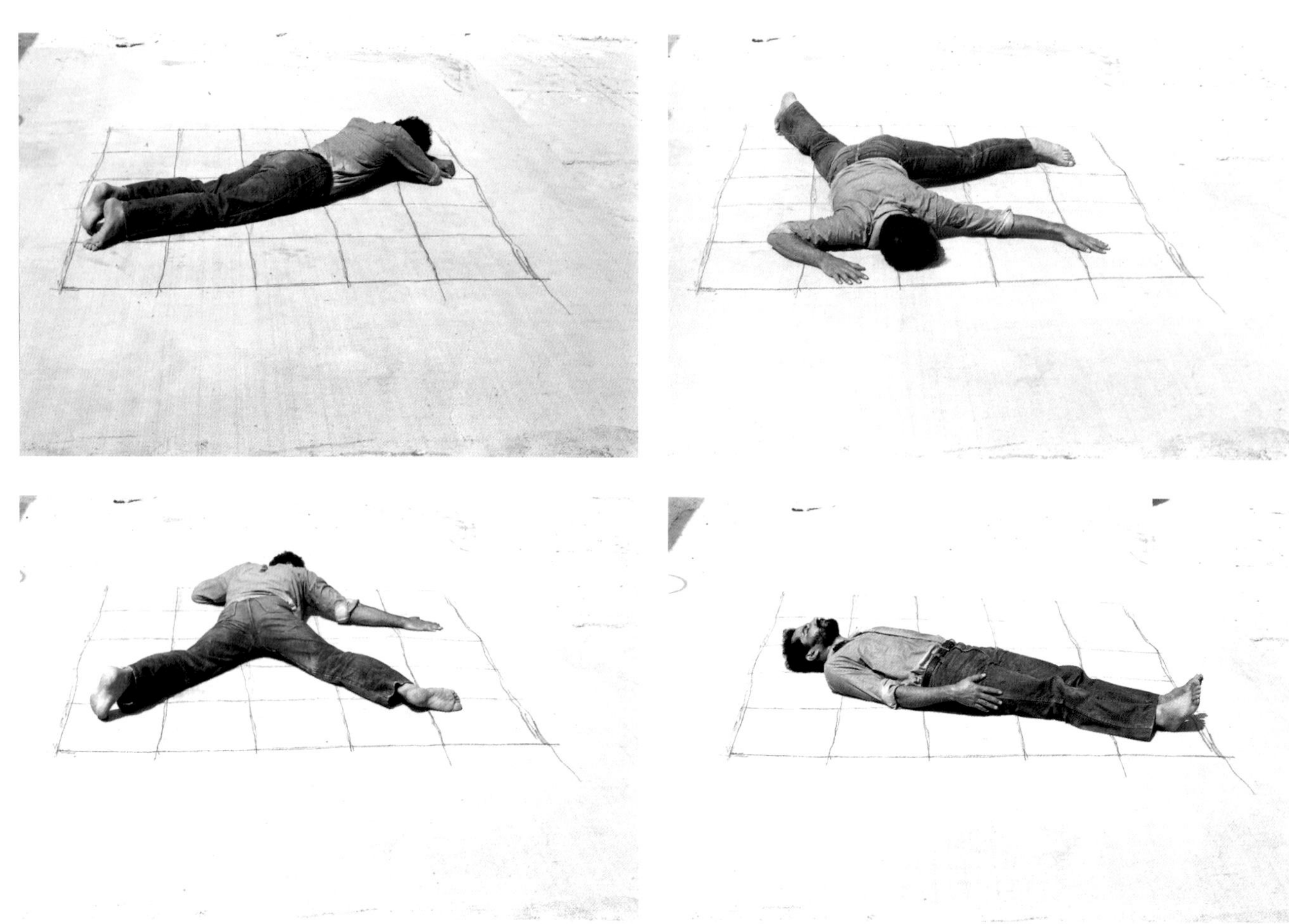

Hassan Sharif, *Body and Squares* 1983, photo documentation of the performance in the artist's studio in Satwa, Dubai

In the United Arab Emirates, the artist Hassan Sharif – who had studied at the Byam Shaw School of Art in London, and who brought RoseLee Goldberg's book on performance back to Dubai to share with peers – made a series of sculptural body-actions in the early 1980s. Using games of his own devising, Sharif applied procedures and rules of repetition based on a visual grid to test his own physical presence as form. His works were made both in his bedroom and out in the desert. In *Body and Square* 1983, for example, he lies in a sequence of six different configurations upon a drawing of a square grid: lying flat with one arm stretched in each direction, sitting up with one hand placed in an adjacent square, lying on his side with one foot in the furthermost square in each corner of the bottom of the grid, and so on. Sharif's approach to body-action as sculpture shaped his later, process-based sculptural practice, and influenced a generation of younger artists in the UAE. A notable inheritor of this approach is Mohammed Kazem, whose photography series *Tongue* 1996 documents actions where he sticks his tongue into domestic objects (water jugs, pipes), effecting absurd, temporary connections between his body and ordinary things. Kazem's later series, *Photographs with Flags* 1997–2003, recalls Sharif's 1980s work explicitly, but invokes the contemporary economy of the UAE. We see Kazem standing alone with his back to the camera in the Al Mamzar desert, with monochrome flags planted beside him marking potential sites for future urban developments: the conquering of territory appears to be already completed.

Within the realm of contemporary art, we increasingly understand the artwork in expanded terms to incorporate both object and action. In some cases, action is objectified, mimicking the qualities of material forms. In other cases, objects are made to move, appearing to act. Often, artists set objects and actions into provisional configurations, so that artworks do not necessarily have a fixed form or end. Duration becomes its boundary, rather than a material limit in space. It is telling that one of the makers of the most ambitious material sculpture of the past fifty years, American minimalist Richard Serra – nevertheless, like Robert Morris whom I shall go on to discuss, influenced by the downtown New York performance scene of his peers – manifests a relationship to action in works such as his film, *Hand Catching Lead* 1968, or his drawing titled *Verb List* 1967, which lists the processes of making, 'to roll, to crease, to fold', and so on.

It follows, then, that with the integration of performance into the field of contemporary art, the infrastructural rules of art's 'game' (the language of art as a kind of evolving institution) have come into visibility more clearly. Drawing attention to the agency of the artist as performer (as a kind of doer or demonstrator), performance-related work exposes the elusive chain of actions that underwrite the artwork. After Duchamp, whose acts of designation were more significant than the objects that physically persist (his naming, signing and placement of *Fountain* 1917 being the focus of value more than the shop-bought urinal itself), we begin to see how the power of utterance that is performativity underwrites the matrix of art's network of meanings and relationships. In other words: how we name things might be as important as the materials themselves for art after the 1950s. Lippard and Chandler called historical performance art, 'a no-man's or everyman's land in which visual artists whose styles may be completely at variance can meet and even agree',[2] and this zone of experimentation offered a valuable ground zero for configurations of attention, appearance and action within an interested community; a production of a shared reality that could be framed and temporarily agreed.

But if ideas of performance and performativity move from a simple sense of making, doing or acting, towards the production of a shared reality, we need to ask not only how does the object appear here, but also, how does this attitude objectify or reify action. Artworks can be made of actions, and objects can perform. This can be the case whether the object is literally moving, in, say, Lygia Pape's *Neo-Concrete Ballet* series 1958, where geometric shapes move around on a stage, or is subjected to a conceptual displacement, as in the repetition paintings of Sturtevant, whose very appearance cites their proximity to, and doubling of, works from the (male) canon.

Guy Debord's theory of social alienation builds upon Marx's analysis of political economy, which argues that capitalism is premised upon commodities seemingly taking on lives of their own, independently of the people who make and trade them – what he called 'commodity fetishism'. However, the notion of commodity fetishism has been fundamentally challenged. Anthropologist David Graeber, for example, has put this term in the context of early misunderstandings between European and African traders in the sixteenth century, pointing to the potential to rewrite this historical narrative. Graeber observes that to 'make' a fetish, for the African traders, would involve the use of an arbitrary material object to signify a valuable *social* bond, rather than that object being valued per se.[3] Within this logic, a piece of gold is as valued as a feather, and, with this rethinking of origins in mind, Graeber proposes a reconsideration of social creativity in contemporary capitalism: that is, the means by which social forms and institutions are created. In shifting how objects are framed within contemporary art, performance art arguably contributes to this broader rethinking of social creativity.

As the boundaries of the artwork are redrawn, our sense of aesthetic value changes, too. Performance has provided a reflexive context in which the artwork – whatever form it takes, whether material or immaterial – is taken out of a sphere of apparent disinterestedness or neutrality as far as viewing conditions are concerned, and is placed instead in an explicitly social and temporal setting. If performance and the performative are to do with how things are made to appear, then we might consider that the entire field of art is simply constituted of the investment we make in its meaning: how we give attention, how we place things, how we interact with our surroundings.

Performance, then, opens art to life by enacting scenarios that suggest that the activities of people in relation to objects and in relation to each other constitute the broader work of art. From a 'live' perspective, the material object can be imagined as but one element, albeit often an essential and catalytic one, in this view of the situation. After important critiques of modernism in the second half of the twentieth century, the Western ideal of art as a neutral, transcendental domain has been challenged, and its spaces of encounter have begun to be resituated socially and politically. Our understanding of performance and the performative have played an important role in this, by revealing the ultimately provisional nature of how we do things.

The way things go

In the first chapter I explored how artists' digital avatars embody some of the contradictions of the post-human. Here, I will look at questions of non-human action by materials or things: how the object position, which I have called *It*, is made to perform. A number of works made since the 1950s move away from explicitly positing the individual subject as a centre of meaning and interior consciousness, or even from the idea of social networks as producers of reality, towards the idea that things also act. This has been done in apparently crude ways, through experiments with performing sculpture; in highly speculative ways, presenting objects invested with a performative attitude; and in ways that frame other organic or technological forms of life. What I am referring to as the performative dimension of contemporary art is to do with how artists draw attention to the way in which all the elements of the art encounter act within a work or situation. The field of contemporary art is entangled with performance and the performative, in terms of how things act upon each other, act upon us, and are coexistent with us. It dramatises the question: what kind of reciprocity exists between people and things?

In 1987, the Swiss artists Peter Fischli and David Weiss made a film starring only objects called *The Way Things Go*. An action drama made with tools and materials in their studio – buckets, flammable liquids, balloons, chairs, water, and ropes – playing a variety of roles, the thirty-minute sequence comprises a chain of actions and reactions. It begins with a burning fuse wire, which, when it breaks, releases a black car tyre to roll down, and then up and down, a set of three rudimentary plywood see-saws before it pulls over an aluminium ladder it has passed through.

Water, fire and a toy train continue the process. This improbably successful chain of reactions keeps moving, as we will it to with some sense of suspense. Fischli and Weiss's approach to sculpture has often shown a highly playful and performative dimension, bordering on magical trickery. Here, the materials in the artists' studio are given apparent agency, as they seem to perform on their own while their masters are absent. Yet with a nod to the kinetic art of their Swiss forbear Jean Tinguely the piece also offers a critique of the fantasy of the autonomous object. We infer the artists' precise planning in every detail of the set-up, their determination in coaxing the objects to play their parts, and the sequence to work.

The study, collection and display of objects – utilitarian, decorative or symbolic – has been central to the evolution of Western modernity and to the way in which the modern or contemporary art museum understands itself, its holdings and its exhibitions. In the realm of 'modern and contemporary' – or 'visual' – art, though, the anthropological context that frame objects in museums such as the British Museum or the Metropolitan Museum of Art in New York is erased in favour of an increasingly globalised conceptual and formal language of object-immanence. A problem with this contemporary model – evolved after modernism – is that, unlike those ethnographic objects with ritual associations, art human agency is somehow out of the picture. In combination with a denigration of manual skill after the readymade, the contemporary artwork becomes untouchable, almost un-made. And, moreover, it becomes out of use: existing only for visual display.[4]

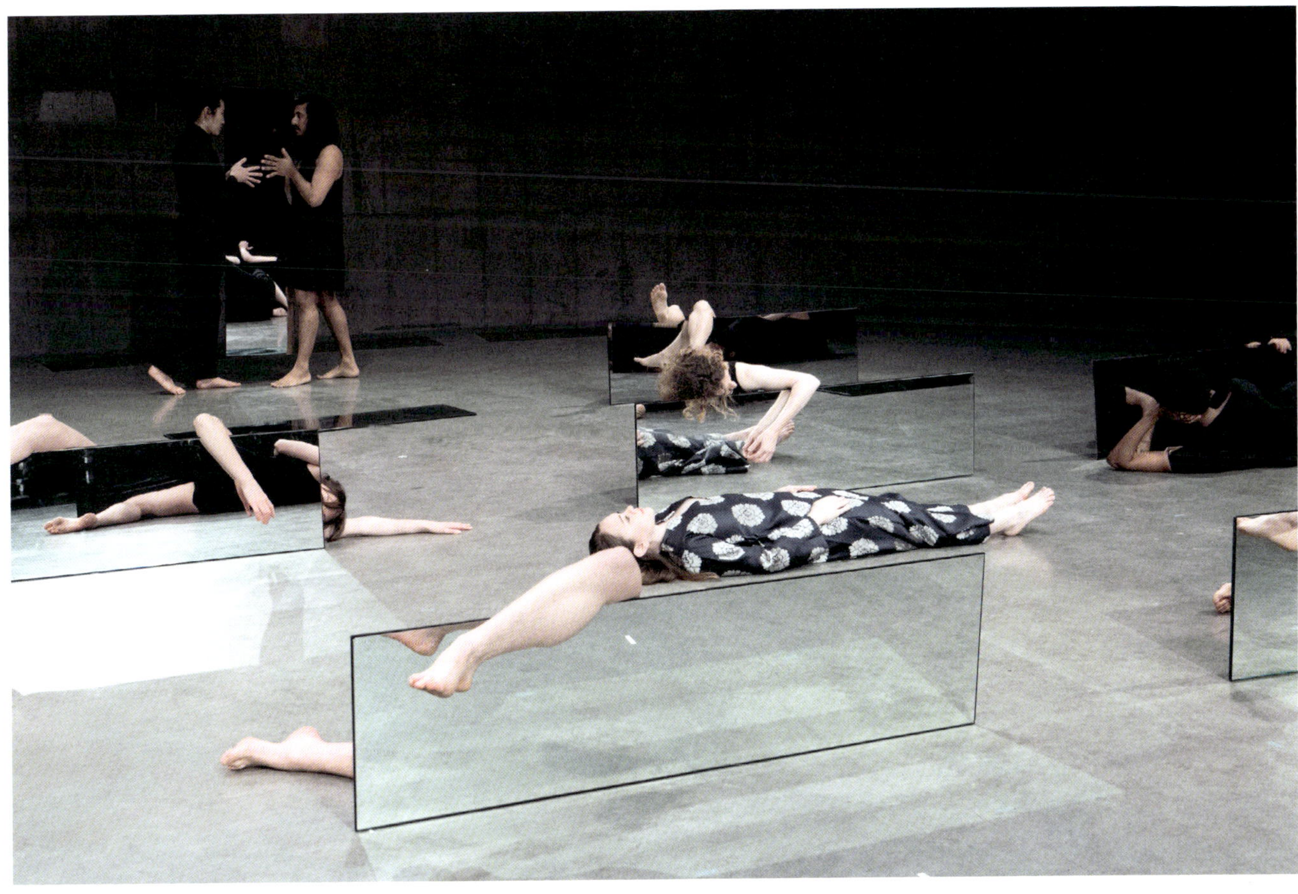

Joan Jonas, *Mirror Piece II* 1970, performed as part of BMW Tate Live Exhibition *Ten Days Six Nights*, Tate Modern, 20 March 2018

To understand the role of the object in the context of performance, and in parallel to understand how it can be performative, it is necessary to think about again how the object is related to action in contemporary art. In the 1960s and 70s, artists enacted process: they staged objects or things as moving entities, often as series of permutations via photography and film; from here, objects began to appear as a kind of prompt or prop that elicits action; and, more recently, objects themselves have been cast as actors in performances that draw attention to organic movement by non-human actors. Lastly, we will look at works that stage objects within narrative or conceptual frameworks, casting them as quasi-characters or stage sets.

Post-1950

Props and prompts

The theatre set provides a ready-made image of how the art object might relate to action. If the visual arts have remained averse to theatricality, long after the term was used pejoratively by American critic Michael Fried in the late 1960s to characterise minimalist sculpture, it might be because the notion of the prop, as a kind of short-hand symbol within a story, represents a denigration of an object's status.[5] Yet there are many interesting ways in which artists have played with art objects as props of sorts, or as prompts to initiate action.

Writing about the artistic working process in 1980, British artist and filmmaker Sally Potter – who collaborated with significant peers in this field, including performance-maker Rose English, and choreographer Jacky Lansley – argued for the use of the art object as a prompt for the creation of live work: 'The sculptor turned performance artist might start with making or finding an object, and working outwards from there; in some sense activating it in time, or giving it space, a room, or a set, which suggests a scenario.'[6] While Potter was moving between, and cross-contaminating, discrete disciplines (dance, visual art and film), American artist Joan Jonas was a pioneer of what, in the 1970s, was labelled 'mixed-media performance', in which all elements (sculpture, video, live action) coincided within a single work (see p.66). Jonas's practice emerged from sculpture. In live form, she often dramatised her own relationship to the so-called traditional media, which she and her peers were moving away from, by incorporating minimal sculptural objects as props. She also performed the actions of drawing and painting. Painted ink symbols, chalk markings and rudimentary sculptural forms – bricks, slats, wooden blocks, cones – would be fundamental to Jonas's sequences of action and allusive narrative. She would also incorporate found things – a doll, a mask or a Japanese fan – to work and improvise with. In her work of this period, Jonas invented a surreal and personal world, a parallel to the exhibition space, populated by symbols, objects, animals and human action, and mediated by lenses and screens.

In her important early performances *Mirror Pieces* 1968–71 (p.183), Jonas used multiple large mirrors as actors of sorts, and also as a way of proposing a form of expanded sculpture. These rectangular mirrors became substitute figures, carried by performers on stage who would slowly, deliberately shift and rotate

Senga Nengudi, R.S.V.P sculptures activated by the artist and Maren Hassinger in *Performance Piece – Nylon Mesh and Maren Hassinger*, Pearl C. Wood Gallery, Los Angeles, 1977

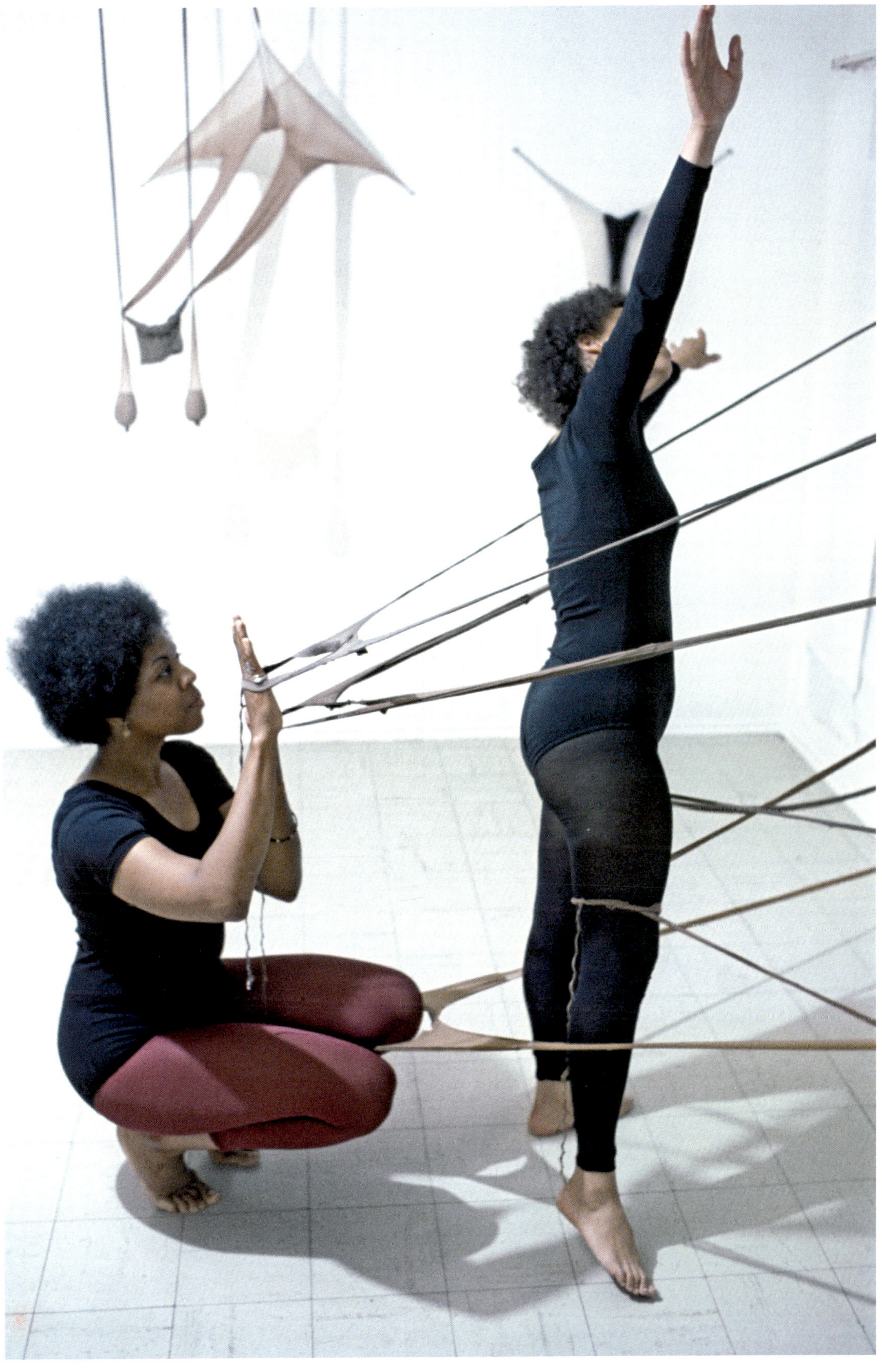

them so as to capture the audience as a fragmented image on glass. Jonas was interested in how the effect of a mirror could disrupt and alter space, as well as in the psychological dimension of mirrors in relation to self-portraiture. As I have discussed in chapter 1, Jonas has since used video in a similar way – to what David Joselit called 'de-synchronised'[7] effect. Her later work *The Juniper Tree* 1976 is a performance and subsequent installation woven through a fairytale. The work takes painting's symbolic function and the ritual use of objects in ancient world cultures as a method for exploring subjectivity and myth, extending the feminine masquerade begun in the early 1970s. In this performance and later installation, Jonas hangs her paintings like ceremonial banners or flags, and displays a collection of objects including percussion instruments, dolls and an embroidered kimono, to designate a space with transformative capacity, where something might happen. For Jonas, such objects represent not an end point but as a set of possibilities.

African American artist Senga Nengudi invented a new language of biomorphic sculpture in her *R.S.V.P.* series, begun in 1977 (p.185). The sculptures are typically made of everyday found materials, such as women's nylon mesh tights which she would select in a variety of skin tones. Nengudi would improvise in situ, pinning and stretching the tights into changing positions, or would fill them with sand to weight and distend them, creating ritual performances with and around the sculptures. In tune with her later emphasis on live process via performance, and influenced by having studied dance, Nengudi favoured the extreme portability of her sculptural materials and method, which could be assembled onsite, carried in her handbag.

Nengudi was affiliated with a radical group of African American artists known as Studio Z, including David Hammons and Maren Hassinger, who took an experimental and improvisational approach to performance. In works such as *Performance Piece* 1978, Nengudi invited Hassinger to activate her sculptures by becoming entangled with the fabric, representing how women were socially restricted via the expectations of gender, and also commenting on the elasticity of the (female) body as it stretches and comes back into shape in pregnancy, or indeed – often exhausted and over-used – does not. In Nengudi's work, the biomorphic nature of the sculpture is proposed as a material equivalent for the body, and a state of dynamic equilibrium is enacted in the performances. As a kind of second-skin, the sculptures perform as bodily equivalents.

From the late 1970s, American artist Mike Kelley's work – as an artist, thinker, writer and performer – acknowledged the legacy of female pioneers in performance such as Jonas, as well as Judy Chicago and her Womanhouse peers. Kelley's early performances and installations staged significant new ways of looking at the making of things in art, and demonstrating them in use, from a rudimentary, or perspective (p.187). In the performance and subsequent installation *Monkey Island* 1982–3, Kelley conjures an image of primates occupying positions in relation to art normally designated for the human spectator. In this work, Kelley referenced the situations set up by psychologist Harry Harlow to test the behaviour of primates in the 1950s, and the installation version conflates modernist sculptural form with Harlow's curiously sculptural scientific equipment. The more recent installation *Test Room Containing Multiple Stimuli Known to Elicit Curiosity and Manipulatory Responses* 1999 elaborates on Harlow's experiments by creating a setting for improvisational dance. The title of the performative element of this project, developed in collaboration with choreographer Anita Pace,

Mike Kelley, *Perspectaphone*, performance, Los Angeles Contemporary Exhibitions, 1978

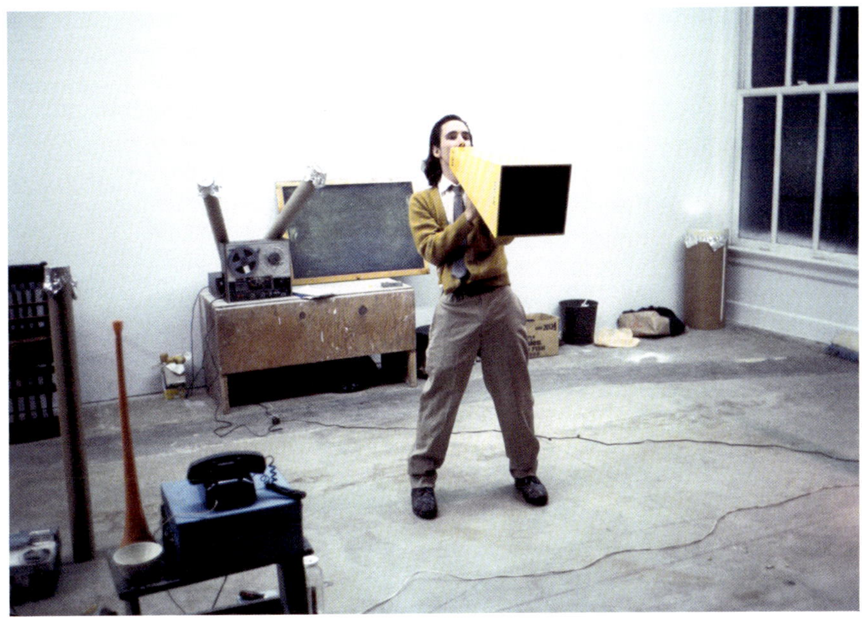

is self-explanatory: *A Dance Incorporating Movements Derived from Experiments by Harry F. Harlow and Choreographed in the Manner of Martha Graham*.

Kelley's staging of this primary relationship to art, like his 1978 wooden birdhouse sculptures made from DIY manuals, was a way of rethinking the place of art within culture, and its relation to craft and other kinds of making. Kelley spoke of the sculptural object as a rudimentary prop or prompt towards thinking, manifest in certain kinds of behaviour. He made visible a continuum between the artwork, the viewer and the architectural space that was not about neutral display, but rather about the activation of curious sets of pivots, repressions, prompts and psychological states. Kelley was significantly influenced, too by the French artist Guy de Cointet, whose scripted plays using minimalist props represented an early instance of the coming together of material object and improvisation in the 1970s, to conjure surreal situations that staged new kinds of behaviours and fictions. In his performance and later installation and video work, Kelley established an important understanding, for artists after the 1980s, of border crossings between genres and genders, between high and low culture. The difference between Kelley's approach and the dematerialisation of art in the 1960s and 1970s is that, rather than being displayed as the results of action-derived process, objects appear here clearly as catalysts that suggest or determine behaviour. In addition, found objects chosen not just for their form but for their associations play roles that deliberately allow the potential contamination of high culture with 'trash'.

Like Jonas, Los Angeles-based artist Channa Horwitz also worked with drawing, but her work suggests a very different relationship to performance (p.188). Rather than being used as prompts in a direct way, her intricate, repetitive score drawings from the *Sonakinatography* series 1968–2012 act as latent notation for performance or dance, which might never be realised: they contain the potential to work as a score, but can also be looked at as abstract patterns that are self-contained.

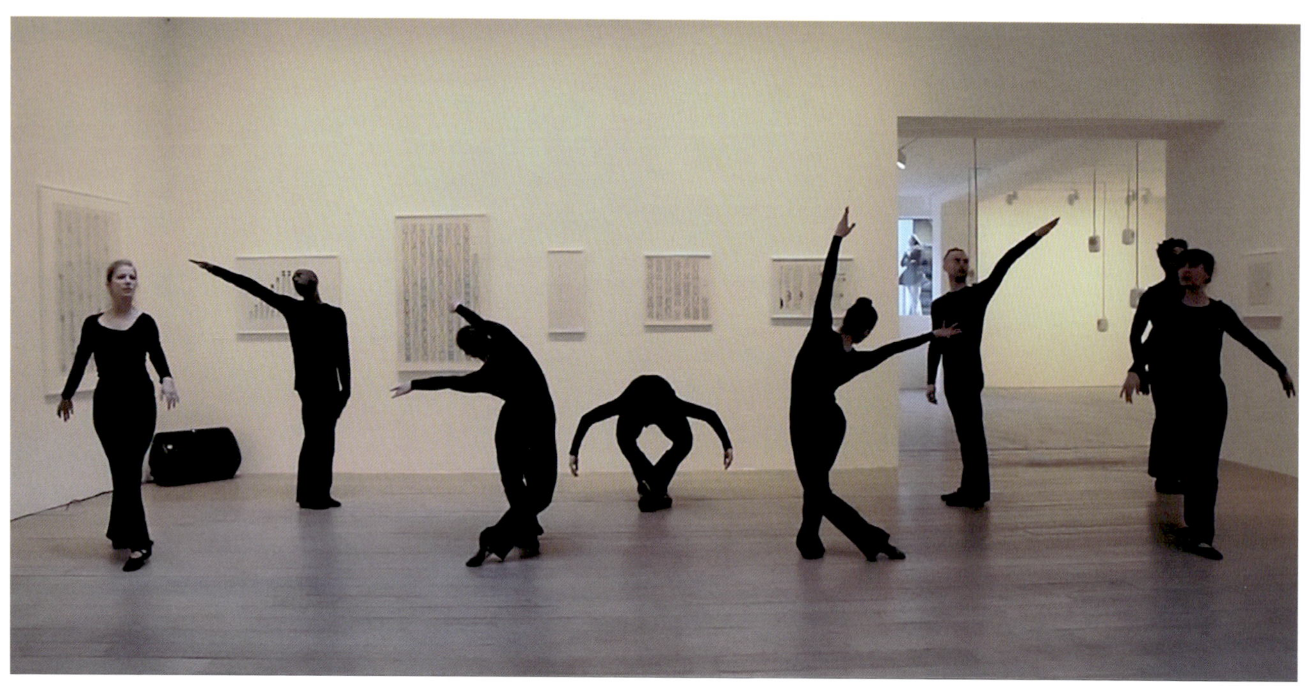

Channa Horwitz, a choreographic interpretation by Ellen Davis of Channa Horwitz's *Sonakinatography Composition III*, performed at Raven Row, 13 March 2016

Horwitz's 'Sonakinatographies' resonate with the compositional strategies of her artist contemporaries Sol LeWitt and Agnes Martin; as notation, they could be read in relation to the musical scores of Charlemagne Palestine, or the abstract scores of elder choreographers such as Mary Wigman and Rudolf Laban. In their intricate numerical grids, they also resemble the then-emergent language of computer programming, nodding to the nascent idea of the thinking machine.

Being works that encapsulate and compress a time-based medium such as dance within static form, and nod to the digital, Horwitz's drawings make new sense today. In the past decade, through our use of lens-based technology, images have come to be understood not as ends in themselves, but as modes of communication. Horwitz's works occupy a unique place in this evolving territory, because they reject and at the same time embrace their own potential as conduits. In acting as latent scores for imagined choreographies, and for the transmission of information in encrypted form, they go beyond the question of performance and its material trace as instruction or documentation. Horwitz's drawings are, simultaneously, end points and potential beginnings, carrying codes that might initiate movement or sound improvisation.

If the American and Western European artists mentioned here worked in contexts in which disciplinary boundaries were severely defined, even fetishised, an important counter-model can be found in the work of the Laboratoire Agit'Art, founded in Dakar in 1974 (p.189). This was a revolutionary and subversive art collective established by the artist Issa Samb, the filmmaker Djibril Diop Mambéty, painter El Hadji Sy and the playwright Youssoupha Dione. While Horwitz or Jonas opened up new performative activations of painting and drawing within the gallery, these artists built a context for the coexistence of action, poetry, painting and sculpture from scratch, in an informal, social set-up. The collaborators, working freely across disciplines, sought to combine what they called traditional 'African performance and creativity'[8] with a modern aesthetic, devising street performances, improvisational happenings, installations and workshops. Although diverse in their practice, they were united in challenging the philosophy of Négritude, promulgated by then Senegal president Léopold Sédar Senghor and others, whose principles were to do with 'the conscience of being black, the simple recognition of a fact which implies its acceptance, charged with its destiny of blackness, its history and culture'.[9] The members of Laboratoire Agit'Art worked against this national policy in the arts, which they saw as being too indebted to the dominant history of Western civilisation. Instead, they wanted to embrace African heritage and tradition as part of making art, on its own terms. Their work offers a model that speaks to contemporary concerns about sustainability and the relative values of the material and immaterial in art.

The outlook of the Laboratoire Agit'Art was political and community-focused: they published manifestos and created installations out of street detritus that raised issues about contemporary African society. The participating artists wanted to propose a new experience of 'total art', often through performative and ritualistic processes in which objects played a significant part within the total *mise en scène*, but were not valued per se. The making of objects was conceived as a continuation of the performances and conversations taking place in the artists' studio – an open courtyard space, in which people could come and go, which was part studio, part café, part performance arena, part exhibition space. Such an attitude represented a microcosm of the wider political shifts occurring

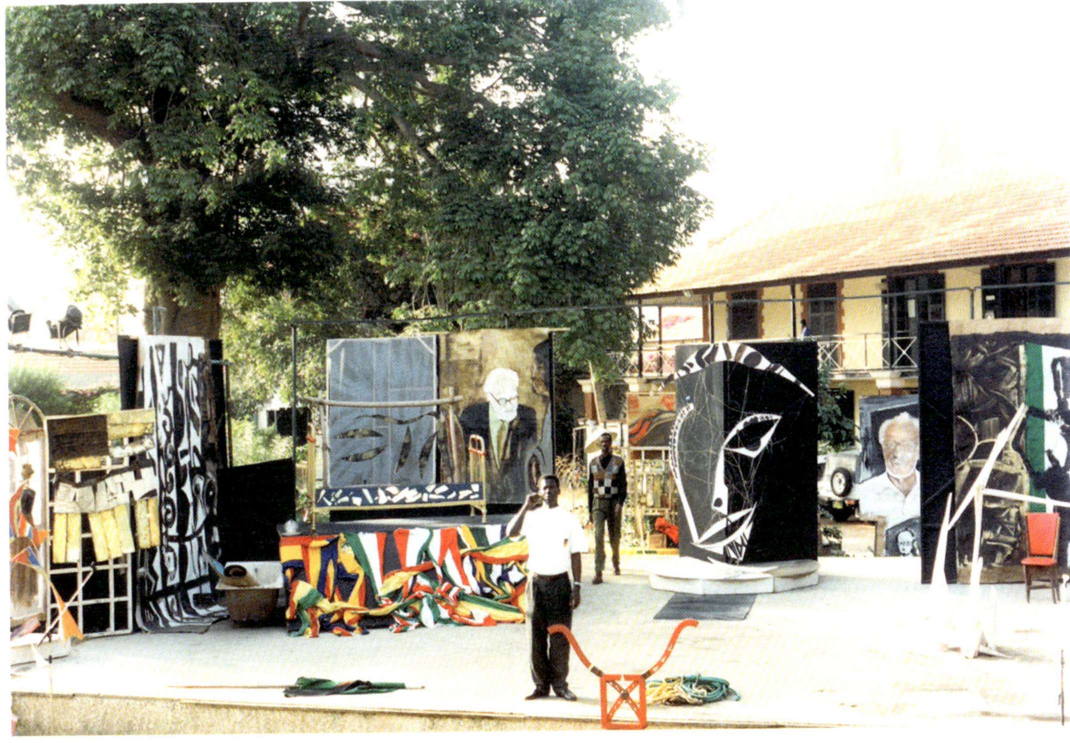

Laboratoires Agit'art: Plehanov 7, Les Cendres de Pierre Lods, 19 January 1990, Théâtre de Verdure du Centre Culturel, Dakar. Reproduced with kind permission of the Weltkulturen Museum, Frankfurt am Main, Collection Axt/Sy

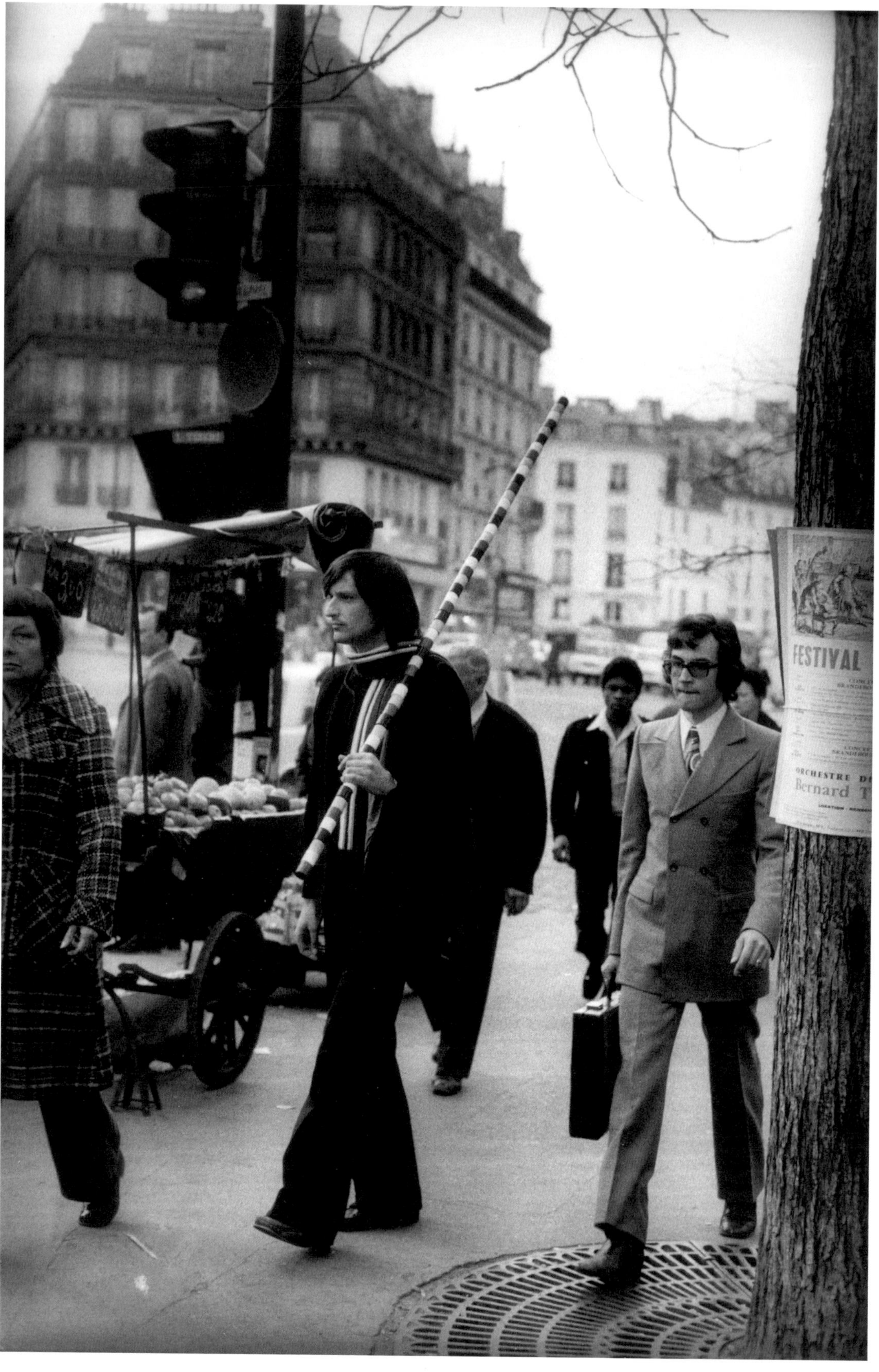

André Cadere, *Exposition avec La Galerie des Locataires*, Avenue des Gobelins, Paris 3–8 April 1973 (photographed by Bernard Borgeaud)

in Senegalese institutions at the time, in its radical questioning of values and rearrangement of aesthetic and social relations.

Crucial to our contemporary understanding of the role of performance in art is the fact that one of the key protagonists of Laboratoire Agit'Art, artist El Hadji Sy, 'made multimedia assemblages of *objets trouvés*, which he used to *symbolically restore the life of those objects*', as curator Elvira Dyangani Ose has observed. By being handled and performed with, objects were not made less valuable but were, in fact, imbued with greater significance. The art object's meaning was directly related to how it was 'performed'. According to Dyangani Ose, this mode of working also offers a nod to everyday Senegalese life, 'in which that reutilisation of objects is part of people's routine'.[10]

The Laboratoire Agit'Art offered a dynamic approach to art-making which did not rest upon the formalisation of any element into a finished product, but emphasised instead shared experience and a deferral of material fixity. Its members were interested in placing the spectator at the centre of every action, as an active participant, and choosing an outdoor location was a part of creating a space that was distinct from Western theatre's separation of spectators and actors. Curator Okwui Enwezor has noted that, 'whilst in Western art the cycle of art is completed in the aesthetic realm of display, in African traditions this finale is achieved through a desublimation strategy that perpetually displaces the object and places greater significance on non-visual codes and performative actions'.[11]

The objects made by Polish-born, Romanian artist André Cadere were also imbued with a quality of magic potency via their use in actions. His *Round Bar of Wood* series, made in 1971–8, consisted of painted object-sculptures that the artist perpetually displaced, in a playful manner, by carrying them with him, in and out of formal gallery spaces. Each one of these stick-like artworks was made in the same way: he cut wooden dowels into segments, painted them different colours, and then strung them like beads onto a thin baton before gluing them together. He worked according to a rule of painting with only eight colours (red, orange, yellow, green, blue, violet, black and white) and then arranged these into patterns using mathematical systems that he called 'permutations'.

This process-based composition was common in post-minimalist art, but the power of Cadere's work was, arguably, more to do with how his objects were used: how they interacted with the institutional functions of the artist, the museum and the market. Having no specific orientation, and being in between painting and sculpture, the bars were carried about by the artist to museums and galleries, and positioned in different ways: propped up against the wall, lying horizontally on the floor, and so on. Contravening norms of exhibition practice, Cadere would sometimes insert them into other people's exhibitions without having been invited. In this way, he underscored the mechanisms of inclusion and exclusion of the museum and gallery system, as well as casting the object not so much as a separate, finished entity but as an extension of his own presence. Even when they were static, the bars connoted a trickster-like possibility of movement, or imminent disappearance, working against the atemporal fixity implied by the gallery. Though he did not play this role in the way that Joseph Beuys did, the stick-sculptures lent his practice a shamanistic quality.

Object actors

As we have seen, since the 1950s, documentation of artists at work in the studio shed light upon artistic process and began to cast the making of art as a kind of proto-performance. In parallel, artists making sculpture began to experiment with what might be seen as a crude legacy of stop-motion animation techniques. The object choreographies of early twentieth-century figures such as Oskar Fischinger created impressions of things moving by themselves, in patterns and sequences. From the 1960s, minimalist artists began to use sequential photography to document the potential permutations of their work: for example, Sol LeWitt's modular open cubes from the late 1960s – sculptures in which the variable arrangements of a three-dimensional grid of cubed shapes were played out in series. Pushing the idea of serial permutation further, the German artist Charlotte Posenenske had her steel and cardboard Square Tubes sculptures photographed in different permutations and at different locations, including on the tarmac at Frankfurt Airport in 1967. Posenenske – who gave up making art objects after 1968 to engage in social work, and to organise trade unions – was concerned with the social substrate of art, and she deliberately contextualised the variable

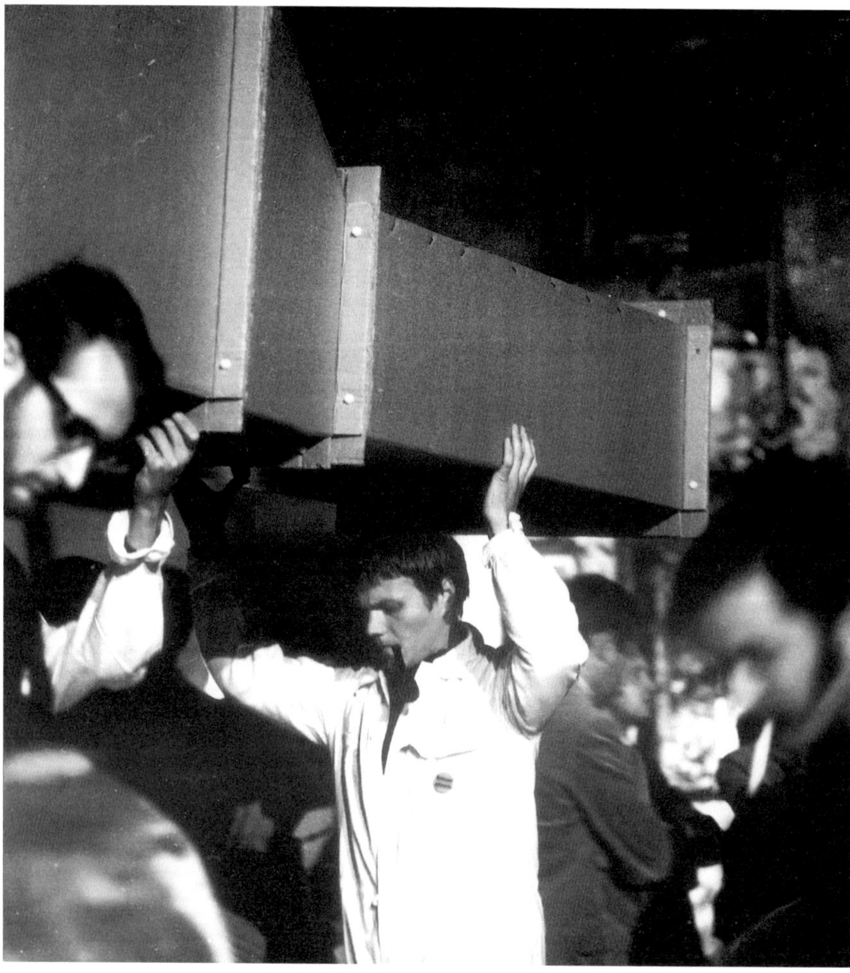

Charlotte Posenenske, *Serie DW Vierkantrohre [Square Tubes]*, corrugated cardboard, Galerie Dorothea Loehr, Frankfurt am Main, 1967

Rasheed Araeen, *Zero to Infinity* 1968–2007, in the process of rearrangement at Tate Britain, 2016

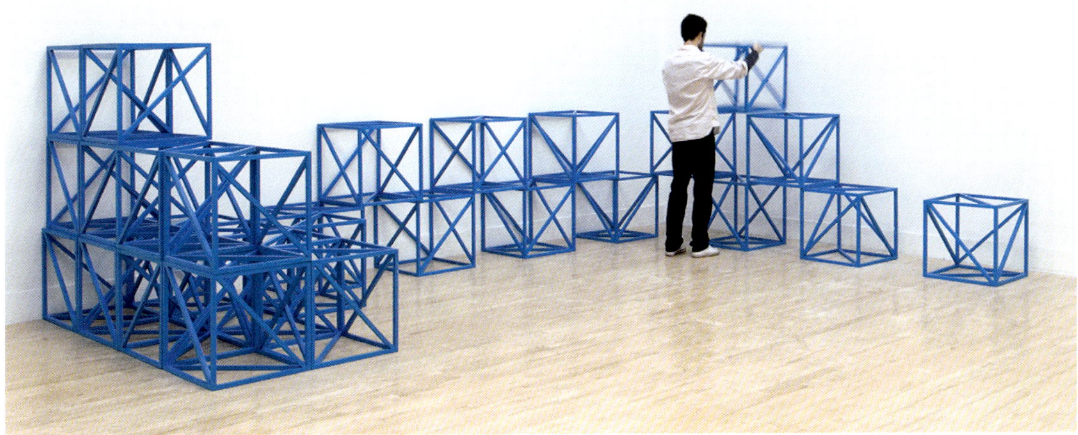

configurations of her industrially produced works, photographed in sequence, by placing them in sites that connoted modern technology and transportation. She also staged photos of 'workers' moving and manipulating them. Pakistani-born artist Rasheed Araeen made interactive sculpture, exemplified in his one hundred open-framework lattice cubes painted blue, titled *Zero to Infinity* 1968, which were occasionally redistributed and photographed in different arrangements, working with participants. His early actions of the 1970s are similarly transient: cut-out circular or geometrically shaped objects were placed in the landscape, or on the surface of a river, to form a sequence of temporary active sculpture constellations. In parallel, making more explicit the performance dimension, Araeen planned an (as yet) unrealised project titled *Disco Sailing* 1970–3, in which the sculptures became surfboards for costumed enactors swathed in fabric.

In the late 1960s and early 1970s, the Japanese artists loosely associated with the group Mono-ha (literally, 'school of things') used photography to document sculpture in a manner that was distinct from these mathematically inspired approaches to process or seriality. And, instead of emphasising the idea of creating something from scratch, or of staging an object against a distinct ground, Mono-ha artists conceived of sculpture made by rearranging the elements of given reality. These ranged from organic to man-made materials: 'things' that were bare and untransformed. The materials were usually easily replaceable: stones, sticks, wooden blocks, earth. For the Mono-ha artists, it was the score for their arrangement or placement that was significant: the way that they appeared – often nakedly provisional – in an art context, and the viewer's inference of the trace of the artist's labour through both their precarious arrangement and the photographic evidence. The work focused on the interdependency of the elements within the arrangements they created, as much as in their relation to the space they were presented in.

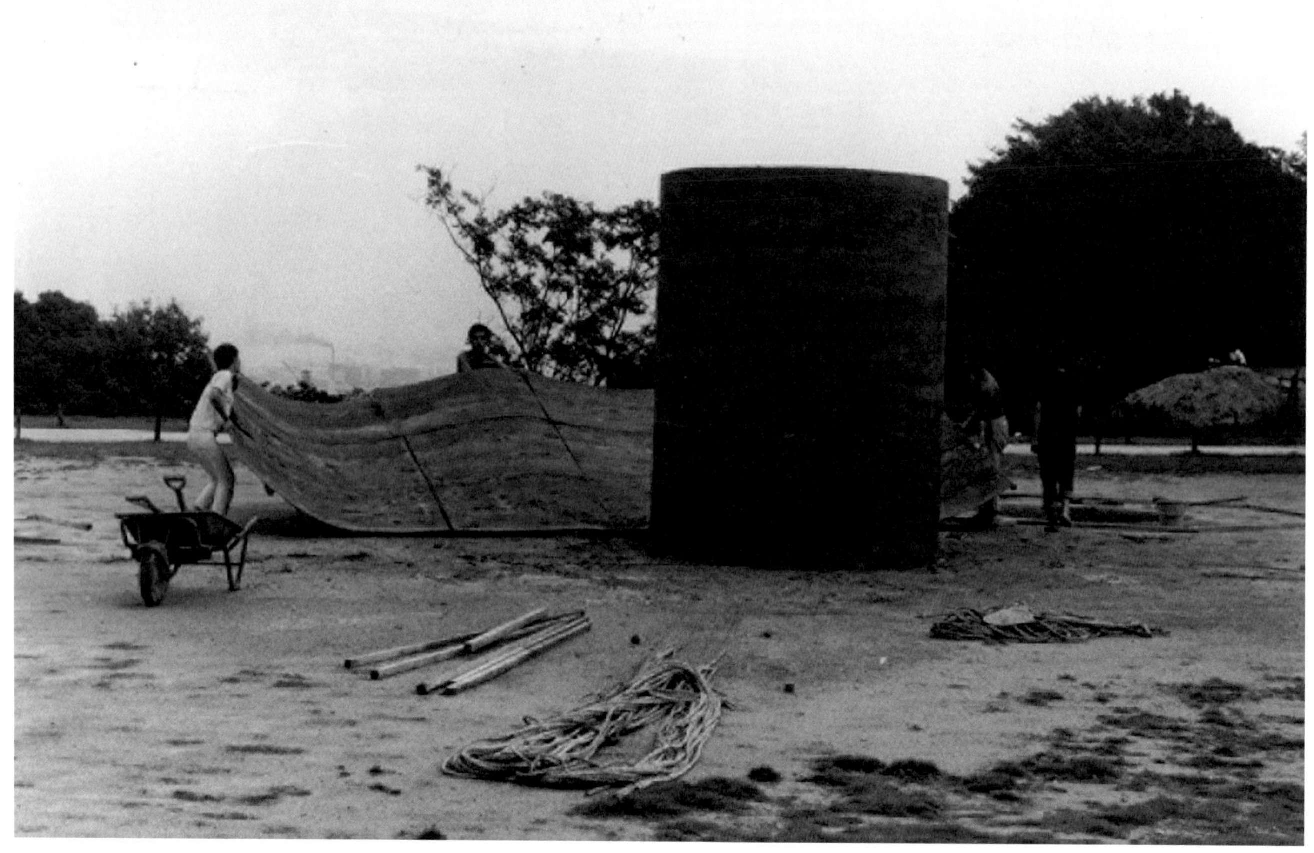

Nobuo Sekine, *Phase-Mother Earth* 1968, production shot, 1st Kobe Suma Rikyu Park Contemporary Sculpture Exhibition, 1 October – 10 November 1968

One of the most important figures within Mono-ha was Nobuo Sekine, whose *Phase – Mother Earth* 1968 is seen to be the piece that established the movement. This work was staged in a public park in the city of Kobe, as part of the *First Open Air Contemporary Sculpture Exhibition* in 1968. It consisted of a precisely dug hole in the ground, in the shape of a column, which was approximately 270 cm in depth and 220 cm in diameter. Alongside the hole was placed a column of the exact same proportions and shape, composed of the excavated soil. It was the movement of earth, documented in photographs, that constituted the work.

Kishio Suga's work is also characterised by the use of simple, everyday materials to create physical and conceptual structures within which the artist's process is made manifest. His practice stressed the interdependence of the materials' weight, form and presence within specific situations. In 1970, he made a piece by propping open two windows in the National Museum of Modern Art in Kyoto with two blocks of wood of different lengths. *Infinite Situation 1 (window)* was intended to draw active attention to the connection between inside and outside, thus incorporating into our experience of the work the room itself, the circulating air and the window as a two-way supporting frame.

In the State of Equal Dimension 1973 is a work made of two tall, forked tree branches, leaning against a corner of the gallery walls, which support a length of rope at their four uppermost points. At each end of the rope, a rock is bound, as though to weigh the sculpture to the floor. Of his understanding of the active relations between things, characteristic of the approach of the Mono-ha artists, Suga has written, 'The thing (*mono*) cannot exist as an isolated single body. Each singular piece is related and must rely on each other. [...] When the related objects are put in sequence, the value of each is realised. [...] The sequentiality of each individual piece expresses the state between the things and also between the thing and cognition.'[12] Mono-ha's focus on the interaction between objects seems to prefigure, in low-fi fashion, the twenty-first-century understanding of the connectivity of electronic objects in the so-called internet of things. Though human actors do not appear in the works, these installations represent a record of action and an acute sensitivity to material temporariness rather than fixity: the binding of a rope around a rock, the digging and moulding of earth, or the balancing of wooden beams. Mono-ha offers an alternative attitude towards 'relationality'.

For many artists in the postwar period, including the American minimalists and Brazilian neo-concretists, as well as Mono-ha, the influence of Maurice Merleau-Ponty's phenomenology was highly significant. Merleau-Ponty emphasised the body as the primary interface through which we get to know the world, implying that one's body is first and foremost situated in space, in relation to things. This offered a corrective to the long-held philosophical tradition of placing consciousness as the source of knowledge and prioritising opticality. Phenomenology proposes that the body and that which it perceives cannot be disentangled from each other, and are bound together within a continuously shifting interrelationship. In this context, the body came to be seen as a sensorial apparatus in itself, rather than being one more thing.

Lygia Pape was a key artist in the Brazilian neo-concrete movement, a group formed in 1959 by Lygia Clark (p.196), Ferreira Gullar and others, and joined later by Hélio Oiticica. Wanting to resituate the art object in lived experience, these artists approached sculpture by 'destroying the base' and creating an object that could be positioned more directly in relation to the viewer, on the same floor plane. Equally, paintings – unframed – would seem to move out in real space and time. In their manifesto, the neo-concretists wrote, 'We do not conceive of a work of art as a "machine" or "object" but as a "quasi-corpus"' that could only be fully understood through a direct, phenomenological encounter.'[13] The work of art was recast by these artists as having something in common with a living organism. The absence of a frame or support encouraged viewers' interaction with the object of art, so that the work would be continually recreated. Eventually, the support even became attached to the body itself, as in Oiticica's cloak-like *Parangolés* from the mid-1960s, conceived in relation to the exuberant dance of carnival.

In the 1950s, Pape made paintings, prints and sculptures but also a number of related performance experiments. Two important projects that challenged the notion of the artwork as an inert object and instead posed it as a living entity were her geometric *Neo-Concrete Ballets* 1958 (p.197), influenced by the mechanical ballets of Oskar Schlemmer in the 1920s, and her large-scale performance piece *Divider* 1968. Pape's ballets differed from Schlemmer's in that they appeared to cast the objects themselves as performers, rather than presenting the performers as objects via costume. In her first piece, *Neo-Concrete Ballet I*, four white cylinders and four orange-red parallelograms appeared onstage. Each was two

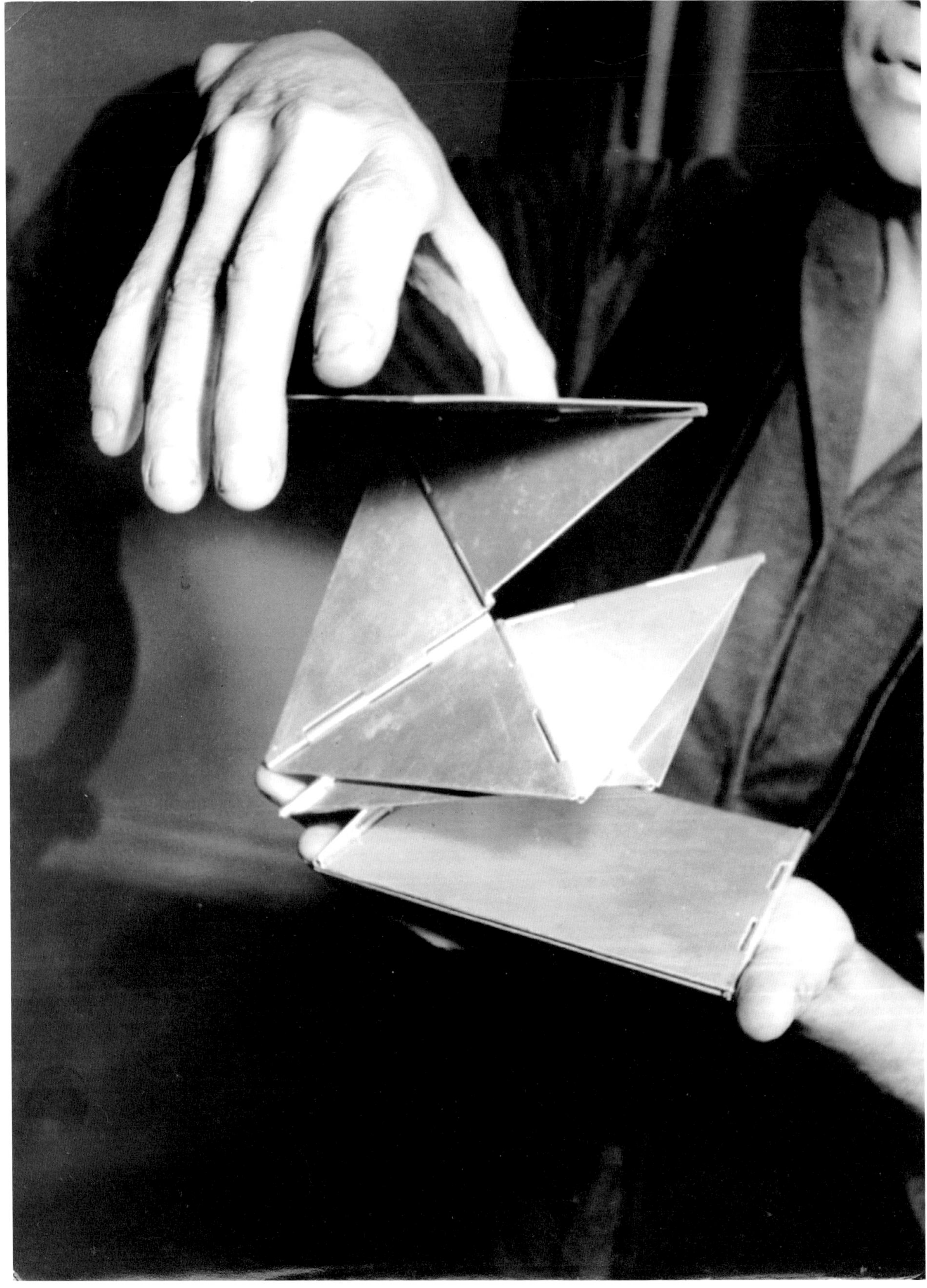

Lygia Clark, *Bicho de Bolso (Pocket Animal* 1966, aluminum, 15 x 37 x 10.5

Lygia Pape, *Ballet Neoconcreto I (Neoconcrete Ballet I)* 1958; performance at Fundação de Serralves – Museu de Arte Contemporânea, Porto, 2000

metres tall and set on wheels, moved by people hidden inside them. Scored according to the two-word poem 'Olho/Alvo' (*olho* meaning 'eye', *alvo* meaning 'target') by Reynaldo Jardim, the choreography was made up of simple repetitive movements enacted by the geometric shapes, as two notes sounded on the piano, which was used as a percussion instrument. The second ballet involved two large pink squares – one distinguished by a blue stripe along the tip – set against a black background. In these works, Pape experimented with an idea of total composition that was related to painting and sculpture, but merged the human actor and object to propose an organic-geometric totality. Such an approach might be seen in relation to action painting, as an alternative disclosure of the artist's process – a kind of live staging of composition. But here the process is clearly presented as the work in itself, a kind of composition in movement, which never becomes fixed.

Pape's *Divider* radically extended the idea of a user-led work, formed entirely by a crowd of participants whose heads slot into holes in a large, square, white sheet. They then proceed to walk down the street, forming a collective action and sculpture in motion. The work prefigures similar works in this period that make visible ideas of social networks as a corpus, such as James Lee Byars's *Ten in a Hat* 1969, a collective mobile sculpture enacted by ten participants wearing an extended piece of pink cloth fixed to each person's head by a cap, and Nicola L's *The Red Coat* 1969, a performance work in which a group of participants wear a multi-part red raincoat, expressing the artist's proposal of a 'desire to share a collective skin': each of these fuse the notion of a collective 'we' with that of the art object.[14]

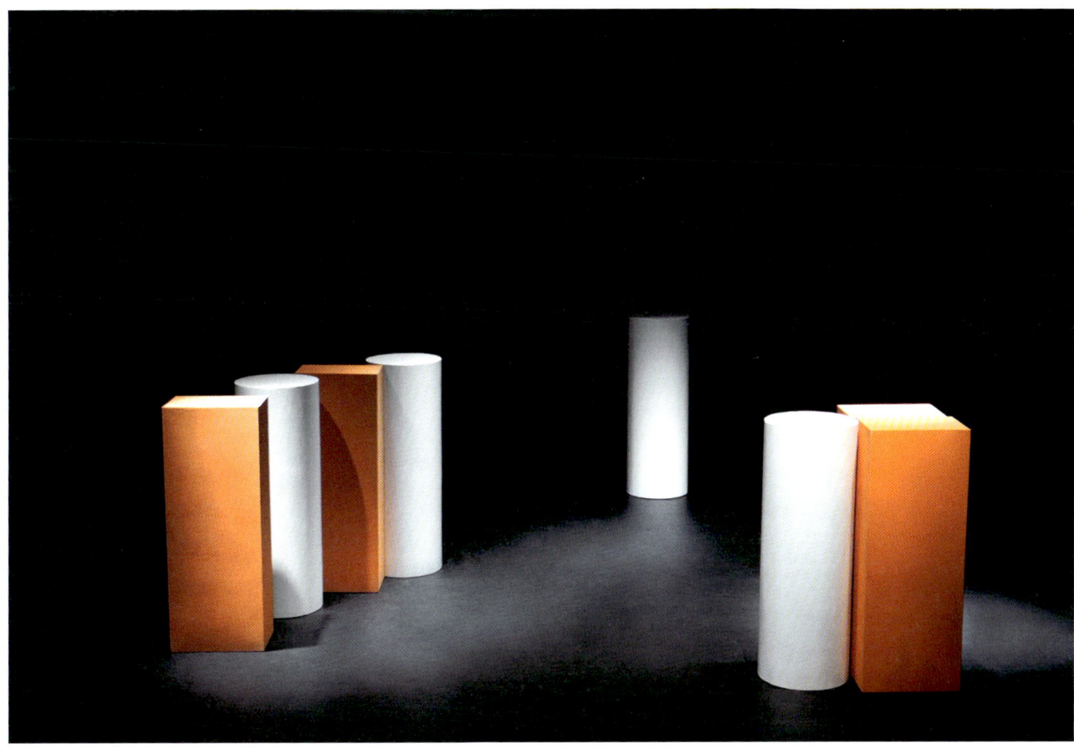

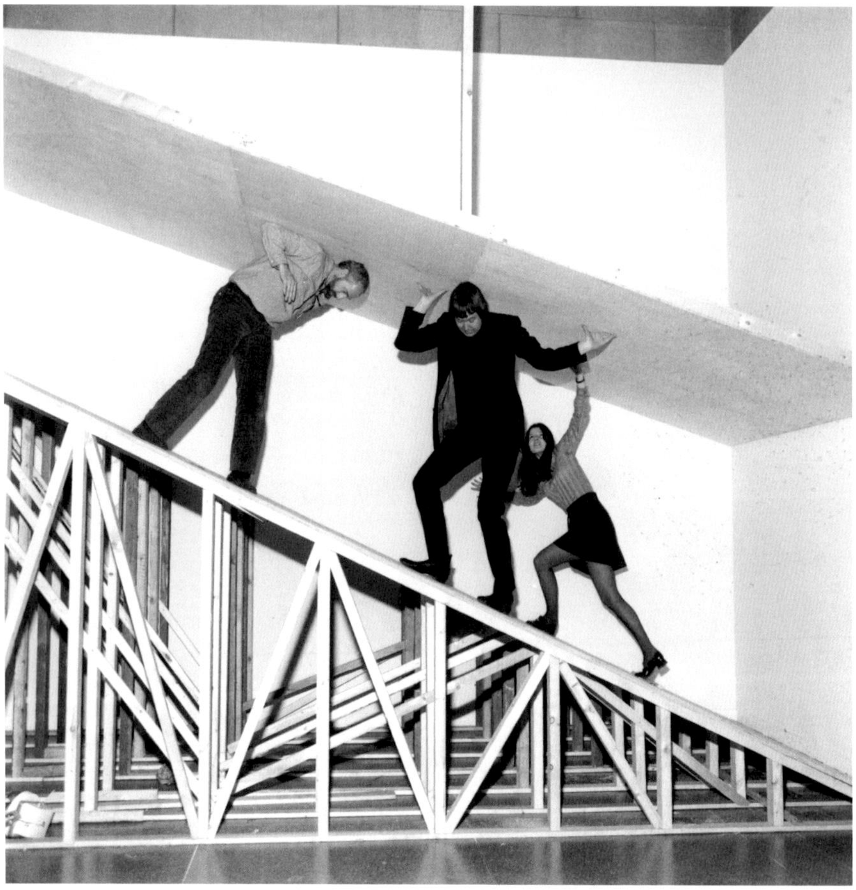

Robert Morris, *Robert Morris* 1971, exhibited at the Tate Gallery 28 April – 7 May 1971; Tate staff demonstrating interaction with the work

American minimalism, by artists including Donald Judd, Robert Morris, Tony Smith and Carl Andre, was also influenced, to different degrees, by Merleau-Ponty's ideas of embodied perception, as well as Gestalt theory and Russian constructivism. Much of Morris's early work had specifically been conceived within a context of theatre, such as the performance *Column* 1961, which happened directly through his involvement in dance theatre alongside Simone Forti and Yvonne Rainer. As Rainer notes in her autobiography: 'The column had originally been constructed and painted yellow by George Sugarman as décor for one of my early solos, *The Bells*. [...] Bob found it in the wings and painted it grey.'[15] In *Column*, Morris presented the newly grey plywood box, built to human scale, centre-stage. After the theatre curtains opened, the box stood upright for three minutes, then, manipulated by a wire, fell over and lay prone for a further three minutes, before the curtain closed again. In the work of both Morris and Rainer, presentations of the body-as-object and object-as-body tested a continuum between inertia and movement, or between the individual and the industrial, often with laconic, deadpan humour. (Like Pape, Morris had originally imagined being inside the box himself, but had been injured in the rehearsal through the falling, and so used a wire on the day.)

Morris's first sculptures, of sorts, were made as props for Forti's dance works *See Saw* and *Slant Board*, presented in Yoko Ono's New York loft in 1961, and he even made five of his own performance or dance works between 1963 and 1966.

His writings and interviews in the late 1960s and early 1970s frequently emphasise the importance of sculpture's 'essentially tactile' nature, distinct from the 'optical sensibilities involved in painting', as well as the viewer's 'physical participation' in contemporary sculpture's 'extended situation'.[16] These early experiments were brought to bear upon his later participatory sculpture, its most ambitious iteration having been realised for his famed Tate Gallery retrospective in 1971, which was, due to the 'exuberant' behaviour of members of the audience and fear of injury and accidents, closed down after just four days.[17]

As Morris's work developed in the direction nevertheless of sculpture and away from performance, this performative approach remained. His important installation of *Untitled (L-Beams)* 1965 at the Jewish Museum in New York, as part of the 1966 exhibition *Primary Structures: Younger American and British Sculpture*, was founded upon the active interplay between material objects and the viewer's embodied perception. By placing a pair of two-metre-long fibreglass L-beams in a gallery space, Morris demonstrated that a division existed between our perception of the object and the actual object because, although viewers perceived the beams as being different shapes and sizes, in actuality they were identical. In direct opposition to modernism's focus on the internal syntax of the object – that is, how the object can be understood as something self-contained – Morris chose instead to examine the external syntax: the theatricality of the object, the way an object extends out from itself into its environment, and how it is perceived in relation to a wider apparatus. Like some of the artists already mentioned, Morris documented these works photographically, creating a sequence of different configurations,

Simone Forti, *Slant Board* 1961, performed at the Stedelijk Museum, Amsterdam, 1982

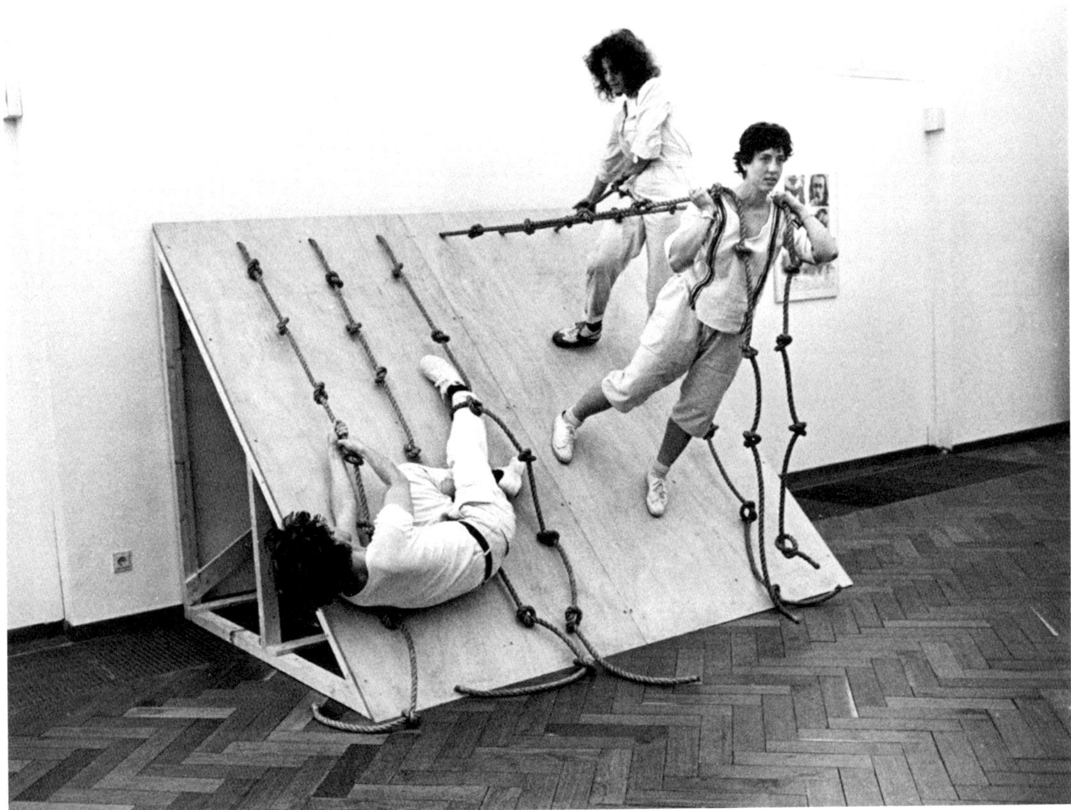

which show all possible orientations of the same unit, and how we perceive them differently – the sculptures themselves as performers in a form of object choreography.

Animal and organic movement

The neo-concretists professed to be interested in finding an organic relationship between art and life through breaking the conventional frames that separated the two spheres. But while Hélio Oiticica and Lygia Pape composed using geometric abstract principles, artists such as Jannis Kounellis, Simone Forti and Fujiko Nakaya invited the 'performance' of organic reality into their work in different ways. These artists staged forms of live action not enacted by manmade objects, but by other non-human actors: animals, plants and natural elements, including the weather.

Kounellis was associated with the Italian arte povera movement, which, like Mono-ha, incorporated the use of simple, raw and found materials, whether cotton, rock or glass, a plant or a piece of ironwork. In 1967, at Galleria L'Attico in Rome, Kounellis displayed live birds in cages with rose-shaped, cloth cut-outs pinned to canvas alongside his painting. In this way, the artist transformed the gallery into a stage, dramatising an unresolvable meeting point between real life and fiction, the spectators becoming a part of the scene.

Two years later, in the same space, Kounellis famously exhibited twelve live horses for his *Untitled (12 horses)*. Inspired by surrealist writer André Breton telling a story about the Tartars bringing their horses to drink at the fountains of Versailles, he wanted to bring horses into the space of a private gallery. The horses were displayed in formation, tethered around the space, and despite being

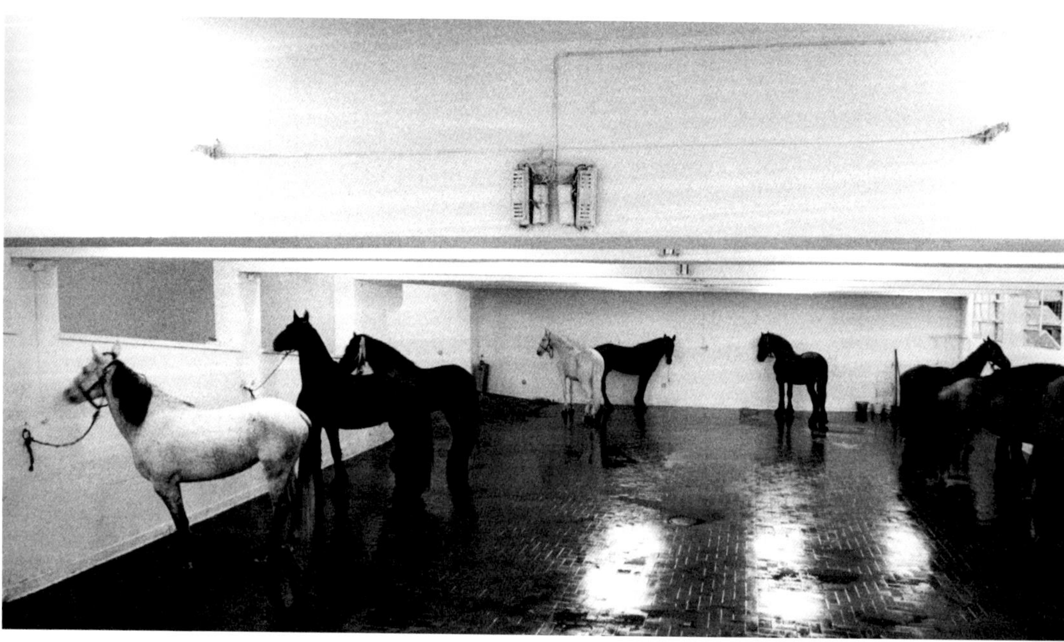

Jannis Kounellis, *Untitled (12 Horses)*, Galleria l'Attico, Rome, 1969

domesticated appeared nevertheless intimidating, while also being sadly impotent in their tamed state. This piece pre-dates Joseph Beuys's 1974 New York action, *I Like America and America Likes Me*, which involved a wild coyote in the gallery. The transgression of Kounellis's piece, as with Oiticica's inclusion of live parrots in his installation *Tropicália* 1967, rests in its opening up the experience of art to a sensual, wild or natural dimension, beyond human control. In 1976, British artist Rose Finn-Kelcey made a piece titled *The Magpie's Box* – a performance presented at Acme Gallery in London, where the artist occupied the window space of the gallery in an attempt to establish a dialogue with two live magpies. Instead of using human language, she employed different sounds to invoke an order of communication and meaning that was non-verbal. Finn-Kelcey's interest in a different type of language was part of her exploration of a feminist position in the UK in the 1970s: proposing alternative voices to the dominant male voice.

Likewise, Simone Forti has been fascinated by animal movement, in parallel with her experiments with human balance, co-operation and participation from the early 1960s, when she worked with both Yvonne Rainer and Robert Morris as collaborators. Forti studied the movement of cats, went to the zoo to observe bears and monkeys, and used her research as a basis for improvisation, as is evident in her video *Three Grizzlies* 1974. She also created other kinds of object-based, or organic, 'choreography'. Made in collaboration with Hollis Frampton, her five-minute film *Cloths* 1967 displays a sequence of patterned and plain squares of fabric, which are mesmerisingly arranged and rearranged in layered sequences, appearing to the camera like semaphores in succession without revealing the human manipulator.

Forti's *Onion Walk* 1961 (p.202) is an intriguing and simple piece, in which a sprouting onion is allowed to grow atop a glass bottle until that growth forces it to fall off its perch. Considered alongside her investigation of animal behaviour, this piece's curious experiment-cum-vegetable 'performance' suggests a relationship to nature that was somewhat ahead of its time, given its interest in movement across both the human and non-human spheres. Anthropological studies tell us that people have been imitating animals for as long as the two have co-existed, but there is a sense that Forti never sought to simply imitate these creatures, impersonate them, or even perform them as ready-made impressions. Rather, she seems to have wished to learn by observing them, to extend her own capacities as a dancer by incorporating their forms of locomotion, as 'non-stylistic movement',[18] into a human repertoire of movement and into human experience – suggesting, in the process, a perceptual paradigm untethered to the upright human body (or to the ostensibly anthropomorphic objects it mirrors).

Conversely, in her artificial fog sculptures developed in the late 1960s and early 1970s, the Japanese artist Fujiko Nakaya drew attention to the broader currents of the atmosphere: the weather, and, more specifically, currents in the air (p.203). Moving to New York in the 1960s, Nakaya was part of the avant-garde group Experiments in Art and Technology (E.A.T.), alongside Robert Rauschenberg, Billy Klüver, and others. Rauschenberg himself was fascinated with how technology might perform: with Klüver, he created moving and sound sculptures such as the *Money Thrower for Jean Tingueley's H.T.N.Y* 1960, and the multi-part *Oracle*, 1962–5, while his 1971 work Mud Muse was a large vat of liquid Bentonite that bubbled and splattered according to patterns triggered by sound recordings attached to its valves and nozzles. Nakaya's first major fog sculpture enveloped the architecture of the group's Pepsi Pavilion (named after its sponsor) at the World's Fair in Osaka,

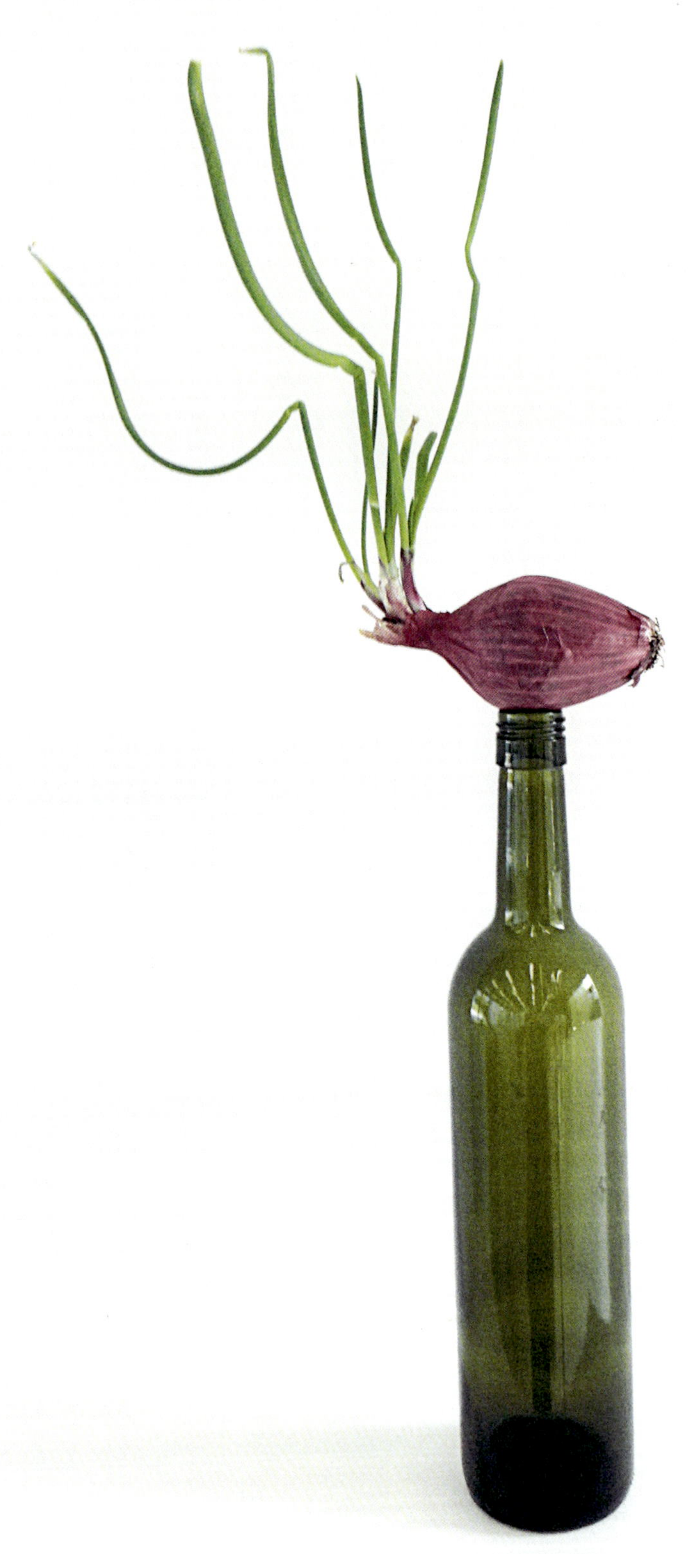

Simone Forti, *Onion Walk* 1961/2014. Exhibition view of *Simone Forti Thinking with the Body: A Retrospective in Motion*, Museum of Modern Art, Salzburg 18 July – 9 November 2014

Japan, in 1970. Her project was emblematic of E.A.T.'s vision of a new kind of relationship between art, science and engineering. In what might be thought of as an organic version of institutional critique, she worked with cutting-edge technology to create immaterial architectures of water-based, artificial fog that allowed us to see the invisible structures governing the atmosphere, and to track their shape in mist. The 'performers' in this work are the vectors and currents of air themselves, which Nakaya makes visible. The work's liveness derives from its continuous, shifting unpredictability as an installation, as well as its literal use as a space for performance in collaboration with others: dancers, musicians and theatre-makers including Trisha Brown and Dumb Type have inhabited the fog as a stage-set. Nakaya's use of technology interacting with the biosphere also significantly precedes a generation of artists including Philippe Parreno and Pierre Huyghe.

Nakaya understands her work as an observational and revelatory process, born of her study of what is already in the environment, and bringing into visibility its constituting elements through the insertion of the fog-object. She has said: 'The fog installations ... [would] interact with and reveal the air, wind. [...] The atmosphere itself gives the fog its shape, movement and volume. The fog disappears if the conditions or air currents change. It's a collaboration with the

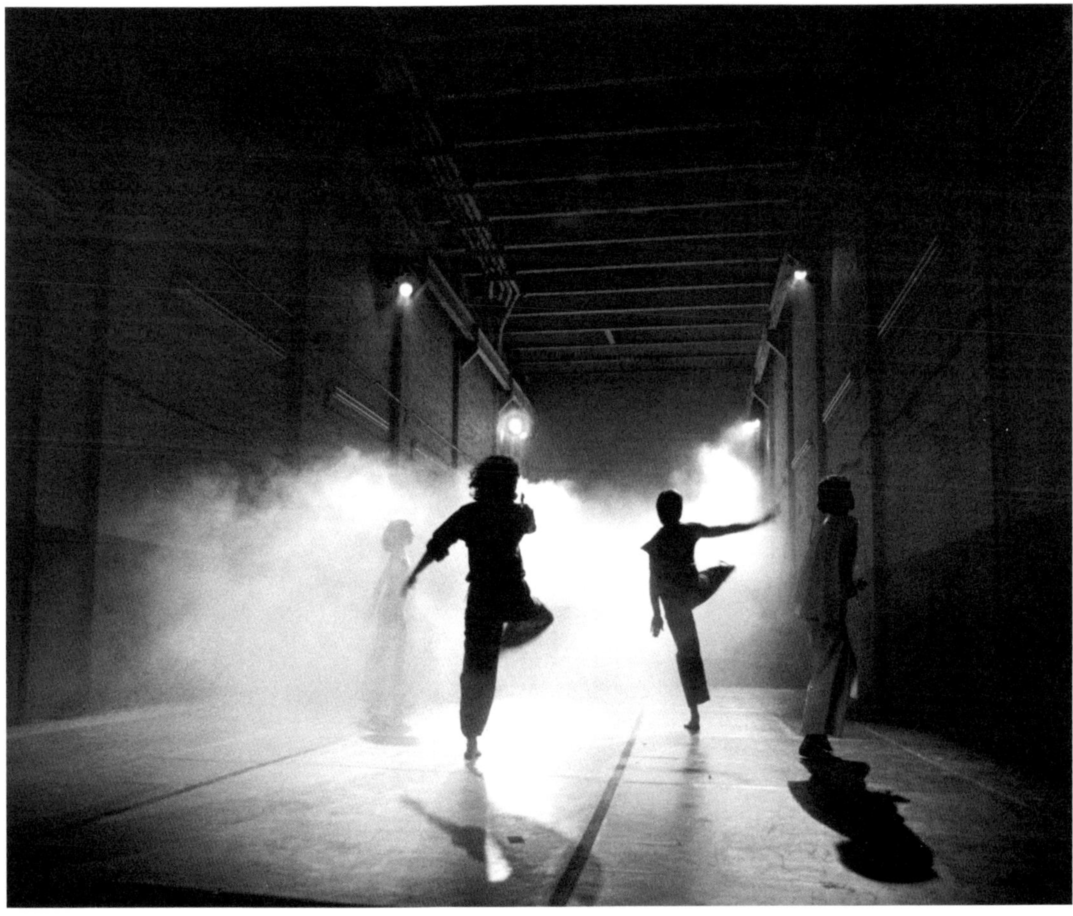

Fujiko Nakaya/Trisha Brown, *Opal Loop: Cloud Performance No.72503* 1980, performance by Trisha Brown and Fujiko Nakaya, New York, 16 June 1980

air.'[19] Nakaya's approach to the elements, as with Forti's approach to non-human or organic performance, could be linked to John Cage's *4'33''* 1952, whose non-music 'composition' of apparent silence was intended to attune the auditory capacity of the audience to the many sounds that would nevertheless fill the air during this ostensible interval.

Argentine artist Nicolás García Uriburu also intervened in, and drew attention to, the environment by making a form of expanded painting-cum-land art in the late 1960s, but with an activist dimension. For the 1968 edition of the Venice Biennale,

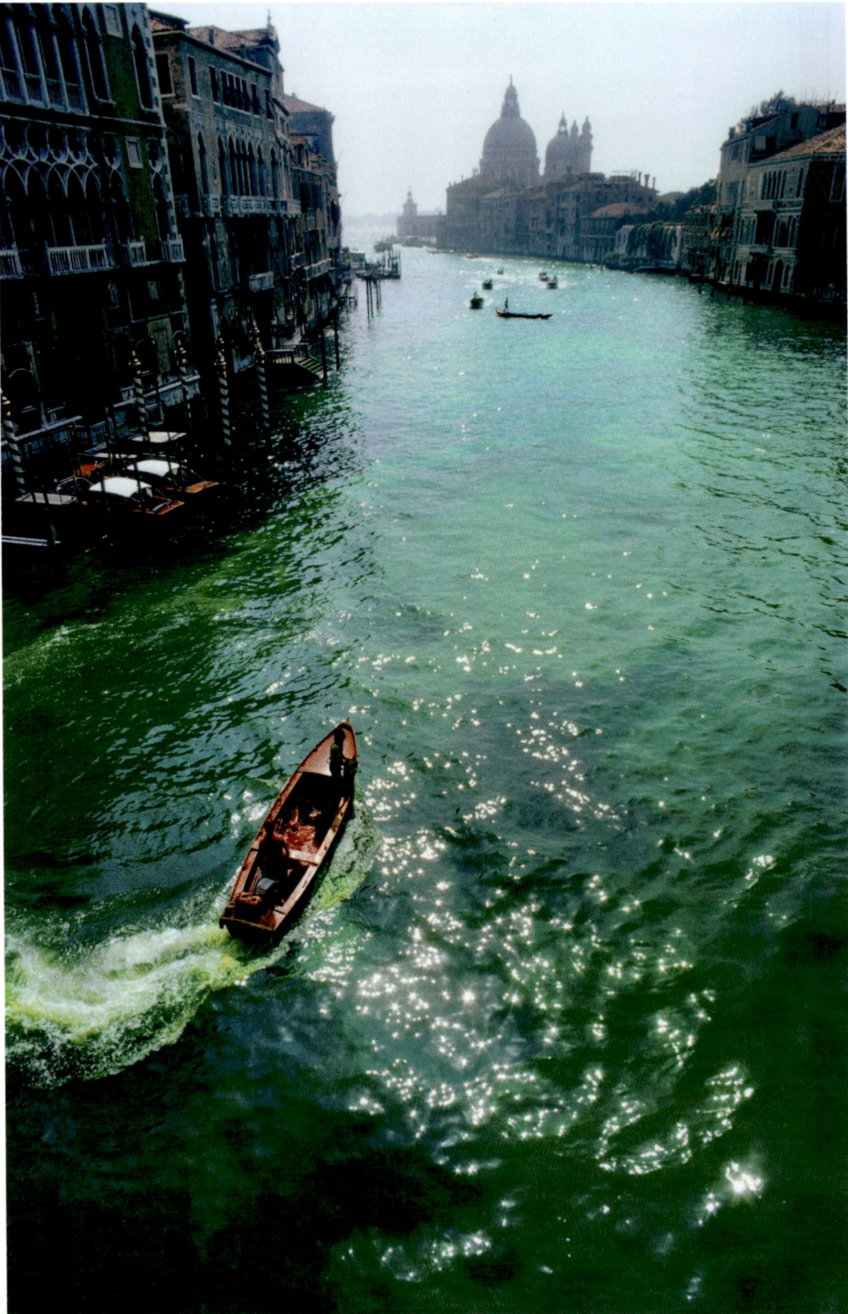

Nicolas Garcia Uriburu, photo documentation of Nicolás García Uriburu's colouring of the Grand Canal in Venice, 1968

he dyed the Grand Canal green using fluorescein, a pigment which turns a bright green when synthesised by micro-organisms in the water. He repeated similar actions in New York's East River, the Seine in Paris, Germany's Rhine (during Documenta 7 in Kassel) and at the mouth of Buenos Aires's polluted south-side Riachuelo. In 1974, he dyed the fountains at Trafalgar Square in London green (and was fined £25 for 'offending the British Empire'). As an early form of performative protest, García Uriburu was involved in raising awareness of water pollution, endangered species and habitat loss, at times in collaboration with Greenpeace. His work was pioneering in its consideration of ecological issues: he used artistic methods to underscore his own capacity, as an individual, to affect the environment around him in strikingly visible ways.

Performing structure

In recent years, a certain kind of object-based or installation work has come to be understood in terms of the 'performative', in a way that has very little to do with performance or action in any other sense.[20] To understand this idea of performativity, we must look back at the history of institutional critique, as it was developed by Daniel Buren, Hans Haacke and Michael Asher from the 1960s onwards, in works that attempted to expose institutional conventions, as well as to make visible the historically and socially constructed boundaries between inside and outside, public and private, and so on. The architectonic answer to Fujiko Nakaya's fog sculptures which circulated within natural air currents was perhaps Asher's contribution to the 1969 group show *Anti-Illusion: Procedures/Materials* at the Whitney Museum of American Art in New York. The artist simply concealed a blower above a door to create a slab of air that visitors passed through when they moved from one gallery to the next. In the 1970s, Asher began to remove elements from exhibition spaces. In 1973, at Galleria Toselli in Milan, he sandblasted away paint on the walls, revealing the layers underneath, while for *Installation* 1970 at Pomona College, he reconfigured the interior space of the gallery and then left it open, without a door, twenty-four hours a day. The light and noise and activity of the street were thus experienced inside the gallery.

If Asher, Buren and others worked performatively on the architecture and set-up of the gallery or museum as *mise en scène*, drawing attention to its hidden codes as carriers of meaning, Elaine Sturtevant (known just as Sturtevant) played on the performative language of painting and sculpture, and on the performance at stake in being an artist, even. Around 1965, Sturtevant began to reproduce paintings and objects created by her New York artist contemporaries, by hand. She copied them so faithfully that it was hard to distinguish them from the originals, thus deliberately turning the concept of originality on its head. She dressed up as another artist, too, when she appeared in costume as Joseph Beuys in her piece *The Revolution Is Us* 1988 (p.206).

An important factor in determining an artwork's value in the art market – and hence its status as a commodity – is its originality, both in the sense of unique expression and in authenticity (that an artwork is, in fact, made by the artist who signs it, or whose style it resembles): to be an 'It' there must be an 'I' certifiable. From her first solo show at the Bianchini Gallery in New York in 1965, Sturtevant worked on the reproduction of iconic contemporary paintings, sculptures and installations. She is credited with marking the beginning of the 1980s Simulationist

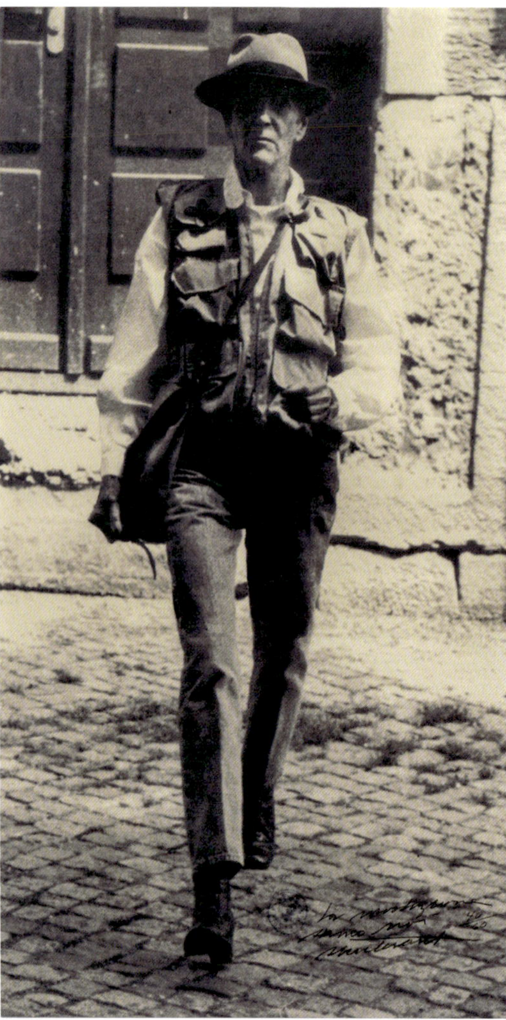

Sturtevant, *Beuys La Rivoluzione siamo noi* 1988, screenprint on paper, 95.5 x 51

movement, but unlike the work of some of her peers, such as Mike Bidlo and Richard Pettibone, her reproductions are neither appropriation art nor homages. 'The brutal truth … is that it's not a copy', Sturtevant has said.[21] Instead, she flagrantly fakes the works of other artists. Her aim is to somehow overidentify with the idea of the signature brand to show the hidden reverse of the apparently legitimate art economy. Where the artist's genius ought to be is a hollow brand that permanently shifts, as it identifies with different works at different times, in a performative manner. By 'passing' as originals by Frank Stella, Roy Lichtenstein, Keith Haring or Andy Warhol, her works reveal originality and authenticity as myths, which the art system does its best to mask. The artists she fakes have sometimes, themselves, been complicit in the process. Warhol, always one step ahead, allowed her to make her *Warhol Gold Marilyn* 1973 on his own silk-screen press. And when Sturtevant met Marcel Duchamp and showed him an early 'Duchamp' that she had made, the artist recalls that he didn't bat an eyelid, playing the game by simply asking, 'How did you get that?'[22]

Even Sturtevant's name sounds like a brand, while maintaining, like VALIE EXPORT, a kind of genderless anonymity for the artist. Her individual works set in motion a heightened awareness of the entire economic system of value and meaning in art. Her doubling of iconic works – usually works by male artists re-fabricated by a female artist – injects a silent virus in the system, a doubling of cells that corrodes and destabilises its structures and support bases via an apparently passive, but in fact excessive and loaded, complicity with the very foundations of its value system. Sturtevant's paintings might look like straightforward museum objects, but their meaning rests upon a theatrical suspension of disbelief.

Contemporary

Object actors II

If artists working in the postwar period expanded the realm of the performative to incorporate the moving object, as well as animal and organic life, the current generation take this complex ecology as a point of departure to make the object 'perform' in a variety of ways. One of the key questions that the presence of performance in the field of contemporary art prompts is: how can we read the history of art in the past century from a live, performance-inflected point of view? Instead of subordinating action to objects, from this perspective, objects appear as catalysts and mediators in an expanded form of practice. Contemporary work is often concerned with the ways in which actions and objects are imperfectly co-existent, even inseparable, and certainly mutually influencing.

In his book *Reassembling the Social* (2005), Bruno Latour challenges sociology's traditional separation of the social from the material as an absurd impossibility. He asks instead, how do all manner of objects influence behaviour, both psychologically and practically? How do they play a part as actors in making us do things? He notes the 'convoluted attachment of primates with objects for the past one million years', and distinguishes between the agency of the tool (a hammer or a door handle) and the symbolic object (the religious icon painting), demonstrating complex convergences of the two.[23] How might things 'authorise, allow, afford, encourage, permit, suggest, influence, block, render possible, forbid, and so on', rather than simply 'express' or 'symbolise' power relations or hierarchies?[24] After Latour, Erik Davis observes that we customarily apply the idea of object-consciousness to social media, software and smart technology, meaning that we behave as though technological devices could speak back to us. In this way, he says, quasi-life is increasingly distributed through the world of objects, from which we infer intelligence and responsiveness.[25]

On the one hand, then, as early twenty-first-century subjects, we are surrounded by objects that seem to address us and talk to us. On the other hand, Bernard Stiegler's conception of the 'technic' considers how we extend our own capacities through technological tools, which he describes as 'organised inorganic matter': a kind of virtual prosthetic that mediates experience.[26] For Stiegler, this is evident in the prosthetic nature of written language in relation to speech, in how we use technological gadgets, and even in styled, formalised gestures. But rather than straightforwardly imagining the prosthetic extension of the human subject as a simple means of adaptation to the world, these theories demonstrate the state of social, material and technological entanglement we are in. Building upon the

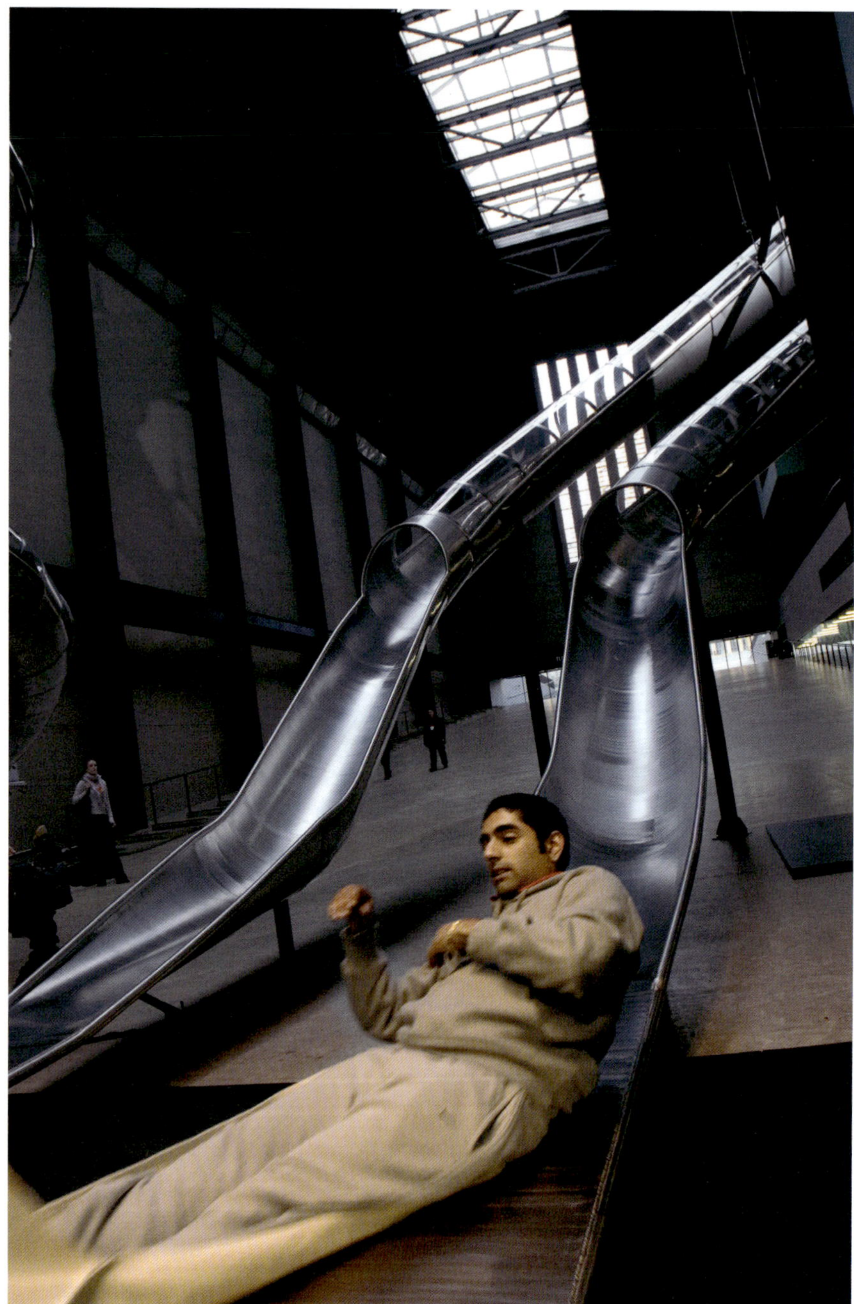

Carsten Höller, *Test Site*, Tate Modern, October 2006 – 9 April 2007

experiments with performative objects – what we might want to call, after Latour, 'object-actors'[27] – that occurred in the 1960s and 1970s, contemporary artists face an increasingly complicated territory for producing art, and considering where the artwork – if not a fixed entity – might begin and end.

Besides being associated with relational aesthetics, Carsten Höller's work resonates with Latour's conception of the object-actor. His installations use elaborate forms of sculptural installation as deliberate prompts for behaviour:

for example, by inviting viewers to pass through multiple sets of electronic sliding doors, mirrored on one side, creating extreme disorientation (*Sliding Doors* 2003), or to whizz down vertiginous, twisting tube slides inside the museum or gallery (a series begun in 1998, whose most spectacular manifestation was *Test Site* 2006–7 at Tate Modern). Holler is fascinated by how people might negotiate physical environments in ways that affect their emotions and their apparent control of a situation. He instigates a physiological passage to a kind of transcendence.

In a similarly experimental vein, animals have also been a feature of Höller's work. In his 2010 exhibition at the Hamburger Bahnhof in Berlin, titled *Soma*, two herds of reindeer were housed in the large main exhibition hall, along with canaries, mice and flies, and a scattering of Höller's giant toadstool sculptures. Some of the reindeers were, purportedly, being fed with hallucinogenic mushrooms. Visitors were invited to enter a raffle to stay the night and drink urine collected from the reindeers, though they could not be sure whether it was from the hallucinogen-fed ones or not. Modelling the exhibition after a scientific experiment, Höller ventured that, through such an experience, art might open people's minds more than drugs can. In these different ways, Höller uses test situations to force an awareness on his viewers of patterns of shared consciousness through forms of participatory feedback. Höller borrows scientific methods and plants them within the space of art in order to stimulate new insight into the borderlines between our sense of self (*I*), communality (*We*) and the built environment (*It*).

Brazilian artist Ricardo Basbaum experiments with art as a connecting device that links sensory experience, sociability and language. His work takes the form of objects, diagrams, drawings, text and sound used in relation to participatory

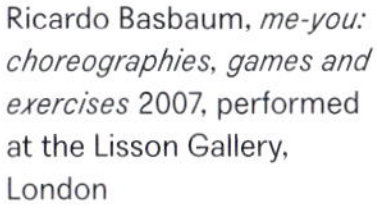

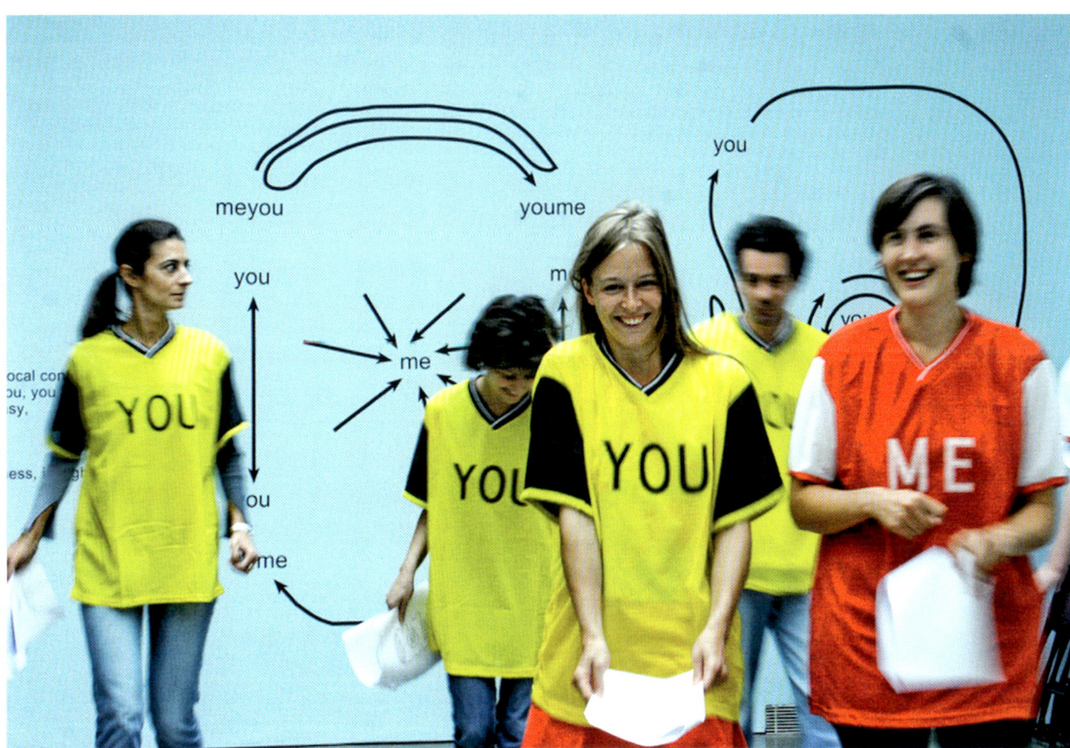

Ricardo Basbaum, *me-you: choreographies, games and exercises* 2007, performed at the Lisson Gallery, London

actions within which individual experience is key, for example in his 'You & Me' exercises. In his major project, *Would you like to participate in an artistic experience?*, initiated in 1994, Basbaum offers an object devised by the artist – a white-painted, rectangular steel structure resembling a large cake tin, measuring 125 x 80 x 18 cm – to be taken home by the participant (whether an individual or a group), who will have around a month to realise an artistic experience with it. During this period of time, the participant's role is to decide how to use it, if at all – where it should be taken, what should be done with it. The results that emerge are radically open. The only requirement is that the participant sends documentation to be archived and made accessible on the project's website.[28]

Uses have been myriad: the object has appeared as part of theatrical performances and dance routines, been shown as outdoor sculpture and been used as a musical instrument, but it has served practical functions, too: as a cat's bed, a clothes basket, a fish tank, or to collect water in. Basbaum's interest in producing such an object as an artwork is to do with a desire to intervene in and reshape the basic protocols of relations between artist, object and participant, and to stimulate creativity. He observes that his predecessors – artists such as Hélio Oiticica and Lygia Clark, but also David Medalla, Antonio Dias, Luis Camnitzer and Cildo Meireles – helped, in different ways, to build up the 'thickness' of this contact zone, allocating greater responsibility to the viewer.[29]

Japanese artist Koki Tanaka creates experimental situations and forms of improvisation that relate to processes of art-making. His earliest works take everyday objects as prompts. In *Everything Is Everything* 2006, for example, the artist documents a sequence of actions using found things: a ladder, a plastic jelly mould, some shaving foam and a broom are tested and played with, transforming them into props for micro-performances. The ladder is kicked over, slapstick-style; the jelly mould is crushed by a foot; the shaving foam makes a picture on a welding mask; the brush is twirled on the fingers like a cheerleader's baton. Tanaka's is a low-fi approach, influenced by the use of things in Mono-ha, or

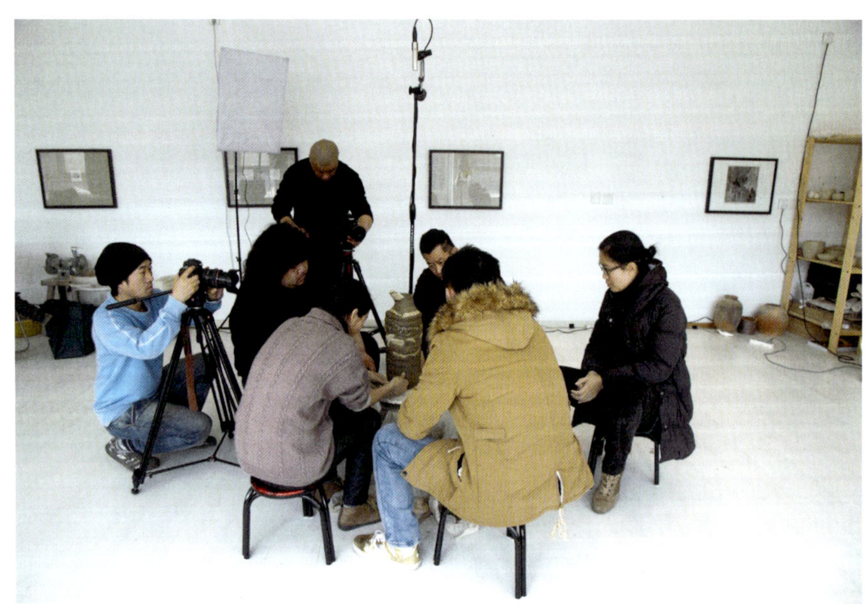

Koki Tanaka, *A Pottery Produced by 5 Potters at Once (Silent Attempt)* 2013; collaboration: video documentation (75 min.) at the Studio of Wang Feng and Han Qing, Beijing; curated by Hu Fang and Mika Kuraya; commissioned by The Japan Foundation; created with Vitamin Creative Space, Guangzhou, and The Pavilion, Beijing; participants: Wang Feng, Yuan Liang, Han Qing, Duan Ran, and Tan Hongyu

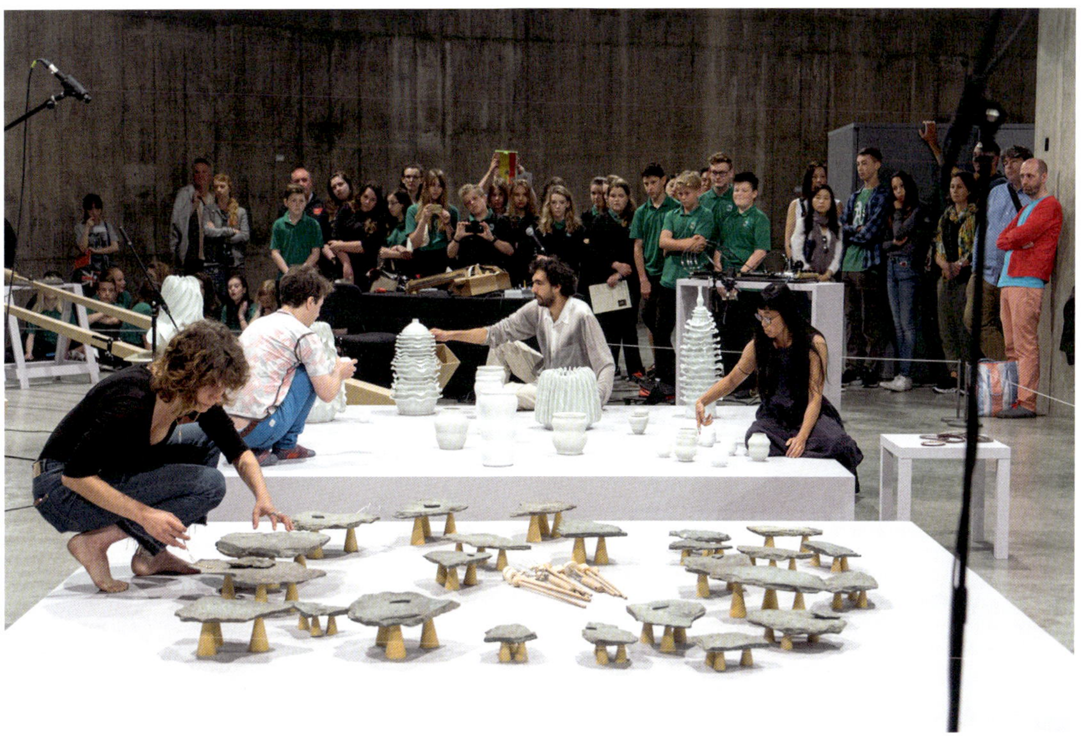

Tarek Atoui, *The Reverse Collection*, South Tank, Tate Modern, 17 June – 5 October 2016

akin to the activation of found materials as sculptures and theatre sets by Robert Rauschenberg. His DIY aesthetic was also dictated, in part, by the economic recession in early 2000s Japan, prompting Tanaka to respond to cheap everyday items that were easily available and to transform their status through use.

More recently, especially since the Fukushima disaster of 2011, Tanaka has explored co-operation. He has created patterns out of the activities of daily life, devising collective tasks. In the Japanese Pavilion for the Venice Biennale in 2013, his video installation documented groups of people collaborating on assignments instigated by the artist: five potters took on the challenge of producing one piece of pottery together, five poets wrote a poem at once, and so on. The second part of the work involved the staging of various collective actions, such as a night walk in the city with some fifty participants, or a discussion in which the topic was the participants' own names. Tanaka's work, like Basbaum's, takes the object (or ready-made social convention) as a focus, in order to unsettle habitual behaviour. But distinct from the custom-designed prop that Basbaum's object represents, Tanaka treats domestic utilities or construction tools as a means of interrupting ordinary movement when encountered out of context. His work sets up loops of apparent dysfunction or absurdity, while at the same time instigating new aesthetic diversions, and new kinds of interaction – or 'social creativity', as David Graeber puts it – where unexpected permissions, solicitations and suggestions are inferred from tasks or cheap, mass-produced things.

Lebanese-born, Paris-based artist Tarek Atoui is an electroacoustic composer who works with sound as material (p.211). Atoui frequently collaborates with artists from other disciplines to create live events, concerts and workshops. For Atoui, the instrument is a special category of object, and one that reflects upon the status of the artwork and its relationship to action. Atoui custom-builds electronic instruments and computers, but also works with historical instruments and archives. He uses the status and capacity of the instrument as a tool to explore different social and political realities, and to create education projects. For the Sharjah Biennial in 2013, Atoui devised a sound programme based on research into the ways in which deaf people experience and perceive sound, titled *WITHIN*. For the Berlin Biennial in 2014, he invited eighteen musicians to record solos performed on historical instruments housed in the Ethnological Museum in Dahlem, Berlin, which were then catalogued into a research archive. In turn, these sound samples became source material for a selected group of instrument makers and composers, who directly and indirectly worked with this archive to produce a new set of instruments capable of producing equivalent sounds, and subsequently compositions.

As part of this project, titled *The Dahlem Sessions* 2013–14, Atoui inverted the idea of the musician eliciting sound from the capacities of an instrument and instead invited instrument makers to use a given sound as a kind of template from which to create instruments which could approximate to that sound. A variety of instruments were produced: ceramic vessels, a lithograph stone hit by cow bones, air-pipes and plastic horns. Through this inversion, Atoui proposes that particular sounds pre-exist the instruments which apparently produce them. In this scenario, the sound is the real carrier of history as a live process, echoing the importance of oral tradition in the history of Arab music, so that the instrument becomes one iteration of the sound rather than the other way around. In the third step of the project, musicians improvise with the new instruments at intervals, creating a gradually building composition which is recorded by the artist and played back in the space.

Atoui's conception of the relationship between instrument and player offers another, music-related metaphor for rethinking how the artwork might be encountered and conceived through performance. Atoui imagines musical performance not only as a way to channel the given capacity of the instrument (the object in question) but also as a way to 'extend or improve the instrument': to imagine capacities beyond what is visibly given, and to indicate future directions for its adaptation.[30] In this sense, the instrument is imagined as an adaptive object whose social use might determine its potential shape.

South Korean-born, New York-based artist Sung Hwan Kim also thinks about the adaptability of the body as a perceiving agent, torn between the consumption of moving images and the inhabitation of physical space, or between eye and body. Taught by Joan Jonas, and rooted in performance, Hwan Kim links the studio practices of drawing and sculpture with a theatrical approach to video and installation. For his large-scale installation in the Tate Modern Tanks in 2012, he created an environment which brought into equilibrium all of the elements that were to be found there: the round architecture of the space; the visitors' presence; his previous work in video, sculpture, drawing and installation; and even functional elements, such as sound cladding or seating furniture.

Whereas in a gallery one is accustomed to clear, white lighting revealing all aspects of the work and its spatial container, and in a theatre or cinema to blackness with a focus on the lit stage or screen, Hwan Kim created a continuously gradating shift in attention via a conflation of space and stage. He eliminated the separation between a theatrical understanding of spectatorship and an embodied one, or between seeing and being seen, using a kind of sculptural furniture to create a bridge, or obstacle, between the imaginative space of video and the physical experience of the setting. The 'world' of his work was expanded beyond representational fiction (within the drawings or films) to incorporate a fictive casting of real-time experience. To view the central film, *Temper Clay* 2012, for example, visitors had to adjust their bodies to the plinth-like sculptures that doubled as viewing furniture, with titles such as *Corner Plinth that Becomes Seating*, *Seat Shaped like Will's Limbs*. In this setting, the shadowy presence of other bodies moving around the space felt essential to the experience. The figure, in this scheme of things, is not a clumsily unwelcome intrusion to a realm concerned with transcendental viewing, as artist and author Brian O'Doherty imagines it in his evaluation of the ritual of the white cube, with its emphasis on retinal experience.[31] Hwan Kim knows that we are embodied viewers performing roles of our own, and plays to the duality of this experience.

Danish choreographer Mette Ingvartsen works mainly within the conventions of theatre, though her work has also been presented in gallery spaces. She has taken an unusual approach to the field of dance by occasionally casting things, rather than people, as performers. Belonging to a new generation of dance practitioners coming after Jerôme Bel, Eszter Salamon and Xavier LeRoy, she considers the expanded potential of choreography towards an installation-like situation onstage. Her piece *Evaporated Landscapes* 2009, for example, is a performance designed to be exclusively played by non-human actors, such as foam, fog, light and sound. It might equally sit in a gallery, were it not designed with a specific, event-like duration, so that it becomes a pictorial form of installation.

In the 2012 performance *The Artificial Nature Project*, Ingvartsen reintroduced the human performer as part of a network of connections between human and non-human actors, asking: 'What does it mean to make a choreography for materials

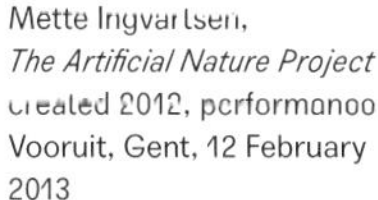
Mette Ingvartsen,
The Artificial Nature Project
created 2012, performance
Vooruit, Gent, 12 February
2013

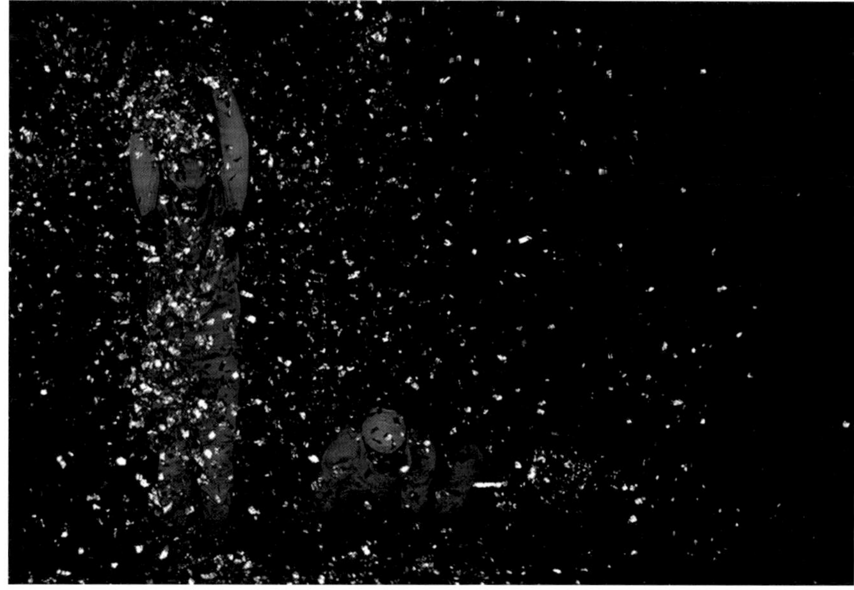

where human movement is no longer in the centre of attention? How can one address the force of things, materials, objects and matters as something that acts upon humans? What is the relationship between the animate and the inanimate world?'[32] In this piece, Ingvartsen uses simple materials, such as silver confetti, spectacularly dispersed in the air by the gust of air from a leaf blower, to create a shimmering firework effect, or the scrunching of glinting gold foil energy blankets to create a landscape in constant transformation.

Interested in what might happen onstage if the focus is shifted away from the human actor – as it typically would be in a gallery, but not onstage – Ingvartsen creates scenarios within which different material elements are foregrounded. There is sensitivity to their textures and shapes, and also drama as they swirl and fly around the stage. Theatre is conjured with only the most rudimentary of means. In this environment, the dancers onstage are paradoxically cast as magicians of sorts, who, Prospero-like, direct the climate and form of this temporary vision before us, and at the same time as passive subjects, vulnerable to the changes in climate, as they are affected by and try to move within this situation.

Within a gallery context, the French artist Philippe Parreno has built upon the groundwork of an earlier generation of artists associated with Experiments in Art and Technology (E.A.T.), Korean-American pioneer of video Nam Jun Paik and the Zero group from the 1960s, to consider the question of liveness as it emanates from electricity and digital technology. Parreno's work dramatises an emerging world of artificial intelligence, as well as the merging of organisms and machines in biotechnology. In his actor-less performative installations, such as *Anywhere, Anywhere Out of the World* 2013, pianos play themselves, lights go on and off, and LEDs and neon lights flicker in time to music. Human instigators are absent, yet the show moves by an invisible force that shapes our movements and attention in turn, ghostly and mysterious. The unpredictable activity of a hidden culture of live yeast in a petri dish, for example, determined the pattern of the lighting and sound at the centre of his commission for Tate Modern's Turbine Hall, *Anywhen* 2016, while the electrical circuits of the museum's lighting were rewired to pace a rhythm of flashes in tune with his suspended marquee sculpture and alternating with the automated rise and fall of his video and speaker system, hung on wires from the ceiling. Parreno's world acknowledges our contemporary condition as that of what writer Jace Clayton has described as 'homo digitalis: online beings whose habitat spans the global information stream'.[33]

Pushing to a maximum this ceding of avant-garde improvisation strategies to computing, American artist Ian Cheng works on the potential of a computer algorithm to have a 'live' presence that self-generates in unpredictable ways and becomes autonomous. His project for the Liverpool Biennial in 2016, *Emissary Forks for You*, was what he describes as a 'mixed reality simulation', in which a virtual pet – a small dog, called Shiba Emissary – verbally commanded visitors to follow it throughout the exhibition. Personal tablets were loaned to visitors, upon which they could interact with the virtual pet, in a kind of deductive narrative video game. For his exhibition at the Serpentine in London in March 2018, Cheng presented a digital life-form called BOB, interacting similarly. Using digital technology, Cheng creates a new form of smart liveness: digital organisms (as images, animations or virtual pets) assume a life and autonomy of their own, continuing to perform, grow and generate behaviours so long as they are connected to a supply of electricity, independently of either viewer or maker.

Installation view of Ian Cheng's *BOB* at the Serpentine Gallery, London, 6 March 2018 – 22 April 2018, with a visitor interacting with the work

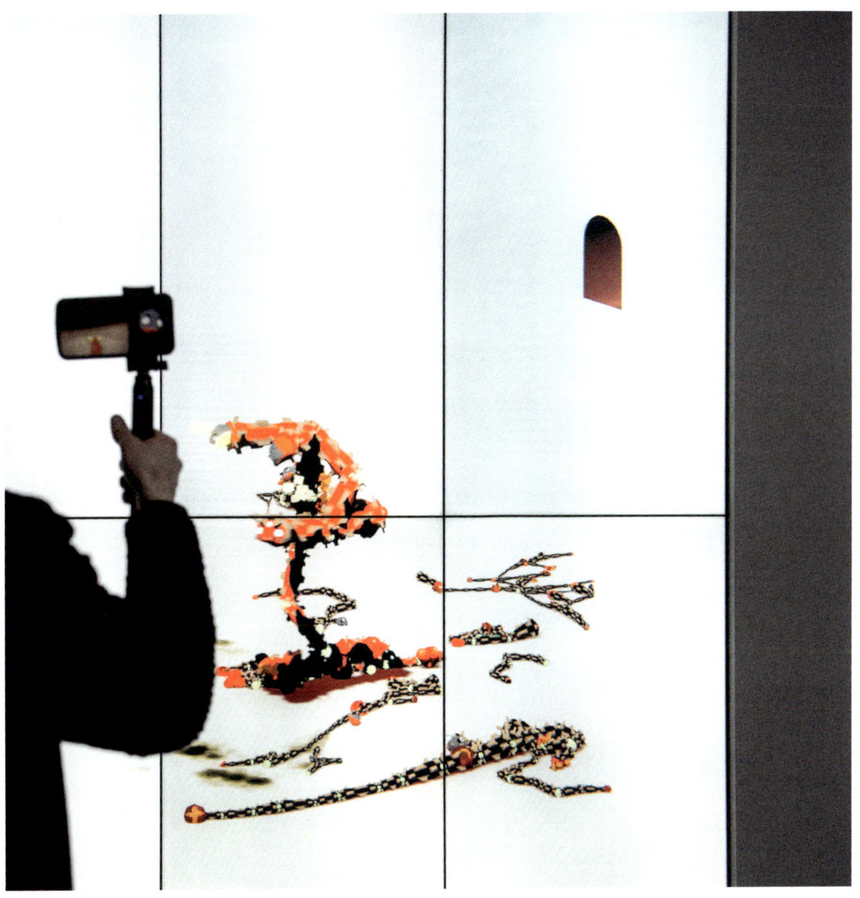

Acting on the infrastructure

Extrapolating the concerns of an earlier generation who drew attention to art's infrastructure through institutional critique, Brazilian artist Renata Lucas extends the idea that the material things around us in the street, or park, likewise serve as prompts and tools that influence our behaviour. Lucas realises ambitious installation projects that embed her sculpture, inconspicuously, in the built environment, to theatrical effect. To make *Crossing* 2003, she covered the entire centre of a large crossroads in Rio de Janeiro with plywood, laid flat on the tarmac (p.216). Lucas's sculptural intervention brought the crossroads's shape and function to the foreground so that it became a kind of temporary stage for the cars passing, because it made a noise as each vehicle drove over it and also created a kind of plinth-like display of the passing traffic. This work might be related to the experimental actions of Chilean artist Lotty Rosenfeld, who since 1979 has transformed the discontinuous white lines dividing driving lanes into crosses, as a means of altering the codes of urban movement, whether in the Chilean desert or in front of the White House in Washington, DC. A related work by Lucas, *Failure* 2003, is a gallery-based installation comprised of multiple hinged sheets of plywood laid onto the floor, wall to wall. It resembles an expanded version of a neo-concrete sculpture, with its geometric principles of composition.

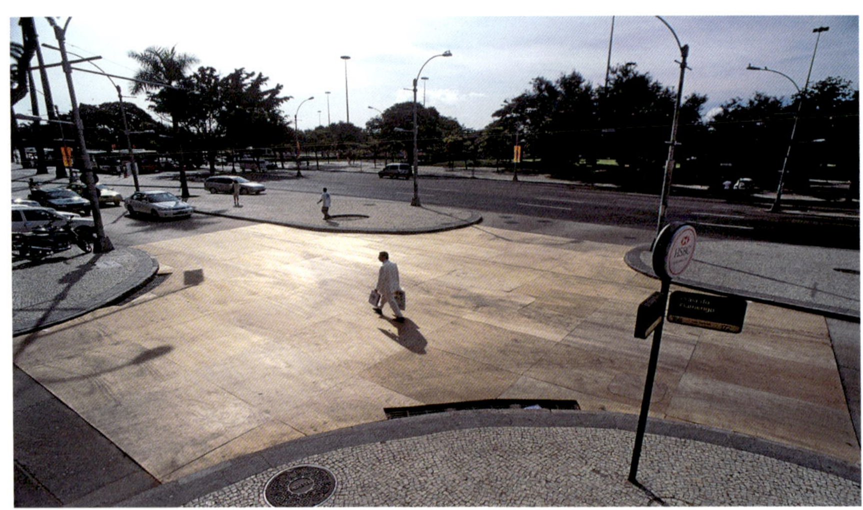

Renata Lucas, *Cruzamento (Crossing)* 2003, plywood. Intersection of Rua Dois de dezembro and Praia do Flamengo for Centro Cultural Oduvaldo Viana Filho (Castelinho do Flamengo), Rio de Janeiro

But Lucas's installation fills the space and can be manipulated by visitors, initiating an ongoing series of live interactions with the site, and reconfigurations thereof.

In *Quick Mathematics* 2006, made in her neighbourhood in São Paulo, Lucas constructed a whole new pavement alongside the existing one in the street: adding replicas of the paving stones, the lamp posts, the trees and flowers, which produced a surreal sense of confusion as to this double vision of the street. Like the artists of Mono-ha or arte povera, Lucas favours basic building materials (plywood, bricks, concrete), but she uses them to manipulate urban spaces and architecture, to insert new scenographic narratives or liminal spaces that disturb perception. The artist is fascinated by the question of how the things around us – our built environment determine actions, behaviour and social relationships. By extension, she is intent on disrupting prescribed definitions of space, property and order. Lucas's attention to the psychosocial substrate of the city environment digs at our perception of everyday activities by leading us to see them afresh through her interventions. Ordinary people and things become actors and players on a giant, often surreal, stage set. Through this way of looking at the world, its malleability and our potential for dreaming of changes come into view.

Rooted in a practice of inventing elaborate architectural façades and follies as drawings, the work of Argentinian-British artist, Pablo Bronstein, also includes temporary sculptural forms, elements of architecture, furniture, video and live performance. Bronstein's skill with pen, ink and wash enables him to depict his imaginings in elaborately detailed renderings that in most aspects convincingly mimic historical precedents. Related to his honing of virtuosic skill with the anachronistic reed pen, Bronstein's playful, performative attitude underpins the other elements of his work, including his ability knowingly to try on period styles. But beyond his often camp or super-stylised choreography, in the work's broader evolution from postmodern pastiche, Bronstein flaunts an exuberant confidence in the contemporary notion that the copy precedes the original, and in the Google-era interchangeability of images and authentic things. Such a quintessentially digital-age mindset is countered, nevertheless, by the eccentricity – and even unfashionability – of his plundered preferences.

Bronstein's work masquerades at surface level as classical, harmonious homage to past glories: the high-art forms of the Baroque, the formalised movement vocabulary of courtly manners, and early Italian ballet – forms that are apparently at home in the seventeenth-century courtyards of Turin or the Munich opera theatre. The work appears to be, and might perhaps be mistaken for, a form of revivalist complicity. But the artist's appropriation of these forms and styles derives from a fascination with their forbidden status within the realm of contemporary good taste. They were meant to be dead, but Bronstein reminds us of their illicit, phantom presence. His work shows how they lurk behind the truth-to-materials approach of modern architecture, or the stripped-back manifestations of the body in contemporary dance gestures, which, in Yvonne Rainer's words, substituted ordinary, 'work-like' movement for virtuosity, 'magic and make believe'.[34] As his project progresses – in works such as *Magnificent Triumphal Arch in Pompeian Colours* 2010 (p.218), in which a single performer dances and gestures elaborately towards a painted architectural fragment as a kind of monolith, or *The Birth of Venus* 2011, a two-part ballet presenting dancers in historical costumes and masks within an architectural *mise en scène* – his complicity resembles a form of resuscitation rather than liveness, and is enacted in a highly performative manner, through different layers of simulation and drag. In work such as *Plaza Minuet*, presented at Tate Britain in 2006, or within a corporate lobby in Performa, New York, in 2007, the artist organised dancers to walk in diagonal patterns performing Baroque gestures with a nod to Voguing – movement that appears exaggerated against a context of pedestrian activity. Such decorative *détournement* works against notions of urban or visitor flow. Bronstein's is a deliciously wasteful and decorative activity amid so much busy efficiency, and, in this insertion of embellishment, his performance offers up a queering of public space.

It seems relevant to his broader practice that Australian artist Gerry Bibby, like Bronstein, began by studying architecture before becoming an activist, prior to studying art. Bibby has expressed doubts about the dogmatic character of the activist strategies he encountered, seeking instead a queered approach, one that he has subsequently developed in his art practice.[35] Bibby's work is fugitive in its restless movement across formats and situations, but he exhibits a consistent fascination with process and system, from both poetic and political perspectives. Bibby explores what he describes as the 'distance between language and representation, or language and action, or language and object'.[36] Rather than departing from the linguistic approach of conceptualism, he begins with concrete objects and systems that he finds in given contexts, and deduces the structures in which they are set or that they imply.

Inspired by finding shards of oyster shells in the soil of Regent's Park in London, in his work for Frieze Projects in 2013, Bibby explored the history of labour and economic exploitation connected to the consumption of oysters in London. He planted clusters of oyster shells in public areas of the fair, which acted as the record of a pre-fair performance, in which art fair workers and building staff were invited to eat oysters, making them participants in, rather than providers of, the decadent pleasures associated with art fairs. For his project at The Showroom in London in 2014, rather than creating an exhibition for the display space, Bibby worked behind the scenes with the organisation to explore potentially different work dynamics between the institution and the artists it supports. Bibby approached the organisation's set-up, its apparatus and capacity as creative material and, through this perspective, he came to focus upon the Showroom's

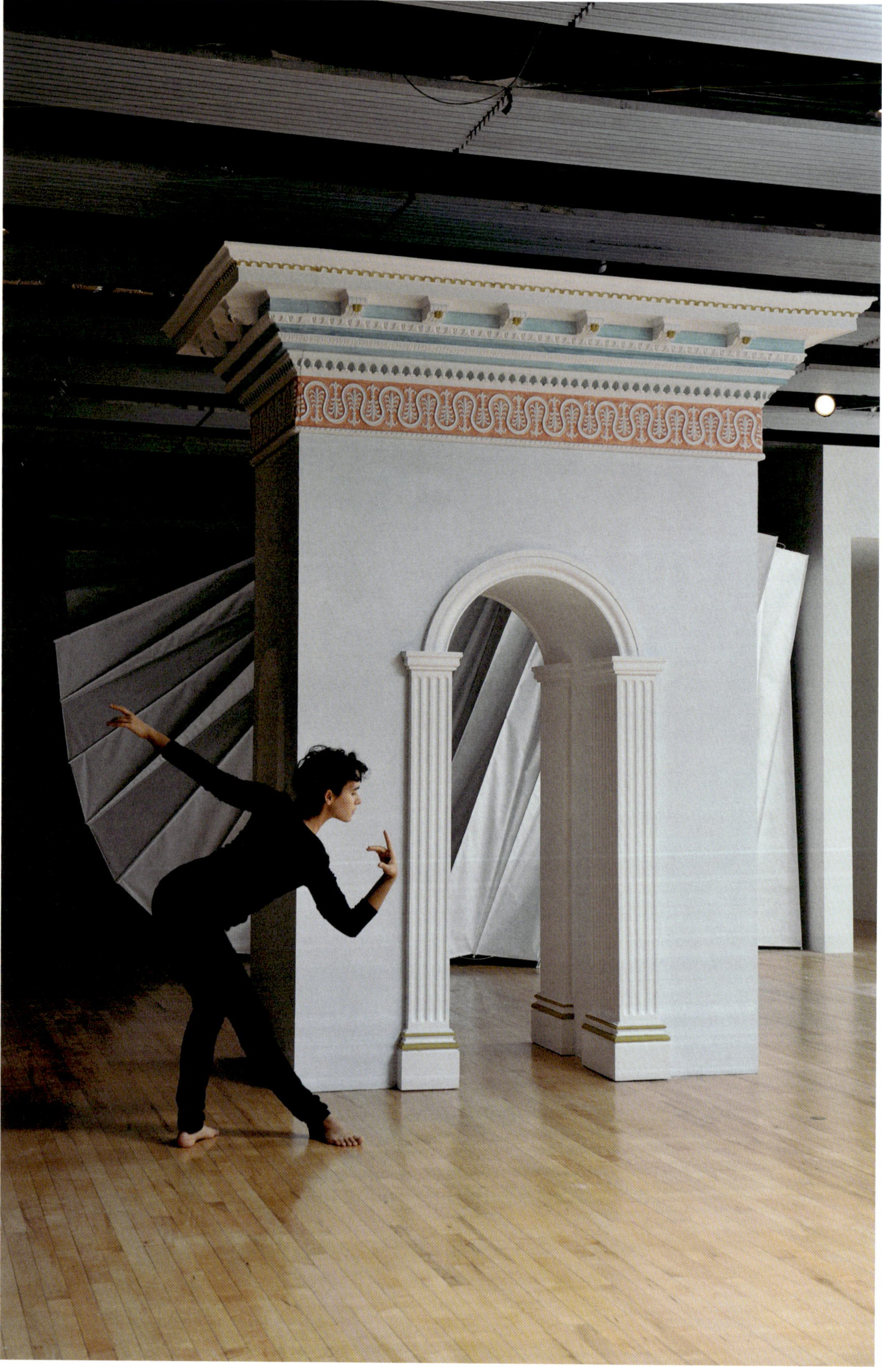

Pablo Bronstein, *Magnificent Triumphal Arch in Pompeian Colours* 2010; the dancer featured in the image is Irene Cena

heating system – a relatively invisible yet essential component of the organisation's infrastructure for its community of workers and participants. Bibby set about bleeding radiators, dismantling pipes, draining the entire system, potentially rethinking it from scratch. He also researched possible alternative measures to make the system more efficient, such as installing double glazing. Through this project, the artist might have initially appeared to instigate measures and physical changes in the environment that build upon Hans Haacke's or Michael Asher's type of institutional critique. But his interest is less in deconstructive criticism (say, measuring real economic and physical constraints that surround the exhibition of art) than in exploring the practical and psychological relations at play in such a set-up, as well as the social dimension of production in an art context, including 'forms of intimacy, intrusion and estrangement'.[37] How far could such an initiative go while maintaining some form of social equilibrium? In parallel to this work behind the scenes, Bibby displayed his work-in-progress novel, in fragments, on a series of constructed panels in the gallery space, interspersed with assemblages of ordinary found objects from the gallery – coins, tickets, rugs and a radiator. There was a sense, through this, of turning the institution inside-out: not only reconstructing its circulatory system through the heating, but also moving things from backstage to display.

Nigerian-born, Antwerp-based artist Otobong Nkanga makes drawings, installations, sculptures and performances that, variously, examine ideas around raw materials, land and the value connected to natural resources (p.220). Nkanga explores how meaning and function are culturally specific, and demonstrates different roles and histories for the same products, as they relate to her own biography and memories, as well as drawing upon art history. Though she often works with materials such as rocks, earth, soap or pigment to create gallery-based sculpture and installation, action and performance permeate Nkanga's approach to diverse media and often form the impetus for her work. She uses her own presence – her body and voice – in live performance, as well as in video, as a kind of narrative catalyst. For Nkanga, the relationship between making, performing and exhibiting is a dynamic one that should remain contingent.

Her work *Baggage* 2007–8 was a response to the happening of the same name by Allan Kaprow in 1972, a work in which earth was moved from one place to another. Nkanga's remaking of the piece involved the parcelling of sand from Lagos and its shipment to the Netherlands, and vice versa, arguably re-politicising Kaprow's original approach to a simple action performed with apparently raw materials. Nkanga also understands the piece in terms of apparent sameness and difference: sand is sand, on one level, yet 'at a particle level we can define the geographical origins of a grain of sand by its chemical composition. At the same time, I talk about flux; the flow of water moving sands through manmade boundaries, breaking constructed borders.'[38] The notion of the 'raw material' is used, by Nkanga, in a way that is almost akin to the role of the flesh-and-blood body in earlier performance art: to suggest, and then deconstruct, a degree zero of locatedness or origin, something which is an impossibility in reality. Nkanga observes: 'None of us exist in a static state. Identities are constantly evolving. African identities are multiple. When I look at, for example, Nigerian, Senegalese, Kenyan, French or Indian cultures, you cannot talk about a specific identity without talking about the colonial impacts and the impact of this exchange – of trade and goods and culture.'[39]

Otobong Nkange, *Diaoptasia* 26 November 2015, as part of BMW Tate Live: Performance Room, Tate Modern

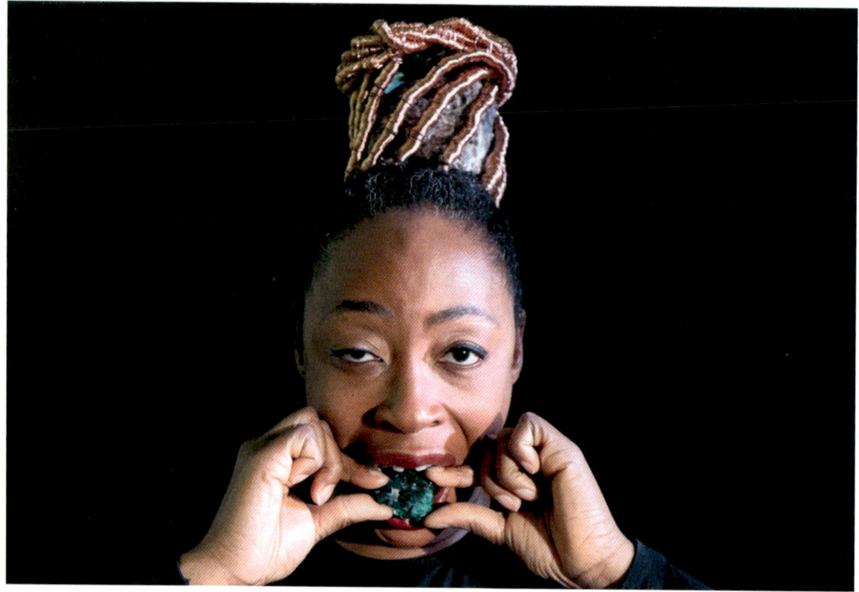

At the Weltkulturen Museum in Frankfurt, for the 2012 exhibition *Object Atlas: Fieldwork in the Museum*, Nkanga selected a number of different African weapons, currencies and body armours from the museum's collection and used them to devise a photographed performance series, staged from a feminist and decolonial perspective. The ritualistic significance of certain things – vessels, knives, jewellery – was not invoked to point towards a past social context, but rather was taken as licence to open up new perspectives on the contemporary. As an artist working with a German national collection that has claimed ownership of artefacts related to her heritage, Nkanga poses and improvises with the objects to remediate their function and reclaim them as part of her own narrative.

Theatre of things

While the artists discussed above, broadly speaking, make works that draw attention to the broader infrastructures of the world as they connect to art's theatre, a number of contemporary artists continue to experiment with the more formal question of display as it relates to the gallery. Guatemalan-born artist Naufus Ramírez-Figueroa makes sculpture and performance that are influenced by his childhood experience of activist theatre in Guatemala, and that often have a set-like appearance, using temporary materials such as painted polystyrene. Ramírez-Figueroa's surreal world is conjured from folklore mixed with conspiracy theories, mythology and magic, and the Guatemalan civil war of 1960–96 is a recurring subject in his work, softened only by the at-times absurdity or humour.

In the Gwangju Biennale, 2014, Ramírez-Figueroa's installation *Props for Eréndira* 2014 takes on the story from Gabriel García Márquez's 1972 novella *The Incredible and Sad Tale of Innocent Eréndira and her Soulless Grandmother*, a story about a girl who is forced into prostitution by her grandmother after accidentally burning down the family home. The installation appears as a stage-set for a drama that is about to unfold, but without live action. Vividly painted polystyrene sculptures of objects from the life of the protagonist are set against pink wallpaper in a static display.

The artist's 2015 exhibition at Gasworks in London, *God's Reptilian Finger*, focused on the amateur archaeology practised by Mormon missionaries in Guatemala since 1947 and by current followers of contemporary British conspiracy theorist David Icke. Geometric polystyrene shapes titled Babylonian Fantasy, were inspired by Icke's view that the global ruling classes are the descendants of the 'Babylonian Brotherhood' – the name he invented for a supposedly ancient extra-terrestrial reptilian race, originating in the Middle East. In the second installation, *God's Reptilian Finger*, an oversized, lit-up sculpture of 'God's finger' hovered in mid-air within an ultra-violet-lit gallery, surrounded by floating stones painted in phosphorescent colours. In this work, the artist referenced the dubious mythology of the Mormon missionaries in Guatemala who sought to conjure up evidence of Western influence upon pre-Columbian civilisations. Ramírez-Figueroa's work often presents art objects as curious fragments from a personal, invented mythology. The significance of the forms themselves are always to be understood in relation to the conjuring of narrative, but often in unsettling or dissonant ways.

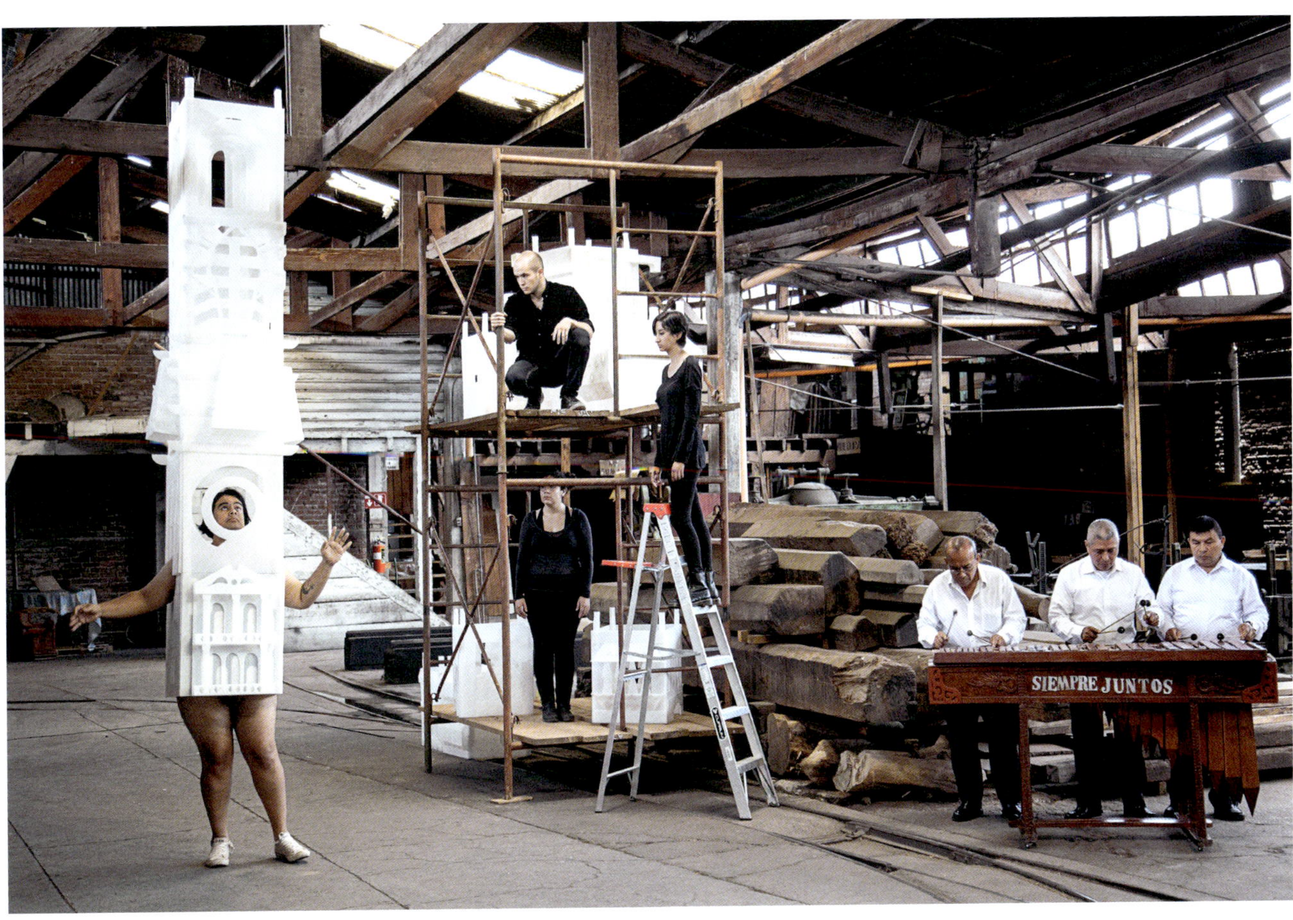

Naufus Ramirez-Figueroa,
Incremental Architecture
2015

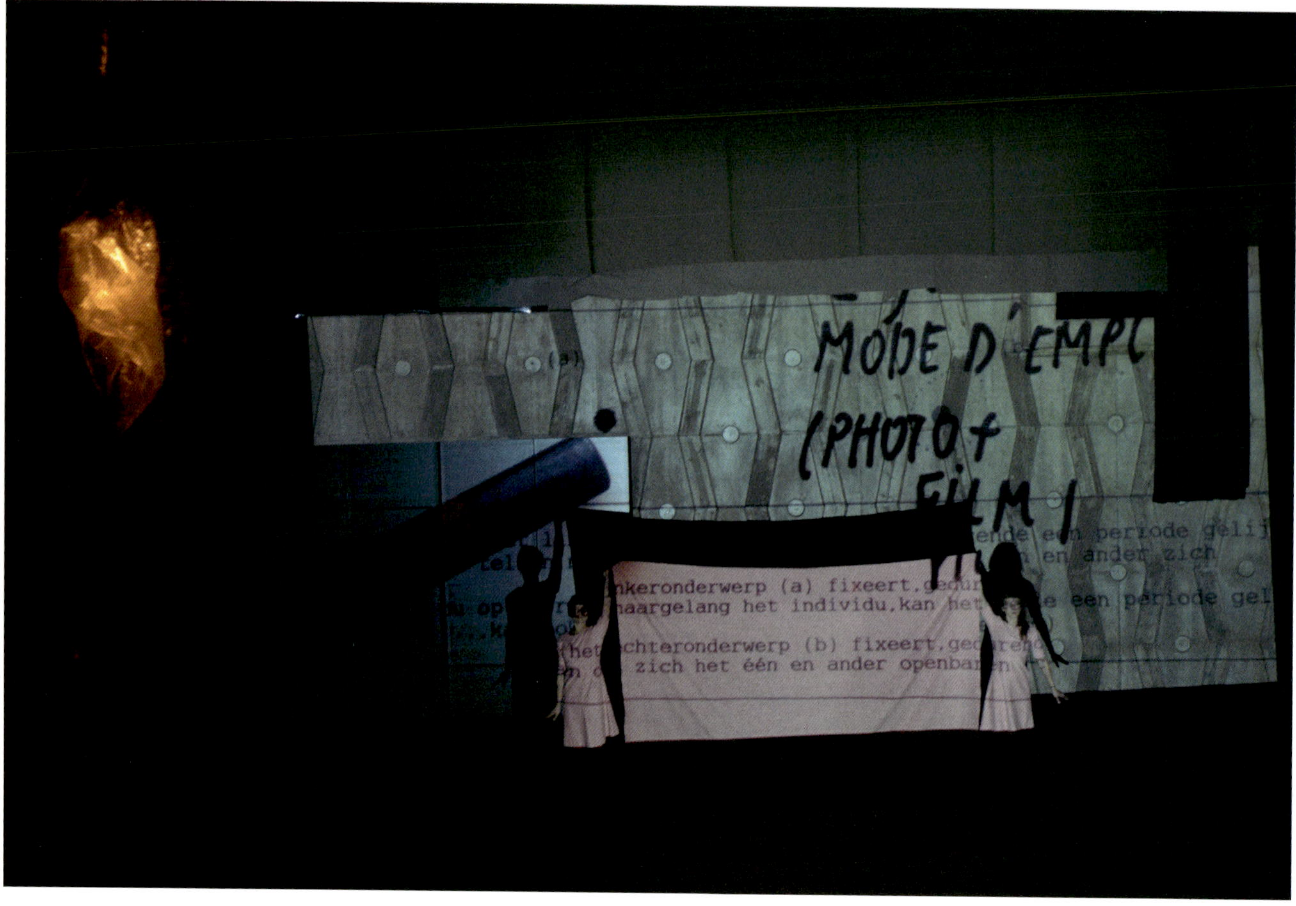

THAT'S IT! (+3 FREE minutes), STUK, Leuven, BE 2014; lecture on a work by Joëlle Tuerlinckx; soundtrack by Christoph Fink accompanied by Valentijn Goethals; interpreted by Francesca Chiacchio, Juliette Thomas and Estelle Labes; commissioned and produced by Corpus

Belgian artist Joëlle Tuerlinckx's installations comprise choreographies of found and handmade objects, manipulations of gallery lighting or framed shafts of sunlight, film and slide projections, pencilled graffiti text and marks, paper screens, and scattered card or paper shapes that the artist describes as 'confetti'. Tuerlinckx's considered placement of these objects in the exhibition space lifts them from the ordinary, often throwaway status they occupy in real time. Her environments become a theatre of things that compress and expand the viewer's experiences of time, scale and light to heighten and disorientate perception. Tuerlinckx has said: 'When I am offered an exhibition space it is as though I receive a kind of parcel, a packet of air.'[40] Her work is perhaps best described as a material manifestation of the patterns and processes of thought itself: she tries to bring mind and body into a unified space.

The 'things' that Tuerlinckx uses range from cheap, mass-produced stuff, such as a plastic football or a cutting from a magazine, to more primary materials, such as sheets of thick white cartridge paper or cardboard. Balls, boxes and buckets are familiar parts of her ecology, alongside, say, a stick used to stir paint, or a sheet of tracing paper with fine lines drawn upon it. Sometimes a piece of wood is marked with the word *objet*, in a not-quite Magritte way. In her gallery exhibitions, Tuerlinckx stages her material collections and arrangements in ways that destabilise our perception, opening up a sense of wonderment owing to our shifting understanding of them as three-dimensional artefacts and images. In her recent lecture opera *"That's It!" (+3 FREE minutes)* 2014, Tuerlinckx exaggerates this masquerading quality by turning an exhibition into a ninety-minute live theatre piece whose backbone is a slide show featuring her personal archive of collage and drawing, interspersed with choreography, music, spoken texts and moving or manipulated objects (a bucket, a trolley, an orange rope).

The performative dimension of Tuerlinckx's work is twofold: she both addresses the exhibition set-up and ritual, and creates exhibitions as a performed theatre-style event. The question of visual display remains central, but she experiments freely with the mode in which we might encounter it. In this sense, her practice can be related to that of German artist Jutta Koether, Colombian-born Oscar Murillo or Scottish artist Lucy McKenzie, artists who use the parameters of painting as both a performative space in itself – articulating the language of the medium knowingly within individual works – and at the same time as a prompt to create social events, performances and film, involving music or other actions.

Though the practice of painting is central for McKenzie, she also, and equally, designs clothes and co-directs an interior design practice. In addition to this, she has founded a record label, as well as choreographed and appeared in performances made in collaboration with other artists, notably Paulina Olowska and the filmmaker Lucile Desamory. McKenzie's painting is anchored in finely honed architectural décor techniques learned at a traditional school for artisanal painting, which includes simulating marble or wood grain, but the deliberately worn surfaces of her canvases are somehow continuous with the painted surfaces of the city: a graffitied wall, blocks of colour on a train door, a printed T-shirt. The one-to-one-scaled realism of her works shifts painting from the window-like illusionistic space of early modern art towards a situation whereby the painted plane of her picture protrudes into, or exists within, the space of the viewer. This combination of convincing representation and its disruption through the layering of mimetic elements – the clouds, the apartment walls, the painted drips – creates a poetically impossible sense of place that is, paradoxically, full of potential. McKenzie's broader practice is, arguably, grown from capacities unique to painting: she builds and inhabits new realities from its fictional foundation (p.224). Emblematic of McKenzie's attitude, the clouds layered into the domestic interior of the Galerie Buchholz in Cologne, in her 2010–11 exhibition *Slender Means*, hold a special place in the history of painting as a portal to elsewhere – somewhere between the magical parting of the sky at the beginning of the hand-drawn world of *The Simpsons* and the cherub-filled heaven of Titian's *Assumption of the Virgin* 1515–18. The window view of sky within this picture frame is not one of spatial depth, nor a Magritte-style surrealist trick, but a prompt towards a dream space that encroaches into the reality of the space inhabited by the viewer.

The use of traditional techniques and dense emblematic composition in McKenzie's approach belies the fact that she shares a common attitude with artists of the same generation who are engaged in an open-ended form of research-based practice. In this kind of work it is common that found materials are assembled in a space and juxtaposed with narrative intention which it is left to the viewer to articulate or activate. In this mode, Canadian artist Kapwani Kiwanga brings her research in anthropology and literature to a practice looking at colonial histories and Afrofuturism – a cultural movement featuring science fiction themes drawn from elements of black history – weaving together material from different sources.

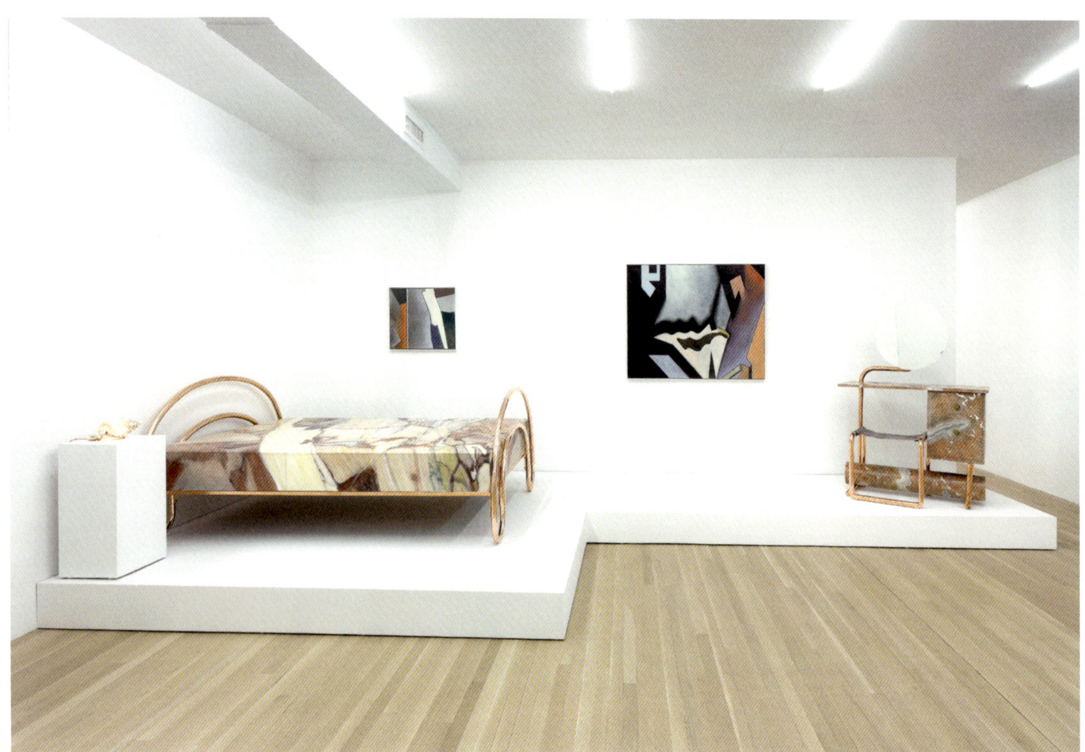

Lucy McKenzie, 'Inspired by Inspired by', installation view Galerie Buchholz, New York, 2016

Kapwani Kiwanga, *Nursery* 2016, plants, wood, oral transmissions; view of the exhibition *Ujamaa* La Ferme du Buisson, Noisiel (FR), 2016

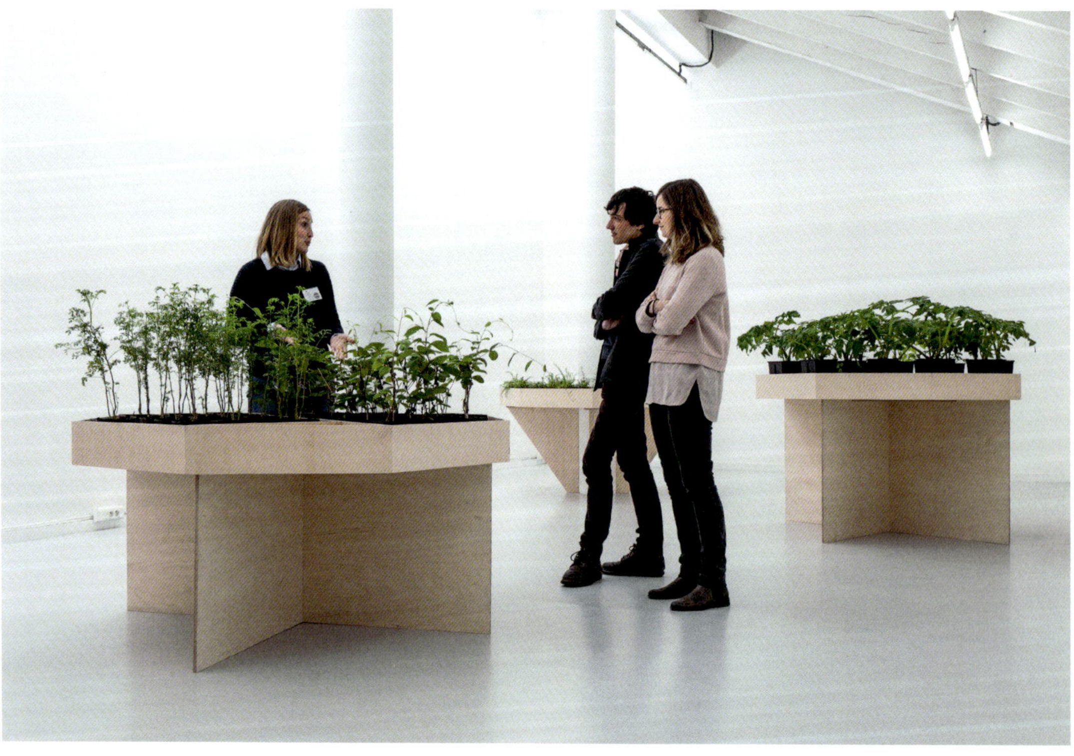

Archival documents, found objects, instruments and performed actions or spoken words are employed in her installations. For her exhibition at the South London Gallery in 2015, *Kinjiketile Suite*, Kiwanga staged a display of ephemera and archival photographs and documents related to the Maji Maji War in 1905–7, an armed revolt against German colonial rule in present-day Tanzania. These documents were set within a plywood and sisal rope construction, interspersed with a collection of castor oil plants, and were accompanied by live readings by actors in English and Swahili. As curator Nataša Petrešin-Bachelez has noted: 'By conceiving the exhibition as a subjective archive through which the artist queries the act of compiling, organising and categorising, she mixes a narrative and subjective ordering that rejects the illusion of totality or exhaustiveness.'[41]

Kiwanga's exhibition thus becomes a stage-set for political narratives and a format for reordering how we might encounter them. It is a theatre of competing narratives; a discursive space in which objects are prompts to explore stories, issues, different voices that meet and clash. These perspectives might emanate from apparently neutral, natural things – a plant, for example – with a hidden historical association. But Kiwanga also allows space for the poetry and potency of absences. Her approach is emblematic of a kind of contemporary practice that makes little distinction between the texture and presence of objects and those of a live reading or action performed in their midst. Kiwanga's work proposes the world of ideas, objects, actions and conversations to be in a state of circulating connections – not directionless, but open in its emphasis on how networks of meaning and relations are configured, and how the space of art not only connects with the external world, but breathes it in and out.

Kiwanga's practice fits within a current trend of artists adopting the role of curators, since it deals with questions of display, juxtaposition, object-based narrative and research, which are to do with editorial selection. But what is the specific role that the combined web of referential fragments and the insertion of performance into the exhibition format plays here? What is drawn out through dialogue and through the staging of this kind of network? Do these juxtapositions elicit a conversation between its elements, interpellated by the viewer? If McKenzie's or Koether's individual paintings, after Kippenberger's, are what David Joselit has labelled as 'transitive painting' – he understands the individual paintings as nodes articulating the art-world networks to which they are connected – the objects assembled in Kiwanga's installations are hyper-transitive: they are conduits to manifold competing global narratives.[42] As a set of provisionally arranged prompts, they keep us moving to deduce a narrative, and are simultaneously puzzle-like and generative.

Just as a performance event puts forward a provisional vision, so the open-endedness of this approach implies the potential for switching positions, for rearrangement. Twenty-first-century artists working in this vein understand their work to be a live process that offers shifting ways of looking and making connections. This process is not only contingent, but one that necessarily includes the viewer as an interlocutor. The question is: how do they intend us to use it? In his *Peterlee Project* in the 1970s, Stuart Brisley invited residents of the then-new town in the north of England to make contributions of materials about their own histories, and created a common archive for residents. This was not initiated with the idea of keeping an archive for posterity, but simply to generate a body of remembrance material to use as a prompt for live reflection and discussion, for looking back, and forward, among a community: a way for a displaced community to perform their history. Kiwanga's mode of aggregate exhibition might be thought of as an active space with a similar, discursive mode of spectatorship. Just as the role of the artist-as-author is evolving, so too is that of audiences.

In a study of audience behaviour and spectatorship at Tate Modern, ethnographer Peter Tolmie observed the prevalence, even in the painting and sculpture galleries, not of individual contemplation (as high modernism imagined it) but of visiting and discussing in pairs. Irish artist Gerard Byrne made a work about this shifting attitude to art. Modelled upon an acting exercise devised by Bertolt Brecht, *An Exercise for Two Actors and One Listener* 2006 involved two actors improvising dialogue using artworks as props: for example, recalling the scene in a Peter Doig painting in narrative terms, as though it had been a dream. Through the incorporation of performances in the gallery space, but also through a broader understanding of performativity, a new mode of exhibition-making is emerging whose provisional arrangement proposes a newly energised take on the props set out for performance, charging viewers with the task of inferring the script. If the ideas at stake in Umberto Eco's *The Open Work* (1962) or Roland Barthes's 'The Death of the Author' (1967) have been hugely influential for postmodern art, the deductive role of the reader that they imagined is being enacted literally in contemporary art.[43] Such enactments may take the form of choreographed gestures that have symbolic presence within an installation, as sound or text interventions, or as public discussion and debate, coaxing silent objects to speak.

Summary

This book has asked what we mean by performance within contemporary art, which has led us to the more fundamental question: how has the rise of performance since the 1950s changed the field of art? We have seen how the model of the artist has shifted away from the figure of the lone individual towards that of a collaborator engaged in experiments with sharing, reciprocal dialogue and networks of exchange. We have also noted how the status of the audience has been altered, transforming supposedly passive observers into participants. And our understanding of the art object as the locus of value and experience has been recast, too: its boundaries are constantly being challenged, and we encounter it in myriad forms. The work of art emerges, as a result, as an ever expanding notion. We have moved from a definition of performance as medium to a more pervasive understanding of the performative. New awareness of the ritual structures that regulate our relation to the work of art is also significant. The assumed behavioural codes of the gallery are changing with these changes of practice. How does performance show the framework of art as being 'made' – whether of architecture, bodies or attention – as much as the object that it foregrounds? All of these questions, today, must be understood against a backdrop in which the broad notion of performance has become more and more important to both work and life, and points back to something ancient.

In the early 1970s, Lucy R. Lippard described performance as 'the most immediate art form, which aspires to the immediacy of political action itself', and noted that 'performance means getting down to the bare bones of aesthetic communication'.[44] If, at that moment, performance offered a new alphabet of forms that foregrounded the patterns of attention, forms of community and dynamic potential for reconfiguration of relations within the art encounter, the effects of these experiments are still in motion today, working their way through art's DNA. Across the world, experiments with action, liveness and performance have enabled new representations of individuality, new shapes for social contact, and new parameters for encountering and understanding art, both born of and reacting against many different psychological, political and artistic contexts. The poet and theorist Fred Moten speaks of the need to find new social forms that redress inherited power structures and biases by 'renewing our habits of assembly' and finding new ways of 'getting together'.[45] His suggestion that even vernacular forms of communal living, such as a neighbourhood barbeque, might make us think about the social bonds within black American communities, and serve as foundations for rethinking institutions, has far-reaching relevance.

Arguably, the new habits of assembly initiated by performance in the second half of the twentieth century have impacted the entire field of contemporary art, rendering the art encounter itself as a set of acts. It is not only that the question of appearing and being visible is fundamental to being an artist, but that the act of exhibiting or showing is understandable as a ritual that is underwritten by both ideological and theatrical protocols, behaviours and expectations.[46] Live performance becomes a metaphor for how life might be played. In a context of dispersed biopolitical power, performance becomes increasingly important as an assertion of 'minor modes of life', as philosopher Peter Pál Pelbart has described them, against dominant pressures to conform or participate as a consumer.[47]

But if performance history supposedly has its origins in a high period of one-off, live events that foreground the palpable, often vulnerable living body, performance now is not only about liveness in that essentialist sense. From an emphasis on the real-time presence of bodies, performance has morphed into a metaphorical texture that represents a provisional state of things, suggesting the possibility of change and transformation through iteration – what I have been calling the 'performative'. This spread of liveness to encompass both human and non-human elements of the art situation is indicative of a constant, deliberate restlessness that serves as resistance to notions of possession. Performance in the twenty-first century might not be anti-market or anti-institutional in an explicit way (performance editions are now bought and sold, museums and galleries are its home) but nevertheless liveness often injects a degree of unruly evasiveness that possibly allows for a more accurate representation of the conditions of life than something that is fixed and can be possessed in its entirety.

Performance, then, is pervasive within art of the twenty-first century. But if everything has become performative, what comes next? Perhaps the critical and revelatory dimension of performance, which initiated such profound shifts within the field of contemporary art in the first place, will push things to a limit. My account of the art zone as a free space for experimentation across disciplinary boundaries might help us to see everything in its frame as a specific set of values and relations, but will it also force awareness of the deceptive freedom and flexibility of contemporary art's own frame? Writer Suhail Malik has argued persuasively that we should begin to see contemporary art as a limited genre with a very specific set of attitudes and practices.[48] Its apparent freedom, indeterminacy and cross-disciplinary character makes it all the more voracious in its consumption of other disciplines, but not neutral as an ideological structure. Indeed, as many artists acknowledge critically, these qualities potentially bring it closer to the immaterial nature of the experience economy, within whose framework it operates. Such profound questions remain in play.

Jumana Emil Abboud, *O Whale Don't Swallow our Moon!*, video performance 7:40 min., 2011, commissioned by the Sharjah Art Foundation. This Project was part of Sharjah Biennial 10

What is certain is that our idea of art as it is represented in the gallery and museum is shifting at its base. Thinking back to some of the earliest uses of painting and sculpture that we know of, for example within Egyptian funerary rituals, we understand that objects were arranged elaborately and reverently in mausolea with a view to their future activation in the afterlife. These mausolea offer a kind of inverse metaphor for the state of art now: we infer that art objects in museums have come from a lived context, which we reflect upon imaginatively, but assume that no future life is possible outside of this static display. The attitude of 'performance' – in fact, a refusal of the segregation of objects and actions that is a relatively recent, largely western, phenomenon in world art history – thrusts the artwork back into ritual, and into life again.

As the art world grapples with globalism and attempts to formulate new cultural narratives and network patterns, the canon is fundamentally in question. It is not possible, with this wider perspective, to assume a universalist understanding of the artwork's origin and meaning. On this point Western museums can learn from the approaches of indigenous art specialists such as Wanda Nanibush, curator and activist, who in working to 'make space' for the artistic legacy of her First Nation ancestors, makes the point that everyone, in fact, should 'locate themselves from where they are speaking.'[49]

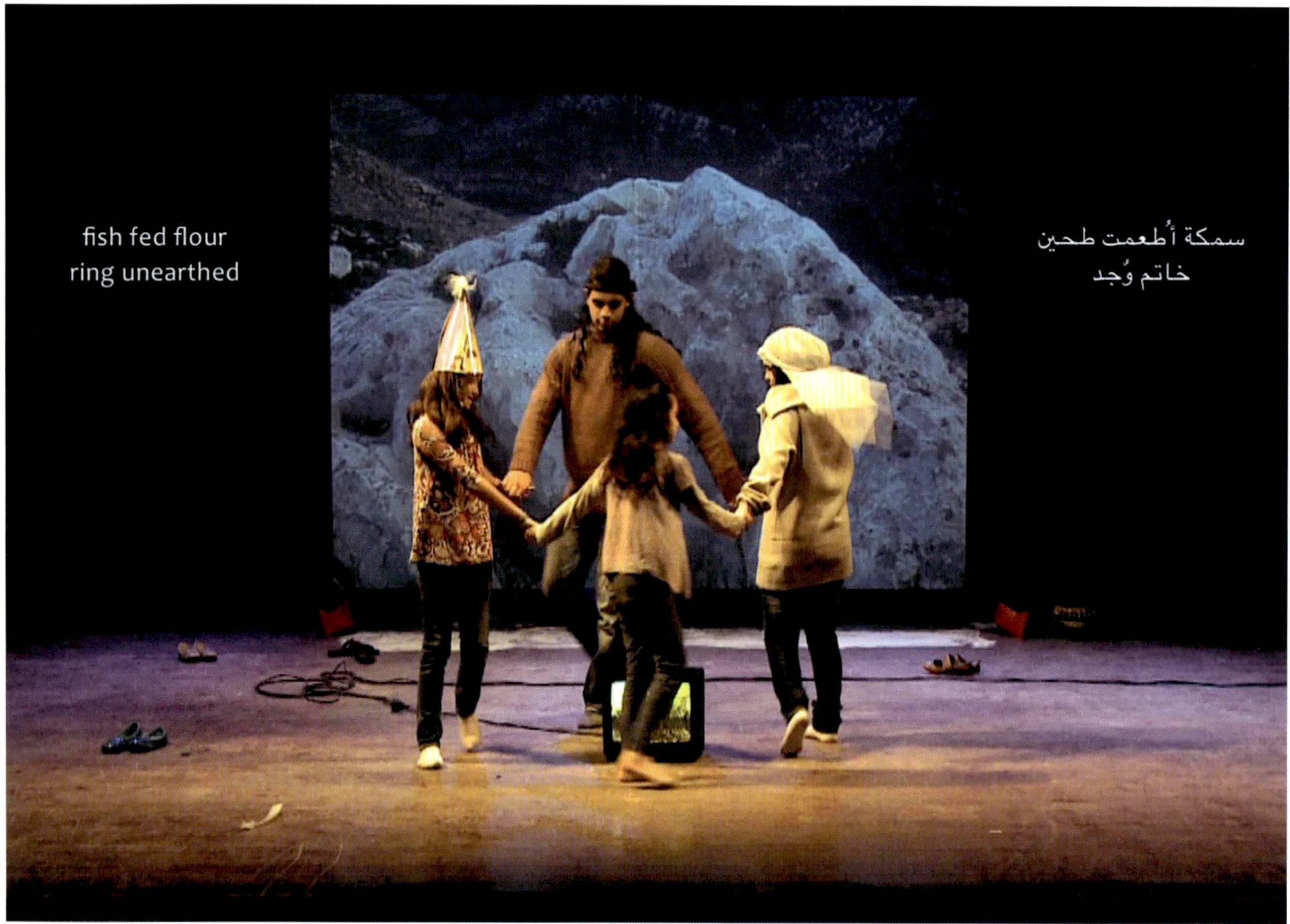

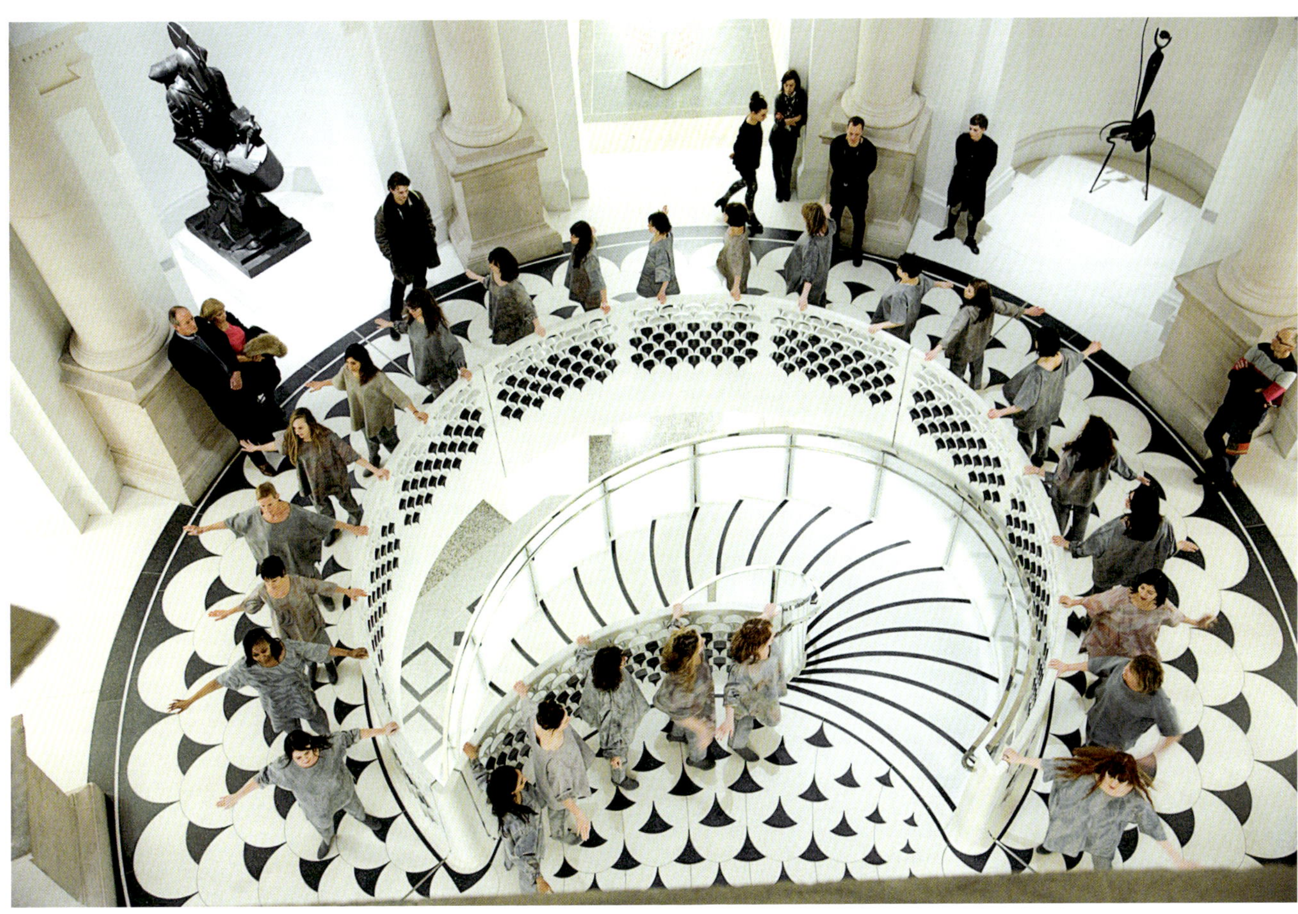

Cally Spooner, *And You Were Wonderful, On Stage* 2014, performed as part of BMW Tate Live, Tate Britain, 21 January 2014

Questions of value are difficult to ascertain without acknowledging that we are in a time of huge – at once necessary, thrilling and unsettling – social shifts. There is a need to act out new positions and experiment with new kinds of encounter. Have we been mistaking the object of art for what it symbolises socially? Have we been confounding the outcome with the act: art not as a thing but as a prompt to enlarge the imagination, art as a form of belief and communal value? It becomes evident that in order to understand 'it', we must recognise the provisional nature of any 'we'.

Performance represents a powerful way in which artists have tried to situate the work of art within an – often temporary – community of belief, to make the production of aesthetic meaning visible. If there is no attempt to understand how relations with others, situated in time, shape the experience of what art is, there is a risk of making assumptions that universalise particularities, prioritise certain forms of cultural power or simply ignore the way that meaning is produced for, between and by people, even while the experience of this deep communion with a work of art might feel transcendent. Ultimately performance registers the shifting state of contemporary reality – moving with it, or reshaping relations to change its course – to make representations of what it means now to live.

Notes

Introduction, pp.6–29

1 Cally Spooner, interview with the author, 21 January 2014. Her words echo the phrase used by Robert Rauschenberg in the 1960s, describing his own approach to improvised assemblage.

2 This question is explored by Thierry de Duve in his series of essays on the Avant Garde and the Invention of Art. Part 6 of 6 essays, *ArtForum*, beginning in October 2013, http://artforum.com/inprint/issue=201404&id=45761; see the April 2014 text.

3 Thomas Berghuis discussed this during his lecture, 'Place, Time and Media in Performance Art in Indonesia', 25 May 2017, SOAS, London. See also Ferial Afiff's research report on performance art with Asia Art Archive; *Singapore: Open Ends*, a documentation exhibition of performance art in Singapore at the Substation's Septfest, 7–21 September 2001.

4 Examples include: Adrian Henri's *Total Art: Environments, Happenings, and Performance* (London 1974); *Studio International*'s special issue on 'Performance Art' (vol.192, July 1976); *La Performance* (exhibition catalogue, Galleria Comunale d'Arte Moderna, Bologna, 1977); 'Performance Art Festival', held in Brussels in October 1978, and then in the US; the magazine *High Performance*, founded in Los Angeles in 1978; *Performance by Artists* (ed. AA Bronson and Peggy Gale, Toronto 1979); RoseLee Goldberg's book *Performance: Live Art, 1909 to the Present* (New York 1979); and *Performance Art Magazine*, published in New York from 1979, and retitled *LIVE* in 1980.

5 'Artist Talk with Graciele Carnevale' 10 March 2012, within the exhibition *Moments: A History of Performance in 10 Acts*, ZKM Karlsruhe, 2012.

6 Guy Debord, *The Society of the Spectacle*, trans. Donald Nicholson-Smith, New York 2006, p.12.

7 Yvonne Rainer, 'Statement', programme notes for *The Mind Is a Muscle*, Anderson Theater, New York, 11, 14 and 15 April 1968; reproduced in Yvonne Rainer, *Work 1961–73*, Halifax 1974, p.71.

8 William Marotti, 'Creative Destruction', *Artforum*, vol.51, no.6, February 2013, p.193.

9 Notable examples include: Performa festival in New York since 2005; Performatik in Brussels since 2009; the event 'Performance Days', organised by the curatorial agency If I Can't Dance in Amsterdam in 2014; as well as numerous performance programmes of major international biennials, as well as Documenta in Kassel.

10 States further explains that these words simultaneously 'belong to the fields of both ideology and methodology: they are at once an attitude and a tool', Bert O. States, 'Performance as Metaphor', *Afterall*, no.3, Spring/Summer 2001, p.65.

11 See J.L. Austin, *How to Do Things with Words*, Cambridge, MA 1964.

12 See Judith Butler, *Gender Trouble*, New York 1990.

13 Richard Schechner, *Performance Studies: An Introduction*, 2nd edn, Hoboken 2012, p.31.

14 Marvin Carlson, *Performance: A Critical Introduction*, London and New York 1996, p.4.

15 RoseLee Goldberg, *Performance Art: From Futurism to the Present*, London 1979 (third edition, 2011), pp.12, 32. However, Goldberg – perhaps because she was writing at a moment during which such disciplinary crossover was taking place – blurs the boundaries of this definition somewhat by including straight dance, theatre and music in her larger-format book *Performance: Live Art since the 60s* (London 1998), without attempting to define more specifically how they intersect with visual art. Alongside Goldberg's book, an important publication defining this area of practice was Lea Vergine's *Body Art and Performance: The Body as Language* (trans. Henry Martin, Milan 2000).

16 Birgit Pelzer, 'Performance or The Integral Calculus of Ambiguities', in Chantal Pontbriand (ed.), *Parachute: The Anthology*, vol.2, Zürich 2013, pp.44–63.

17 Bruce McLean, interview with Vincent Honoré, *Spike*, no.38, Winter 2013, p.58.

18 Diana Taylor, *The Archive and the Repertoire*, Durham, NC 2003, p.12.

19 Harper Montgomery, 'Conceptualism, Dematerialization, Arte no-objetual? Historicizing the 1960s and 1970s in Latin America', *Post: Notes on Modern and Contemporary Art around the Globe*, 11 July 2013, http://post.at.moma.org/content_items/246-conceptualism-dematerialization-arte-no-objetual-historicizing-the-60s-and-70s-in-latin-america, accessed 19 September 2017.

20 Joan Kee, 'Why Performance in Authoritarian Korea?', *Tate Papers*, issue 23, Spring 2015, http://www.tate.org.uk/research/publications/tate-papers/23/why-performance-in-authoritarian-korea, paragraph 12, accessed 19 September 2017.

21 Bojana Kunst, 'The Troubles with Temporality: Micropolitics of Performance', *Stedelijk Studies*, no.3, Autumn 2015, p.1.

22 Dorothea von Hantelmann, *How to Do Things with Art: The Meaning of Art's Performativity*, trans. Jeremy Gaines and Michael Turnbull, Zurich 2010.

23 The question of format has been dealt with in much recent art history, see B. Clausen (ed.), *After the Act: The (Re) Presentation of Performance Art*, Vienna 2007.

24 Goldberg 2011, p.8.

25 *Out of Actions: Between Performance and the Object 1949–79*, exhibition catalogue, Museum of Contemporary Art, Los Angeles, February–May 1998 (11).

26 Peggy Phelan, 'performance cannot be saved, recorded, documented, or otherwise participate in the circulation of representations *of* representations: once it does so it becomes something other than performance', *Unmarked: The Politics of Performance*, London 1993, p.146.

27 Jonah Westerman, 'Between Action and Image: Performance as "Inframedium"', *Tate Online*, 20 January 2015, http://www.tate.org.uk/context-comment/articles/between-action-and-image-performance, accessed 19 September 2017.

28 An event exploring this phenomenon, titled 'Performance Year Zero: A Living History', was staged in the Tanks at Tate Modern, 5–6 October 2012.

29 For example, in his introduction to *Performance: A Critical Introduction*, Marvin Carlson writes, 'my emphasis will remain on the United States ... because, despite its international diffusion, performance art is both historically and theoretically a primarily American phenomenon, and a proper understanding of it must, I believe, be centred on how it has developed both practically and conceptually in the United States'. Carlson 1996, p.2.

30 David Joselit, '*International Pop* and *The World Goes Pop*', *Artforum*, vol.54, issue 5, January 2016, pp.230–1.

31 Glissant cited in Hans Ulrich and Asad Raza (eds.), *Mondialité, or the Archipelagos of Edouard Glissant*, Paris and New York 2017, p.21.

I: the individual (pp.30–111)

1 Marina Abramović makes these remarks in the documentary film *The Artist Is Present* (Matthew Akers, 2012).

2 Marina Abramović talk, *Talking Art*, Tate Modern, 16 October 2010.

3 Ulay, interview with the author, Institute of Contemporary Arts, London, 6 March 2015.

4 Allan Kaprow, 'The Legacy of Jackson Pollock' (1958), Jeff Kelley (ed.), *Essays on the Blurring of Art and Life*, Berkeley and Los Angeles 1993, pp.1–9.

5 Walter Benjamin, 'The Work of Art in the Age of Mechanical Reproduction' (1936), Hannah Arendt (ed.), *Illuminations*, trans. Harry Zohn, New York 2007, pp.217–52.

6 Leo Steinberg, *Other Criteria: Confrontations with Twentieth-Century Art*, Chicago 2007, p.62.

7 In Yves Alain Bois, 'Klein's Relevance for Today', *October*, vol.119, Winter 2007, p.79.

8 Helen Westgeest, 'No Meaning, No Composition, No Colour: From Zero to Gutai', in *Gutai: Painting with Time and Space*, exhibition catalogue, Museo Cantonale d'Arte, Lugano, October 2010 – February 2011, p.125.

9 Saburo Murakami, 'Gutai bijutsu nit suite' (On Gutai Art), *Gutai*, no.7, 1957, quoted in Ming Tiampo, 'Gutai Experiments on the World Stage', in *Gutai: Painting with Time and Space*, p.31.

10 As Alexandra Munroe has noted, Gutai should not be positioned only in relation to expressionism, as is common in Western art historical accounts. Of the canonical survey *Art since 1900: Modernism, Antimodernism, Postmodernism* (ed. Hal Foster et al, London 2004), for example, Munroe comments: 'The authors cite Gutai and the Brazilian Neo-Concretists but misread both as derivative. Their terms "dissemination" and "reinterpretation" preserve the construct of Euro-America as the dominant centre.' She observes, instead: 'Gutai offers a paradigmatic example of a non-Western art movement and aesthetic discourse that was, as it saw itself, "at the cutting edge of world culture"' (p.23), and indeed increasingly appears so in retrospect because it offers a different starting point that paves the way towards an understanding of performance as an end in itself. Alexandra Munroe, 'All the Landscapes: Gutai's World', in *Gutai: Splendid Playground*, exhibition catalogue, Guggenheim Museum, New York, February – May 2013.

11 A significant early influence was Toju Nantembo, a Zen priest born in the late nineteenth century who devised the idea of the 'body as a brush' and lived in Osaka near to Yoshihara. Marco Franciolli, 'Gutai: Painting with Time and Space', in *Gutai: Painting with Time and Space*, p.13.

12 Jirō Yoshihara, 'Gutai Art Manifesto', 1956, in *Gutai: Splendid Playground*, p.18.

13 Midori Yoshimoto, *Into Performance: Japanese Women Artists in New York*, New Brunswick 2005, p.195.

14 Ming Tiampo, 'Gutai Chain: The Collective Spirit of Individualism', *Positions*, vol.21, issue 2, 2013, pp.383–415.

15 Phelan 1993, p.1.

16 Peggy Phelan, lecture at Tate Modern, London, 29 March 2003.

17 Lea Vergine, *Body Art and Performance: The Body as Language*, trans. by Henry Martin, Milan 2000, p.8.

18 Carolee Schneemann, 'Eye-Body: 36 Transformative Actions', http://www.caroleeschneemann.com/eyebody.html, accessed 19 January 2017.

19 Kristine Stiles, 'Uncorrupted Joy: International Art Actions', in *Out of Actions: Between Performance and the Object, 1949–1979*, p.296.

20 Carolee Schneemann, *More than Meat Joy: Complete Performance Works and Selected Writings*, ed. Bruce McPherson, New Paltz 1979, p.235.

21 Stuart Brisley, 'And for today… nothing', http://www.stuartbrisley.com/pages/27/70s/Works/And_for_today____nothing/page:7, accessed 19 September 2017.

22 As described in *Live Art in LA: Performance in Southern California, 1970–1983*, ed. Peggy Phelan, New York and London 2012. The Barbara T. Smith reference is in the extended caption for plate 55 (unpaginated); additional references to this piece pp.144–5.

23 Tehching Hsieh, interview with Adrian Heathfield, *Tehching Hsieh: Doing Time*, exhibition leaflet, Taiwan Pavilion, Taipei Fine Arts Museum, 57th Venice Biennale, May – November 2017.

24 Sandra Llano Meija, interview with the authors, 5 February 2016, in Andrea Giunta and Cecilia Fajardo Hill, *Radical Women: Latin American Art 1960–1985*, exhibition catalogue, Hammer Museum, Los Angeles 2017, p.264.

25 Ibid.

26 Zdenka Badovinac, 'Body and the East', in *Body and the East*, exhibition catalogue, Museum of Modern Art, Ljubljana, July – September 1998, p.14.

27 Ibid., p.15.

28 Kristine Stiles, 'INSIDE/OUTSIDE: Balancing Between a Dusthole and Eternity', in ibid., p.24.

29 Ibid.

30 *Performance Art of Korea: From Happening to Event*, 1967–2007, exhibition catalogue, National Museum of Contemporary Art, Korea, August – October 2007, pp.69, 84.

31 Ibid.

32 Joan Kee lecture for Tate Research, 2015.

33 Kee 2015, paragraph 45.

34 Kee 2015, paragraph 49.

35 See Thomas J. Berghuis, *Performance Art in China*, Hong Kong 2006; and Meiling Chang, *Beijing Xingwei: Contemporary Chinese time-based art*, Kolkata 2013.

36 Huang Yong Ping, interview with Jane DeBevoise, 15 October 2010, http://www.aaa-a.org/programs/conversation-with-huang-yongping/, accessed 19 September 2017.

37 Berghuis 2006, p.66.

38 Ibid.

39 Ibid., p.37.

40 Ibid., p.48.

41 Ibid., p.51.

42 Ibid., p.56.

43 Jack Smith, 'The Memoirs of Maria Montez or Wait for me at the Bottom of the Pool', 1963–4, *Wait for me at the Bottom of the Pool*, New York and London 1997, p.37.

44 Ibid., p.37.

45 Douglas Crimp later reconfigured *Pictures* as an important article in the journal *October* (vol.8, Spring 1979, pp.75–88).

46 'David Bowie: Five Years', BBC Four, 18 July 2015.

47 *Joan Jonas Works 1968–94*, Stedelijk, 1994.

48 Helena Reckitt, Peggy Phelan, *Art and Feminism*, London 2012.

49 Adrian Piper, 'Xenophobia and the Indexical Present II', in Jan Cohen-Cruz (ed.), *Radical Street Performance: An International Anthology*, London 1998.

50 Adrian Piper, *Out of Order, Out of Sight: Selected Writings in Meta-Art, 1968–1992*, Cambridge, MA. 1996, vol.1, p.263.

51 MoMA caption Gallery label from *Contemporary Art from the Collection*, 30 June 2010 – 12 September 2011: https://www.moma.org/collection/works/130862.

52 *Tseng Kwong Chi: Performing for the Camera*, exhibition text, Grey Art Gallery, New York, April – July 2015, https://greyartgallery.nyu.edu/exhibition/tseng-kwong-chi-performing-for-the-camera/, accessed 19 September 2017. Amy Brandt discusses this issue, and its minority and queer politics, in more detail in her essay in Amy Brandt (ed.), *Tseng Kwong Chi: Performing for the Camera*, New York 2015, pp.26, 32.

53 In critical theory, the post-human is a speculative being that seeks to reconceive the human. It is the object of post-humanist criticism, which critically questions Renaissance humanism, a branch of philosophy which claims that human nature is autonomous, rational, capable of free will, and unified in itself as the apex of existence. Thus, the post-human position recognises imperfectability and disunity within the individual, and understands the world through heterogeneous perspectives while seeking to maintain intellectual rigour and a dedication to objective observations. Key to this post-human practice is the ability to fluidly change perspectives and manifest oneself through different identities. The post-human, for critical theorists of the subject, has an emergent ontology rather than a stable one; in other words, the post-human is not a singular, defined individual, but rather one who can 'become' or embody different identities and understand the world from multiple, heterogeneous perspectives. See Donna J. Haraway, 'Situated Knowledges', *Simians, Cyborgs, and Women*, New York 1991.

54 Jacques Lacan, *The Seminar of Jacques Lacan: Book VII: The Ethics of Psychoanalysis 1959–60*, trans. Dennis Porter, London 1992, p.139. Lacan coined the term 'extimité'.

55 Pope.L, interview with Adrienne Edwards, http://www.walkerart.org/magazine/2015/william-popel-will-exhaust, accessed 19 September 2017.

56 Regina Galindo EARTH 2013.

57 Tania Bruguera, 'Self-sabotage', http://www.taniabruguera.com/cms/index.php?article_id=111&clang=0, accessed 19 September 2017.

58 Holland Cotter, 'Chinese Art, in One Man's Translation', *The New York Times*, 7 September 2007, http://www.nytimes.com/2007/09/07/arts/design/07zhan.html, accessed 19 September 2017.

59 In November/December 1985 a large Rauschenberg exhibition was held at the China Art Gallery in Beijing. Financed by Rauschenberg himself, and not subject to same control by the state that was often imposed by central authorities, it was one of the largest exhibitions held by a single overseas artist in China. Over twenty-two days the exhibition attracted over 300,000 people including artists from all over the country. From around 1981, several Chinese art journals published a series of articles on the concept of self-expression in painting and other forms of art. In February 1981 Meishu (Fine Arts) published an article about the concept of 'self-expression' in relation to Sartre. A month earlier, they had printed images of German expressionist work, and articles on dada and surrealism.

60 Lu Hong and Sun Xhuanhoa's book *Alienated Body / Flesh: Chinese Performance Art* 2006 notes the 'premature' arrival of body art in China. Cited in Meiling Cheng, *Beijing Xingwei: Contemporary Chinese Time-Based Art*, Los Angeles 2013, p.9.

61 Berghuis 2006, p.57.

62 He Yunchang, Chinese performance catalogue in Asia Art Archive, Hong Kong.

63 Berghuis 2006, p.102.

64 See Catherine Malabou, *The Future of Hegel: Plasticity, Temporality and Dialectic*, trans. Lisabeth During, London 2005; and Catherine Malabou, *The Ontology of the Accident: An Essay on Destructive Plasticity*, trans. Carolyn Shead, Cambridge 2012.

65 Jerzy Grotowski, *Towards a Poor Theatre*, preface by Peter Brook, 1968.

66 Moe Satt, interview with Enoch Cheng, 1 November 2009, https://www.aaa.org.hk/en/ideas/ideas/interview-with-moe-satt, accessed 19 September 2017.

67 Moe Satt, F&F: video interview about his work, and notes sent by email to the author, March 2018.

68 Luca Cerizza, 'Roberto Cuoghi', *frieze*, no.116, June–August 2008, https://frieze.com/article/roberto-cuoghi, accessed 19 September 2017.

69 Astrida Neimanis, 'Hydrofeminism: Or, On Becoming a Body of Water', in Henriette Gunkel, Chrysanthi Nigianni and Fanny Söderbäck (eds.), *Undutiful Daughters: Mobilizing Future Concepts, Bodies and Subjectivities in Feminist Thought and Practice*, London 2012, pp.85–100.

70 Hal Foster, *Bad New Days: Art, Criticism, Emergency*, London 2015, p.196.

71 See the interpretation of Alison Gingeras, Jack Bankowsky and Pop Life: Art in a Material World, 2010 at Tate Modern.

72 See Dorothea Von Hantelmann (ed.), *Pierre Huyghe: Celebration Park*, exhibition catalogue, Tate Modern, 2006.

73 The way in which these artists performed aspirational images of assimilation to the mainstream has a structure (if not a political imperative) that relates to the notion of 'passing', albeit in a very different social context. Passing was a term that, in the early twentieth century, was used to describe mixed-race Americans, most often black, identifying as other ethnicities, most often white. But in the 1980s, it was appropriated by queer and transgender African American and Latino communities – as documented in the film *Paris Is Burning* (Jennie Livingstone, 1990) – to describe their masquerading performances, in which they enacted various drag characters, from glamorous divas to sharp businessmen.

74 In email correspondence with the author, October 1998.

75 Artist's talk, British Film Institute, London, 17 October 2015.

76 Paulina Ołowska, email to the author, December 2012.

77 Paulina Ołowska, email to the author, December 2012.

78 Artist's website, http://www.nikhilchopra.net/home/?page_id=1615, accessed 19 September 2017.

79 Ibid.

80 Andrea Fraser, 'Art Criticism in Action', in *Museum Highlights: The Writings of Andrea Fraser*, Cambridge, MA 2007.

81 Subuhi Jiwani, 'Hijrotic: Towards a New Expression of Desire', *Mayday Magazine*, no.2, Winter 2010, http://maydaymagazine.com/issue2scholarjiwanihijrotic.php, accessed 19 September 2017.

82 In 2006, Tejal Shah and Varsha Nair performed a collaborative action at Tate Modern. Swathed in a custom-designed shell of white embroidered fabric, their two bodies appeared to be bound together, set within an urban context, approximating to the lines of the architecture. The straitjacket exoskeleton devised by the artists and joined at the arms forms an outstretched bridge to span the distance between being connected and being able to touch.

83 Amalia Ulman, personal interview with the author, London, October 2016.

84 See Jonathan Crary, *24/7: Late Capitalism and the Ends of Sleep*, London 2014.

85 Haraway 1991, p.149.

86 Pierre Huyghe, Stefan Kalmar, Philippe Parreno, Beatrix Ruf, and Hans Ulrich Obrist, 'Conversations', in Pierre Huyghe and Philippe Parreno (eds.), *No Ghost Just A Shell*, The Netherlands 2003, pp.28–9.

87 'Ceding our rights to the Annlee Association is what seals her definitive liberation', in Luc Saucier, 'Annlee Association Articles, Assignment of Rights Contract Governing the Author of Annlee', in Huyghe and Parreno, ibid., p.303.

88 Tiqqun, *Preliminary Materials for a Theory of the Young-Girl*, trans. Ariana Reines, Cambridge, MA 2012.

89 Ed Atkins, interview with Joline Platje, *Glamcult*, 9 April 2015, http://glamcult.com/interview-ed-atkins/, accessed 19 September 2017.

90 Ed Atkins, *Recent Ouija*, exhibition leaflet, Stedelijk, 21 February – 30 May 2015.

91 Ibid.

92 *Sidsel Meineche Hansen: INSIDER*, exhibition leaflet, Cubitt, London, October – November 2014.

93 See Bernard Stiegler, *Technics and Time*, vol.1, trans. Richard Beardsworth and George Collins, Stanford 1998.

94 Phelan 1993.

We: the social (pp.112–73)

1 Tino Sehgal in conversation with the author as a part of *Characters, Figures and Signs* at Tate Modern 2008.

2 See Bruno Latour, *Reassembling the Social: An Introduction to Actor-Network Theory*, Oxford 2005.

3 Tino Sehgal in conversation with the author as a part of *Characters, Figures and Signs* at Tate Modern 2008.

4 Westerman 2015.

5 Ricardo Basbaum, 'Post-Participatory Participation', *Afterall*, no.28, Autumn/Winter 2011, https://www.afterall.org/journal/issue.28/post-participatory-participation, accessed 19 September 2017.

6 Will Bradley and Charles Esche (eds.), *Art and Social Change: a Critical Reader*, London 2010, p.227

7 Vitaly Komar, conversation with the author, Tate Modern, London, November 2014.

8 See Andrew Hewitt, *Social Choreography: Ideology as Performance in Dance and Everyday Movement*, Durham 2005; and Judith Butler, *Towards a Performative Theory of Assembly*, Harvard 2015.

9 Brook continues, 'Yet when we talk about theatre this is not quite what we mean. Red curtains, spotlights, blank verse, laughter, darkness, these are all confusedly superimposed in a messy image covered by one all-purpose word.' Peter Brook, *The Empty Space*, New York 1968, p.7.

10 Jacques Rancière, *The Politics of Aesthetics*, trans. Gabriel Rockhill, New York 2004, p.12.

11 *Emily Roysdon: Positions*, 'Art in General', New York, March – May 2011, http://www.artingeneral.org/exhibitions/506, accessed 19 September 2017.

12 Vergine 2000, p.26.

13 Jérôme Bel in conversation with Roselee Goldberg (ed.), *Everywhere and All at Once: An Anthology of Writings on Performa 07*, Zurich 2009, p.124, and online: http://performa-arts.org/magazine/entry/why-dance-in-the-art-world-jerome-bel-and-roselee-goldberg-in-conversation.

14 Anne Teresa de Keersmaeker in conversation with Nick Mauss, Heimo Zobernig and Catherine Wood for *Mousse* magazine 60, Autumn 2017, p.80.

15 Interview with John Cage by Mary Emma Harris, 1974, quoted in Richard Kostelanetz, *Conversing with Cage*, New York 1988, p.104.

16 Katsuhiro Yamaguchi, quoted in Miwako Tezuka, 'Jikken Kōbō (Experimental Workshop): Avant-Garde Experiments in Japanese Art of the 1950s', unpublished Ph.D. thesis, Columbia University, New York 2005, pp.54–5.

17 Ibid.

18 Chris Burden, quoted in RoseLee Goldberg, *Performance: Live Art since the 60s*, London 1998, p.107.

19 In these works Graham explicitly invokes theories of structural linguistics, especially the work of Jacques Lacan.

20 Michael Fried, 'Art and Objecthood', *Artforum*, vol.5, no.10, June 1967, pp.12–23.

21 Beth Citron describes the happenings of Bhupen Khakar in her article, 'Experiencing Performance Art in India', Spring/Summer 2008, https://www.mutualart.com/Article/Experiencing-Performance-Art-in-India/608DA39ABF298790, last accessed April 2018.

22 A notable example is Steve Paxton's *Satisfyin' Lover* 1967, in which a large group of non-dancers were directed simply to walk back and forth between the theatre wings across the stage.

23 This was a common rallying cry used by feminist groups in the US and the UK in the late 1960s and 1970s. Feminist writer Carol Hanisch's essay 'The Personal Is Political' appeared in the anthology *Notes From the Second Year: Women's Liberation* in 1970, though she credits the editors of the anthology, Shulamith Firestone and Anne Koedt, with the title.

24 Gorgona Group included the artists and art historians Mangelos (Dimitrije Bašičević), Miljenko Horvat, Marijan Jevšovar, Julije Knifer, Ivan Kožarić, Matko Meštrović, Radoslav Putar, Đuro Seder and Josip Vaništa.

25 Collective Actions Group is comprised of the artists Nikita Alekseev, Elena Elagina, Georgy Kizevalter, Igor Makarevich, Andrei Monastyrski, Nikolai Panitkov, Sergei Romashko and Sabine Hänsgen.

26 Claire Bishop, 'Zones of Indistinguishability: Collective Actions Group and Participatory Art', *e-flux journal*, no.29, November 2011, http://www.e-flux.com/journal/29/68116/zones-of-indistinguishability-collective-actions-group-and-participatory-art/, accessed 19 September 2017.

27 Ibid.

28 *Beyond Memory: Photography and Photo-Related Works of Art from the Norton and Nancy Dodge Collection of Nonconformist Art from the Soviet Union*, exhibition catalogue, Zimmerli Art Museum at Rutgers University, New Brunswick 2004, pp.95–8, 123–4, 127–8, 279. http://conceptualism.letov.ru/CONCEPTUALISM.htm, accessed 9 February 2014.

29 Gabriela Jauregui, 'No-Grupo', *frieze*, no.137, March 2011, https://frieze.com/article/no-grupo, accessed 19 September 2017.

30 Maris Bustamante, 'Non-Objective Arts in Mexico 1963–83', in Coco Fusco (ed.), *Corpus Delecti: Performance Art of the Americas*, London 2000, p.235.

31 Huang Yongping interview: http://www.aaa-a.org/programs/conversation-with-huang-yongping/
Jane DeBevoise speaks with Huang Yongping about his work and practice in the 1980s, recorded 15 October 2010, 6:30 p.m., Museum of Modern Art (MoMA), New York. Translated on site by Vincent Cheng and recorded by MoMA. To celebrate the co-launch of MoMA's recent publication *Contemporary Chinese Art: Primary Documents* and AAA's archive and website project *Materials of the Future: Documenting Chinese Contemporary Art in the 1980s*, MoMA and AAA came together to engage visiting speakers in the field.

32 Carol Linghua Yu, introductory text panel to New Measurement Group exhibition, Shenzhen Ocat 2015.

33 Ibid., text panel.

34 Author in conversation with the artist.

35 José Díaz Cuyás, 'The Everyday Fact as Peripety', *Afterall*, no.26, Spring 2011, p.72.

36 Ibid.

37 Graciela Carnevale interview with Fabian Cerejido – quoted in *e-flux journal* no.30, Grant Kester, 'The Sound of Breaking Glass, Part 1: Spontaneity and Consciousness in Revolutionary Theory'.

38 Augusto Boal, *Theatre of the Oppressed*, trans. Charles A. and Maria-Odilia Leal McBride and Emily Fryer, London 2000, p.119.

39 Ibid., 'invisible theatre' is a term used throughout *Theatre of the Opressed*.

40 Boal 2000, p.145.

41 Ibid.

42 C. Ondine Chavoya, 'Orphans of Modernism: The Performance Art of Asco', in Fusco 2000, p.245.

43 Claire Bishop, 'Antagonism and Relational Aesthetics', *October*, no.110, Autumn 2004, pp.51–79.

44 Nicolas Bourriaud, *Relational Aesthetics*, trans. Simon Pleasance and Fronza Woods, Dijon 2002, p.113.

45 Ibid., p.13.

46 'David Hammons by Kellie Jones, *REAL Life* magazine, no.16, New York, Autumn 1986, p.8.

47 Jenny Schwarting, *The Brooklyn Rail*, April 2007, http://brooklynrail.org/2007/4/artseen/david-chie-hammons, accessed 19 September 2017.

48 Salvoj Žižek, 'Why are Laibach and Neue Slowenische Kunst Not Facists?' in *The Universal Exception: Selected Writings*, vol.11, London, Continuum 2006, pp.63–6.

49 *The Neo Naturists*, exhibition leaflet, Studio Voltaire, London, July – August 2016, p.16.

50 The Neo Naturists, interview with the author, 29 July 2016.

51 Saul Anton, '1000 Words: Francis Alÿs talks about *When Faith Moves Mountains*', *Art Forum*, vol.10 , no.40, 2002, pp.146–7.

52 Artist's website, www.zhanghuan.com/worken/info, accessed 2 February 2018.

53 Andrew Hewitt, 'Social Choreography: Ideology as Performance in Dance and Everyday Movement' in *Dance and Everyday Movement*, Duke, 2005.

54 Pierre Bourdieu, *The Field of Cultural Production: Essays on Art and Literature*, ed. Randal Johnson, Cambridge 1993.

55 The sum of 3.1 million euros was widely reported in the press, including 'Why Weiwei?' in *Der Spiegle*, 13 June 2007.

56 Ai Weiwei, 'Why I'll stay away from the Opening Ceremony of the Olympics', *Guardian*, 7 August 2008.

57 Chto Delat, https://chtodelat.org, accessed 2 February 2018.

58 Agata Pyzik, 'What is to be done? Radical collective Chto Delat confront the paradoxes of political art', *The Calvert Journal*, 2 October 2013, http://calvertjournal.com/comment/show/1578/what-is-to-be-done-chto-delat-art-collective, accessed 19 September 2017.

59 Artists' website, https://studio.camp/, accessed 19 September 2017.

60 Artists' website, http://www.goldinsenneby.com/gs/, accessed 19 September 2017.

61 Brian Doitcourt, 'Interview with Goldin+Senneby', *Rhizome*, 4 February 2009, http://rhizome.org/editorial/2009/feb/4/interview-with-goldinsenneby/, accessed 19 September 2017.

62 Roman Ondak, interview with Evi Baniotopoulou, 16 October 2004, http://www.tate.org.uk/art/artworks/ondak-good-feelings-in-good-times-t11940, accessed 19 September 2017.

63 Nevin Aladağ, interview with Walter D. Mignolo, *Ibraaz*, 27 February 2004, http://www.ibraaz.org/interviews/116, accessed 19 September 2017.

64 Ei Arakawa, interview with the author, 18 December 2012.

65 Wall texts and leaflet text for Japanorama, Pompidou Metz, November 2017.

66 Emily MacDermott, 'Maria Hassabi's Premiere League', *Interview Magazine*, 4 November 2013, http://www.interviewmagazine.com/art/maria-hassabi-premiere/#_, accessed 19 September 2017.

67 Michel Serres, *The Parasite*, trans. Lawrence R. Schehr, Minneapolis 2007.

68 Isabel Lewis, quoted in Ben Luke, 'Making waves: choreography moves into the museum', *The Art Newspaper*, 19 June 2014, http://ec2-79-125-124-178.eu-west-1.compute.amazonaws.com/articles/Making-waves-choreography-moves-into-the-museum/32988, accessed 19 September 2017.

69 http://www.berlinartlink.com/2012/11/19/making-space-marinella-senatores-rosas/
Making Space: Marinella Senatore's ROSAS, Melissa King in Berlin; 19 November 2012.

70 Claire Tancons, *En Mas': Carnival and Performance Art of the Caribbean*, 2016.

71 Sven Lütticken, 'Dance Factory', *Mousse*, no.50, Summer 2015, pp.90–7.

72 Artist's website, http://www.taniabruguera.com/cms/609-0-.htm, accessed 19 September 2017.

73 Ibid.

74 Meschac Gaba, *Tate Shots* interview www.tate.org.uk, accessed 1 February 2018.

75 Artist's website, www.borischarmatz.org/en/faire/bocal, accessed 19 September 2017.

76 B. Charmatz, 'Manifeste pour un Musée de la danse', 2009, http://www.museedeladanse.org/fr/articles/manifeste-pour-un-musee-de-la-danse, accessed 19 September 2017. Trans. the author.

77 Shannon Jackson, *Social Works: Performing Art, Supporting Publics*, London 2011, p.9.

78 Einar Engström, 'Hu Xiangqian: A Ridiculous Business', *Leap: The International Art Magazine of Contemporary China*, 16 October 2012, http://leapleapleap.com/2012/10/hu-xiangqian-a-ridiculous-business/, accessed 19 September 2017.

It: the object (pp.174–229)

1 Lippard and Chandler however, admit that despite 'immaterial' themes of 'water, steam, dust, flatness, legibility [and] temporality', 'little art is really conceptual to the point of excluding the object altogether'. Lucy R. Lippard and John Chandler, 'The Dematerialization of Art', *Art International*, vol.12, no.2, February 1968, p.34.

2 Ibid., p.31.

3 David Graeber, 'Fetishism as Social Creativity: or, Fetishes are gods in the process of construction', *Anthropological Theory*, vol.5, 2005, p.411.

4 At the same time, there has been a rise in interest in the idea of objects having consciousness or intention in 'object-oriented ontology', theorised by Graham Harman and others. Artists have borrowed from this theory in ways that do not necessarily literally concern themselves with whether objects have such capacity, but often rather as a poetic metaphor of sorts to try to reanimate the field, fantasising new relationships between people and the things around them.

5 Michael Fried, 'Art and Objecthood', *Artforum*, vol.5, no.10, June 1967, pp.12–23.

6 *About Time: Video, Performance and Installation by 21 Women Artists*, exhibition catalogue, Institute of Contemporary Arts, London, October – November 1980, unpaginated.

7 Introduction in *Joan Jonas: Scripts and Descriptions*, 1968–1982, p.8.

8 Elvira Dyangani Ose, 'Tracing Community', unpublished conference paper, 2011.

9 Elizabeth Harney, quoted in ibid.

10 Ibid. Emphasis in the original. The work of the Laboratoire Agit'Art was not widely publicised in a Western context until relatively recently, after Clémentine Deliss's exhibition *Seven Stories About Modern Art in Africa* (1995) at the Whitechapel Gallery in London. In its wake, the work of El Hadji Sy has had significant international exposure, including his participation in the 31st Bienal de São Paulo in 2014 and Documenta 14 in 2017.

11 Owkui Enwezor, quoted in Dyangani Ose ibid.

12 Kishio Suga, quoted in Rachel Taylor, 'Ren-Shiki-Tai', *Tate Online*, January 2009, http://www.tate.org.uk/art/artworks/suga-ren-shiki-tai-t13336, accessed 19 September 2017.

13 This manifesto was written by Ferreira Gullar, signed by Lygia Clarke and others. Published 22 March 1959 in *Journal do Brazil*. See also; Yve-Alain Bois, and Lygia Clarke, 'Nostalgia of the Body', Cambridge, MA, Summer 1994, pp.85–109.

14 Elsa Coustou, 'Nicola L', *Tate Online*, September 2015, http://www.tate.org.uk/whats-on/tate-modern/exhibition/ey-exhibition-world-goes-pop/artist-biography/nicola-l, accessed 19 September 2017.

15 Yvonne Rainer, *Feelings Are Facts*, Cambridge, MA 2006, p.253.

16 Robert Morris, 'Notes on Sculpture Part 1', in Gregory Battcock (ed.), *Minimal Art: A Critical Anthology*, New York 1968, pp.224, 231.

17 Michael Compton, quoted in Dennis Barker, 'Tate – Where the Action Was', *Guardian*, 4 May 1971.

18 This is a term commonly used by Forti in relation to her work. See *Simone Forti. Thinking with the Body: A Retrospective in Motion*, exhibition catalogue, Museum der Moderne Salzburg, July–November 2014.

19 Michelle Kuo and Julian Rose, 'Atmospheric Disturbance: Michelle Kuo and Julian Rose on Fujiko Nakaya at the glass house', *Artforum*, November 2014, vol.53, no.3, p.131.

20 See von Hantelmann 2010.

21 Bernard Blistène, *The Brutal Truth*, Frankfurt 2004, p.37.

22 Sturtevant, interview with the author, 2009.

23 Latour 2005, pp.82–3.

24 Ibid., p.72.

25 Erik Davis, 'The Thing is Alive', in Mark Leckey (ed.), *The Universal Addressability of Dumb Things*, exhibition catalogue, Hayward Touring (The Bluecoat, Liverpool, February – April 2013; Nottingham Contemporary, April – June 2013; De la Warr Pavilion, Bexhill on Sea), p.90.

26 Stiegler 1998, p.49. I am grateful that this writing was introduced to me by the artist Cally Spooner.

27 Latour 2005, p.72.

28 See www.nbp.pro.br, accessed 19 September 2017.

29 Pablo Lafuente, 'Ricardo Basbaum, or that Elusive Object of Emancipation', *Afterall*, no.28, Autumn/Winter 2011, p.82.

30 Tarek Atoui in conversation with the author and Andrea Lissoni, published in *Tarek Atoui: The Reverse Collection / The Reverse Sessions*, Milan 2017.

31 See Brian O'Doherty, *Inside the White Cube: The Ideology of the Gallery Space*, Berkeley, CA 1986.

32 Artist's website, http://www.metteingvartsen.net/performance/the-artificial-nature-project/, accessed 19 September 2017.

33 Jace Clayton, 'One Take: Ian Cheng's Emissaries', *frieze*, 22 April 2017, https://frieze.com/article/one-take-ian-chengs-emissaries, accessed 19 September 2017.

34 A year before creating *Trio A*, Yvonne Rainer wrote her 'No Manifesto' (1965). Through it, she declared her opposition to the dominant forms of dance of the period – typified by Martha Graham – and outlined the tenets of her radical new approach.

35 Gerry Bibby, interview with Hans Ulrich Obrist, 18 July 2001, https://vimeo.com/26605971, accessed 19 September 2017.

36 Ibid.

37 *Gerry Bibby: Combination Boiler*, exhibition text, The Showroom, London, April – June 2014, http://www.theshowroom.org/exhibitions/gerry-bibby, accessed 19 September 2017.

38 Otobong Nkanga, interview with Louisa Elderton, *The White Review*, October 2014, http://www.thewhitereview.org/interviews/interview-with-otobong-nkanga/, accessed 19 September 2017.

39 Ibid.

40 *Pas d'histoire, Pas d'histoire*, exhibition text, Witte de With Centre for Contemporary Art, Rotterdam, November–December 1994.

41 *Kapwani Kiwanga: Maji Maji*, exhibition text, Jeu de Paume, Paris, June – September 2014, http://www.jeudepaume.org/?page=article&idArt=2017, accessed 19 September 2017.

42 David Joselit, 'Painting Beside Itself', *October*, no.130, Autumn 2009, p.129.

43 Umberto Eco, *The Open Work*, trans. Anna Cancogni, Cambridge, MA 1989; Roland Barthes, 'The Death of the Author', in *Image Music Text*, trans. Stephen Heath, London 1977, pp.142–8.

44 Lucy R. Lippard, quoted in Gregory Battcock and Robert Nickas (ed.), 'Introduction', *The Art of Performance*, New York 1984, p.12.

45 Fred Moten, interview with Sharon P. Holland, *south*, Spring 2015, http://southjournal.org/talk/poet-fred-moten/, accessed 19 September 2017.

46 See von Hantelmann 2010.

47 Peter Pál Pelbart, 'Modes of Existence, Modes of Resistance', lecture as part of 'Event and Duration', organised by If I Can't Dance I Don't Want to Be Part of Your Revolution, Cygnus Gymnasium, Amsterdam, 24 January 2016.

48 Suhail Malik, 'On the Necessity of Art's Exit from Contemporary Art', talk series, Artists Space, New York, 3 May – 14 June 2013.

49 'Indigenous Art in the Museum' symposium, Tate Modern, 29 May 2018, where Wanda Nanibush was speaking on teh J.S Mclean Centre for Indigenous and Canadian Art.

Credits

Copyright

All works © the artist/s with the exception of the following:

© Marina Abramović, courtesy Marina Abramović and Sean Kelly Gallery, New York. DACS 2018 p.33
© Marina Abramović, courtesy Marina Abramović and Sean Kelly Gallery, New York. DACS 2018 / Ulay © DACS 2018 p.35
© Kanayama Akira and Tanaka Atsuko Association p.26
© Francis Alÿs, courtesy David Zwirner, New York / London / Hong Kong p.145, back cover
Joseph Beuys © DACS 2018 p.117
© Trisha Brown Dance Company / © Fujiko Nakaya / Harry Shunk © J.Paul Getty Trust (photo) p.203
© Chris Burden, licensed by the Chris Burden Estate and DACS 2018 p.36
Daniel Buren © DB-ADAGP Paris and DACS, London 2018 p.22
© Estate of André Cadere p.190
Lygia Clark © The World of Lygia Clark Cultural Association p.196
VALIE EXPORT © DACS 2018 p.46
© Damien Hirst and Science Ltd. All rights reserved, DACS 2018 p.91
Carsten Höller © DACS 2018 p.208
© Estate of Channa Horwitz (score and installation) / © Ellen Davis (choreographic interpretation) p.188
Pierre Huyghe © ADAGP, Paris and DACS, London 2018 / © Philippe Parreno p.105
Joan Jonas © ARS, NY and DACS, London 2018 pp.66, 183
© Mike Kelley Foundation for the Arts. All rights reserved / DACS, London / VAGA, NY 2018 p.187
Kapwani Kiwanga © ADAGP, Paris and DACS, London 2018 p.224 (bottom)
© Estate of Yves Klein c/o DACS, London 2018 / Shunk-Kender © J. Paul Getty Trust (photo) p.39
Jannis Kounellis © DACS 2018 p.200
Tseng Kwong Chi © Muna Tseng Dance Projects Inc., New York p.73
© Estate of Pi Lind p.178
Paul Maheke © ADAGP, Paris and DACS, London 2018 pp.88–9
© Estate of Ana Mendieta Collection, L.L.C. p.48
© Marta Minujín / Shunk-Kender © J. Paul Getty Trust (photo) p.126
© Robert Morris / Artists Rights Society (ARS), New York / DACS, London 2018 p.198
© Estate of Sadamasa Motonaga p.40
Lorraine O'Grady © ARS, NY and DACS, London 2018 pp.14–15
Gina Pane © ADAGP, Paris and DACS, London 2018 p.47
© Projeto Lygia Pape, courtesy Hauser & Wirth p.197
© Estate of Leticia Parente p.49
© Estate of Charlotte Posenenske p.192
© Estate of Hassan Sharif p.180
© Jack Smith Archive p.62
© Estate Sturtevant, Paris p.206
© Nicolás García Uriburu, reproduced by permission p.204

Photo Credits

Courtesy the Marina Abramović Archives p.35
Marco Anelli, courtesy the Marina Abramović Archives p.33
Courtesy the artist/s pp.50, 59, 64 (bottom, both), 72, 78, 81, 82, 87, 92, 119, 131, 144, 148, 172, 221, 228
Courtesy the artist and Arcadia Missa p.75
Courtesy the artist and Gavin Brown's enterprise, New York / Rome p.140
Courtesy the artist and Cabinet, London. Photo: Alessandro Raho p.177
Courtesy the artist and Chatterjee & Lal. Photo: Teena Lange p.98
Courtesy the artist and Ronald Feldman Gallery, New York p.118
Courtesy the artist and gb agency, Paris p.135
Courtesy the artist and Goodman Gallery p.101
Courtesy the artist. Photo: Gus Gustafson p.129
Courtesy the artist / Koenig & Clinton, New York / The Breeder, Athens. Photo: Thomas Poravas p.158
Courtesy the artist. Photo: Susumu Koshimizu p.194
Courtesy the artist / Lévy Gorvy, New York and London / Thomas Erben Gallery, New York pp.174–5, 185
Courtesy the artist and Lisson Gallery p.209
Courtesy the artist and Luhring Augustine, New York p.69
Courtesy the artist and Metro Pictures, New York p.64 (top, both)
Courtesy the artist and Mitchell-Innes & Nash, New York p.77
Courtesy the artist and Galerie Nagel Draxler, Berlin p.222
Courtesy the artist and galerie Jérôme Poggi, Paris. Photo: Émile Ouroumov p.224 (bottom)
Courtesy the artist. Photo: © Nadine Fraczkowski front cover
Courtesy the artist & Sfeir-Semler Gallery Hamburg / Beirut p.95
Courtesy the artist / Vitamin Creative Space, Guangzhou / Aoyama Meguro, Tokyo p.210
Courtesy the artist and Wentrup, Berlin p.154 (bottom)
Courtesy the artists / Auto Italia / Theo Cook p.109
Courtesy the artists and Cabinet, London p.97
Courtesy the artists and Marian Goodman Gallery, New York / Paris. Photo: Angel Art Ltd. p.105
Courtesy the artists and KOW, Berlin p.151 (top)
Jom Tob Azulay p.49
Dawoud Bey, courtesy Tilton Gallery, New York p.141
Courtesy Boers-Li Gallery and the artists p.60
Courtesy Galerie Buchholz, Berlin / Cologne / New York p.224 (top)
Nicholas Burrough p.157
Courtesy the Estate of André Cadere and Galerie Hervé Bize, Nancy. Photo: Bernard Borgeaud p.190
Courtesy Carlos / Ishikawa p.154 (top)
Archivo Graciela Carnevale. Photo: Carlos Militello p.137
Andrea di Castro p.132
Monika Chojnicka-Bodzianowska p.85
Eduard Constantin p.169
Courtesy Electronic Arts Intermix (EAI), New York p.46
Erró, courtesy Carolee Schneemann, Galerie Lelong & Co., and P.P.O.W, New York p.43
Courtesy Gallery Isabelle van den Eynde, Dubai p.180
© Nadine Fraczkowski. Courtesy the artist and the German Pavilion 2017, Venice p.115
© Harry Gamboa, Jr., courtesy the artist and the UCLA Chicano Studies Research Center p.138
Getty Research Institute, Los Angeles (2014.M.14) p.52
Courtesy Gladstone Gallery, New York / Brussels p.62
Hugo Glendinning p.215
Hugo Glendinning, courtesy the artist and Herald St, London p.218
Courtesy Alexander Gray Associates, New York pp.14–15
Courtesy Barbara Gross Galerie p.102
Courtesy the Hammer Museum, Los Angeles. Photo: Brian Forrest p.55
© Jeremy Hilder, courtesy Kurimanzutto and Estudio Amorales p.163
© Jeremy Hilder, courtesy Sadie Coles HQ, London p.90
Minoru Hirata, courtesy Galerie Lelong & Co., New York p.11
© Linda Hollingdale Photography p.139
Mingu Jeong p.110
Courtesy Mike Kelley Foundation for the Arts p.187
Kinetikon Pictures, courtesy the artist and Galerija Gregor Podnar, Berlin p.143
Courtesy Archivio Kounellis. Photo: Claudio Abate p.200
Courtesy Galerie Lelong & Co. p.48
© Jan Lietaert p.213
Courtesy Lisson Gallery pp.22, 124
© Moderna galerija, Ljubljana p.57
Courtesy Long March Space p.170
© mumok – Museum moderner Kunst Stiftung Ludwig Wien, donation of the artist p.44
Babette Mangolte p.6
Giles Moberly p.91
© 2018 The Museum of Modern Art, New York. Photo: Julieta Cervantes p.167
© 2018 The Museum of Modern Art, New York / Scala, Florence p.199
Courtesy Galleria Lorcan O'Neill p.63
Courtesy Osaka City Museum of Modern Art, GA1805 p.26
Akiko Ota p.162
© Seiko Otsuji, courtesy Musashino Art University Museum & Library and Tokyo Publishing House (from the portfolio *GUTAI PHOTOGRAPH 1956-1957*) p.40
© Adrian Piper Research Archive Foundation Berlin p.67
Courtesy the Estate of Charlotte Posenenske and Mehdi Chouakri, Berlin. Photo: © bpk / Abisag Tüllmann p.192
Judy Price, courtesy Raven Row p.188
Michael Rees, courtesy Sadie Coles HQ, London p.93
Rocco Ricci, courtesy Museu d'Art Contemporani de Barcelona (MACBA) p.179
Courtesy Galerie Thaddaeus Ropac, London / Paris / Salzburg and Gavin Brown's enterprise, New York / Rome. Photo: Charles Duprat p.206
Courtesy Richard Saltoun Gallery p.47
Courtesy Museum der Moderne, Salzburg. Photo: Sabine Breitwieser p.202
Katrin Schoof, courtesy the artist pp.30–31, 83
Harry Shunk, courtesy the Getty Research Institute, Los Angeles (2014.R.20) p.203
Shunk-Kender, courtesy the Getty Research Institute, Los Angeles. (2014.R.20) pp.39, 126
Moderna Museet, Stockholm p.178
Courtesy Galeria Luisa Strina p.216
Ashok Sukumaran p.151 (bottom)
El Hadji Sy p.189
© Tanz im August / HAU Hebbel am Ufer. Photo: Vitali Wagner, 2015 p.160
© Tate 2018 pp.9, 19, 54, 66, 70, 100, 112–113, 164, 166, 193
© Tate 2018. Photo: Brotherton-Lock pp.88–9
© Tate 2018. Photo: Oliver Cowling p.229
© Tate 2018. Photo: Lucy Dawkins pp.153, 211, 220
© Tate 2018. Photo: Andrew Dunkley p.183
© Tate 2018. Photo: Oliver Leith p.208
Tate Archive Photograph Collection p.198
Tate Archive Photograph Collection. Photo: Simon Wilson p.117
© Anne Van Aerschot p.122
Courtesy Video Data Bank, School of the Art Institute of Chicago – www.vdb.org p.13
Courtesy Museum of Modern Art in Warsaw p.17
Courtesy The World of Lygia Clark Cultural Association p.196
Courtesy Huang Yong Ping p.134
Courtesy David Zwirner, New York / London / Hong Kong p.145, back cover
Courtesy David Zwirner, New York and Sadie Coles HQ, London. Photo: Gert Jan van Rooij p.106

The publishers have made every effort to trace all copyright holders, and apologise for any omissions that may have been made.

Acknowledgements

I can only try to imagine what it takes to stand up in front of an audience and share one's private world: whether literally, or at one remove. This thought makes me all the more grateful to the many artists I acknowledge here, for daring to give me, and many others, such extraordinary images and experiences to love, get lost in, and try to process. So to the artists: thank you. This book is an attempt to set a wild variety of approaches and attitudes into a pattern; to make sense of the shift I have been fortunate to witness and be part of in the past two decades. Of course, there is also much more to say and do.

I am hugely appreciative to have had a small amount of time out from the live side of curating and producing to think about this book, through the support of Tate's 2014–16 Performance at Tate research project, in cooperation with Exeter University, Gabriella Giannachi, and supported by the AHRC. http://www.tate.org.uk/about-us/projects/performance-tate-collecting-archiving-and-sharing-performance-and-performative. Sincere thanks to my colleagues Jennifer Mundy, Head of Research at Tate, for making this project possible, and to Achim Borchardt-Hume, Director of Exhibitions at Tate Modern, for granting me a sliver of space in the portfolio during the run-up to the opening of the Blavatnik Building at Tate Modern to engage with it.

I am enormously indebted to our then-resident research fellow on this project, Dr Jonah Westerman, for many rigorous, probing (and often fun) discussions on what performance is, where its edges are, and what it means in the museum, as well as for extraordinary generosity in reading through and discussing an early draft and helping me shape it.

Thanks are due, too, to Nikki Columbus for her useful preliminary feedback on an earlier draft; to Thomas Berghuis for generously reading the manuscript and for his fantastic insight into Chinese and Indoneisan practices; Martin Hargreaves for ongoing conversations on dance as it intersects with art, and for kindly reading through the second draft; Elvira Dyangani Ose and Clementine Deliss for formative discussions about the Laboratoires Agit Art; to Joan Kee for her insight into Korean performance history; Anthony Yung at the Asia Art Archive for help during my visit whilst in Hong Kong, and RoseLee Goldberg not just for her foundational book, but also for ongoing conversation and collaboration. Thanks to the authors of many specific histories of performance in different regions globally – from the former Yugoslavia, to Latin America, to China – that have been published in the last few years, and who offer depth where I have, in attempting an overview, only skimmed the surface. Much gratitude, also, to my colleagues on the production side of performance: Kathy Noble for talking about performance and art over many years, both whilst in the thick of the production process and in theory; Isabella Maidment for rich conversations emanating from her meticulous PhD research and beyond, and also Sook-Kyung Lee, Stuart Comer, Andrea Lissoni, Nada Raza, Inti Guerrero, Vanessa Desclaux, Marie de Brugerolle, Capucine Perrot, Ana Janevski, Cosmin Costinas, Claire Bishop, Dorothea von Hantelmann, Barbara Clausen, Adrienne Edwards and Frederique Bergholz and my Corpus colleagues for significant conversations and collaboration. And thanks to Gil Leung for an important, if passing, discussion of the title some years ago!

I am very grateful to the Tate Publishing team: my patient and fastidious editor, Nicola Bion, who has demonstrated extraordinary calm and good humour through a drawn-out and often challenging process; Deborah Metherell, who undertook the masterful picture-research detective hunt with equal good cheer; Juliette Dupire, who took such good care of the image proofing, and the overall production; and Jacky Klein for her bracing and very welcome feedback in the earlier stages. I am immensely appreciative of the rigorous copy-editing and refining of the text by Helena Vilalta, whose questions and comments helped to improve the flow of the text; and would particularly like to thank Sarah Boris, whose thoughtful approach has resulted in such a striking design.

Lastly, my love and thanks to Alessandro, Roman and Belle: for giving me time to 'work on my computer' and teaching me so much about the related areas of painting and play.

Index

Page numbers in italic type refer to pictures.